Primary Elections in the United States

The direct primary stands as one of the most significant and distinctive political reforms of the Progressive era in American history. In this book, the authors provide the most comprehensive treatment available on the topic and utilize new data on election outcomes, candidate backgrounds, incumbent performance and behavior, newspaper endorsements, and voters' preferences. They begin by studying whether primary elections have achieved the goals set by progressive reformers when they were first introduced over a century ago. They then evaluate the key roles these elections have played in the US electoral system, such as injecting electoral competition into the regions that are dominated by one of the two major parties, helping select relatively qualified candidates for office, and, in some cases, holding incumbents accountable for their performance. Finally, they study the degree to which primaries are responsible for the current, highly polarized political environment. Anyone interested in US primary elections, US political history, or electoral institutions more generally, should read this book.

Shigeo Hirano is Professor of Political Science at Columbia University. He has published in the leading political science journals. He was a visiting scholar at the Russell Sage Foundation, the Yale University Center for the Study of American Politics, and the Princeton University Center for the Study of Democratic Politics.

James M. Snyder, Jr. is Leroy B. Williams Professor of History and Political Science in the Harvard Government Department, a Research Associate at the National Bureau of Economic Research, and a Fellow of the American Academy of Arts and Sciences. He has published more than 100 scholarly articles, many appearing in the leading political science and economics journals. He taught previously in the Department of Political Science and the Department of Economics at the Massachusetts Institute of Technology, and in the Department of Economics at the University of Chicago.

POLITICAL ECONOMY OF INSTITUTIONS AND DECISIONS

Series Editors

Jeffry Frieden, *Harvard University*
John Patty, *Emory University*
Elizabeth Maggie Penn, *Emory University*

Founding Editors

James E. Alt, *Harvard University*
Douglass C. North, *Washington University of St. Louis*

Other books in the series

(*continued after the Index*)

Primary Elections in the United States

SHIGEO HIRANO
Columbia University

JAMES M. SNYDER, JR.
Harvard University

CAMBRIDGE
UNIVERSITY PRESS

CAMBRIDGE
UNIVERSITY PRESS

University Printing House, Cambridge CB2 8BS, United Kingdom

One Liberty Plaza, 20th Floor, New York, NY 10006, USA

477 Williamstown Road, Port Melbourne, VIC 3207, Australia

314–321, 3rd Floor, Plot 3, Splendor Forum, Jasola District Centre,
New Delhi – 110025, India

79 Anson Road, #06-04/06, Singapore 079906

Cambridge University Press is part of the University of Cambridge.

It furthers the University's mission by disseminating knowledge in the pursuit of education, learning, and research at the highest international levels of excellence.

www.cambridge.org
Information on this title: www.cambridge.org/9781107080591
DOI: 10.1017/9781139946537

© Shigeo Hirano and James M. Snyder, Jr. 2019

First published 2019

Printed in the United Kingdom by TJ International Ltd. Padstow, Cornwall

A catalogue record for this publication is available from the British Library.

ISBN 978-1-107-08059-1 Hardback
ISBN 978-1-107-44015-9 Paperback

Contents

Acknowledgments

For reasons that are still not entirely clear, this book has taken more than ten years to write. Along the way we have been helped by so many people that we cannot remember them all. We will try to thank as many as possible, and we apologize to those who we have overlooked.

First, we thank our collaborators Steve Ansolabehere, J. Mark Hansen, Gabriel Lenz, Maksim Pinkovskiy, and Michael Ting, with whom we co-authored several articles that form the basis of key parts of the book. Our work with them has helped shape our thinking about primaries.

Second, we thank the many people who have provided useful comments on earlier versions of the manuscript, or on papers that have been incorporated into the manuscript. In 2014, Markus Prior generously arranged a book conference for us at Princeton University where Matias Iaryczower, Nolan McCarty, Bob Erikson, Tom Romer, Marc Meredith, and Talia Stroud discussed earlier versions of various chapters. Their comments were extremely valuable. Toward the end, Anthony Fowler and Daniel Smith gave us detailed suggestions on the entire manuscript. Other colleagues who have offered us their thoughts and advice on various projects that have become part of the book include: James Alt, Christopher Berry, Ethan Bueno de Mesquita, Devin Caughey, Olle Folke, Justin Fox, Jeff Frieden, Alan Gerber, Gregory Huber, David Lewis, David Mayhew, Soccoro Puy Segura, Pablo Querubin, Ken Shepsle, Matthew Stephenson, Craig Volden, and Dustin Tingley. We have also benefited from the comments on our work at invited seminars at various institutions, including Columbia, LSE, MIT, Russell Sage

Foundation, Stanford, University of Chicago Harris School, University of Bocconi, University of Essex, University of Malaga, University of Virginia, Vanderbilt, Washington University and Yale, and various academic conferences, including: Erasmus political economy conference, EPSA annual conference, Latin American and Caribbean Association annual conference, MPSA annual conference, Trento Festival of Economics, Yale CSAP conference, and Wallis conference on political economy.

Many of the key insights and findings in the book draw on newly created datasets that span decades of US political history. We have been working on some of these datasets for over two decades and they could not have been created without the help of many excellent research assistants at various institutions. Among those who have collected, scanned, coded, checked, and cleaned data are the following: Abuchi Agu, Brittany Allison, Jonathan Backer, Pamela Ban, Geoffrey Buller, Philip Burrowes, Daniel Campos, Jessica Cui, Alina Dunlap, Erin Fackler, Mason Fitch, Michael Gill, Stacy J. Hall, Sarah Hamilton, William Hennessey, Sean Hirose, Jaclyn Kaslovsky, Patricia Kirkland, Aaron Kaufman, Danielle Kehl, Scott Kim, Mayya Komisarchik, Cynthia Lee, Rebecca Lee, Simone Leeper, Chad Levinson, Elaine Li, Karen Li, John Lovett, Margaret Mattes, Aidan McCarthy, Ashley Mehl, Laura Mills, Ester Min, Kelly Murdock, Cody Nager, Pin–Quan Ng, Farrah Ricketts, Sophia Rogers, Jungho Roh, Melissa Saldana, Amy Semet, Adria Schulman-Eyink, Alexis Schustrom, Noah Schwartz, Jasmine Senior, Jessica Soberman, Byung Kwon (BK) Song, Dean Spirito, Victoria Steger, Kendall Tucker, Tony Valeriano, Nida Vidutis, Miranda Yaver, Hye Young You, and Adam Zelizer. We also thank Stephen Pettigrew, Gary Jacobson, Marc Meredith, Jeffrey Mondak, and Brian Gaines for sharing data with us.

We have also received institutional and financial support from multiple sources. Large portions of the data collection were funded through two National Science Foundation (NSF) grants. Shigeo gratefully acknowledges the institutional and financial support from Columbia University, the Russell Sage Foundation, and the Yale University Center for the Study of American Politics. Jim thanks Harvard University and the Massachusetts Institute of Technology for institutional and financial support. We would also like to thank Alan Gerber, Greg Huber, Pam Lamonaca, Pam Greene, and Yale's Center for the Study of American Politics for providing us with office space, library access, and other Yale amenities when we met to work on the book roughly midway between Cambridge and New York City.

A number of people have been instrumental in helping transform our manuscript into a book. Tricia Vio in particular has read and re-read and edited and re-edited the manuscript so many times that she must have whole sections memorized by now. Michael Auslen, Peggy Chen, Fred Dalzell, Kelly Friel, Michael Olson, Connor Phillips, Shiro Kuriwaki, Tyler Simko, and David Simpson helped clarify and clean the prose. We thank the editorial team at Cambridge University Press and Newgen Publishing for their work producing the book, and in particular Robert Dreesen and Helen Flitton for managing the whole process. We also thank John Patty, Maggie Penn, and Jeffrey Frieden for having us as part of the Political Economy Institutions and Decisions series.

We would like to thank our families for their support and for putting up with our endless conversations about US politics. Shigeo's children, Serena and Leo, were born while the book was being written and literally grew up listening to these conversations. Finally, we thank our parents, Asao Hirano, Keiko Hirano, James M. Snyder, and Jean May Snyder, to whom we dedicate this book.

1

More Democracy

"The cure for the evils of democracy is more democracy."
~ H.L. Mencken

"If the people can only choose among rascals, they are certain to choose a rascal."
~ V.O. Key, Jr.

To win a political office in the US – virtually any office, from US senator to state treasurer to county sheriff – candidates must win two elections. First, they must win in a primary election, and then they must win in a general election. Do these first elections, the primaries, matter? How? Do they help the US electoral system select more qualified individuals? Do voters use them to reward good behavior in office and punish poor performance? Do primaries need to be reformed and if so in what ways?

We argue that the answers are *yes, read the book to find out, yes, yes, and perhaps.*

Primary elections do three things. First, in many states and even more legislative districts and localities, primaries constitute the only "real" elections for most offices. Consider the following examples: (1) in Kansas, no Democrat has won a US Senate general election since 1932; (2) of the 442 general elections for governor or US senator held in the ten states of the "Solid South" between 1878 and 1960, the Republicans won just once; (3) there are more than 400 counties in the US in which the same party has won a majority of the two-party vote in every presidential election for the past 50 years. A list of the one-party bastions today would include many of the most populous cities and suburban areas in the country – New York, Philadelphia, Boston, Baltimore, Detroit, Milwaukee, St. Louis, San Francisco, Oakland, Phoenix, and Tulsa.

Since state and local governments in the US have enormous power, we care about the quality of democracy at the state and local level. One minimal requirement of a democracy is that there is enough electoral competition that incumbents face a real possibility of being defeated at the polls. If the general elections in a state or locality dominated by one party are rarely in doubt, then these elections fail to contribute meaningfully to democratic accountability.

This is where primaries come in. As we show below, competition in primary elections is quite lively in the cases that matter most. In particular, competition is often spirited in the primaries of the dominant party, in states and districts dominated by one party. Primary competition is especially vigorous when the incumbent is not running. In these cases, two or more candidates run 84 percent of the time, and many of the contenders appear highly qualified for the office sought.

The second thing primaries do is provide an electoral arena that encourages voters to weigh the relative qualifications of the candidates running, rather than partisan or ideological divisions, when deciding how to vote. The contenders in Democratic primaries are (almost) always all Democrats, so party identification cannot govern voting. The situation is analogous in Republican primaries. Also, compared to the large ideological cleavages between parties, the ideological or issues differences between candidates within a party tend to be small. This makes it more likely that voters will base their decisions on other possible attributes, such as prior experience, energy, intelligence, and qualification for office. A loyal Democratic voter who would never cross party lines to vote for a Republican in the general election – even a Republican who is more qualified than the Democrat on many key dimensions – might pay close attention to qualifications when choosing among Democrats in the primary. In fact, a loyal Democratic voter living in a competitive constituency has an additional incentive to focus on qualifications in the primary, since a more qualified Democratic nominee should have a better chance of winning in the general election.

As we show below, primaries help the overall electoral system select and retain more-qualified office holders due to three factors. First, when voters in a primary are presented with a choice between one candidate with clear qualifications for the office sought and another who lacks such qualifications, they nominate the more-qualified candidate about 80 percent of the time. Second, this leads potential entrants to respond strategically, as one might expect – candidates with the qualifications that voters reward often run, especially in areas that are safe for their party. Third, the "pool" of potential candidates also varies systematically with voter partisanship, and, in particular, in areas where a party is electorally strong that party will tend to have a larger number of qualified candidates.

The resulting bottom line – combining voters' decisions, the strategic behavior of potential candidates and other political elites, and variation in the parties' pools of talent – is that the politicians elected in areas that are safe for one party and those elected in areas with robust two-party competition are approximately equally qualified. During the first half of the twentieth century, in fact, in states with primaries the winners in safe areas were even more likely to be qualified. If primaries were adding little to the electoral system compared to general elections, then we would have expected to find that politicians in safe areas were systematically less qualified than those in competitive areas. We do not.

The third thing primaries do is give a party's rank-and-file the opportunity to help resolve, in a democratic fashion, issue conflicts within the party. This is especially important for issues that cut across partisan lines, but on which there is significant variation in preferences within the party. Prominent examples include the contests between progressives and stalwarts in the early 1900s through the 1920s, especially among Republicans; battles over prohibition in both parties from the 1900s through the 1930s; conflicts between proponents and opponents of the New Deal, especially among Democrats; and abortion politics in the 1970s and 1980s.

We study several of these cases below, and show that a significant share of voters appears to vote on the basis of these issues in primaries, when the issues are salient and the candidates competing espouse different positions.

This points to a tension between the second and third things that primaries can do. When deep factional or issue cleavages exist within a party and drive primary election voting, then candidate qualifications almost by definition will have less influence on nominations. However, as V.O. Key, Jr. showed for the "Solid South," and as we will show more broadly below, stable intra-party factions are rare in the US, and persistent issue cleavages also tend to be more the exception than the rule.

Skeptical readers may be shaking their heads at this point. What about the fact that incumbents are almost never seriously challenged in the primaries? That turnout in primaries is often dismally low and skewed toward ideological extremists, exacerbating today's dysfunctional polarized politics? How can primaries possibly function well given that they demand so much of citizens – the same citizens who, by many accounts, lack adequate information even when deciding how to vote in general elections?

Regarding the first question, it is true that incumbents rarely face serious primary challenges. But is this a problem? As we show below, in terms of qualifications we can measure, the typical incumbent is much better than a "random draw" from the pool of candidates who typically run for open seats. This is because in open-seat races the winning candidates tend to be more qualified than the losers, and, as in most professions, there is on-the-job learning in political offices. Open-seat winners become the incumbents who draw little opposition in subsequent races. Why should we want to replace them, when we know that (i) the potential replacements are on average less qualified than the incumbent was when he or she was first elected, and (ii) the potential replacements lack the on-the-job learning that incumbents have acquired in their current positions?

There is another consideration as well. Do we want incumbents to fear for their jobs even when they are performing as expected? We already complain about the lack of talent in our political classes. How many talented people would choose a career in politics if there was a substantial chance of being kicked out of office every few years – by ones' co-partisans in a primary election – even while doing a good job?

Finally, we also find that incumbents are opposed in primaries much more often when they are performing especially poorly, and in these cases they often lose. This is especially true for incumbents in states or districts where their party is dominant.

Regarding the third question above, it is true that only a small percentage of the electorate is attentive and well-informed. This is especially true when we consider down-ballot races. The question is, how many voters must be informed – or act "as if" they are informed – in order for the outcome of an election to be the same as it would be if all voters were actually informed? If the uninformed voters generally cancel one another out – voting randomly or based on idiosyncratic factors and therefore splitting their votes roughly equally across the candidates – then those who are informed will usually be pivotal and determine the outcome, even if they constitute a small fraction of the electorate.

As noted above, when more- and less-qualified candidates compete in primaries, the more qualified candidates win about 80 percent of the time. It is extremely unlikely that this happens because 80 percent of the voters know each candidates' qualifications at the time of the election. Rather, it probably happens because a much smaller percentage of voters know the candidates' qualifications, or behave as if they did, and the remaining voters tend to spread their votes across candidates in ways that cancel one another out. Another indication that information makes its way into the electorate is that when primary candidates clearly have distinct ideological positions (or different positions on prominent issues), large numbers of voters cast ballots as if they knew these positions.

Regarding the second question above, as we show below, primary election turnout actually tends to be quite high in the primaries that matter – that is, in open-seat primaries in the dominant party, in constituencies where a dominant party exists. Moreover, as others have shown, those who vote in primaries are ideologically representative of party identifiers as a whole. In particular, primary election voters are not significantly more ideologically extreme than party identifiers.

Much of the current debate surrounding primary elections is focused on the problem of polarization and gridlock in government. Many observers argue that primaries "cause" polarization. But they do not state the counterfactual. Primaries compared to what? If we removed the current system of direct primary elections, we would still have to nominate candidates somehow. Would polarization and gridlock decrease under the alternative system? While the evidence is sparse – because caucuses and conventions are rare these days – when we analyze the data that exists we find that caucuses and conventions do not produce nominees who are any more moderate than those elected in primaries. The evidence also suggests that the differences between open and closed primaries are quite small, and that a shift to open primaries – which has been happening in any case – would not significantly increase the number of moderate nominees.

Other reforms are possible. One is the top-two system, in which all candidates run together in a first-round election (the primary) and the top two vote-getters go on to the second-round election (the general) regardless of party. A variant of this system has been used in Louisiana since 1975, and it was adopted more recently in Washington state and California. There is not yet enough data to assess with confidence how the system performs. The existing evidence suggests that top-two systems might reduce polarization, but only modestly.

Another option is to move entirely to non-partisan elections. While this might reduce polarization, the costs might also be substantial. All offices under this system would tax voters with two informationally demanding elections – a non-partisan first-round election followed by a non-partisan second-round election – rather than just one. Under this system even the second-round (general) elections are likely to be low-information contests with relatively low voter participation, except perhaps for offices at the top of the ticket.

Where does this leave us? Imperfect as they are, primaries on balance enhance the US electoral system. They bring an essential element of democracy – competitive elections from time to time that offer the voters of at least one party a real choice – to the vast areas of the US where the general elections do not. Thus far, our limited imaginations have not come up with anything obviously better.

2

One-Party Dominance, 1880 to 1950

Two months before the 1903 Pennsylvania Republican state convention, state party leaders met in US Senator Boies Penrose's Philadelphia office to discuss the party's slate for the general election. To no one's surprise, the group backed loyal party men for the top two positions on the ticket – William L. Mathues for state treasurer and William P. Snyder[1] for state auditor. Neither candidate had resumés indicating that they were particularly qualified to manage or audit the state's funds. Mathues was a prothonotary and chairman of the Delaware County Republican Committee. Snyder was a state legislator whose first political appointment was as postmaster; he had also served as a Republican county committee chair. However, they both had the support of key party leaders: Mathues was backed by US Senator Matthew S. Quay, and Snyder was supported by state Attorney General John P. Elkin. Media speculation about other potential nominees for these positions (most of whom were also party insiders with little relevant experience) ended after the leaders' meeting.[2] Two months later Mathues and Snyder were uncontested at the Republican convention in Harrisburg, and were nominated by acclamation.

As noted in the press, the Pennsylvania state auditor and treasurer were essentially selected in Penrose's office, eight months prior to the general election. At that time the state was completely dominated by

---

[1] No relation to the author.

[2] One potential nominee who had relevant experience and also expressed interest in the state treasurer position was Edmund B. Hardenbergh, the incumbent state auditor. He withdrew his name from consideration at the convention a few days after this meeting.

the Republican Party. During the four decades prior to the New Deal, the Republicans won all but one election for statewide executive office, and controlled the state legislature by overwhelming majorities. In the previous decade, the average margin of victory for Republican candidates for state auditor or treasurer was close to 20 percentage points over their Democratic challengers. Mathues and Snyder both won their general elections as expected, accumulating more than twice as many votes as their closest competitors. In an important sense, voters had limited direct input in determining who held these offices.

If the Republican party leaders had selected qualified and dutiful officials, then there might have been less cause for concern. However, in addition to not having experience managing public funds, both Mathues and Snyder turned out to be corrupt. They were later convicted on charges of conspiracy and false pretense for their role in the state capitol graft scandal.[3] The scandal surfaced in part because of a partial, temporary break in one-party control of the state government. In 1905, William H. Berry was elected state treasurer, the only non-Republican to hold statewide office during this period of one-party dominance. During the campaign Berry exploited the growing suspicion that state funds were being mismanaged, and although no single party gave him enough votes to win, the combined support of the Democratic, Independent, Lincoln, and Prohibition parties did.[4] Berry is often credited with uncovering the inappropriate use of public funds of the previous administration.

Mathues and Snyder represent extreme examples of how the caucus-convention system could be vulnerable to abuse by a dominant party. Indeed, even in decades before the capitol graft scandal, there were reports that Pennsylvania Republican state treasurers had engaged in questionable activities.[5] Moreover, Pennsylvania was not the only state vulnerable to such abuses. One-partyism was widespread in state politics around the turn of the twentieth century. Observers often remarked that the dominant party nominations in these states were equivalent to election.[6] The popular perception was that when candidates were

---

[3] See Klein and Hoogenboom (1973) for a discussion of the scandal. In brief, $4 million was appropriated for capitol building, but the final cost was inflated to nearly $13 million.

[4] See Klein and Hoogenboom (1973). Counting only Democratic and Republican votes, Berry would have lost the election by close to 10 percentage points. The support from the minor parties gave him an extra 20 percent of the total vote.

[5] Klein and Hoogenboom (1973, 421).

[6] In commenting on a primary election law bill, Wisconsin State Dairy and Food Commissioner H.C. Adams stated, "in the great majority of cases, the nomination of the

nominated at caucuses, conventions, or party meetings, party elites had significant influence, if not direct control, over nominations. In drawing connections between the nomination process and cases of corruption and inefficiency, progressive reformers sought to increase popular support for a transition to a direct primary system.

In this chapter, we document the dearth of two-party competition in the decades before and after the introduction of primaries. We examine party competition between 1880 and 1950. The partisan balance in many states, counties, and congressional districts around the turn of the century made general elections largely uncompetitive. The absence of inter-party electoral competition continued to be a concern even through the New Deal. Thus, to the degree that primaries are particularly relevant in uncompetitive areas, their adoption had potentially far-reaching consequences for the electoral system.

While the caucus-convention system was not designed to give party elites undue influence over the nomination process, in practice it provided a variety of avenues for elites to manipulate the outcomes. In Section 2.2 we discuss some of the ways party leaders could exert this influence as well as some of their motivations for preferring certain types of nominees.

The final section of this chapter examines the relationship between the absence of inter-party electoral competition and the introduction of primaries. Since the concerns associated with the caucus-convention system were likely to be particularly acute in states dominated by one party, we might expect the pressure for nomination reform to be highest in these states. While we cannot establish a causal link between general election competition and primary adoption, we show that they are at least highly correlated.

2.1 DEMOCRACY OUT OF COMMISSION

Following Reconstruction, partisan loyalties in the US largely reflected the Civil War alignment, making states in the South Democratic and other states Republican.[7] This sectional cleavage became even more

---

candidate of a dominant party is equivalent to an election, nominations of candidates and selection of delegates to conventions are more important than election itself." *Oshkosh Daily Northwestern*, March 4, 1901, p. 7.

[7] In describing this period, Key (1964, 288–9) writes, "[In the South the] Civil War gave impulse to unity in national politics to defend the peculiar regional practices against the North. To support Republicans in national affairs was to support the sectional enemy.

evident in voting patterns in the late 1890s, and some scholars see 1896 as particularly important.[8] The electoral success of the Populist Party in the late nineteenth century motivated the two major parties to further solidify their control over state politics. Between 1892 and 1896, the Populist Party won more than 40 US House elections and control of several state legislatures and governorships.[9] The Populists were particularly successful in areas traditionally dominated by one party when their candidates ran on fusion tickets. For example, the Populist–Republican ticket in North Carolina won control of the state government during this period. The Populists pursued this strategy nationally by supporting the Democratic candidate for president, William Jennings Bryan, in 1896.

In reaction to the success of the Populist movement, Southern Democrats were willing to pursue strategies to keep Southern conservatives in control – even if this meant reducing the party's appeal outside the South and making control of the national government less likely. As Schattschneider (1960, 77) writes, they accomplished this by "reviv[ing] the tensions and animosities of the Civil War and the Reconstruction in order to set up a one-party sectional southern political monopoly in which nearly all Negroes and many poor whites were disfranchised." Schattschneider notes that a similarly conservative reaction outside the South strengthened the Republican Party in the Northeast and Midwest and "decimated" the Democratic Party in large sections of those regions. He describes this period as "one of the most sharply sectional political divisions in American history." Following Schattschneider's seminal work, this electoral period has been known as the Fourth Party System, and it lasted until the New Deal realignment.[10] A wave of states introduced primary elections during this period.

The case of the "Solid South" is well known. In every state of the former Confederacy, in almost every year between 1880 and 1950 the Democrats won virtually every statewide elective office – 2271 out of 2291

The maintenance of partisan unity in national affairs destroyed, or at least prevented the development of, Republican parties for the purposes of state politics. The necessities of unity against an external threat compelled a degree of unity at home ... In the states of the North the war had a similar impact whose effects, though felt for decades, have by now largely worn away."

[8] For example, Walter D. Burnham described this as a period when democracy was "effectively placed out of commission – at least as far as two-party competition was concerned – in more than half the states" (Burnham, 1965, 26).

[9] Hirano (2008).

[10] Mayhew (2002) critiques the re-alignment and critical elections literature and argues that fundamental electoral changes tend to be more gradual.

elections – and held overwhelming majorities in both houses of the state legislature. Republicans were so weak that in 53 percent of the elections for statewide offices during this period they did not even nominate a candidate.

Two-party competition was also weak in many states outside the South. Democrats won 95 percent of the statewide contests in Arizona and Oklahoma during the period between 1880 and 1950. Republicans dominated in much of the North, Midwest, and Far West prior to the New Deal realignment. While the Republican vote margins were not as overwhelming in the northern tier as the Democratic margins in the South, Republicans won office to nearly the same degree. For example, in 12 states[11] Republicans won 96 percent of the statewide elections between 1894 and 1928.[12]

To study the patterns of two-party competition, we use election returns for all available major statewide offices – including US senator, governor, lieutenant governor, attorney general, secretary of state, state treasurer, state auditor or comptroller, and various elected agency heads or commissioners.[13] We describe constituencies with uncompetitive general elections as "uncompetitive" or "safe," and classify states as uncompetitive in year t if the difference between the moving averages of the Democratic and Republican vote shares during the years $t-4$ to $t+4$ is larger than 15 percentage points.[14] In uncompetitive states, the candidate of the advantaged party is expected to win the general election.

The decline in two-party competition around the turn of the century is apparent in the state electoral data. Classifying states according to the average vote share definition above, in 1890 there were 19 uncompetitive

[11] California, Iowa, Kansas, Maine, Michigan, Minnesota, New Hampshire, North Dakota, Oregon, South Dakota, Vermont, and Wisconsin.

[12] One Pennsylvania newspaper, *The Daily Notes*, made the following comparison: "A Republican nomination in Pennsylvania is usually equivalent to election, having been compared in this respect to a Democratic nomination in South Carolina." Appeared on May 19, 1926, page 1 under the headline "Beideleman Named for Governor."

[13] The set of partisan elected offices varies across states. A list of all of the offices for each state is given in Ansolabehere et al. (2010). We do not include judicial offices. We also include all at-large US House races.

[14] We drop cases for which less than ten races are used to calculate the vote shares. Our threshold is halfway between the two most common thresholds used to classify elections as competitive or not (45–55 percent and 40–60 percent). For candidates who receive votes under more than one party label (for example, in states that allow cross-filing such as New York) we only include the votes reported under the major party label. In a small number of cases neither the Democratic nor the Republican Party had the second-highest vote share. In these cases we use the vote margin with the third party.

states, while 25 were competitive. By 1904 the situation was reversed, with 28 uncompetitive states and 17 competitive states (see the top-left panel of Figure 2.1). Thirteen states switched from being classified as competitive to uncompetitive, while only four states switched in the opposite direction.[15] The newly uncompetitive states were mostly Midwestern, Western, and Northeastern states that became solidly Republican.

State-level measures do not necessarily reflect the competitiveness of elections for local offices or legislative districts. Since counties, cities, and legislative districts cover much smaller geographic areas than states, we might expect them to have more homogeneous preferences. Gerrymandering could exacerbate the problem, if, for example, the majority party "packs" the minority party's districts in order to waste minority votes, or a bipartisan, incumbent-protecting gerrymander produces additional safe districts for both parties.

We study competitiveness below the state level using two measures, one for counties and one for congressional districts. For counties we lack comprehensive data on election results for all statewide offices, but we do have a complete dataset of county-level results for all races for president, governor, US senator, and US House representative. Thus, we can create a moving average of the two-party vote similar to that defined above for the states. The top-right panel of Figure 2.1 plots the share of counties classified as competitive over time. More than half of the counties were uncompetitive for the entire period 1880 to 1950.

Constructing a measure of competition for congressional districts is more complicated due to both redistricting and data availability. Because of reapportionment and redistricting that occurs after each decennial census, for congressional districts we construct the underlying measure of two-party competition as simple averages of the vote shares in all available elections by decade. Also when constructing these averages we use only presidential and (in some cases) gubernatorial elections.[16]

---

[15] The states that became uncompetitive are California, Connecticut, Iowa, Illinois, Massachusetts, Michigan, Minnesota, North Carolina, New Hampshire, Pennsylvania, Virginia, Washington, and Wisconsin. The states that became competitive are Colorado, Kansas, Nebraska, and Nevada.

[16] To construct the average presidential and gubernatorial vote for each congressional district we began with the county-level results. Relatively few counties were split across congressional districts in the pre–World War II period, and all of these were in New England or in major cities. We found ward- and precinct-level presidential and/or gubernatorial data for most years for most of the cities in split counties outside New England, and town-level data for all years for all of the New England states with split

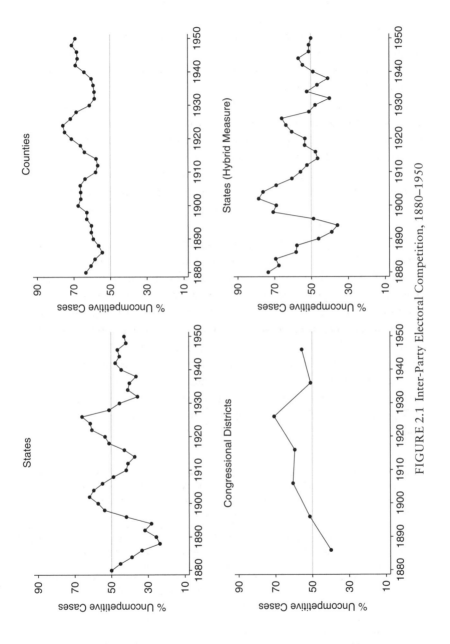

FIGURE 2.1 Inter-Party Electoral Competition, 1880–1950

13

The bottom-left panel of Figure 2.1 plots the share of congressional districts classified as competitive over time. After 1890 more than half of congressional districts were uncompetitive.[17]

Measures of competitiveness that focus only on average vote shares do not account for the stability or volatility of the vote, and therefore might misrepresent the extent of one-party dominance. If one party consistently receives, say, 54 percent of the vote, then it would still dominate electoral outcomes in terms of winning offices and therefore controlling the government. We therefore constructed another, "hybrid" measure of electoral competition that incorporates the percentage of offices won in addition to vote shares. More specifically, we classify a state as "uncompetitive" in year t if the difference in the moving average of the two-party vote share is greater than 15 percent, or if one of the two major parties wins 95 percent or more of the statewide races over the years $t-4$ to $t+4$.

The bottom-right panel of Figure 2.1 plots the hybrid measure for the period 1880 to 1950. Compared to the vote share based measure in the upper-left panel, the hybrid measure indicates an overall higher level of one party dominance. The difference between the measures is especially prominent in the 1880s, but is noticeable even into the 1910s. According to the hybrid measure, one-party dominance was a prominent feature of the political landscape even in the 1880s. As with the gap in vote share measure alone, two-party competition was noticeably absent in the decade following 1896. Between 1898 and 1906, roughly 70 percent of states were classified as uncompetitive according to the hybrid measure.

The patterns in Figure 2.1 highlight the extent to which one-party dominance prevailed during the period 1880 to 1950. This was especially

---

counties. For the remaining cases we impute competitiveness based on the congressional results. We deal carefully with redistricting, using Martis's (1982) *The Historical Atlas of Congressional Districts, 1789-1983, Redistricting in the 1980s*, the *Congressional District Atlases* published by the US Census Bureau, and other books and reports.

[17] The analysis above treats large and small states, and large and small counties, equally. However, the situation looks only slightly better if we weight by population. During the period 1880 to 1950, the percentage of state-years classified as competitive is 48.7 percent, while the fraction of people living in competitive states is 54.0 percent. Similarly, the percentage of county-years classified as competitive is 34.9 percent, while the fraction of people living in competitive counties is 41.8 percent. Thus a substantial majority of the population lived in uncompetitive counties. Although the pre-1950 period is before the Supreme Court decisions equalizing congressional district populations (for example, *Baker v. Carr*), even during the period under investigation the differences in population across congressional districts were smaller than the variation across states or counties.

true at the county and congressional district level, although it also held at the state level in many years. Thus, for a large number of constituencies during this period, the general elections did not appear to give voters a choice between two viable alternatives, leaving them with little apparent influence over the selection of their elected officials.

2.1.1 Why So Much One-Party Domination in the US?

Although stable two-party competition is considered one of the hall-marks of the US political system, below the national level many constituencies maintained one-party dominance well into the twentieth century. In Chapter 7 we show that uncompetitive general elections are a prominent feature of US politics even into the twenty-first century.

Why is there so little general election competition locally in US politics? A number of prominent scholars have weighed in on this question. The most straightforward explanation is based on party identification. Many voters in the US have strong party attachments that are heavily influenced by national historical events, national public policy choices, group attachments, and perhaps ideologies, which interact with various social, economic, and cultural characteristics. The distribution of social, economic, and cultural characteristics varies considerably across geographic areas, and therefore the distribution of party attachments varies as well. Thus, there is no reason to expect that in any given area the distribution of partisan attachments will be the same as the national distribution. Even if the national division in the support for the two major parties is close to 50–50, in many localities the division may be far from 50–50. For example, these days, Massachusetts and New York City are heavily Democratic, while Wyoming and Lubbock County, Texas, are heavily Republican.

This argument dates back at least to Key (1964, 289):

A state's social and economic characteristics may drive it toward one-partyism in both national and state affairs. To take an extreme hypothetical instance, a state dominated by industries organized by the CIO would have been in recent decades strongly Democratic nationally. It would also have probably been overwhelmingly Democratic in state affairs. Given the potency of the issues of national politics in shaping popular attitudes, the circumstances fixing the cleavages in national politics may incidentally form the divisions within state politics.

Sorauf (1972, 42) also observed the trend of "the formation of party loyalties along lines determined by national or statewide political debate." He provides an example of how "party loyalties and identifications grow out of national politics," arguing: "If the Democratic Party is identified nationally with the aspirations of the poor and minority groups, its appeal in a homogeneous, affluent suburb may be limited. Increasingly, national politics may thus rob the local party organization of the chance to develop strength based on its own issues, personalities, and traditions." The nationalization of politics can therefore undermine local two-party competition.

The political psychology literature maintains that important events or policy choices may continue to affect the distribution of partisanship long after they occur. Partisan identifications formed out of profound experiences are durable through individuals' life cycles, and even across generations through socialization.[18] Thus, one-party dominance in an area may persist long after the initial cause has faded.

The pockets of one-party dominance expected from the uneven geographic distribution of interests associated with party labels is perhaps most applicable to periods when parties and the electorate are nationalized. While some argue that US politics became significantly more nationalized following the New Deal, local electorates – particularly in the South, according to Schattschneider (1960, 87) – were still attached to particular national parties based upon the social, economic, and cultural characteristics of their geographical areas even earlier.[19] The South/non-South partisan divide during the Fourth Party System could be viewed as reflecting the differences in the national parties' positions in the Civil War.[20]

Elites' strategic choices can exacerbate pre-existing partisan imbalances and often reinforce the tendency toward one-party domination. If Democrats or Republicans have a clear electoral advantage in a particular area, then talented individuals who live in that area and want to run for office will tend to join the advantaged party. Interest groups or individuals who control electorally valuable resources – money, endorsements, campaign workers, votes – that they would like to exchange for favorable government policies or other political "favors" will also gravitate toward the party that is more likely to be in the majority, since it will typically be in a better position to deliver policies

[18] Campbell et al. (1960); Green, Palmquist, and Schickler (2002).

[19] See Claggett, Flanigan, and Zingale (1984) for a review of the early work on the extent to which the electorate has become nationalized over time. See Hopkins (2018) for a more recent analysis of nationalization of US politics.

[20] Schattschneider (1960, 76, 80) argues that even during the "1896 party cleavage" there was at least tacit collusion between "the northern conservative Republicans and the southern conservative Democrats."

and favors.[21] Sorauf (1972, 42) writes, "a party trying to pull itself into competitiveness may find itself caught organizationally in a vicious circle of impotence. Its inability to win elections limits its ability to recruit resources, including manpower, because as a chronic loser it offers so little chance of achieving political goals." Thus, a party that is advantaged due to the underlying distribution of voters' partisan loyalties may often be further advantaged by its ability to attract talent and resources.

These explanations for the prevalence of uncompetitive constituencies are most salient when there are two political parties. In principle, third parties – especially regional parties or those with geographically concentrated groups of supporters – can substitute for competition between the two major parties. Prior to the New Deal, some third parties did so, at least to a limited degree. The Greenbacks, Populists, and Progressives all attracted regional support in the late nineteenth and early twentieth centuries. Overall, however, third parties in the United States have generally been too weak and short-lived to provide a sustained alternative to two-party competition. Even the limited support these parties received at the turn of the twentieth century had essentially disappeared by the New Deal.[22]

The US is relatively unique in its lack of third-party competition. Schattschneider (1942, 60) calls this "the most conspicuous and perhaps the most important fact about the system." The absence of viable third parties even in the one-party-dominated constituencies in the US is one of the enduring puzzles in American politics. While a number of explanations have been proposed in the literature, none seem particularly satisfactory. One popular explanation is that the US is limited to two parties because the prevailing electoral system in use is simple plurality rule. The application of Duverger's Law to the national level is appealing, but it does not explain why third parties do not gain strength in states and localities that lack two-party competition.[23] State and local governments in the US control vast resources and have extensive policy-making capacities, and this was even more true prior to the New Deal. Why are there not two viable parties competing to control each state and local government throughout the US?

---

[21] Grossman and Helpman (1996) provide a formal model that shows how resource allocation and policy choices by elites can exacerbate pre-existing partisan imbalances.
[22] Hirano and Snyder (2007).
[23] Also, other countries with similar electoral institutions have more successful third parties, which suggests that these institutions alone cannot explain their absence.

Resolving the puzzling absence of third parties in US electoral politics is beyond the scope of this book. We return to this issue in the next chapter, when we examine whether the introduction of primaries may have helped limit the appeal of third parties. For now we simply accept the fact that third parties have not offered a durable alternative to one-partyism.

2.2 THE CONVENTION SYSTEM

The US nomination system has evolved significantly over time.[24] Before the introduction of direct primaries, parties typically nominated their candidates through a two-stage system commonly referred to as the caucus-convention system. (For the remainder of the book, we refer to this as simply the "convention system.") In the first stage, localities would select delegates to meet at a nominating convention using a variety of methods including caucuses, or indirect primaries in which voters elected delegates. The delegates then gathered at party conventions to nominate candidates for offices at different levels – for example, state, county, or congressional district. The system had significant theoretical appeal, and even some of its critics acknowledged that it initially functioned well.[25] However, by the turn of the twentieth century there were widespread claims that the system was being abused and in need of reform.

When functioning as intended, the convention system has the potential to produce responsible party organizations with high-quality nominees. The conventions are an opportunity for delegates, who are presumably more informed and engaged than the typical voter, to formulate a coherent party platform and to choose high-quality nominees to represent this platform. In their deliberations, delegates could also identify and propose qualified candidates, which would likely expand the pool of suitable individuals considered for nominations.[26]

The system also gives party elites the opportunity to balance the representation of different interests and factions on their ticket. When

---

[24] See Dallinger (1897); Meyer (1902); Sait (1927); Ware (2002); Reynolds (2006).
[25] Sait (1927, 325), however, argues that the convention system was problematic from the beginning: "The wire-pullers and manipulators were always there."
[26] Meyer (1902, 51) writes, "[M]en of special merit have found in the meetings of delegates fortunate opportunities for acquiring prominence without great loss of time or money. To these time is often more important than money. The necessary personal advertising required for a preliminary canvass, aside from its disagreeable features, would have consumed a forbidding amount of time if done with sufficient thoroughness to insure a nomination; while many a young man of ability would have found the drain upon his finances in conducting a protracted personal campaign too severe to enable him to win the day for himself in the usual way."

asked to nominate candidates for multiple offices, convention delegates could log-roll, allocating the positions across the competing groups within the party. In the nineteenth and early twentieth centuries, these interests were often geographically based, but they could also be based on other demographic or religious attributes.[27]

Of course, in practice caucuses and conventions did not always function as intended. The system provided multiple avenues for narrow interests to exert undue influence over the nomination process. Critics of the system claimed that elites easily dominated caucuses and indirect primaries. Since the rules for selecting delegates were typically not clearly defined, party leaders had a wide range of tools with which to manipulate the caucus, beyond bribing or offering patronage. These included adjusting the timing or location of the caucus (holding "snap" delegate selection meetings or elections), providing alcohol, and outright intimidation.[28] The belief that the system was open to fraud or corruption may also have deterred well-intentioned individuals from participating in either the caucus or indirect primary.

While local elites may have manipulated the delegate selection process, state party elites were widely suspected of influencing the outcomes at conventions. For example, party leaders could circumvent the decisions of the caucuses and indirect primaries altogether by controlling the committee responsible for certifying delegates. This committee, usually referred to as a Committee on Credentials, determined which delegations would be seated at the convention in the event that multiple delegations claimed to represent the same localities.

Party elites would often simply resort to buying the support of convention delegates.[29] One Pennsylvania historian writes (Roberts, 1904, 318):

---

[27] For example, Hand (2002) discusses how the Vermont Republican Party managed the factions within the party by rotating positions between candidates from different sides of the Green Mountains.

[28] Meyer (1902, 41–2).

[29] Various news outlets reported claims about bribery or corruption in conventions. The following headlines are illustrative: "Mr. Hanna's Methods – Grave Scandal Comes to Light in Washington – Alleged Bribery of National Convention Delegates," *Salt Lake Tribune*, June 24, 1897; "Democratic Delegate Bribed," *New York Tribune*, April 8, 1899; "Delegates Bribed – Witnesses Substantiate Charges of Mayor Weaver," *Wilkes-Barre Record*, September 25, 1906; "Charges of Bribery by both Onondaga Factions at Rochester Convention," *The Post Standard*, October 1, 1910; "Delegate Bribed, Folk Charges, to Vote for Parker: Missourian Blames Ryan, Belmont, Murphy–Hearst, Clark and Tammany in Deal," *St. Louis Post-Dispatch*, June 25, 1912; "Did Send $1,000 to Negro Delegate: Chairman McKinley Admits Paying Expenses of the Delegation from Mississippi," *New York Times*, June 16, 1912; "The 'Lily Whites' –

Conventions, where nominations are made, have become in our counties bargain counters where candidates openly buy votes, and the delegates boastfully exhibit the money they secure by selling them. Sums from $75 to $200 were recently paid and the men receiving the money attempted not to conceal the fact. An ex-boss in politics in one of our counties in a recent public address protested against bribery, corruption and commercialism in politics and said that the electors were sold "as sheep in the shambles." A man in the crowd said: "He ought to know; a few years ago he brought into the county $10,000 to buy up delegates for the state machine."

In his autobiography, Robert M. La Follette attributes his difficulty in being elected governor in Republican-dominated Wisconsin to his unwillingness to rely on elites to gather convention delegate support. He lost the Republican gubernatorial nomination three times – in 1894, 1896, and 1898 – despite his own perceived majority support among the convention delegates and among the electorate. He describes the 1898 gubernatorial nomination as follows (La Follette, 1913, 220):

When the convention met I should have been nominated on the first ballot, except for the use of money with delegates exactly as in the convention of 1896. Senator Stephenson, then a Scofield supporter and a power in the old organization, stated many times to my friends that the total amount of money required to handle delegates the night before the balloting began was $8,300. I was again defeated.

To some extent the pathologies of the convention system might also have reflected changes in the types of candidates seeking the nominations. Reynolds (2006, 10) argues that there was a sharp rise in the number of ambitious office-seekers – which he calls "hustling candidates" – and this further distorted the system from one based on deliberative meetings over carefully considered options to an arena for rent seeking. He writes:

The appearance of a more visible and active body of elective office seekers posed a special problem for the convention system. Candidates recruited scores of paid and unpaid agents, traveled extensively to meet with local notables, took a more active part in conventions, and most importantly worked to elect delegates committed to their candidacy … and conventions became more unruly as aspirants struggled for control.

Presumably in some cases the party elites could therefore extract more rents from the hustling candidates, leading to enhanced incentives to manipulate the system, as discussed above. In other cases, the new

Report that Some Convention Delegates Will Have Their Expenses Paid," *News Journal* (Wilmington, Delaware), September 19, 1912.

ambitious candidates were challenging the power of established party leaders by bypassing them and appealing directly to local notables and delegates.

It seems evident that elites' incentives to intervene in the caucus-convention process were stronger in one-party-dominated areas compared to competitive constituencies, since nominations in these areas were tantamount to winning the office. In competitive areas, elites had a stronger incentive to select high-quality candidates and avoid accusations that the nomination process was corrupt, since the parties had to worry about how well their nominees appealed to the general electorate.

2.3 ADOPTION OF PRIMARIES

Criticism of the convention system increased steadily during the nineteenth century, as this system became increasingly viewed as a source of corruption, fraud, and inefficiency. The direct primary appealed to many as a straightforward reform that would limit the ability of political and economic elites to manipulate and profit from the nomination process. During the first two decades of the twentieth century, almost all US states abandoned conventions in favor of direct primaries, ushering in what Ranney (1975, 121) describes as "the most radical of all the party reforms adopted in the whole course of American history."[30]

Popular accounts of the adoption of direct primaries often give substantial credit to progressive leaders. Progressive reformers sought to weaken political parties, which they claimed were under the control of bosses and corrupt machines. To accomplish this they worked to influence public opinion and mobilize local elite support, and they sponsored legislation and lobbied for its passage. The direct primary was in fact just one in a bundle of anti-party reforms, and as Ranney (1975, 81) notes, "The Progressives' arguments – and formidable political clout – won the day."

More recently, scholars have raised important questions regarding how the reform could have been enacted if all entrenched interests were against it.[31] There must have been support for the reform among those holding power. In the absence of direct democracy, a majority of state legislators and the governor must have supported the legislation in order

[30] Merriam and Overacker (1928) describe the relatively rapid adoption of this mechanism throughout the country.
[31] Ware (2002); Reynolds (2006).

for it to pass.[32] Why would incumbent politicians be willing to pass mandatory direct primaries?

One argument is that certain types of conservative, stalwart, or "organization" politicians would benefit personally from weakening the party bosses' control over nominations. Politicians who were charismatic campaigners or who were popular among the rank-and-file could expect to win in primaries and, under the primary system they would feel less pressure to pander to the party machine. Ware (2002) gives the examples of governors Charles Deneen of Illinois and William Sulzer of New York – they were not progressive reformers, but believed that direct primaries would improve their positions within their respective parties.

Another argument is that some party leaders supported primaries hoping to thwart challenges that were emerging from third parties and/or the other major party. Ware (2002) discusses how the Republican Party's dominance in Pennsylvania was threatened when a dissident faction left to form the City Party. In response, Governor Samuel W. Pennypacker expanded his reform proposals to include direct primaries. Ware (2002, 145) writes: "Pennypacker's overall strategy of moderate reform as a way of restoring trust in the Republicans worked. After Berry, no Democrat was elected to statewide office until 1931, and the City Party had collapsed by 1907. Republican dominance was restored."[33] Key (1949) and Kousser (1974) argue that in many Southern states Democrats promoted primaries as a way to consolidate the party's political monopoly particularly in response to threats from populists. Relatedly, Democratic Party elites sought to prevent factions within the party from bolting and aligning with third parties.[34]

A third argument is that conventions had lost their value to many local party elites. Since US state parties were typically decentralized organizations, incumbent politicians needed control over local party organizations and – in order to "bring home the bacon" – they

---

[32] In at least one case (Oregon), the entrenched interests could be bypassed by appealing to voters directly and passing the law by initiative.

[33] Another argument follows from the claim in Reynolds (2006) that politics was becoming increasingly candidate-centered around the turn of the twentieth century. As party leaders had to worry more about the electability and campaigning ability of their nominees, they might have used primaries to help them identify candidates with these attributes. Serra (2011) and Carey and Polga-Hecimovich (2006) apply this argument to use of primaries by parties in Latin America.

[34] See Kousser (1974). Other scholars have argued that parties sought primaries as a way to manage intra-party conflicts (Hortala-Vallve and Mueller, 2015; Kemahlioglu, Weitz-Shapiro, and Hirano, 2009).

had to make deals with politicians in other parts of the state. Two forums for making these deals were the state legislature and the state party conventions. For example, at party conventions nominations for different statewide offices could be divided across areas of the state or across party factions, and inter-temporal log-rolls, such as the "mountain rule" in Vermont, could be implemented. As Ware (2002) and Reynolds (2006) both argue, party conventions had become increasingly unwieldy, chaotic, and unpredictable. Ware (2002) points to factors such as population growth and increasing population heterogeneity due to immigration, while Reynolds (2006) highlights the role of ambitious office-seekers. Both also note the increase in claims of fraud and bribery. Also, in states that used indirect primaries, large blocs of delegates would enter the convention already pledged to particular candidates or slates. Thus, over time party conventions had become less and less useful as spaces for deal-making and log-rolling, reducing their value to many "regular" politicians.

The direct primary was also generally popular among voters, and some "regular" politicians might have hoped to win votes by attaching themselves to the reform movement.[35] In the states where there were initiatives or referendums to adopt primaries, the system was supported overwhelmingly: Oregon voted in favor of primaries by 56,325 to 16,354 in 1904; Illinois voted 590,976 to 78,446 in 1904; Wisconsin voted 130,699 to 80,192 in 1904; Maine voted 65,810 to 21,774 in 1911; and Montana voted in favor of primaries by 46,473 to 12,879 in 1912. Politicians in states that were late to adopt primaries might have felt additional pressure to reform. Critics and political opponents could easily argue, "What is wrong with our representatives? Most states have already adopted primaries and they seem to be working well. Why hasn't our state adopted them? I guess our politicians must be corrupt."

Finally, while progressives were focusing on direct primaries as a simple and intuitive solution to the problems caused by the caucus and convention system, non-progressives did not offer any alternative reforms with similar appeal. Ware (2002, 204) argues that "the key to the eventual success of the direct primary was the absence of serious rivals to it. Consequently, amid the complexity of the issues surrounding nomination reform, attention came to be focused on the supposed 'solution' rather than on anything else."

---

[35] Ware (2002).

2.3.1 Primary Adoption and One-Partyism

V.O. Key, Jr. originally argued that the introduction of direct primaries was related to the absence of inter-party competition. Southern states dominated by the Democratic Party were early adopters of direct primaries. Key (1949) and Kousser (1974) argue that primaries were designed to preserve one-party rule by white elites and middle-class citizens in the South. The success of populist third parties in the late nineteenth century raised concerns that a coalition could form between black voters and lower-income white voters to defeat Democratic Party candidates. Kousser (1974, 74) explains how primaries offered party leaders a way to maintain the one-party-dominant system and further disenfranchise blacks and lower-income voters: "Deciding party nominations in semi-private primaries rather than in backroom caucuses, would legitimate the nominees, settle intra-party differences before the general election and greatly reduce the power of opposition voters – most often Negroes – by confronting them with a solid Democratic party."[36]

Key later extended his argument that inter-party competition is connected to the adoption of direct primaries to include non-Southern states.[37] Key (1964, 375–6) writes:

The spread of the direct primary is commonly attributed to its appeal as an instrument of popular rule, yet probably the nature of the party structure in the area of its origin stimulated its growth. In the 1890's the party system had broken down in the sense that a single party dominated many states and localities... The ties of party – given the recency of the Civil War – made it simpler to advance popular government by introducing the direct primary to permit intra-party competition than to proceed by a realignment of parties. The convention system

---

[36] Many accounts of the all-white primary as a means to disenfranchise black voters are too simplistic, because they implicitly *assume* the existence of primary elections. For example, Scher (2015, 37–8) writes the following: "The all-white primary was another mechanism designed to disenfranchise blacks during the Jim Crow era. It was the product of the one-party system in the old South ... after 1896 ... the Democratic Party was the only political game in the region. As a result, electoral politics were centered in the Democratic primary; the winner of this contest would inevitably prevail in the general election." But this begs the question: Why did southern Democrats need all-white *primaries* to disenfranchise blacks, when they already had all-white (Democratic) *conventions* doing this? All-white primaries were not required to exclude black voters from the Democratic Party's nomination process. Thus, something *else* must have been driving the need to adopt primaries (for example, the fear that large numbers of Democrats would defect to the Populist Party or another third party in the general election if the current convention system was retained). In the South, once primaries were being adopted, limiting participation to whites was natural.

[37] Key (1956, 1964).

in a one-party situation does not serve well to produce acceptable decisions on contests that stir the multitude.

Others have echoed this sentiment.[38] If this relationship exists, then we would observe primaries being adopted first in those areas where they have the greatest potential to increase electoral competition.

The literature does not fully develop the logic of why one-partyism outside the South would facilitate the adoption of primaries. The need to maintain one-party dominance to disenfranchise certain groups was less apparent for the Republican parties in non-Southern states. However, the various problems associated with the convention system highlighted by progressive reformers were most likely made worse by the absence of general election competition. By allowing party elites to determine general election winners through their influence over nominations, the convention system provided strong incentives for special interests, such as business groups, to direct their resources toward the dominant party. In turn, the leaders of the dominant party, who did not have to be as concerned about the quality of their nominees in order to win the general elections, were also less constrained in extracting rents through the nomination process.

These problems were recognized by some progressive reformers and political observers, including newspaper editors. For example, *The Des Moines Register* wrote in 1899, "When party strength is more equal the instinct of self-preservation and the fear of defeat are generally strong enough to compel parties to nominate fit men for public office."[39] Another example, from a pamphlet distributed by the Citizens Union in 1909, stated: "As Governor Hughes pointed out in a recent speech in New York City, three-fourths of the members of the present legislature come from districts where the nomination of the dominant party is equivalent to election. When, in such districts, the candidates are nominated by a method which places the real selection in the hands of a

---

[38] Sorauf (1972, 210) writes, "The quick success of the direct primary movement happened during the years of the greatest one-partyism in American history. In the early years of the twentieth century sectionalism was rampant, and one party or another dominated the politics of many states. One-partyism made the nomination of the major party crucial. Although the failings of the conventions might be tolerated when a real choice remained in the general election, they could not be borne when the nomination of the dominant party was equivalent to election. The convention could choose the weariest party hack without fear of challenge from the other party. And so the Progressives who fought economic monopoly with antitrust legislation, fought political monopoly with the direct primary." See also Burnham (1965).

[39] *The Des Moines Register*, October 25, 1899, page 4.

few men, then in soberest earnest we may say that the forms of popular government are become but a sham."[40]

Ware (2002) challenged the notion that the lack of inter-party competition was a particularly important factor for explaining the introduction of direct primaries outside the South. In an empirical analysis of non-Southern states, Ware (2002, 195) claims that "there was absolutely no connection between the absence of competition and the likelihood of a state adopting the direct primary ... while competition can be important in understanding the rise of the direct primary in particular states, it is not an explanatory variable that can account for developments in all states."[41]

In fact, the relationship between one-party dominance and the adoption of primaries is quite tight, at least statistically. We document this clearly, using new measures of party safety and dominance based on state-level electoral and legislative data, as well as new information on when states introduced primaries.

Somewhat surprisingly, it is not straightforward to determine when and where direct primaries were used in every US state. In some cases, determining the date primaries were introduced involves an element of judgment. The most difficult cases are states in which the primary was optional but used routinely as a matter of party practice. The dates for when primaries were adopted in Southern states are particularly difficult to identify; in many Southern states, primaries were allowed by law or party rules and were used at the discretion of party leaders. Further complicating the coding, some states used primaries for only some offices. For example, for many years, Indiana and New York used primaries to nominate candidates for the US House but not for the US Senate or statewide office. We employ a variety of sources, including historical works, state manuals, and newspapers, to provide a detailed

---

[40] This pamphlet was discussed in several New York newspapers at the time, including the *New York Times* on February 21, 1909, page 10 and the *Buffalo Commercial* on February 20, 1909, page 1.

[41] Even Ware (2002, 178) acknowledges the relationship between the introduction of primaries and constituency safety, stating that "when examining the timing of the introduction of primary laws that covered virtually all state offices, it appears as if there may be a link between their early introduction and Republican party strength ... Those states that were safely Republican in 1910 ... were much more likely to have given an early passage to such legislation ... Underlying the apparent relationship between the two variables is a different factor – region." While there does appear to be some regional clustering in the adoption of primaries, it is not clear what the "region" variable represents theoretically. This variable may simply be capturing areas with more dominant parties.

coding of the dates and types of primary elections used in each state and year.[42] Appendix Table 2.A shows the year of adoption of mandatory and optional primaries for statewide offices, the US House, and the US Senate.[43] In some cases, we include the date when primaries were optional but were used in virtually every statewide election. For the mandatory and optional primary laws, the dates reflect the year the law was passed. We use these dates in various analyses throughout the book.

Table 2.1 shows the underlying distribution of voter partisanship – based on voting in statewide elections as above – and party control of government at the time each state adopted direct primaries. For all states outside the South, the year of adoption is the year the state passed a mandatory statewide direct primary law. For some Southern states, the year of adoption is the first year that the Democratic Party began the continuous use of primaries to make nominations statewide.

We define party control in the usual way. A state is under Unified Democratic control if the governor and a majority of the legislators in each chamber are Democrats or if the Democrats control more than two-thirds of the seats in both legislative chambers. Unified Republican control is defined similarly. All other situations are classified as Divided control. To measure the underlying partisanship in each state, we use the results for all available statewide elections that took place during the years $t-8$ to t, where t is the year of adoption. We then classify states as follows: Advantaged Democratic if the average Democratic vote over the years $t-8$ to t is greater than 57.5 percent; Leaning Democratic if the average Democratic vote is between 50 and 57.5 percent; Leaning Republican if the average Republican vote is between 50 and 57.5 percent; and Advantaged Republican if the average Republican vote is greater than 57.5 percent.

[42] We inspected tables published in other works, such as Merriam and Overacker (1928); Galderisi, Ezra, and Lyons (2001); Ware (2002), and Harvey and Mukherjee (2006), and find noticeable discrepancies. Building on these tables, we have done our best to resolve the discrepancies. We used the following materials: Joint Committee of the Senate and Assembly of the State of New York (1910); Aylesworth (1908, 1912); Merriam (1908). We also checked a large number of newspaper articles that report primary dates, lists of candidates running, and primary results.

[43] In Table 2.A we exclude some of the very early legislation regarding the conduct of optional primaries. Some states used primaries in certain elections for certain offices. For example, South Carolina used primaries in 1892 for governor but no other statewide offices. North Carolina used primaries for US Senate in the Democratic Party in 1900 and 1912, but not in other years prior to passing the mandatory primary law in 1915. In Virginia, which had optional primaries, the Democratic Party nominated candidates through conventions instead of primaries.

Table 2.1 makes clear that most states adopted primaries when one of the parties was advantaged, 31 out of 45 cases. Moreover, in most of these states the advantaged party also had full control of the state government. In general, primaries tended to be adopted when one party had unified control over the state government, 40 out of 45 cases. The table also suggests that primary laws were adopted later, and were more likely to be repealed or weakened, in states without an advantaged party. Of the 28 states that adopted a law prior to 1910, which are in bold italics, 23 had an advantaged party.[44] All of the early adopters were under unified party control. In a majority of the late adopters, the state did not have an advantaged party at the time the reform was introduced. For many of the late adopters, the parties may have felt additional pressure to adopt the reform already adopted in neighboring states.[45] All of the early adopting Southern states (9 out of 11) were solidly Democratic and under unified Democratic control at the time of primary adoption. Even outside the South, the early adopting states were likely to be uncompetitive, 14 out of 19.

These tables and figures do not, of course, demonstrate that the absence of two-party competition *caused* the adoption of primaries. Some states had advantaged parties for many years prior to the reform, which suggests that the absence of inter-party competition alone does not explain the relationship. Nonetheless, the two variables do have a strong association. Primaries were initially introduced in states in which we would expect them to have made the most significant contribution to the electoral system.

2.4 CONCLUSION

V.O. Key, Jr. described the direct primary as "at bottom an escape from one-partyism."[46] In the absence of this "escape," voters in one-party-dominated constituencies were to some extent merely spectators in the process of selecting elected officials. Political historians have long documented the frustrations reformers expressed concerning

---

[44] Only two of the five case studies in Ware (2002) examine states where primaries were adopted prior to 1910.

[45] Two states sharply weakened their initial primary laws and did not strengthen them again for many decades. In 1929, Indiana eliminated primaries for governor and US senator, and did not reinstate them until 1975 (Indiana never adopted primaries for statewide down-ballot offices). In 1921, New York eliminated primaries for all statewide offices, and did not reinstate them until 1967. Note that neither of these states had an advantaged party and neither was an early adopter of the reform. South Dakota had an advantaged party that had unified control of the state government at the time primaries were introduced, but later eliminated primaries for down-ballot offices.

[46] Key (1956, 88).

TABLE 2.1 *Partisanship and Control When Statewide Primaries Adopted*

Partisanship	Party Control at Time of Adoption		
	Unified Democratic	Divided	Unified Republican
Advantaged Democratic	*AL, AZ*[1]*, AR* *FL, GA, LA* *MS, SC, TX* *VA*, NM, NC TN, UT		
Leaning Democratic	*MD, MO, NV*[2] *OK*[1], IN[2], KY NY[2], OH		
Leaning Republican	CO, ME	MT, NJ, WV	*NE*
Advantaged Republican		MA, WY	*CA, ID*[2]*, IL* *IA, KS, MI* *ND, NH, OR* *PA, SD*[2]*, WA* *WI*, MN[3], VT

Only states that adopted primaries prior to 1940 are included. So, AK, CT, HI and RI are not shown. DE is not shown because it adopted optional primaries that neither major party used during this period. States that adopted primaries prior to 1910 are in bold italic font.
[1] AZ and OK adopted primary laws at statehood. Therefore, the underlying partisanship is based on the elections to the constitutional conventions and the first two statewide elections after statehood.
[2] IN (1929) and NY (1921) eliminated primaries for governor and US senator, and did not reinstate them for over 40 years. SD eliminated primaries for statewide down-ballot offices in 1929. ID eliminated statewide primaries in 1919 and then reinstated them in 1931. NV repealed its primary law in 1915, replacing direct primaries with indirect primaries, but restored direct primaries in 1917.
[3] In 1901 MN adopted a statewide primary law that included US House seats, state legislative seats, and local offices, but not statewide offices.

the abuses of the convention system by various elites who could manipulate the convention delegates. The combination of one-party dominance and the convention system was particularly problematic.

Political observers have debated whether primaries provided an effective solution to the problems associated with one-partyism in the decades after they were introduced. The evidence has tended to be in the form of anecdotal accounts. The following chapters provide systematic evidence that primaries helped alleviate many of the problems associated with one-partyism, and that this had a significant impact on representation in the first half of the twentieth century.

TABLE 2.A *Adoption or Major Modification in Use of Primaries*

State	Year	Events
Alabama	1902	Democratic Party begins using primaries regularly for statewide offices and US House
	1915	Major law regulating the conduct of primaries
Alaska	1958	Mandatory primary law (in constitution at statehood)
Arizona	1909	Mandatory primary law (in constitution at statehood)
Arkansas	1900	Democratic Party begins using primaries regularly for statewide offices and US House
	1909	Major law regulating the conduct of primaries
	1957	Mandatory primary law
California	1909	Mandatory primary law
	2010	Adopted Top-Two System (effective in 2012)
Colorado	1910	Mandatory primary law
Connecticut	1955	Mandatory primary law, under "challenge primary" system
Delaware	1913	Passes optional primary law, but neither major party used them for statewide office or US House
	1969	Mandatory primary law, under "challenge primary" system
Florida	1902	Democratic Party begins using primaries regularly for statewide offices and US House
	1913	Mandatory primary law
Georgia	1898	Democratic Party begins using primaries regularly for statewide offices and US House
	1908	Major law regulating the conduct of primaries
Hawaii	1959	Mandatory primary law (in constitution at statehood)
Idaho	1909	Mandatory primary law
	1919	Repeals mandatory primaries for statewide offices and US House
	1931	Restores mandatory primaries for statewide offices and US House
Illinois	1908	Mandatory primary law (laws passed in 1905, 1906, and 1908 were struck down by state Supreme Court; primaries were held in 1908, under the 1908 law; the 1908 law was rewritten in 1910 to satisfy the Court).
Indiana	1915	Mandatory primary law (effective in 1916) for governor, US senator, and US House, but not down-ballot statewide offices
	1929	Repeals mandatory primaries for governor and US senator
	1975	Restores mandatory primaries for governor and US senator
Iowa	1907	Mandatory primary law
Kansas	1908	Mandatory primary law

TABLE 2.A *(cont.)*

State	Year	Events
Kentucky	1912	Mandatory primary law (state made primaries optional from 1920 to 1935, but both parties used primaries for statewide offices and US House throughout this period)
Louisiana	1904	Democratic Party begins using primaries regularly for statewide offices and US House
	1906	Mandatory primary law
	1975	Switch to Louisiana "Top-Two" system (effective in 1978 for federal offices)
Maine	1911	Mandatory primary law
Maryland	1910	Mandatory primary law
Massachusetts	1911	Mandatory primary law
Michigan	1909	Mandatory primary law for governor, US Senate, US House, and lt. governor, but not other down-ballot statewide offices
Minnesota	1899	Mandatory primary law for Hennepin County only (including 5th congressional district)
	1901	Mandatory primary law for US House but not statewide offices
	1912	Mandatory primary law for statewide offices
Mississippi	1902	Mandatory primary law
Missouri	1907	Mandatory primary law
Montana	1912	Mandatory primary law
Nebraska	1907	Mandatory primary law
Nevada	1909	Mandatory primary law
	1915	Replaces mandatory direct primaries with indirect primaries
	1917	Restores mandatory direct primaries
New Hampshire	1909	Mandatory primary law
New Jersey	1911	Mandatory primary law
New Mexico	1939	Mandatory primary law
New York	1913	Mandatory primary law
	1921	Repeals mandatory primaries for statewide offices
	1967	Restores mandatory primaries for statewide offices
North Carolina	1915	Mandatory primary law
North Dakota	1907	Mandatory primary law
Ohio	1908	Mandatory primary for offices that do not span multiple counties
	1913	Mandatory primary law
Oklahoma	1908	Mandatory primary law
Oregon	1904	Mandatory primary law (effective in 1906)

(continued)

TABLE 2.A *(cont.)*

State	Year	Events
Pennsylvania	1907	Mandatory primary law for US House
	1913	Mandatory primary law for statewide offices
Rhode Island	1947	Mandatory primary law
South Carolina	1892	Democratic Party begins using primaries regularly for US House
	1896	Democratic Party begins using primaries regularly for statewide offices
	1915	Major revision to primary election law
South Dakota	1907	Mandatory primary law
	1929	Repeals mandatory primaries for down-ballot statewide offices
Tennessee	1909	Mandatory primary law (struck down by state Supreme Court)
	1917	Mandatory primary law
Texas	1905	Mandatory primary law (Terrell Law)
Utah	1937	Mandatory primary law
Vermont	1915	Mandatory primary law
Virginia	1905	Democratic Party begins using primaries regularly for statewide offices
	1912	Major law regulating the conduct of voluntary primaries
Washington	1907	Mandatory primary law
	2004	Adopted Top-Two System (effective in 2008)
West Virginia	1915	Mandatory primary law
Wisconsin	1903	Mandatory primary law (effective in 1906, and subject to referendum; referendum passes in 1904 by vote of 62 percent to 38 percent)
Wyoming	1911	Mandatory primary law

Tennessee passed legislation requiring primaries in 1909. In 1910 this was struck down by the state supreme court. Primary elections were held in 1908 and 1912, but we found no evidence that they were held in 1914 or 1916. Georgia passed a law that introduced the county-unit rule system in 1917. Maryland's original primary law included the county-unit rule system. In the Louisiana top-two system, the candidates proceed to a second round only if no candidate receives a majority in the first round.

3

Introduction of Primaries and Electoral Competition, 1892 to 1950

In May 1914, the Pennsylvania Republican Party held its first direct primary for statewide offices. As discussed in the previous chapter, Republicans dominated Pennsylvania politics at the turn of the twentieth century. They won the general elections for all but one statewide office in the four decades prior to the New Deal. The 1914 primary was the first opportunity for the state's voters to "escape from one-partyism."

At the state level, the first direct primaries in Pennsylvania were a success, at least in terms of offering the electorate more options. Of the four statewide offices that were up for election, three had contested Republican primaries – the nominations for governor, US senator, and lieutenant governor – and in the one that was uncontested, for secretary of internal affairs, the incumbent was seeking re-election. For those hoping for more competition, however, the primaries fell short, as none of the three contested races were competitive. The nominees, all supported by party boss Boies Penrose (himself the nominee for US senator), won at least 66 percent of the primary vote in their respective races. The gubernatorial primary was the most lopsided, the nominee winning almost 80 percent of the vote. As in the past, all four Republicans were elected easily with over 62 percent of the vote in the general election. Thus, Pennsylvania state politics in 1914 remained largely uncompetitive.

Two years later, Republican primaries were held for three statewide offices: US senator, state treasurer, and state auditor. The Republican primaries for US senator and state treasurer again offered disappointing levels of competition. In both races, the party leaders lined up in support of a favored candidate. The party elite endorsed Senate candidate Philander Knox, who was a former US senator, US attorney general, and

33

US secretary of state; he faced no primary competition.[1] Party bosses also endorsed state treasurer candidate Harmon M. Kephart, who easily won his primary with roughly two-thirds of the vote.[2] As in previous elections, both Republican candidates faced little general election competition, winning office with close to 60 percent of the two-party vote.

The one statewide office for which the Republican nominee did face significant competition was state auditor. The Republican party elites were divided in their support; Governor Martin G. Brumbaugh was among the prominent party leaders backing Charles A. Ambler, while Senator Boies Penrose and much of the state party organization backed Charles A. Snyder.[3] Both candidates had state legislative experience, but Ambler had a more traditional pedigree for a party loyalist, having been a Republican Party county committee member and former postmaster. Snyder appeared to have more relevant experience, as he was formerly a county comptroller. The primary was relatively close; Snyder won with less than 53 percent of the vote. Of course, Snyder went on to easily win the general election, also with close to 60 percent of the two-party vote.

Some of those skeptical of the direct primary were concerned that primaries would not be competitive, and thus would not provide an "escape" from one-partyism. They argued that the high costs associated with running primary campaigns would limit the pool of potential primary entrants to those with substantial campaign resources. In areas with party machines, the party leaders could endorse their preferred candidates and back them with the machine's resources, allowing them to dominate the nomination process. In the first two electoral cycles under

[1] On January 17, 1916, four months before the Republican primary, page 6 of the *Harrisburg Telegraph* stated, "Governor Brumbaugh made a wise move when he got behind Mr. Knox for the United States Senate. This at once brought not only all Republicans, but the Progressives as well, together on common ground and eliminated the possibility of a serious contest for the most important office to be filled in Pennsylvania at the November elections ... Every day finds the prospects brighter for Republican harmony at the primaries in May and for Republican success at the elections in November."

[2] There was some confusion as to whether Kephart's opponent J. V. Clark had the support of the governor due to slate cards distributed in certain parts of the state indicating Clark was on the governor's slate, which may explain why Clark was able to attract some electoral support in the primary (*The Pittsburgh Press*, May 14, 1916, page 1). Subsequent reports indicate that the governor did not consider Clark as being part of his slate.

[3] In a *Harrisburg Daily Independent* front-page article that appeared on February 14, 1916, a list of Ambler's supporters included Governor Brumbaugh, Congressman Vare, Senator Vare, Mayor Smith of Philadelphia, and Public Service Commissioner Magee. Snyder's supporters included Senator Penrose, Senator James McNichol, Mayor Armstrong, former Secretary of the Commonwealth McAfee, former Highway Commissioner Bigelow, and "a majority of the State organization."

direct primaries, six of Pennsylvania's seven statewide primary races were non-competitive, and the presence of party organizations was evident.

However, the 1916 Pennsylvania state auditor race demonstrates that primaries, at least in certain situations, had the potential to inject competition even into systems with long histories of one-party dominance and strong party organizations. Was this race indicative of how primaries were operating in other states, and how they might have increased the overall competitiveness of the electoral system in the country? If so, how much competition did primaries introduce across states and over time?

In this chapter we investigate primary competition across all states during the first half of the twentieth century. We have constructed a dataset of electoral results that includes virtually all primary elections for all statewide and federal offices since primaries were introduced in each state. This allows us to present a comprehensive description of primary competition overall and across different electoral circumstances. As noted throughout this book, primaries have the potential to play an especially important role in the US electoral system in areas that lack two-party competition. Also, when elections function largely as a selection rather than an accountability mechanism, we should be particularly concerned with the outcomes of open-seat races. Thus, we compare primaries in safe versus competitive constituencies, and incumbent-contested versus open-seat races.

In addition to documenting the competitiveness of primaries, we investigate the extent to which the new nomination system increased the overall competitiveness of the US electoral system where it was arguably most needed – that is, constituencies where the partisan loyalties significantly advantaged one political party in the general election. We seek to determine the percentage of elected officials who would not have faced any electoral competition in the absence of primaries. We document the percentage of cases in which an office holder faced electoral competition in only the primary, only the general, both the primary and general, or neither the primary nor the general election. Categorizing the electoral experience of office holders in this way highlights the contribution of primaries to the overall competitiveness of the US electoral system. During the first half-century after the reform, over 40 percent of all statewide and federal officials elected in open-seat races faced competition only in the primaries. By this metric, primaries added significantly to the competitiveness of the system as a whole.

Several scholars have speculated that primaries may also indirectly affect the overall level of competition by influencing the level of general election competition. Two prominent hypotheses in the literature are: (i) primaries increase support for incumbent parties; and (ii) primaries reduce competition by third-party candidates. Both of these claims suggest that the introduction of primaries may have had a negative effect on general election competition, and may even have helped perpetuate one-party dominance. While there are theoretical and intuitive reasons why primaries may have had these effects, we find little supporting evidence. One possible exception is the decline in third-party competition in the South.

In the final section we examine whether primaries affected the nature of electoral politics more generally – in particular whether the reform increased candidate-centered voting in general elections. Although few scholars have explicitly linked primaries to the growth of candidate-centered politics, the conventional wisdom is that primaries helped weaken political party organizations. This might have reduced the ability of parties to influence voter behavior – thereby increasing the incentives for candidates to campaign on their own – which might have led to an increase in ticket splitting. We provide evidence that the introduction of primaries is correlated with more split-ticket voting in general elections.

The bottom line is that primaries had a significant, direct impact on the competitiveness of the US electoral system in the first half of the twentieth century. Especially in areas dominated by one party, they injected intra-party electoral competition into advantaged parties' nomination contests. The indirect effects of primaries on general election competition are more ambiguous.

3.1 PRIMARY COMPETITION BY CONSTITUENCY TYPE

During the first half of the twentieth century, the overall level of primary competition was relatively modest when we average across all cases. Only 49.4 percent of US House primaries were even contested, and only 21.2 percent could be considered competitive. Also, the overall level of primary competition was relatively stable over time, aside from an increase in the 1930s. Thus, we do not examine the over-time variation in primary competition in this chapter.[4] Instead, here we focus on cross-sectional variation. For example, we sometimes separate

---

[4] We return to the over-time variation in Chapter 7, where we document the more dramatic shift in primary competition that occurred between the first and second half of the twentieth century.

open-seat primaries for advantaged parties in safe constituencies from other primaries, since these are likely to contribute the most to the US electoral system.

Theoretically, we expect there to be substantial variation in primary contestation and competition across constituencies depending on the expected level of general election competition. In areas that are safe for one party, where winning the primary almost guarantees being elected to office, potential candidates have a clear incentive to run. In areas with more two-party competition, winning the primary is more like winning a lottery with a 50–50 chance of being elected to office. This is of course valuable, but less so, and therefore fewer candidates will find it worth the effort to run. Where a party's nominee is expected to lose the general election, the incentives to run in the primary are even weaker.

Previous empirical studies typically find evidence consistent with these expectations. In safe states and districts, advantaged-party primaries are more contested and competitive especially in open-seat races, and disadvantaged-party primaries are less competitive. For example, Key (1949) famously described the vigorous competition for nominations in Democratic primaries in the one-party South during the first decades of the twentieth century. Also, in his classic study of American state politics, Key (1956) examined open-seat gubernatorial primaries in 25 states during the period 1906 to 1952. For this set of races he found that, "such factors as urbanism and incumbency may affect the frequency of primary competition through time but ... in the long run the incidence of primary competition is chiefly a function of the prospects for victory in the general election."[5] One limitation of these studies is that they typically only provide snapshots of primary competition for specific years, states, or offices.[6]

We employ data on primary and general election returns for all statewide and federal offices during the half-century after primaries were

[5] Key (1956, 79). Key (1956, 117) also notes that "as states deviate from equality of strength between parties, the frequency of sharp competition within the stronger party increases." Similarly, Sorauf (1963, 111) states, "The basic determinant of primary competition in Pennsylvania remains the prospect of victory in the [general] election." See also Ewing (1953); Turner (1953); Key (1956); Standing and Robinson (1958); Jewell (1967); Sorauf (1972); Schantz (1980); Grau (1981); Jewell and Olson (1982); Rice (1985); Jewell and Breaux (1991); Berry and Canon (1993); Herrnson and Gimpel (1995); Hogan (2003); Boatright (2014).

[6] Two exceptions are our own previous work with Stephen Ansolabehere and J. Mark Hansen (Ansolabehere et al., 2006, 2010).

first adopted.[7] These data were collected from official state election reports, state manuals, newspapers, and almanacs.[8] For the period prior to 1950, we have primary electoral returns and/or candidate lists from 8,923 statewide races and 15,782 US House races. These data allow us to give a relatively comprehensive account of primary competition during this period.

We use the statewide general election data introduced in the previous chapter, as well as a newly assembled data set of presidential election returns aggregated at the congressional district level, to measure constituency partisanship in a way that is arguably less prone to measurement error and/or endogeneity concerns than prior analyses of primary competition.[9] More specifically, we consider a party to be advantaged in a given state and year if its candidates won more than 57.5 percent of the vote, on average, across all available statewide races in a nine-year window around the given year ($t-4$ to $t+4$). The opposing party in such constituencies is considered disadvantaged. We refer to all other cases – that is, those in which the average Democratic (or Republican) vote share is between 42.5 and 57.5 percent – as parties-balanced constituencies.[10] For US House districts we use the presidential vote for all available years, and the same window around 50 percent to define safe and parties-balanced constituencies.[11] By combining these measures of constituency partisanship with measures of primary competition, we can assess not only whether primaries introduced competition into the US electoral system, but also in what types of constituencies.

---

[7] Only two states in our data, South Carolina and Georgia, had primaries before 1900. We include these races in the decade labelled 1900 in the figures below.

[8] See Ansolabehere et al. (2006) and Ansolabehere et al. (2010) for a list of most of the official sources used for the primary data.

[9] The measures used to define safe versus competitive constituencies in prior empirical studies often relied on previous general election outcomes for the office of interest. Our measure of constituency partisanship exploits general election outcomes for offices other than the one being investigated. This limits the problems that might arise from factors such as incumbency or the idiosyncratic personal appeal of particular candidates.

[10] The patterns look similar when we use the hybrid measure discussed in the previous chapter that includes winning percentages as well as vote percentages for the statewide offices, rather than the measure based exclusively on vote percentages.

[11] For the US House, we aggregated county-level returns, together with precinct- and ward-level returns where available for counties that were split across districts. In a few cases, we added or substituted gubernatorial precinct- or ward-level returns. In the remaining cases, we imputed the presidential vote based on congressional district votes. We do not classify some districts for some years because of large discrepancies in the partisanship implied by the presidential and congressional votes.

In describing different types of primaries, we use the following terminology. First, when an incumbent is running in a party's primary, we refer to it as an "incumbent-contested primary." Second, when an incumbent is running in the other party's primary, we refer to it as a "challenger-party primary." Third, we refer to situations where no incumbent is running in either party's primary as "open-seat primaries." Finally, in some analyses below we group together all primaries without incumbents – that is both open-seat primaries and challenger-party primaries – and refer to these collectively as "non-incumbent primaries."

Given the findings in previous literature as well as the theoretical arguments about where primaries can potentially contribute most to the electoral system, we are most interested in assessing how the level of competition in a party's primary varies with the general election prospects of the party's nominee, and also whether or not there is an incumbent in the race.[12] Thus, we divide primary races into seven types: (i) advantaged-party open-seat primaries; (ii) advantaged-party incumbent-contested primaries; (iii) parties-balanced open-seat primaries; (iv) parties-balanced challenger-party primaries; (v) parties-balanced incumbent-contested primaries; (vi) disadvantaged-party open-seat primaries; and (vii) disadvantaged-party challenger-party primaries.[13]

We consider four aspects of primary competition: (i) the percentage of races that were contested – that is, at least two candidates received more than 1 percent of the vote;[14] (ii) the percentage of races that are "competitive" – that is, if the winner received less than 57.5 percent of the total votes;[15] (iii) the number of candidates who received more

---

[12] Previous studies have also examined factors such as whether a state employs a primary and runoff system, or whether parties endorse candidates in pre-primary conventions (Canon, 1978; Wright and Riker, 1989; Berry and Canon, 1993). While these are likely to influence the level of primary competition, here we focus on documenting the relationship between primary competition and the partisanship of constituencies.

[13] There are two other types of primaries: advantaged-party challenger-party primaries and disadvantaged-party incumbent-contested primaries. Since there are so few cases of these types we do not include them in the figure.

[14] We drop cases in which a nomination was made by convention, including where one party nominated its candidate by convention but the other party held a primary election. All of these cases involve the Republican Party in Southern states. Alternatively, we can include them and count them as cases with "uncontested primaries." When we do this, the overall patterns are similar to those shown below.

[15] Uncontested elections are of course classified as uncompetitive, as are any primary elections in which *no* candidates ran for the nomination. We also drop cases in which the winner was nominated by a caucus or convention.

than 1 percent of the primary vote; and (iv) the votes cast for all losing candidates as a percentage of the total votes.[16]

Figures 3.1 and 3.2 display the four measures of primary competition averaging over the period 1892 to 1950 for statewide and US House races, respectively.[17] Each figure has three curves. One curve connects the average level of competition in open-seat primaries across the three types of constituencies: advantaged, parties-balanced, and disadvantaged. Another curve connects the average levels of competition for challenger-party primaries in disadvantaged and parties-balanced constituencies. The third curve connects competition in incumbent-contested primaries in parties-balanced and advantaged-party constituencies.

First, consider open-seat primaries for statewide offices in Figure 3.1. Advantaged-party primaries were more likely to be contested and also more likely to be competitive than disadvantaged-party primaries – 84.5 percent of advantaged-party primaries were contested, compared to just 32.9 percent of disadvantaged-party primaries. Similarly, 64.2 percent of advantaged-party primaries were competitive, compared to just 17.7 percent of disadvantaged-party primaries. Open-seat primaries in parties-balanced states were, on average, less competitive than advantaged-party primaries and more competitive than disadvantaged-party primaries. The other two measures of competition – the average number of candidates, and the percentage of votes won by losing candidates – exhibit the same relationship with constituency type. Also, Figure 3.2 shows that essentially the same pattern between the four measures of competition and constituency type is present for open-seat primaries for the US House.

Turning to incumbent-contested primaries, we see two clear patterns. First, the level of competition is noticeably lower in incumbent-contested primaries than in open-seat primaries. Second, as we move from parties-balanced constituencies to advantaged-party constituencies the level of competition generally increases but by less than in open-seat primaries. This is especially true for the US House. The gaps between

---

[16] That is, 100 minus the vote percentage of the winning candidate. When the primary is uncontested, the losing candidates' vote percentage is zero.

[17] The statewide offices included are US senator, governor, lieutenant governor, attorney general, secretary of state, treasurer, auditor (or controller or comptroller), superintendent of education, and any commissioners of public utilities, commerce, corporations, insurance, labor, lands, mines, or agriculture who are elected statewide. We also divided the statewide offices into four groupings: governor, US senator, "High Offices" (lieutenant governor, attorney general, and secretary of state) and "Low Offices" (all other statewide offices). The patterns look very similar across all four groupings.

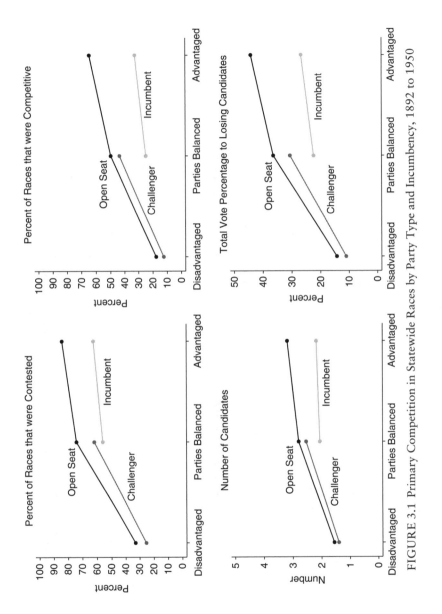

FIGURE 3.1 Primary Competition in Statewide Races by Party Type and Incumbency, 1892 to 1950

41

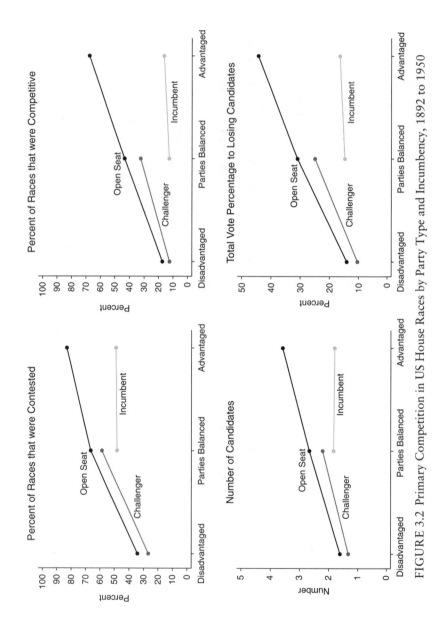

FIGURE 3.2 Primary Competition in US House Races by Party Type and Incumbency, 1892 to 1950

incumbent-contested primaries and open-seat primaries indicate that there was a sizable incumbency advantage in primary elections even in this early period.

Finally, in challenger-party primaries, the level of competition was slightly less than that observed for open-seat primaries in both parties-balanced and disadvantaged-party constituencies. The fact that these differences were small suggests that potential candidates were responding strategically to the electoral environment at the time. More specifically, there was little reason for candidates to be deterred by the prospect of facing an incumbent in the general election, since the general election incumbency advantage was small.

Overall, the patterns in these figures are consistent with the logic highlighted above and with previous findings in the literature. They provide further support for our argument that primaries contribute to the electoral system by allowing candidates to enter and compete in constituencies that would otherwise lack electoral competition. Some observers lament the low level of primary competition when an incumbent is present. However, as we discussed in the introduction, this might not be too much cause for concern. In fact it might even be desirable. If elections are effective selection mechanisms and/or service in office generates job-specific human capital, then incumbents may lack competition because they are better qualified for the position than the pool of potential entrants.

3.2 PRIMARY VERSUS GENERAL ELECTION COMPETITION

We now examine competition in primaries and general elections with the following two questions in mind. Did elected officials face moderate to serious competition at some point on their way to winning? If so, did this competition arise in the primary election, the general election, or both? The proportion of elected officials that faced a significant challenge only in their primary elections provides one measure of the extent to which primaries contributed to the overall competitiveness of the electoral system.

We divide the cases into four categories based on where (and whether) the ultimate winner faced electoral competition: (i) primary only; (ii) general election only; (iii) both primary and general election; (iv) neither primary nor general election. As above, an election is considered competitive if the winner received less than 57.5 percent of the total votes cast.[18]

---

[18] Only cases in which primaries were in use are included in the analysis.

TABLE 3.1 *Competition in Primary versus General Elections,*
1892 to 1950

	Election that is Competitive				
	Primary Only	General Only	Both	Neither	Number of Cases
Statewide, All Positions	27.7%	18.7%	13.9%	39.7%	4945
Statewide, Open Seats	40.5%	16.3%	20.5%	22.7%	1713
Statewide, Incumbent Present	20.9%	20.0%	10.3%	48.8%	3232
US House, All Seats	13.3%	23.5%	6.9%	56.3%	7823
US House, Open Seats	41.3%	17.1%	19.7%	21.9%	736
US House, Incumbent Present	10.4%	24.1%	5.6%	59.9%	7087

Cell entries give the percentage of cases of each type.

Table 3.1 presents the percentage of races that falls into each of the four categories during the period 1892 to 1950. Since the categories form a partition, each of the rows sums to 100 percent (differences are due to rounding). The top panel covers statewide races and the bottom panel is for US House races.

The top panel shows that elected statewide officials faced significant competition only in the primary election 27.7 percent of the time; significant competition only in the general election 18.7 percent of the time; and in both the primary and general election 13.9 percent of the time. Thus, primary elections probably contributed at least as much as general elections to the overall competitiveness of statewide elections during this period. Although we do not show this in the table, these percentages are relatively stable across decades.

The second row shows that primary elections were even more important in open-seat races. Statewide officials elected in open-seat races were more than twice as likely to face competition only in the primary than they were to face competition only in the general election. The patterns are different for incumbent-contested races (third row). The winners in these races were about as likely to face competition only in the general election as they were to face competition only in the primary.

The sources of competition in US House races were different. Candidates who won US House seats faced significant competition only in the primary 13.3 percent of the time, only in the general election 23.5 percent of the time, and in both elections 6.9 percent of the time. Overall, about half of these winners faced no competitive elections. The relatively low level of competition largely reflects the high proportion of cases that are incumbent-contested. For open seats, the overall patterns of competition in US House races are similar to the patterns in statewide office races. In these cases, House winners were 24.2 percentage points more likely to have faced significant competition only in the primary compared to those who faced competition only in the general election. As is the case with statewide offices, the winners in incumbent-contested races faced significantly less competition than those competing for an open seat: only 40.1 percent faced a competitive primary or general election. The difference is particularly dramatic for primaries – only 16.0 percent of incumbent winners faced significant primary competition.

Table 3.1 does not provide a complete accounting of how primary elections might have contributed to the competitiveness of the electoral system. First, it is not clear how to apportion the cases where the primary and general elections were both competitive. Second, the decompositions in the table ignore the effects that primaries might have had on the level of general election competition (and vice versa). That is, some cases where competition in the primary was especially fierce might have been "shifted" from the Primary Only column to the Both column (or vice versa).[19] In the following sections we examine other avenues through which the introduction of primaries may have affected the overall competitiveness of the electoral system.

3.3 INTRODUCTION OF PRIMARIES AND GENERAL ELECTIONS

As discussed in the previous chapter, recent attempts to explain the adoption of primaries highlight the importance of incumbent politicians' motivations. In particular, it seems puzzling that state governments would pass reforms designed to weaken elite control over party nominations, when, in many cases, these same elites or their allies dominated the state policy-making process.[20] In describing states' efforts to pass direct primary legislation, Ware (2002) claims that elites often expected some type of electoral benefit from the reform. In some cases

---

[19] For example, some scholars and many political observers argue that when a party's primary is "divisive," that party's nominee will tend to suffer in the general election. Despite its intuitive appeal, the literature provides mixed empirical support for the hypothesis. Also, some scholars argue that divisive primaries might sometime help nominees. See Hacker (1965); Johnson and Gibson (1974); Piereson and Smith (1975); Bernstein (1977); Jewell and Olson (1978); Ware (1979); Lengle (1980); Born (1981); Kenney and Rice (1984); Herrnson and Gimpel (1995).

[20] Ware (2002); Snyder and Ting (2011).

the incumbent party might have adopted primaries in order to ward off threats from the opposing major party, especially when it was gaining popularity.[21] In other cases, incumbent politicians might have sought to reduce the potential threats from third parties.[22] If primaries had these effects, then the shift from conventions to primaries would have tended to dampen competition in general elections.

To examine whether primaries improve incumbent parties' electoral results, we plot the vote share of favored parties during the 12 years before and after the introduction of primaries. A party is considered favored if its average vote share across all statewide offices for the eight years prior to and including the year primaries were adopted is greater than 52 percent.[23] States in which neither party was favored at the time primaries were introduced are dropped from the analysis.[24] The prediction is that the favored party's vote share should have increased after primaries are adopted, or possibly that the trend in the favored party's vote share should have increased relative to the pre-primary period.[25]

Figure 3.3 plots the average vote share for the favored party.[26] For each year *t* the average is taken over all races for statewide offices held between years *t* − 1 and *t* + 1. There is no evidence that favored parties benefited electorally from the adoption of primaries. The average vote share for the favored party in the 12 years prior to the reform is lower than the average vote share in the dozen years after the reform. However, this largely reflects an upward trend in the favored party's vote share in the years leading up to the reform. If we focus on the eight years immediately around the reform, we observe a slight drop in the favored party's vote share. The favored party's vote share during the 12 years after primaries were introduced is relatively flat. Thus, overall there is

[21] Snyder and Ting (2011) present a formal model that captures this idea. In the model the electoral benefit for the incumbent party arises through an asymmetry in how primaries affect the nomination of higher quality candidates.
[22] Recall from above the discussion of Pennsylvania Republicans in Ware (2002), who supported primary elections in part to limit the appeal of the City Party.
[23] Averaging over several years hopefully alleviates some of the concerns about regression to the mean.
[24] We drop Maine, Indiana, and Ohio, since the Republican Party was advantaged but the Democratic Party had unified control over the state government at the time primaries were adopted. We also drop states that adopted primaries after 1916.
[25] In all but six cases the favored party had unified control of the state government.
[26] The vote share is defined as the favored party's vote as a share of the favored party and the largest opposition party's vote. In some cases the largest opposition party is not one of the two major parties. Uncontested races are dropped from the calculation.

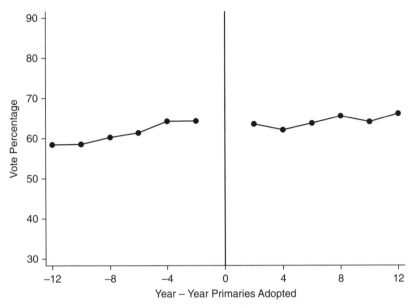

FIGURE 3.3 Favored Party Votes before and after Primaries

little evidence that the introduction of primaries had much of an impact on the level of competition in general elections.

The analysis above drops uncontested general elections. Thus it might understate the effects that primaries had on general election competition, if primaries increased the fraction of uncontested races. This is particularly relevant in the South, where the Democrats were frequently uncontested. To investigate whether this was the case, we estimate a simple linear regression model in which the dependent variable is the fraction of contested races and the independent variables are two variables that indicate whether primary elections were used in a given state and year, one for the South and one for the non-South. We find a significant coefficient on the primary indicator variable only in the South. Thus, outside the South primaries appear to have had no significant effect on the fraction of uncontested races. For the South, it is difficult to interpret the results, because the adoption of primaries often occurred around the time of other reforms that were intended to disenfranchise African-Americans and solidify the hegemony of the Democratic Party.[27]

---

[27] In addition, we studied general election victories for statewide offices, including uncontested races. We find no significant increase in the favored party's probability of winning after primaries.

Primaries might also have affected the competitiveness of general elections by suppressing support for third parties, as discussed above. Some scholars of Southern politics argue that Democrats supported primaries in order to preserve their one-party rule. They were particularly concerned about the populist threat and possibility of factional defections.[28] Epstein (1986, 131) provides a related argument to account for the decline in third-party support outside the South as well:

> It is arguable, therefore, that the also distinctively American institution, the direct primary, is a cause of the distinctively American weakness of third parties. The reasoning is that third-party efforts are discouraged by the opportunity to capture the label of one or the other major party in a primary.

While these arguments seem intuitive, there is little systematic evidence that primaries had an immediate effect on third-party electoral support.[29]

Figure 3.4 displays a simple plot of the average vote share for third-party candidates for all statewide offices in the years leading up to and just after the adoption of the direct primary. Identifying the third-party vote is not straightforward, because these parties sometimes fused with a major-party candidate. The top panel of Figure 3.4 calculates the third-party vote using only votes for candidates who do not have a Democrat or Republican label.[30] Races with fusion candidates are dropped in this case. The bottom panel calculates third-party votes treating fusion candidates as major party candidates.

When fusion candidates are excluded, third-party support is noticeably lower in the 12-year period after primaries are introduced compared to the 12 years prior to their introduction. However, in the figure third-party support is generally trending downward and the largest single decline occurs between years $t-10$ and $t-8$. When fusion candidates are included, there is no obvious decline in third-party support after the introduction of primaries. There is no clear drop in either measure when we narrow the window to six years before and after the introduction of primaries.

Regressions of state-level third-party support on primary introduction provide at best weak evidence that primaries overall are associated with a drop in third-party support.[31] However, the results differ

[28] Key (1949); Kousser (1974).

[29] Hirano and Snyder (2007).

[30] We include races in which the major and third-party votes for candidates were separated.

[31] We hesitate to draw strong conclusions because the regression results are sensitive to time period, specification, and the choice of dependent variable. We estimated a

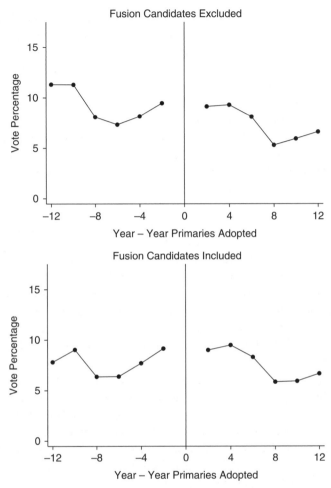

FIGURE 3.4 Third-Party Support before and after Primaries

noticeably between Southern and non-Southern states. The introduction of primaries was associated with a noticeable drop in third-party

variety of different regression models with different sets of controls other than primary introduction, including: (i) a year trend; (ii) state-specific fixed effects plus a year trend; (iii) state-specific fixed effects plus year fixed effects; (iv) state-specific fixed effects, year fixed effects, and state×year trends. We considered both measures of third-party support, with and without fusion candidates. We focus on the period 1880 to 1930. In no case is the primary introduction indicator variable statistically significant at the 0.05 level. When fusion candidates are excluded, in cases (iii) and (iv), the coefficient is significant at the 0.10 level. When we use a narrow range of years around the years of adoption, the coefficient estimates are small and far from statistically significant.

support in the South. This is consistent with the claims about Southern primaries made by Key (1949) and Kousser (1974). However, as noted above, we hesitate to draw strong conclusions about primaries since the introduction of primaries in the South often occurred around the time of other changes in the electoral laws designed to reduce competition. This makes it difficult to isolate the effect of primaries.

Primaries might also have weakened third parties by attracting candidates who would have otherwise run with a third-party label. This does not appear to be the case, however, at least for the 1890-to-1930 period. During this period, 8,929 individuals in our dataset ran as third-party candidates or as independents in the general elections for statewide or federal office under the convention system.[32] Of these candidates, only 116 later ran in one of the major-party primaries. Even this probably overstates the number of third-party candidates who were "shut out" under the convention system – that is, unable to seek major-party nominations – since 32 of these candidates also ran as major-party nominees at some point under the convention system.[33] It is possible that in the long run, primaries made the major parties more flexible and easier to enter, thereby allowing them to absorb some potential third-party movements, but this connection is difficult to establish.[34]

Figures 3.3 and 3.4 suggest that primaries did not have an obvious immediate impact on the competitiveness of general elections. One concern is that the adoption of primaries might have been endogenous. For example, state parties might have passed primary election reforms in anticipation of a strong third-party threat, or when they expected an imminent negative shock to their electoral support. The introduction of primaries may have dampened these threats. Moreover, the influence of primaries on general election competition may have taken more time to develop. Demonstrating long-term effects is extremely challenging since over long periods of time many changes take place in the political environment.

---

[32] Fusion candidates are not counted as third-party candidates.

[33] A number of major-party candidates also appear later as third-party candidates.

[34] For example, in the 1930s, the Democratic Party transitioned rapidly – in less than a decade – from a party with a predominantly conservative ideology to one that supported a significant expansion of government activity. Primaries might have helped the various state Democratic parties to adopt the New Deal ideas and nominate candidates who supported these ideas.

3.4 PRIMARIES AND CANDIDATE-CENTERED VOTING

Primaries might also have influenced general election competition by facilitating the shift from party-centered to candidate-centered electoral politics. The conventional wisdom is that the era of candidate-centered politics took hold sometime in the 1950s or 1960s.[35] However, some scholars argue that primaries might have played a role in the transition. There are two main channels. First, primaries might have weakened party organizations. For example, Jacobson (2004, 15–16) writes:

A fundamental factor [in the decline of parties] is clearly institutional: the rise and spread of primary elections as the method for choosing party nominees for the general election … Primary elections have largely deprived parties of their most important source of influence over elected officials. Parties no longer control access to the ballot and, therefore, to political office. They cannot determine who runs under their label and so cannot control what the label represents … parties typically have few sanctions and little influence [on nominations].

As political party organizations became weaker they would presumably be less able to influence voting behavior – they not only had fewer resources with which to mobilize voters, but they also had less control over the party labels. In response, candidates who could no longer rely on the party had strong incentives to develop their own personal organizations.[36]

In addition primaries might have changed the culture of political campaigning more generally.[37] With no party labels on the ballot,

---

[35] Aldrich (1995); Nie, Petrocik, and Verba (1979); Alford and Brady (1989); Wattenberg (1990, 1991); Jacobson (1992); Shively (1992). Aldrich and Niemi (1990) call the post-1960s era "the sixth party system."

[36] Schier (2000, 24–5) credits primaries with a loss of party control that forced candidates to become "individually responsible for attracting voters." Herrnson (1988, 26) observes that this process "encouraged candidates to develop their own campaign organizations, or pseudo-parties, for contesting primary elections." See also Key (1964: 342).

[37] For example, soon after Minnesota adopted primaries a local newspaper reported that "James A. Tawney has made the acquaintance of several hundred of his Fillmore county constituents in the last week. It is a new thing for the Winona congressman to get around among the rank and file of the voters, shake hands and give them a 'jolly.' It was hard to come down to it, but he did it gracefully, and the honest citizens of this county are in closer touch with their congressman than ever in their lives. Mr. Tawney is visibly worried… He realizes that he is in a fight, one which the new primary law makes doubly uncertain, and although sure that his prestige and organization will win for him, he is taking no chances. He is working like a harvest hand for votes" ("Fillmore is Mixed," *The Minneapolis Journal*, September 8, 1902, page 8).

candidates in primaries were forced to compete for their party's nomination on the basis of their personal attributes and reputations. It seems natural to expect this type of campaigning to spill over to the general election, as candidates learned during the primary how to campaign on the basis of personal attributes. Selection might have reinforced this tendency since the primary winners were presumably even more adept than average at candidate-centered campaigning. Finally, nominees might have carried much of their primary campaign (including the organization) into the general election because, after all, what worked once might work again.

One indicator of candidate-centered voting is the degree to which the electorate engages in "split-ticket" voting. In party-centered systems we would expect voters to vote for all of the candidates of a particular party across offices within an election, that is to cast a straight party ballot. A crude measure of split-ticket voting is the variation in the two-party vote across offices in a given election. This is obviously a lower bound on the total amount of split-ticket voting, since individual voters may split their tickets in different ways that cancel one another out. However, the correlation between split-ticket voting measured at the individual level and the aggregate-level proxies is quite high.[38]

For each state-year in which there are three or more statewide races, we construct the variable *Standard Deviation* as follows:

$$Standard\,Deviation_{kt} = \left[\frac{1}{N_{kt}-1} \sum_{j=1}^{N} \left(V_{jkt} - \overline{V}_{kt}\right)^2 \right]^{1/2}$$

where N_{kt} is the number of statewide races in state k in year t, V_{jkt} is the Democratic share of the two-party vote in race j in state k in year t, and $\overline{V}_{kt}$ is the average of the Democratic percentage of the two-party vote

---

[38] Data from exit polls and the Cooperative Congressional Election Study show that split-ticket voting tends to be higher at the individual level than the aggregate-level differences would suggest. However, the measures of split-ticket voting using state-level data are highly correlated with measures using individual-level data. Consider, for example, split-ticket voting for US senator and governor for the period 1982–2006. For each state-year with both a US Senate and governor race, let s_{ikt} be an indicator variable equal to 1 if respondent i in the exit poll voted for candidates from different parties in the US Senate and governor races (including third-party and independent candidates), and 0 otherwise; let N_{kt} be the number of respondents in the exit poll; and let $S_{kt}^I = (1/N_{kt}) \sum_{i=1}^{N_{kt}} s_{ikt}$ be the overall amount of split-ticket voting at the individual level. Let D_{kt}^G (D_{kt}^S) be the aggregate Democratic share of the two-party vote in the governor (US Senate) race; and let $S_{kt}^A = |D_{kt}^G - D_{kt}^S|$ be the aggregate measure of split-ticket voting. The correlation between is S^I and S^A is 0.72 ($N=157$).

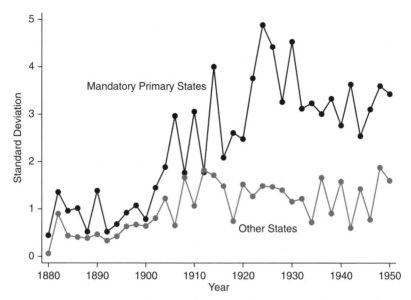

FIGURE 3.5 Split-Ticket Voting in Statewide Elections, 1880 to 1950

across all races in state k in year t. We only include races contested by both major parties, and we drop races in which a third-party candidate received more than 15 percent of the total vote.

Figure 3.5 shows the average value of *Standard Deviation* for each year. The black curve indicates the set of states that adopted a comprehensive, mandatory primary election law during the period 1900–1915 and did not subsequently repeal the law, while the light-gray curve shows the states that did not.[39] As discussed in Chapter 2, the period 1900-1915 was the period in which most states adopted their direct primary laws.

While both curves increase over time, the increase is noticeably larger for states that adopted a comprehensive mandatory primary. A large and persistent gap opens between these states and states without primaries between 1902 and 1914; from 1914 onward (that is, after most states adopted their primary laws) states with comprehensive mandatory primaries exhibit noticeably more split-ticket voting.

The patterns in Figure 3.5 are consistent with the hypothesis that primaries increased split-ticket voting. To explore the hypothesis more

---

[39] Each state is weighted equally in each year. We group the odd-numbered years together with the previous even-numbered year – for example, 1881 with 1880, etc.

thoroughly we estimate a variety of regression models, with split-ticket voting as the dependent variable. The key independent variable indicates whether or not a state had a mandatory primary law in a given year. We also control for other ballot reforms, such as straight-ticket options, office block, and party list. In some specifications we also include state-specific fixed effects and year-specific fixed effects. These are described in the Appendix. The estimated coefficient on mandatory primary variable is large, positive, and statistically significant in all specifications.[40] This analysis shows that: (1) there was a significant increase in split-ticket voting earlier than the conventional wisdom suggests; and (2) this increase was especially noticeable in states that adopted a comprehensive mandatory primary between 1900 and 1915.

Hirano and Snyder (2018) find evidence consistent with the second channel by which primaries might affect candidate-centered voting in general elections – that is, similarities in campaigning across the two elections. In that paper, we analyze county-level voting and find a significant correlation between nominees' electoral support in primaries and their subsequent electoral support in the general election. More specifically, even after controlling for county-decade and race-specific fixed effects (to capture factors such as differences in the normal vote across counties and the overall electoral appeal of the candidates), candidates' primary election vote shares are significantly and positively related to their general election vote shares. Most interestingly, the relationship is relatively large even before the well-known era of candidate-centered politics began in the 1960s, especially for gubernatorial and US Senate races at the top of the ticket.

While the traditional literature focuses on the hypothesis that primaries weakened party-centered politics, recent work suggests that the causal relationship might run in the opposite direction. Reynolds (2006) argues that in the years prior to the adoption of primaries, conventions were becoming increasingly contentious. Ambitious and charismatic "hustling" candidates began actively seeking nominations, lobbying party leaders, local notables, and delegates. Thus, "[t]he rapid and relatively uncontroversial adoption of the direct primary represented an effort by officeholders and party officials to adapt the electoral system to an increasingly candidate-centered political culture."[41] To the extent

---

[40] Throughout the book, unless otherwise specified, when we use the term "statistically significant" we mean statistically significant at the 0.05 level.

[41] Reynolds (2006, 10).

that hustling for nominations translated into more candidate-centered voting in general elections, direct primaries may have been a reaction to an increasing focus on candidates rather than a cause of increasingly personalistic politics. The evidence in Harvey and Mukherjee (2006), Hirano and Snyder (2018), and Hirano et al. (2018) suggests that while this might have been occurring, primaries played an independent role in the process.

In theory, the rise in candidate-centered electoral politics might have increased or decreased the overall level of competitiveness in general elections. On the one hand, open-seat elections in traditionally safe areas might have become more competitive in those cases where disadvantaged parties nominated candidates with greater personal electoral appeal. On the other hand, and perhaps more likely, the advantaged party – which could typically draw from a larger pool of candidates – might select popular nominees more often, solidifying its pre-existing advantage. Candidate-centered elections might have been one of the factors leading to the incumbency advantage. While the incumbency advantage is known to dampen competition in incumbent-contested races, it is not clear how it should affect open-seat races – these could become even more competitive as future-oriented career politicians had even more incentive to acquire the advantages of incumbency. Thus, whether the shift toward personal politics led to an increase or decrease in electoral competition (or had no effect) is unclear. Finally, it is important to remember that even with the rise in candidate-centered politics, partisanship was still the dominant driver of general election outcomes and in most cases only a small minority of voters appear to have split their tickets.

3.5 CONCLUSION

The patterns we identify in this chapter suggest that in terms of electoral competition, primaries were contributing to the system much as we would hope, at least in advantaged-party areas. The low levels of competition in Pennsylvania's first two statewide primaries were not representative of the typical level of primary competition in areas dominated by one party. In fact, in the next cycle of statewide elections in Pennsylvania, in 1918 the Republican nominees for two of the three contested offices received less than fifty percent of the primary vote. In other states with an advantaged party, such as California, Minnesota,

Oregon, and Wisconsin, the primaries for open-seat races were competitive immediately after the new nomination system was adopted. In the first decades of the twentieth century, primary competition facilitated an escape from one-partyism for a substantial segment of the US electorate, and for newly elected officials the primary was often the most challenging electoral hurdle they faced on their way to office.

It is difficult to assess the impact of the direct primary on electoral competition overall. We find little evidence of short-term effects, at least outside the South, on competition between the major parties or on third-party support. There might, however, have been long-term effects. Another possible long-term effect of primaries was to enable the emergence of the highly candidate-centered politics of the late 1950s and 1960s.[42]

3.6 APPENDIX

3.6.1 Regression Analyses of Split-Ticket Voting

Regression analyses show that the difference in split-ticket voting between primary and non-primary states is statistically significant and substantively important. In these analyses we can also compare the relative importance of primary elections and other institutional factors, such as ballot form. The results are shown in Table 3.2. The independent variables are: $DirectPrimary_{jt} = 1$ if state j employed primary elections in year t; $StraightTicket_{jt} = 1$ if state j had a straight party lever/circle on the ballot in year t; $OfficeBlock_{jt} = 1$ if state j used the office block ballot form in year t; $PartyList_{jt} = 1$ if state j used the party list ballot form in year t. We also ran specifications including a measure of party competition. This variable was never statistically significant and did not substantively change the coefficient estimates on our main variables of interest. Note that the coefficients on the two ballot form variables, that is, *OfficeBlock* and *PartyList*, are relative to the excluded category, which is the pre-Australian ballot "party ballot."

In Columns 2 and 4 we include indicators for differences in ballot form – such as whether there is an easy option to vote a straight party ticket or whether candidates are grouped by office or party – which

---

[42] Ware (2002, 244) writes, "without the widespread use of the direct primary, the technological advances – television, computer-analyzed opinion polls, and so on – would not have had the effect that they did, because candidates would have had to work through party leaders to build support for their nomination at a convention."

TABLE 3.2 *Primaries and Split-Ticket Voting*
in Statewide Elections, 1880–1950

	Dep. Var. = *Standard Deviation*			
Direct Primary	1.84	1.52	1.09	0.93
	(0.31)	(0.27)	(0.22)	(0.19)
Straight Ticket		−1.26		−0.60
		(0.34)		(0.39)
Office Block		1.29		0.25
		(0.64)		(0.38)
Party List		1.13		−0.02
		(0.73)		(0.56)
State FE	No	No	Yes	Yes
Observations	986	986	986	986

Table shows OLS regression estimates. Year fixed effects included in all specifications. Standard errors are in parentheses. Standard errors are clustered by state in all specifications.

are often argued to affect split-ticket voting.[43] When state-specific fixed effects are included in the regression, only the introduction of primary elections appears to be associated with a statistically significant change in split-ticket voting. When fixed effects are not included, the direct primary is found to have a similar effect on split-ticket voting as whether a straight party ticket option is included on the ballot.[44]

Clearly, this analysis does not demonstrate that the adoption of a mandatory primary law caused an increase in *Standard Deviation*. For example, the decline of "strong party organizations" might be the real cause of the increase in split-ticket voting. Strong party organizations might have prevented the adoption of primary laws in their states and might also have reduced the amount of split-ticket voting. Of course, since the analysis includes state- and year-fixed effects it must be that party organizational strength *changed* within states over time and in

[43] See, for example, Ansolabehere, Hirano, and Snyder (2007) and Harvey and Mukherjee (2006).

[44] We find no statistically significant evidence that the introduction of the Australian ballot is associated with an increase in split-ticket voting. The estimated coefficients on the ballot form variables are particularly sensitive to the choice of time period and specification. We also ran specifications including the log of total votes cast as an additional control variable, and the basic patterns are the same as those reported here.

different states at different times (that is, not as the result of a nationwide shock such as a transformative presidential election). A plausible alternative explanation of the pattern is that party organizations might have weakened in some but not all states during the 1900s, leading the affected states to adopt primary laws and to experience an increase in split-ticket voting.

4

Primaries and Party Loyalty

Joseph Cannon of Illinois has been reelected Speaker of the House of Representatives. The old vicious rules have been readopted with only a few cheating amendments. His power has hardly been diminished at all, for he will again appoint all committees and again pack them for or against measures. He can control the committee on rules and can interpose his own arbitrary will against the reforms planned by President Taft and demanded by the general public.[1]

For many progressive Republicans, "Uncle" Joe Cannon personified all that was wrong with national politics in general, and their party in particular, in the early 1900s. He had turned the US House of Representatives into a plutocracy of rich industrialists, bankers, and merchants who consistently subverted the democratic process and thwarted the will of the people. Progressive editors denounced the state of affairs: "The Degradation of the House of Representatives – How the Privileged Interests Captured and now Control the National House," "Speaker Cannon and the Destruction of Popular Rule in the House," "Government by Oligarchy," and "The Autocratic House."[2]

Of course, Cannon could not rule alone. Among his supporters was a cadre of lieutenants, who were also odious to progressives. *Colliers* observed with disgust that "some members like the old rules. They like the regime of Cannon. They want Congress to remain a Cannon star chamber of suppression and evasion. Who are these? First of all there is the Cannon Freemasonry, the little group who are the Grand Viziers

---

[1] From the *North American*, as quoted on page 3 in *LaFollette's Weekly Magazine*, "How the People Were Beaten," 1(12):3–4, March 27, 1909.
[2] Titles from *Arena*, 39:615–618, May 1908; *Arena*, 40:89–91, July 1908; *The Outlook*, 89:12–14, March 2, 1908; and *The Outlook*, 91:807–809, April 10, 1909, respectively.

of this regime – Dalzell, Payne, Sherman, Tawney, and a very small number more. They are the Chairmen of his important committees. By fawning, or by identity of interest, or by willingness to do his bidding, they have wormed their way to the inner places of power. They are well satisfied."[3] Below these leaders, rank-and-file Republican representatives supported the party organization and its legislative agenda, at least with their roll-call votes.

Progressives put forward the direct primary to counteract the evils of bossism in general and Cannonism in particular. Reformers argued that taking nominations out of the hands of party elites and machines and placing them in the hands of voters would result in elected officials who would better represent their constituents. Here are two prominent examples:

Senator George W. Norris of Nebraska: "The direct primary will lower party responsibility. In its stead it establishes individual responsibility. It does lessen allegiance to party and increase individual independence, both as to the public official and as to the private citizen. It takes away the power of the party leader or boss and places the responsibility for control upon the individual. It lessens party spirit and decreases partisanship. These are some of the reasons why the primary should be retained and extended."[4]

Governor Charles Evans Hughes of New York: "[The direct primary makes] the elective officer more independent of those who would control his action for their own selfish advantage and enables him to appeal more directly to his constituency upon the basis of faithful service."[5]

In some cases, the reform appeared to work much as intended. One example was John A. T. Hull, a "standpatter," staunch Cannon supporter, and part of the loyal old guard. First elected to Congress in 1890, Hull represented the 7th district of Iowa. Republicans held this seat continuously for over 50 years, winning all of the elections from 1880 to 1930. Hull was re-elected nine times and – reaping the fruits of party loyalty – ultimately rose to become chairman of the House Committee on Military Affairs from the 54th through the 61st Congresses. When the direct primary came to Iowa in 1908, however, Hull's political fortunes began a rapid decline. Challenged that year

---

[3] From *Colliers*, 42: 11, March 13, 1909; as cited in Charles R. Atkinson, "The Committee on Rules and the Overthrow of Speaker Cannon," unpublished PhD dissertation, Columbia University, 1911, page 81.

[4] Gubernatorial acceptance speech, August 8, 1900, quoted in Ranney (1975, 125).

[5] Quoted on page 92 of *The Outlook*, "The Remedy for the Evils of the Present System of Nomination," 91(3):91–92, January 16, 1909.

by Solomon Prouty, a moderate progressive Republican, Hull won by just 40 out of more than 20,000 votes cast. When Prouty ran again in 1910, US Senator Albert B. Cummins, the leader of the Iowa Republican Party's progressive wing, supported Prouty over Hull. In the primary Prouty defeated Hull by over 3,000 votes, carrying every county, and went on to win the general election. Prouty served two terms before retiring, distinguishing himself as "an active, progressive, and useful congressman," according to a later obituary.[6] The difference in party loyalty between Hull and Prouty is evident in their roll-call voting behavior. Hull voted in line with the House party leaders more than 90 percent of the time, while Prouty did so less than 73 percent of the time.

Were such cases exceptional, or relatively common? That is, did primaries reduce loyalty to party leaders in Congress? If so, was this due to replacement as in the case of Hull and Prouty above, or was it due to changes in behavior by individual members of Congress? The massive quantitative literature analyzing party loyalty, party cohesion, and inter-party conflict in Congress and state legislatures has largely overlooked this question.[7] This chapter attacks the question by examining party loyalty in the roll-call voting behavior of members of Congress. We find that members of Congress did exhibit less loyalty to party leaders in Western states such as Iowa, and especially on issues of concern to progressive leaders.

---

[6] "Solomon Francis Prouty" (1928, 311).

[7] To our knowledge, the one exception is our own joint work, Ansolabehere, Hirano, and Snyder (2007), which analyzes whether or not the introduction of the direct primary had a noticeable impact on party loyalty and discipline in Congress. The literature on legislative partisanship includes: Jewell (1955); Clubb and Allen (1967); Brady (1972); Shade et al. (1973); Brady and Althoff (1974); Deckard (1976); Sinclair (1977); Clubb and Traugott (1977); Cooper, Brady and Hurley (1977); Brady, Cooper and Hurley (1979); Rosenthal (1981); Hurley and Wilson (1988); Patterson and Caldeira (1988); Brady, Brody, and Epstein (1989); Cox and McCubbins (1991); Morehouse (1996); Snyder and Groseclose (2000). For example, Brady and his collaborators attempt to account for changes in loyalty over time, and emphasize the importance of intra-party homogeneity and rules. In particular, they argue that the realignment of 1896 produced party delegations in the US House and Senate with much more homogeneous constituency interests – Republicans drawn heavily from manufacturing areas, Democrats from the agricultural South. Even here, the basic facts are in dispute. Rothman (1966) claims that party loyalty was low in the 1870s and 1880s but high in the 1890s, and many authors cite this to support their arguments. However, Shade et al. (1973) show that party loyalty was just as high in the 1870s and 1880s as it was in the 1890s.

62   *Primaries and Party Loyalty*

4.1 EXISTING CLAIMS AND EVIDENCE

Initial assessments were optimistic. In the years immediately following
the widespread adoption of primaries, some observers detected a weakening in the grip of corrupt party organizations. Arthur C. Millspaugh
wrote that the direct primaries took from the party professional "his
most prized powers and have made him the appointee of the candidate,
thus reversing the former relation." Millspaugh observed that party
discipline was diminishing as a result: "Since the candidate is simply
a self-assertive individual who steps out of the ranks and gathers
around him a following which is one of the several factions and often
merely a minority of the party membership, his control is ephemeral
and decentralizing and encourages insubordination."[8] George R. Brown
concurred: "The primary had made the Congressman an individualist
and had deadened the old sense of clanship ... He was no longer
coerced or instructed by the caucus, and the restraining influences of that
instrument of stern discipline no longer held his intellectuality in check.
Inevitably a candidate for reelection, he outlined his own campaign, and
paddled his own political canoe. Gradually he committed himself to his
constituents on an increasingly large number of issues."[9]

The hopeful view that primaries weakened party discipline persisted
even several decades later, albeit with more nuance. V.O. Key, Jr. argued,
"The adoption of the direct primary opened the road for disruptive forces
that gradually fractionalized the party organization. By permitting more
effective direct appeal by individual politicians to the party membership,
the primary system freed forces driving toward disintegration of party
organizations and facilitated the construction of factions and cliques
attached to the ambitions of individual leaders. The convention system
compelled leaders to treat, to deal, to allocate nominations; the primary
permits individual aspirants by one means or another to build a wider
following within the party."[10] In a similar vein, Austin Ranney contended
that the reform "in most instances has not only eliminated boss control
of nominations but party control as well. Whatever may have been
the case before the La Follette revolution, there are today no officers
or committees in the national parties and very few in the state and
local parties who can regularly give nominations to some aspirants and
withhold them from others."[11]

[8] Millspaugh (1917, 173).
[9] Brown (1922, 246–7).
[10] Key (1964, 342).
[11] Ranney (1975, 129).

Not everyone agreed. Some skeptics believed the party machinery had survived the transition. In an early analysis of the situation in Missouri, Loeb concluded that "the direct nomination system has not weakened the party organization nor lessened the influence of the professional politician."[12] McKenzie maintained that while the direct primary was "designed originally to eliminate the evils of a party machine under the convention system," it had probably not "accomplished as much as its supporters claimed for it. Certainly the machine continues to exist in undiminished prestige."[13] Beard agreed that the direct primary "has not fulfilled all the hopes of its advocates. It has not destroyed party bosses, eliminated machines, or led to radical changes in the character of the men nominated."[14] According to Ranney and Kendall the consensus among scholars was that "the party organizations or 'machines' put forward slates of carefully selected candidates, back them in the primaries, and elect them, often with little or no opposition."[15] Pollack provided a more mixed assessment: "I do not find that the party system in Michigan has been weakened by the primary system ... I do find that the primary system has broadened the control over nominations and the control of political parties, although politics is still pretty much of an insider's game even today." He went on to explain that, "The failure of the rank and file of the parties to participate in large numbers in the primary ... has made it easier for organization leaders to control nominations in the primary. But this control has not been absolute, nor steady, and it has always been subject to popular revolts."[16]

The results, in sum, seemed mixed at best. One weakness with the accounts, however, is that proponents and skeptics alike based their assessments primarily on subjective evaluations of particular cases. As Beard wrote in 1924, the direct primary's "actual achievements are difficult to measure. In fact no searching examination has yet been made into the operations of the direct primary throughout the Union."[17] Thirty years later the situation had changed little, as Ranney and Kendall noted: "Few attempts have been made to measure precisely what effects the direct primary has actually had on the control of nominations. What evidence we have on this point consists of statements made by students on

12 Loeb (1910, 171).
13 McKenzie (1938, 318).
14 Beard (1924, 551).
15 Ranney and Kendall (1956, 284).
16 Pollack (1943, 61–2).
17 Beard (1924, 551).

the subject on the basis of personal observation of the general workings
of the system over a number of years."[18] With a few exceptions, the same
can be said about our current state of knowledge.

4.2 WESTERN PROGRESSIVE REPUBLICANS VERSUS THE NORTHEAST ESTABLISHMENT

Most scholars assume – either implicitly or explicitly – that the effects
of primaries would be similar everywhere. On reflection, however, this
assumption seems dubious. Rather, it is likely that the effects of primaries
varied depending upon the political context and circumstances. First,
the national parties did represent large segments of the population,
so in some areas of the country a party's rank-and-file would have
been relatively happy with the overall direction of their party's policies.
Second, as discussed above, it is difficult to believe the heroic story that
everywhere primaries were adopted they represented a victory of weak
progressive outsiders over powerful, stalwart insiders.[19] In some states
even regular party leaders suffered from the defects of the convention
system and sought change (perhaps believing they could control, or at
least personally win under, the primary system). Third, in some states
that were late to adopt primaries, party leaders might have felt compelled
to reform because of increasing public pressure. In such states we should
not expect the introduction of primaries to have had large effects on party
loyalty, because it is not clear that the members of Congress nominated
under the convention system in these states were, in broad ideological
terms, unrepresentative of their districts.

Ideally, in order to measure primaries' impact on party loyalty, we
would want to identify districts and policy issues where the preferences of
local voters diverged significantly from the agendas pursued by national
party leaders. Unfortunately, due to data limitations, we cannot do this
on a district-by-district and issue-by-issue basis. We can, however, take
a broad-brush approach by exploiting variation across regions.

At the time primaries were first introduced, one of the most salient
policy conflicts split the progressive and agrarian interests in the West
and South from manufacturing and financial interests in the Northeast.
This divide was especially pronounced inside the Republican Party.
Progressive reformers argued that state and national party bosses in

---

[18] Ranney and Kendall (1956, 284).
[19] Ware (2002).

many states catered to the dominant economic elites. Elected politicians in turn pandered to the bosses, on whom they depended for nominations, re-nominations, and promotions to higher office. Since Eastern economic elites tended to dominate national politics, the policies pursued by Republicans under the pre-primary nomination system tended to favor Eastern voters, in the aggregate, at the expense of Western voters (see below for the definition of Eastern and Western states). Thus, reforms causing members of Congress to become more responsive to the interests and expectations of local constituents would be expected to have a disproportionate impact on political dynamics in the West.[20]

A large literature argues that the regional economies in the US in the late nineteenth and early twentieth centuries were quite different, and these differences led to substantial differences in political agendas. The economies of the Western states were based heavily on agriculture and mining, while many Eastern states' economies had large manufacturing and financial sectors. The ownership of capital was also concentrated in the East. In 1890 the average manufacturing capital per person was $183 in Eastern and industrial Midwestern states, compared to $51 in Western states and just $25 in the South. Thus, the policies favored by Northeastern industrial and financial elites – such as high tariffs designed to protect manufactured goods, regulatory laws that generally favored capital over land and labor, and laissez-faire policies that fostered highly concentrated oligopolies in investment banking and other industries – would have been especially costly to average citizens in the West.

Support for progressive Republican politicians was especially strong in the rural Midwest and West compared to the industrial East.[21] For example, all members of Congress designated as progressive insurgents by Baker (1973) represented states west of the Mississippi River or Wisconsin. Analysis of the 12 Republican primaries held during the 1912 presidential election reveals that the average vote share for the progressive Republican candidates, Roosevelt or La Follette, was 79 percent in the states west of the Mississippi, compared to only 55 percent

---

[20] Unlike the Republican congressional delegation, which came mainly from the Northeast and West, much of the Democratic delegation came from the agrarian South and border states. Therefore, it is less clear how the salient economic divisions inside the Democratic Party mapped into regions, even broadly. In the analysis below we focus only on Republicans.

[21] See, for example, Nye (1951) and Sanders (1999).

east of the Mississippi.[22] Contemporary observers fully appreciated the regional distinction. One progressive editor argued that Cannonism was doomed because, "The Middle West, supported by the honest, healthy thought of 45 States is against him."[23] Like many others, this writer saw the Middle West leading the progressive charge, with only part (the "honest" and "healthy" part, of course) of other states following.[24]

Meanwhile, from the 1880s through the 1920s, the Republican congressional leadership (and membership) remained under the firm control of members from the industrial East. During the period we study, 1890 to 1928, all but one of the five Republican speakers came from east of the Mississippi River.[25] Members of Congress from the Northeast also controlled numerous other party leadership positions. For example, prior to the revolt against Cannon in 1910, Eastern representatives controlled 82 percent of the top House committee chairs – that is, Ways and Means, Appropriations, and Rules. The same held true in the Senate.[26]

Republican leaders from the industrial East were in a position to offer local state party elites in the West various rents in exchange for nominating members of Congress who would be loyal to the national party leadership. These ranged from small items such as railroad passes to high-level patronage positions, such as appointments to the US judiciary.[27]

Progressive Republican reformers hoped that primary elections would break the grip of the Old Guard, and free members of Congress to make decisions more in line with the interests of their constituents. If primaries were successful in this regard, they should have reduced party loyalty, at least among representatives from the West. Moreover, the decline in loyalty should have been most pronounced on issues that separated Eastern, industrial interests from those of the agrarian West and Midwest.

---

[22] Data are from CQ, except for New York. The data for New York is only for New York county and comes from a *New York Times* article "Republican Bosses for New Candidate?" April 4, 1912, page 1.

[23] *Success Magazine*, January 1910.

[24] Further evidence of the divide between the Western and Eastern states over progressive issues is evident in the ratification of the 16th, 17th, and 18th constitutional amendments.

[25] The exception was David B. Henderson from Iowa. Although Henderson was from the Midwest, he shared many policy positions with Northeastern congressmen – for example, support for high tariffs and a gold standard. He only served for two years.

[26] See, for example, Rothman (1966); Brady, Brody, and Epstein (1989).

[27] See, for example, Aldrich and Hubbard (1884). See Kernell and McDonald (1999) for evidence of the strategic use of the US postal system by Republicans in Congress.

4.3 THE IMPACT OF PRIMARIES ON PARTY LOYALTY

Did primaries reduce loyalty to US House party leaders? As noted above our analysis focuses exclusively on the Republican Party, since the predictions are clearest for Republicans. Also, we limit attention to the period 1890 to 1928 (52nd to 71st Congresses). This interval begins 12 years before the first mandatory primary law covered all US House elections in a state (Minnesota in 1902) and ends 12 years after the last of the "initial wave" of mandatory primary laws went into effect (Indiana in 1916). We chose this period in order to focus on the era of primary reform while ensuring that our sample includes an adequate number of pre- and post-primary years for all states.

We employ a standard measure of partisan loyalty, *Loyalty to Party Leaders*, defined as the percentage of times a member votes in the same direction as a majority of the leadership of their party. The set of party leaders consists of the Speaker of the House (who seldom votes), the majority or minority leader, the majority or minority whip, and the chairs or ranking members of the Appropriations, Rules, and Ways and Means committees.[28],[29]

As noted, we expect to observe a relatively steep decline in loyalty among Western Republican representatives, particularly on those issues related to the progressive agenda. Following the literature, we define Western states as those west of the Mississippi River plus Wisconsin, and Eastern states as those east of the Mississippi (other than Wisconsin). This regional division captures, at least crudely, the key factional split within the Republican Party. Note that Eastern states include both those of the Northeast and the industrial Midwest (Illinois, Indiana, Michigan). We drop Southern and border states since the predictions for these states are unclear, and since there are almost no Republican members of Congress from the South.[30]

---

[28] A large number of roll-call votes are nearly unanimous or very lopsided, but these carry little information about loyalty. We therefore exclude all roll calls with more than 80-percent support on the winning side.

[29] We also studied *Loyalty to the Party Caucus*, defined as the percentage of times a member votes in the same direction as a majority of the members of their party. We focus on loyalty to party leaders in the analyses below, since very similar results hold for the second measure.

[30] These are the 11 confederate states plus Kentucky, Missouri, Oklahoma, and West Virginia. We include Maryland as an Eastern state since it is home to Baltimore, the seventh-largest city in the US during most of the study period.

In addition to studying the overall change in loyalty, we also examine roll-call votes on the progressive agenda. We measure this in two ways. First, we identify roll calls on the following issues: tariffs, anti-trust, railroads, banking and consumer regulations, income taxes, monetary policy, women's and child labor issues, women's rights (especially suffrage), and electoral reform (mainly the direct election of senators). We also include the roll calls related to the Cannon revolt.[31] Second, we analyze roll-call votes for which a majority of progressive or populist leaders voted in opposition to a majority of regular Republican leaders.[32] This second definition also allows us to define a set of roll calls – that is, those on which either a majority of progressive/populist leaders and regular Republican leaders were on the same side or over which one of the faction's leaders were divided – which can form the basis of a type of "placebo" test. More specifically, primaries are not expected to significantly impact party loyalty on these roll calls.

Figure 4.1 displays a simple before-and-after analysis, which shows that direct primaries reduced party loyalty rates in Western, but not Eastern, states. For each state, the x-axis is centered at the year primaries became mandatory for all congressional nominations in the state. Thus, *Years Since Primary* $= 0$ for the year of adoption, t in the tth year after adoption, and $-t$ in the tth year before adoption. We group the odd- and even-numbered years together since some states adopted primaries in election years and some non-election years.[33]

For Western states, the average pre- and post-primary loyalty rates are 89.4 and 77.6 percent, respectively. For Eastern states the corresponding rates are 88.6 and 84.9 percent. Thus, the decline in loyalty was 11.8 percentage points in Western states but only 3.7 percentage points in

[31] We chose issues based on reading the Progressive Party platforms for 1912 and 1924 and the Populist Party platform for 1892. We also included specific issues discussed in the historical literature (for example, the bills identified in Table II.1 in Sanders (1999, 174)). We identified the roll calls using key words and phrases found in the short descriptions of each roll call provided in ICPSR study #9822 *United States Congressional Roll Call Voting Records, 1789-1990: Reformatted Data.*

[32] The progressive and populist leaders are: T. R. Amlie, J. B. Belford, G. J. Boileau, W. J. Bryan, E. H. Campbell, W. M. Chandler, H. A. Cooper, F. W. Cushman, C. C. Dill, W. Everett, C. N. Fowler, J. P. Heatwole, K. Hill, W. H. Hinebaugh, G. Huddleston, T. L. Johnson, P. J. Kvale, R. M. LaFollette, F. H. LaGuardia, C. E. Littlefield, H. C. Lodge, V. Marcantonio, F. M. Maverick, V. Murdock, J. M. Nelson, G. W. Norris, W. Patman, M. Poindexter, C. A. Russell, T. D. Schall, B. N. Scott, J. H. Sinclair, and P. D. Swing.

[33] For the figure we only include states that adopted the primary before 1917, since it shows the before-and-after averages within state for the period 1890 to 1928.

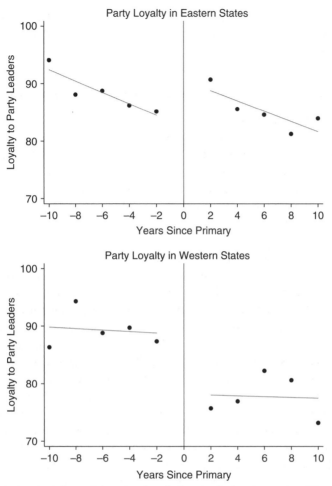

FIGURE 4.1 Loyalty to Party Leaders before and after Primaries, West versus East

Eastern states. Also, while there was some downward trend in loyalty in the East, no such trend is apparent in the West.

We now turn to regression analyses. We exploit the panel structure of the data and the fact that different states adopted the primary at different times. This allows us to estimate models with district-specific fixed effects and congress-specific fixed effects. Including these fixed effects helps control for omitted variables. Such variables might include the overall progressive tendencies of a district's voters, the resources available to congressional party leaders, and the relative popularity of agendas across congresses. This helps us isolate the independent influence of the primary election reform.[34]

We therefore estimate the following model:

$$Party\,Loyalty_{ijt} = \alpha_{ij} + \theta_t + \beta_1 Primary_{jt} \times Western\,State_j + \beta_2 Primary_{jt} + \epsilon_{ijt}$$

where i indexes districts, j indexes states, and t indexes congresses; $Primary_{jt}$ is the same indicator for mandatory primary defined above; and $Western\,State_j$ indicates that state j is in the West (as defined above). The α_{ij} terms are district-specific fixed effects. We include a separate fixed effect for each district for each decade. This captures the partisanship of the district within the decade, as well as other factors, including state-level factors.[35] The θ_t terms capture the congress-to-congress variation in average levels of loyalty. Factors that might affect this include the changing legislative agenda.

Table 4.1 shows the estimates. The first column covers all roll calls. The next column covers roll calls on progressive issues. Column 3 focuses on roll calls for which a majority of progressive/populist leaders voted against the "official" party leadership – that is, the Speaker, majority or minority leader, majority and minority whip, and top committee chairs. The last column focuses on roll calls on which a majority of progressive/populist leaders agreed with a majority of the official party leadership: these constitute the "placebo" roll calls on which we do not expect primary elections to have a large differential effect across regions.

Note first that for all roll calls, the coefficient on *Primary* × *Western State* is negative and both substantively and statistically significant. Thus, the adoption of primaries appears to have had a noticeable impact on party loyalty rates in Western states relative to Eastern states. The estimates indicate that loyalty to party leaders in the West dropped by 9.7 percentage points more than in the East. The estimates are even larger when we focus on roll-call votes related to progressive issues. On these issues, loyalty to party leaders in the West dropped by 14.3 percentage points more than in the East. Finally, the last two columns show a stark difference between the changes in loyalty on progressive roll-call votes compared to other roll calls. The estimate

---

[34] Our regressions are "difference-in-differences" analyses. The key identifying assumption is called the "parallel-trends" assumption – that is, any key omitted variables are trending in a similar fashion across states – which is untestable.

[35] We do not include state or region "main effects" because they are absorbed by the district-fixed effects.

TABLE 4.1 *Effects of Primaries on Loyalty to Republican Party Leaders, 1890 to 1928*

	All Roll Calls	Progressive Issues	Prog. Leaders and Regular Leaders: Disagree	Agree
Primary × Western State	−9.68	−14.28	−11.67	−1.12
	(1.92)	(2.50)	(2.74)	(1.44)
Primary	1.47	2.60	−1.83	1.72
	(1.74)	(3.46)	(2.88)	(1.05)
# Observations	3440	3404	3165	3511

Table shows OLS regression estimates. District-specific fixed effects and congress-specific fixed effects included in all specifications. Standard errors are in parentheses. Standard errors are clustered by state in all specifications.

on *Primary × Western State* for the roll calls on which a majority of the progressive/populist leaders disagreed with a majority of the regular Republican leaders is large and statistically significant. However, for "placebo" roll calls the estimated coefficients are quite small and statistically insignificant.

To put these effects into perspective, recall that the average loyalty rate among Western Republicans on progressive issues before the introduction of primaries was about 89.4 percent. Thus, the decline we report represents a drop in loyalty of more than 10 percent from the average. The estimated change is even more impressive when viewed relative to the standard deviation in party loyalty scores. On average, the standard deviation of party loyalty scores among Western Republicans within a Congress was 15.7, not far from the first coefficient in Column 2 of the table.

4.3.1 Robustness Checks

We conducted a variety of robustness checks, and the patterns shown in Table 4.1 hold in all of the alternative specifications. First, as noted above, the estimates are quite similar when we use *Loyalty to Party Caucus* rather than *Loyalty to Party Leaders* as the dependent variable. Second, it is not the case that the effect of primary elections appears only on relatively lopsided roll calls. When we restrict the sample to the set of roll calls with vote divisions between 40 and 60 percent, we find similar effects as those in Table 4.1. We also find similar estimates when we include border states in the analysis, when we include border states but classify Missouri as a Western state (since it lies west of the Mississippi), and when we either drop Wisconsin or classify it as an Eastern state.

One concern with the difference-in-differences estimates is that the adoption of the direct primary might itself be affected by party loyalty, or by some other variable that is correlated with party loyalty. This could cause the underlying identification assumption – the "parallel trends" assumption – to be violated. Two scenarios seem most likely. In the first, progressive strength among the electorate or key interest groups in a state increases exogenously, and as this occurs the adoption of primary elections becomes more likely and members of Congress simultaneously become less loyal to party leaders. In the second, regular party organizations in a state grow weaker for other reasons, such as increasing factionalism, and as they weaken the adoption of primary elections becomes more likely and members of Congress simultaneously become less loyal to party leaders.

It seems unlikely that the estimates in Table 4.1 are severely biased due to either of these scenarios. First, as noted in Chapter 2 and above, the adoption of primaries was a complicated process involving a variety of different actors and diverse motives. For example, Ware (2002) argues that this process was not driven mainly by pressure from progressive reformers, but was instead a response to the "problem" of nominating candidates in a large and growing society with highly decentralized political parties – together with a variety of idiosyncratic factors including personal goals and rivalries, factional battles, and inter-party conflict. As he and others have observed, states with strong party organizations – where we also expect high party loyalty – were just as likely and almost as quick to adopt direct primaries as those with a progressive or populist streak.

Second, our specifications are really more of a "triple-differences" approach because we compare Western and non-Western states within the difference-in-differences framework. It is difficult to think of simple theories in which the estimates would be severely biased away from zero in Western states, but not in Eastern states. Third, we also estimated specifications that include separate time trends for each state, which allow for non-parallel trends that are somewhat flexible across states. These specifications yield estimates that are very similar to the simple difference-in-differences estimates.

Fourth, we can assess the endogeneity issue directly, at least to some degree, by examining whether short-run changes in the loyalty of a state's delegation help explain the temporal patterns of primary adoption across states. Overall, we find that loyalty rates and changes in loyalty rates do not provide significant leverage in explaining the timing of the adoption of primaries. This is not surprising, especially for Western states in light of Figure 4.1, which reveals no evidence of any trends in loyalty either before or after primaries.

There is evidence of a pre-trend in Eastern states (and a post-trend as well), but two facts make this less troubling. First, the figure is somewhat deceptive, because the apparent steepness of the pre-trend is driven largely by the point at *Years Since Primary* $= -10$. More importantly, neither of the accounts above can explain why the adoption of primary elections should stop the downward trend in loyalty, or why loyalty should increase immediately after primaries are adopted, as the figure indicates. Finally, as discussed in Chapter 2, inter-party competition is correlated with the adoption of primaries. We therefore estimated all of the specifications including a measure of inter-party competition as a regressor. Including this variable does not substantially affect our conclusions.[36]

The analysis above is relatively coarse on at least two dimensions. First, our *Western State* variable only roughly approximates the actual distribution of support for progressive positions. It is possible that some areas of the West – for example, urban centers with important financial and manufacturing interests such Milwaukee, Minneapolis, and San Francisco – had preferences that were often aligned with the urban areas in the industrial Northeast. Similarly, some areas in the East – for example, rural districts in states such as Illinois and Indiana – may have shared preferences with Western progressives.

Second, our categorization of roll calls is also coarse. For example, it is likely that some roll calls on tariff bills or banking regulations did not sharply divide the progressive and regular Republicans. Also, our list of progressive issues is probably incomplete. Fortunately, the estimates in Table 4.1 are similar whether we classify the roll calls based on issues or based on the positions of progressive versus regular leaders. This gives us more confidence in our coding scheme.[37]

---

[36] In addition, the estimated coefficient on the inter-party competition variable is never large or statistically significant.

[37] Since our measures are crude, our estimates might suffer from attenuation bias due to measurement error. With more accurate measures we might find that primaries had an even larger effect.

4.3.2 Replacement versus Conversion

How much of this change in Republican Party loyalty was due to turnover, and how much was due to changing incumbent behavior? Although primary elections might have caused some members of Congress to change their roll-call voting behavior, it is likely that much of the change that occurred was through replacement. One piece of evidence consistent with this hypothesis is the following. We estimated a model analogous to that estimated above, but included member-specific fixed effects rather than district-specific fixed effects. Thus, the coefficient on the interaction term reflects the change in partisan loyalty within continuing incumbents. We find that the estimate for progressive issues is less than 40 percent as large as in Table 4.1 and is no longer statistically significant. This suggests that most of the estimated decline in party loyalty was due to replacement rather than conversion.

It is also interesting to note that primary election defeats were significantly more common in the West than in the non-West, suggesting that Republican voters in the West were more dissatisfied with their incumbents. From 1900 to 1928, 24.6 percent of Western Republican incumbent members of Congress lost at least one primary election, while only 15.2 percent of those in the East and industrial Northwest lost a primary.[38] In addition, members of Congress in the last cohort elected under the convention system in their state were significantly more likely to retire (rather than face a primary) in the West (15.9 percent) than in the East (9.9 percent).

4.4 CONCLUSION

Overall, the evidence above indicates that primaries had a particularly large effect on the party loyalty of Republican congressmen from Western states, especially on issues related to the progressive agenda. We focus on Congress, but of course the progressive reformers also hoped that primaries would weaken the grip party leaders and machines held over state and local politics. Therefore it would be interesting to study whether primaries affected roll-call voting in state legislatures, and to examine whether they facilitated the adoption of progressive reforms by state and local governments. We leave this to future studies.

---

[38] The rates are reversed for general elections, and more similar: 16.5 percent of Western Republican members, and 27.6 percent of Eastern Republican members lost at least one general election.

Our findings are consistent with accounts arguing that the introduction of primaries weakened party leaders' control. For example, Holt (1967, 41) highlights the role of primaries in the defeat of Republican standpatters in Congress: "In the primary election of 1910, 41 incumbent Republican Congressmen were overthrown, almost every one of them standpatters. On the other hand the insurgents maintained and improved their position, especially in the progressive strongholds of the west." At least among Republicans in Congress, the introduction of primaries moved politics in the direction the progressive reformers had intended.

5

Primaries and the Qualifications of Nominees

At the 1902 Kansas Republican state convention, the party considered three potential candidates for state auditor. One candidate, D. Y. Wilson, had served in elected office as a county clerk, but his district was also promoting two other candidates for state offices. Because the party attempted to balance the geographic representation on its ticket, the presumption was that Wilson's district would not receive all three nominations, and Wilson was not considered the strongest candidate of the three.[1] The convention settled on Seth G. Wells, the editor and owner of the *Erie Record*, who was also Erie's US postmaster – typically a party patronage position in this era – and arguably the candidate with the least amount of relevant experience.[2]

Eight years later, in the first open-seat primary election for the Kansas state auditor, two candidates competed for the Republican nomination. In campaigning for this office, one of the candidates, W. H. Cauble, highlighted his home county's lack of representation on past Republican Party tickets. No Republican Party nominee for statewide office had ever come from his home county, despite its large population, high property valuation, and strong support for the Republican Party.[3] Party loyalty

---

[1] C. C. Coleman was considered to be the most likely to be nominated of the three candidates; he was chosen to be the Republican nominee for state attorney general (*The Clifton News*, May 2, 1902, page 1).

[2] The third candidate, S. H. Kelsey, managed a general insurance agency.

[3] One campaign advertisement prominently stated: "SISTER COUNTIES OF KANSAS, for a half century we have graciously assisted you in electing your citizens to various offices in the state house; now we most earnestly ask you to reciprocate and hereby present

W. E. Davis For State Auditor

W. E. Davis, candidate for the republican nomination as state auditor, has served for four years as deputy state auditor. He has been in charge of the important work of the office and has thorough knowledge of all branches of the state's business. The office of state auditor is of the utmost importance. It is the book keeping department of the state. Upon it we must depend for the accurate handling of the state's money. Every dollar expended by any department of the state government must go through the auditor's office. The best experience gets the best service in this class of work, and Mr. Davis has the equipment that comes from experience.

FIGURE 5.1 Campaign Advertisement for William E. Davis (*The Wichita Beacon*, July 23, 1910, page 17)

and geographic representation across a party's statewide ticket were commonly used to justify parties' nomination decisions. The other candidate in the primary, William E. Davis, had never served in elected office. However, his four years of service as assistant state auditor – the top appointed official in the state auditor's office – made him a highly qualified candidate for the state auditor position, as highlighted in his campaign advertisement (see Figure 5.1). Davis went on to win the Republican nomination with 73 percent of the vote; Connelley (1918, 1313) describes his performance in office as "a synonym of efficiency and economy."[4]

According to progressive reformers, the nomination of qualified candidates such as Davis, rather than seemingly less-qualified party insiders such as Wells, was one of the key benefits that direct primaries were expected to bring to the electoral system. As discussed in Chapter 2,

for your consideration our FIRST candidate William H. Cauble for state auditor." *The Topeka State Journal*, July 23, 1910, page 2, reprinted in the Appendix.

[4] Connelley (1918, 1313) further writes that Davis "possesses and exercises a promptness and sureness of decision and a thorough knowledge of details which largely account for the excellence of his administration. While in office he has exercised a careful scrutiny of public expenditures, and it is said that he has put in effect rules governing the expenditure of public moneys that have been helpful to the claimant and beneficial to the state."

there was a common perception around the turn of the twentieth century that nominating conventions and caucuses were easily manipulated by party bosses, who were less interested in high-quality nominees than in nominees who would serve the party machine's interests. Allowing voters to directly select party nominees would not only increase the importance of candidate quality relative to party loyalty in determining nominations; it would also expand the pool of high-quality candidates competing for the nomination. In particular, many progressive reformers expected that some candidates who were unwilling to engage in the corrupt practices associated with the convention system might have been more willing to compete in primaries. Thus, reformers such as Robert M. La Follette, Sr. asserted that primaries would naturally "improve the character of nominees" and "bring into public service the best talent of the times."[5]

Early critics of primaries argued that opening up the nomination process would have the opposite effect. They questioned whether primary voters would actually choose high-quality nominees even if such candidates were available, since voters were largely uninformed and easily persuaded to support candidates based on other characteristics. In addition, they argued that the high costs of running in the primaries, and the negative and personal nature of primary campaigns, would deter many high-quality candidates from entering the race.[6]

After the initial adoption of primaries, a number of political observers claimed that the primaries were having only a limited effect on the quality of elected officials. For example, in 1919 William B. Munro assessed the nomination reform in his popular textbook on American government as follows:

Has [the primary system] proved superior to the convention as a means of securing capable legislators in the several states? On the whole, perhaps it has, although there is no certainty in that direction. At its best the convention was capable of making excellent selections, the fruit of careful deliberation. The primary has not often shown itself able to reach as high a standard. On the other hand the convention at its worst could strike occasionally a plane of arrogance, trickery, and corruption to which a primary rarely if ever descends. In a word, the primary seems to afford protection against the worst fault of the convention,

---

[5] Boots (1917, 62).

[6] In listing the "prominent defects" of primaries to the Texas State Bar Association, William H. Wilson's first concern was that the system "prevents the people from selecting the ablest men and the men of highest character as candidates for office, and restricts the choice of the people to those who are willing to rush forward and inject themselves into what is frequently a vicious election in order to obtain nomination" (Wilson, 1916, 298).

which was the frequent selection of incapable and corrupt candidates at the behest of a few political leaders.[7]

Many assessments were lukewarm in part because they considered the impact of primaries broadly, regardless of the electoral context. As discussed above, reformers should have been most concerned with the performance of primaries in places where they could contribute the most to the electoral system. For example, in many uncompetitive constituencies the outcome of the advantaged party's primary matters more than the outcome of the disadvantaged party's primary.

In the next section, we discuss a simple theoretical framework for thinking about how primaries could affect the quality of nominees. Using a decision theoretic model that assumes politicians make strategic entry decisions, we provide a rationale for why primaries might be an effective mechanism for nominating high-quality candidates in constituencies that favor one party in the general election. We also present some theoretical considerations that can explain why the quality of candidates nominated by the advantaged party might be higher under primaries than the convention system, relative to those nominated by parties that do not have an advantage in the general election.

The remainder of the chapter examines the empirical evidence that primaries affected the quality of party nominees in the years immediately after the nomination system was adopted. One of the key challenges to assessing this relationship is the difficulty of measuring the quality of candidates for public office. We focus on one particular aspect of quality – elected officials' ability to perform the functions of the office they are seeking. We use previous political experience in positions involving tasks similar to the tasks of the office being sought as an indicator of having qualifications for the office. We discuss the appropriateness of relevant experience as a measure of qualifications, both in this chapter and later in Chapter 8.

Our empirical analyses of primaries cover the period 1892 to 1950. However, when we examine the effects of introducing primaries we narrow our focus to the years 1892 to 1928. We chose this period in order to ensure that our sample includes an adequate number of pre- and post-primary years for all states. The period includes four or more presidential elections under each nomination system for all non-Southern states that passed mandatory primary laws during the progressive era.

---

[7] Munro (1919, 419).

Consistent with our model's predictions, candidates with relevant prior experience were more likely to compete (and win) in advantaged party primaries compared to competitive or disadvantaged party primaries. Moreover, this relationship between nominee qualification and constituency type is even more pronounced under the primary system than the convention system.

5.1 THEORETICAL CONSIDERATIONS

How do primaries facilitate the nomination of high-quality candidates in constituencies that favor one political party in the general election? This could be the case if primary voters in these constituencies were somehow better than party elites at selecting high-quality nominees. Even if voters behave similarly in advantaged-party and other primaries, advantaged-party primaries may be more likely to select high-quality nominees if more high-quality candidates compete in these primaries. In this section we provide a theoretical framework to illustrate how politicians who strategically respond to the incentives of the electoral system can increase the likelihood of nominating high-quality candidates in an advantaged-party primary compared to parties-balanced or disadvantaged-party primaries.

We begin with a simple model of strategic entry to illustrate this point and to show how the incentives are affected by the partisan loyalties in a constituency. Since contested primary campaigns are quite costly, in most cases more costly than "throwing their hats in the ring" at a convention, candidates' strategic entry decisions are an especially important issue for primaries.[8] The likelihood that a primary will attract high-quality candidates depends on the incentives that the pool of potential candidates faces in a given election. After describing strategic entry under primaries, we turn to a discussion of how the quality of party nominees may be expected to differ between primaries and conventions.

5.1.1 Strategic Entry and Primary Elections

The intuition for why the advantaged party's nominees in a safe constituency will more often be of higher quality than the nominees

---

[8] Even the bribes sometimes paid in conventions were probably small compared to the costs of a serious primary campaign.

in other constituencies follows from three simple assumptions: (1) candidates will enter an election when they expect the net benefits of winning office to outweigh the costs of running; (2) voters prefer high-quality candidates to low-quality candidates; and (3) there is substantial variation in the costs of running for different candidates, and the costs are low for a considerable number of candidates.[9] The third assumption is intuitive and is consistent with observed behavior. For example, more than 20 percent of candidates who run in contested primaries receive less than 10 percent of the vote and therefore were running even though they probably knew they had little chance of winning.

By high-quality we are referring to candidates' aptitude, prior job experience, and other characteristics that make it more likely that they will be effective in performing the duties of the office they are seeking. We are not referring to electioneering ability *per se*. Of course, the hope is that voters learn about all candidates' attributes and, all else equal, favor those who are high-quality; thus, high-quality candidates will also appear to be good at campaigning.

When voters' partisan attachments in a constituency significantly favor one party over another, giving one party's nominee an advantage in the general election, there will be a significant gap in the expected benefits of being nominated by the advantaged versus the disadvantaged party. This difference should naturally attract more candidates to seek the advantaged party's nomination compared to the disadvantaged party's nomination. Primaries in constituencies where the general election is expected to be competitive should also attract fewer (more) entrants than the advantaged (disadvantaged) party's primary for similar reasons. These differences in the number of entrants alone would not necessarily lead to differences in the quality of nominees across primaries, without making additional assumptions about differences in the pool of high-quality candidates or the behavior of voters across these constituencies.

However, even without making additional assumptions, advantaged-party primaries may lead to higher-quality nominees because the fraction of high-quality nominees in the set of entrants is likely to be higher due to candidates' strategic decisions. Since advantaged-party primaries are expected to attract more entrants (including high-quality

---

[9] The cost could be negative for some candidates – for example, business owners who may benefit from advertising themselves and their businesses during the campaign.

candidates), low-quality candidates may be less willing to bear the costs of entering advantaged-party primaries compared to disadvantaged party or parties-balanced primaries. This strategic behavior would increase the proportion of high-quality candidates competing in the advantaged party's primary. Thus, we should expect high-quality nominees in these constituencies simply because there are relatively more of them competing in the primary.

This pattern should be even more apparent if the "pool" of high-quality candidates who could potentially enter the advantaged-party primary is larger than the pools for other primaries. It should also be more apparent if voters in advantaged-party primaries are somehow more likely to vote for high-quality entrants. However, the basic pattern is likely to exist even absent these additional assumptions.

We capture this intuition by modeling candidate entry in a party's primary, varying the probability that the party's nominee will win the general election. For analytical convenience, in the model we treat this probability as a continuous variable, but the idea is to capture the three types of primary elections defined above. These are: (1) advantaged-party primaries, that is, primaries for the party that is likely to win the general election in safe constituencies; (2) disadvantaged-party primaries, that is, primaries for the party that is likely to lose the general election in safe constituencies; and (3) parties-balanced primaries, that is, primaries in competitive constituencies.

We model one party's primary election taking events in the opposing party as given. There is a pool of potential candidates, some high-quality (H) and some low-quality (L). The fraction of high-quality candidates is θ. We call candidates who run in the primary "entrants," and entrants who win become "nominees." The probability that a high- (low-) quality nominee wins the general election is G_H (G_L). These parameters will vary across constituencies. In particular, they will all be (weakly) larger in constituencies that are safer for the party. If the primary is contested and both entrants are of the same quality, then each entrant wins with probability 1/2. If one entrant is high-quality and the other is low-quality, then the probability the high-quality entrant wins is $P > 1/2$. The value of office is $V > 0$ for all candidates. Each candidate pays a cost of running, C, which is drawn from a uniform distribution on the interval 0, 1. We assume that the parameters that represent probabilities, that is, θ, G_H, G_L, and P, all lie strictly between 0 and 1.

One candidate always enters. Nature then draws a second candidate, who decides whether or not to enter. The second candidate will enter if and only if the expected benefit of holding the office exceeds her cost of running. Let t_1 denote the first candidate's type, and let t_2 denote the second candidate's type. There are four possible cases for the vector (t_1, t_2): (H, H), (H, L), (L, H), and (L, L). For the second candidate, the expected benefits of running in the four cases are, respectively: $VG_H/2$, $VG_H P$, $VG_L(1 - P)$, and $VG_L/2$. Assume that even the largest of these, $VG_H P$, is less than 1.[10] Then, since $C \sim U0, 1$, in each case the expected benefit is also equal to the probability that the second candidate will run.

We want to study what happens in constituencies where the party is advantaged, constituencies where it is disadvantaged, and constituencies that are balanced. Let s denote the general election advantage parties have in a constituency, and assume that G_H, G_L, and θ are functions of s, with $dG_H/ds > 0$, $dG_L/ds > 0$, and $d\theta/ds \geq 0$. Note that we allow $d\theta/ds = 0$, which means that the pool does not have to improve with s.

Let N be the expected number of entrants, let N_H be the expected number of high-quality entrants, let F_H be the expected fraction of entrants who are high-quality, and let W_H be the probability that the nominee is high-quality. It is straightforward to derive the following comparative statics of the model:

Proposition 1. (i) $dN/ds > 0$ and $dN_H/ds > 0$; (ii) the signs of dF_H/ds and dW_H/ds are indeterminate; (iii) if $dG_H/ds > (dG_L/ds)(1 - P)/P$, then $dF_H/ds > 0$ and $dW_H/ds > 0$. ∎

To interpret the condition in part (iii) of the proposition, recall that $P > 1/2$ is the probability that a high-quality entrant will defeat a low-quality entrant in a primary election. Thus, the condition is definitely satisfied if $dG_H/ds \geq dG_L/ds$. More generally, the condition requires that as the party becomes stronger in a constituency, the probability of winning the general election increases for both high- and low-quality nominees, and the probability does not increase markedly more for low-quality nominees than for high-quality nominees. For example, if $P = 3/4$, then the condition in part (iii) is $dG_H/ds > (dG_L/ds)/3$. Thus, it is satisfied as long as the rate of increase in the probability of winning the general election for high-quality nominees is at least 1/3 as large as

---

[10] This clearly holds if $V \leq 1$.

that for low-quality nominees. This seems plausible. If $d\theta/ds > 0$, which seems natural, then the condition in part (iii) can be relaxed.

If part (iii) of the proposition holds, then the predictions are straightforward: as the party's prospects in the general election improve, the expected number of candidates, the expected number of high-quality candidates, the fraction of candidates who are high-quality, and the probability that the nominee is of high quality all increase.[11,12]

Figure 5.2 illustrates the key predictions of the model, as derived in Proposition 1, where we again divide a party's general election prospects, s, into three cases. This is a highly stylized depiction of the result. We do not necessarily expect the relationships to be linear across the full range of constituency types. We do, however, expect monotonically increasing relationships as we move from disadvantaged-party primaries to parties-balanced primaries to advantaged-party primaries.

The model is clearly highly stylized and does not capture all the factors involved in candidates' decisions to run for office. For example, our model does not incorporate candidates' policy or ideological preferences. These are crucial determinants of behavior in the well-known Besley

---

[11] The models in Snyder and Ting (2011) and Evrenk, Lambie-Hanson, and Xu (2013) make similar predictions. Those models go even further on one important dimension, since they model the strategic interaction between parties as well as the behavior of candidates and voters within parties. The model in Castanheira, Crutzen, and Sahuguet (2010*b*) shows that primary elections induce candidates to improve the quality of the policy platforms they offer when general elections reveal little information about platform quality, or when the value of holding the office is low. They note that the second prediction can be interpreted as showing that, in a constituency where one party is strong and the other is weak, primary elections induce the candidates in the stronger party to improve the quality of their policy platforms. In another model, Castanheira, Crutzen, and Sahuguet (2010*a*) show that primary elections can improve the quality of the policy platforms that party-affiliated candidates offer in order to defeat independent candidates.

[12] If the condition in part (iii) does not hold, then it is possible for dF_H/ds to be less than zero. Suppose high-quality candidates are only slightly less likely to win the general election in parties-balanced constituencies compared to constituencies that are safe for their party, while low-quality candidates are much less likely to win in parties-balanced constituencies compared to safe constituencies. Then we might observe low-quality candidates entering at least some of the time in safe constituencies but almost never in competitive constituencies, while high-quality candidates would be entering in both types of constituencies. In this case, the fraction of high-quality candidates could turn out to be lower in safe constituencies than in competitive constituencies. The empirical patterns identified below are consistent with the predictions of Proposition 1, and not with this alternative.

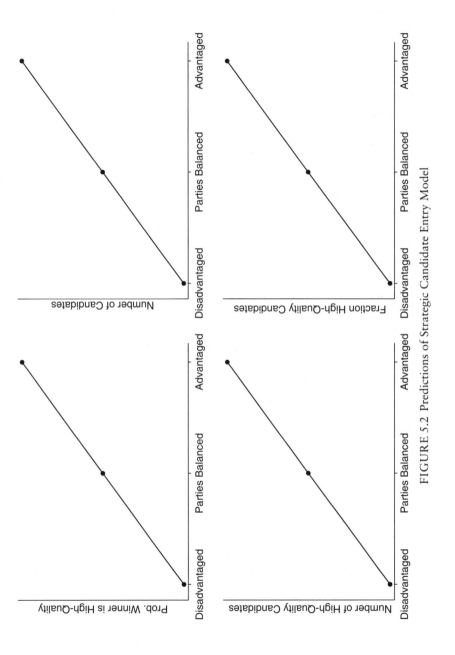

FIGURE 5.2 Predictions of Strategic Candidate Entry Model

85

and Coate (1997) and Osborne and Slivinski (1996) "citizen-candidate" models. Our model also does not explicitly distinguish between incumbents and non-incumbents. Banks and Kiewiet (1989) model challengers and incumbents, and allow potential challengers to delay running for office until the incumbent retires. We abstract from these and other considerations in order to focus attention on the general election environment, and highlight how this environment impacts candidates' entry decisions.

5.1.2 Nominee Quality under the Convention System

Do primaries produce more high-quality nominees than conventions? Developing a theoretical model to capture the relationship between convention nominations and candidate quality is not straightforward. Since convention nominations are often assumed to be under the control of party elites, the predictions from these models will depend heavily on the assumptions about the preferences of party elites and the pool of potential candidates.

Consider, for example, the following simple model: party elites care about both quality and some other attribute, which we call "party service" – that is, an individual's willingness to act in the interests of the party elite. Party service would include activities such as insuring that patronage appointments and government contracts are made in the interests of party leaders, supporting legislation that the party elites support, and supplying resources for the party's electioneering efforts. Party leaders would presumably prefer to increase the number of high-party-service types elected, as long as this does not significantly reduce their chances of controlling the government. In constituencies where parties have an electoral advantage, the elites are especially likely to prefer party service over quality.[13]

If party service is not positively correlated with quality, and the pool of high-quality candidates is the same under both nomination systems, then the model outlined above would make the following predictions. First, the average quality of nominees under conventions would be lower than under primaries. Second, this would be especially true in constituencies where the party is advantaged. We should observe the opposite patterns

---

[13] This assumes that there is little spillover across constituencies in the electoral implications of each constituency's nominee type. However, even if high-quality types are available, party leaders may prefer low-quality nominees if they believe that these nominees have worse outside options, making them more likely to serve the interests of the elites.

for party service. The average party service level of nominees under conventions would be higher than under primaries, and this would be especially true in constituencies with an advantaged party.

A similar argument applies in the context of geographic balancing. Under the convention system, parties were expected to nominate geographically balanced tickets.[14] This is therefore another situation in which it makes sense to assume that party elites value an attribute of potential nominees that is not positively correlated with quality. Moreover, imposing geographic requirements for certain offices would constrain the pool of candidates that elites could consider, constraints that might be more binding for down-ballot offices.[15]

There are, however, several reasons to be skeptical of such a simple model. First, the composition of the pool of potential candidates is likely to be affected by the nomination system. This point was highlighted by those critical of primaries, who often argued that the cost of campaigning in contested primaries would deter high-quality types from seeking any party's nomination. The absence of these campaigning costs under the convention system would presumably expand the pool of candidates, including high-quality types, willing to compete for a nomination. With more options available to party elites, they might be more able to find a candidate who is both a high-party-service type and also high-quality.[16]

[14] Critics of the primary system highlighted the potential loss of geographic balancing that would result from the reforms. Beman (1926, 120) discusses how the Citizens Union made this point during the debates over whether to adopt direct primaries in New York. The Citizens Union claimed: "The statement has been made by almost every opponent of the system that such a law, if adopted here, would result in New York City, Buffalo and Rochester's obtaining all the state offices, and controlling state offices, and controlling state elections, to the exclusion of the smaller cities and the rural districts."

[15] Primaries will tend to produce geographically unbalanced tickets when one area has a disproportionate number of a party's supporters. One such case was Massachusetts prior to the New Deal. Close to, and in some cases more than, a majority of the Democratic primary votes were cast in Boston. By contrast, less than a fifth of the Republican primary votes were cast in Boston. We examine the city or town affiliations of Democratic and Republican nominees for statewide office and US Senate in Massachusetts between 1896 and 1930. After primaries were introduced, the percentage of Democratic Party nominees from Boston rose from 22 percent (n=94) under conventions to 39 percent (n=93) under primaries, and the increase is statistically significant. For Republicans, the percentage of nominees for statewide office from Boston fell from 37 percent (n=90) to 32 percent (n=97), a small and statistically insignificant change. This provides some evidence that primaries could weaken the geographic balance of a party's tickets, when a disproportionate number of a party's voters are located in a particular geographic area.

[16] The pool of candidates may also differ by office. Since higher offices tend to be more attractive, elites may be less constrained in the pool of high-quality candidates who are also high-party-service types willing to run for these offices.

On the other hand, progressive reformers argued that primaries would motivate high-quality types, who previously were deterred by the alleged problems associated with the convention system, to seek their party's nomination. It is not obvious which of these scenarios is more likely.

It is therefore difficult to make tight theoretical predictions about whether the *overall* probability of nominating high-quality candidates would be higher or lower under conventions compared to primaries. It is somewhat easier, however, to make predictions about *relative* probabilities. In particular, there are stronger arguments for comparing conventions and primaries in terms of the relative likelihood each system will nominate high-quality candidates in safe versus competitive constituencies.

In attempting to maximize the number of offices their party will win, party elites have an incentive to nominate high-quality candidates in constituencies where their party does not have an electoral advantage, especially in parties-balanced constituencies. Moreover, under the convention system party leaders are likely to have resources to help achieve this goal. In particular they can offer to subsidize the general election campaigns of their nominees running in competitive constituencies in order to attract high-quality candidates who would not otherwise choose to enter these races.

Party leaders might also have an incentive to select high-quality nominees due to externalities across races. Nominating low-quality candidates for some offices may hurt the party's "brand," reducing the votes for the party's nominees in other races.[17] Externalities might also exist in a legislative context, if each voter's utility depends directly on the quality of all representatives, not only on the quality of the representative from her district. Party leaders are more likely than primary voters to internalize these externalities in their strategic calculations. Thus, in order to attract high-quality candidates, party leaders might also choose to subsidize the general election costs for high-quality nominees even in constituencies where the party has a disadvantage.

Therefore, relative to primaries, under conventions we should expect to observe a higher percentage of high-quality nominees for a party

[17] Externalities may also arise due to imperfect information. For example, voters might not know what fraction of each party's candidates are high-quality. As a result, observed quality in one district or for one office could affect voters' beliefs in other districts or when voting for other offices. In addition, voters might not know how much value party leaders place on quality relative to party service. So, again, observed quality in one district could affect voters' beliefs in other districts.

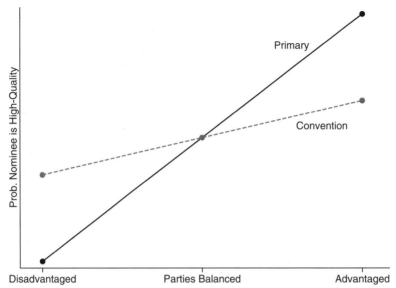

FIGURE 5.3 Theoretical Predictions Comparing Quality under Primaries and Conventions

that does not have an advantage in the general election compared to the percentage observed for an advantaged party in a safe constituency. That is, the relationship between the probability that the nominee is high-quality and the expected two-party vote across constituencies should be flatter under conventions than primaries. This is illustrated in Figure 5.3.[18]

5.2 RELEVANT EXPERIENCE AS A QUALIFICATION FOR OFFICE

One of the key challenges to investigating the effect of primaries on candidate quality concerns measurement. In the early debates over primaries, candidate quality was never clearly defined, although it was commonly understood to include attributes such as honesty, integrity, and capability. We focus on a particular dimension of quality – the candidate's ability to perform the tasks associated with the office they are seeking. Even this is difficult to measure. However, one reasonable indicator that a candidate might have such ability is that she has

---

[18] In the figure the two curves intersect exactly at the point labeled "Parties-Balanced" on the x-axis. This is purely incidental. As discussed above, it is difficult to predict where (or even if) the two curves should actually intersect.

qualifications based on her prior experience – that is, she has served previously in positions that required her to perform similar tasks. In this chapter, we use a measure of quality based on candidates' qualifications to investigate the hypotheses presented above regarding primaries and conventions.

A large body of literature in economics and psychology examines the importance of prior experience for job performance. In the labor economics literature, prior experience is often viewed as building human capital and is used to explain wage differences.[19] In the psychology literature, an individual's ability to perform new tasks is found to be related to their prior experiences. Both literatures highlight the variation in types of prior experience and in how the different experiences are related to expected performance in new positions. In general, the degree to which prior experience is related to the tasks expected of workers has a significant impact on their performance. Various studies find that prior experience that builds human capital for particular industries, occupations, or firms has different effects on worker compensation. These differences are particularly salient when workers move to a new industry or firm.[20] More recently, economists have focused on the implications of task-specific human capital.[21] The personnel psychology literature finds that task-specific prior experience is strongly related to performance.[22]

Although this literature has tended to focus on the private sector, similar arguments presumably hold for public sector jobs, including elected offices. Since the tasks required of public officials, including elected officials, vary across offices, not all prior experience is likely to have the same impact on performance for all offices. The prior experience relevant to being a member of Congress is likely to differ from that relevant to being a state treasurer. For the former, prior experience as a state legislator – where the specialized tasks include drafting and helping pass (or defeat) legislation – is likely to be more relevant than a past position managing funds for a local government. For the latter office, the reverse is likely to be the case. Candidates are occasionally required to have some minimal qualifications for certain offices. For example, candidates for state attorney general are often required to be licensed to practice law in their state. However, this is a minimal qualification,

---

[19] Becker (1964).
[20] Neal (1995).
[21] Gibbons and Waldman (2004).
[22] Quinones, Ford, and Teachout (1995).

and successful candidates often demonstrate their qualifications with additional relevant prior experience, such as being a district attorney.[23]

5.2.1 Measuring Relevant Experience

The analyses in this chapter focus on five offices: US House, US Senate, governor, state treasurer, and state auditor. The first two are legislative offices. To be effective at their job, legislators are expected to have skills such as drafting bills and shepherding them through the committee system, compromising to build broader support for passing bills on the floor, trading favors with fellow legislators, and working with party leaders. For US House and Senate candidates we define relevant experience as prior service as a state legislator or member of Congress.[24]

Governors must do many things, but one of their most important roles is "chief bureaucrat" of the state government. Prior experience as the head of a major statewide executive department or agency should help a politician develop the skills required to run large public bureaucracies, and also expertise about specific areas of state policy-making. Serving as the mayor of a major city should help develop similar skills, since mayors are executive branch heads at the local level. Thus, for gubernatorial candidates we define relevant experience as prior service in a major

---

[23] One example where the attorney general did not have relevant prior experience was in North Carolina. North Carolina Attorney General Zeb V. Walser, who was nominated through a convention in 1896, apparently had no additional prior relevant experience other than being a lawyer and a member of the state legislature. He was criticized during his term in office for being incompetent and for needing to hire additional attorneys to represent the state. An article in *The North Carolinian* states, "If contradictory decisions are what the people desire, then in Attorney-General Walser they have a man after their own heart; but when it comes to performing the duties which were formerly attached to this position, the present official is woefully deficient." (*The North Carolinian*, September 9, 1897, page 8.)

[24] We also include lieutenant governors, since they are typically heads of their state senates. The only other positions that seem potentially comparable are city and county councilors. We do not include these, however, because we do not have comprehensive information about this type of experience. For both offices we disregard previous service known to have occurred more than 30 years prior to an election. For many analyses of US House races, we do not include Southern states because we do not know the exact year in which each congressional district's Democratic Party began using voluntary primaries on a regular basis. We also drop California in some analyses because it permitted cross-filing, allowing candidates to run in several parties' primaries simultaneously. Many US House candidates won both the Democratic and Republican primaries. For example, this was the case in 6 out of 11 congressional races in 1920, and in 9 out of 11 races in 1922 and 1924. It is difficult to code party affiliations and seat safety in such cases.

statewide executive position or as the mayor of a major city.[25] The statewide offices we use are: lieutenant governor, secretary of state, treasurer, auditor or comptroller, and attorney general.[26]

Although it is somewhat simplistic, we treat both state treasurers and auditors as "accountants and guardians of public funds." These offices require a general familiarity with accounting and public finances, as well as a high degree of fiduciary trust. We define relevant experience for these offices as prior service as the auditor or treasurer of a county or municipal government; as a deputy or assistant in the office of state auditor or state treasurer; or as deputy auditor or treasurer at the local level. We also include service in auditing or accounting positions in other state departments and agencies. Serving in these offices not only builds relevant job-specific human capital, but also helps establish a reputation as a trustworthy caretaker of public funds.[27] One issue with this measure is that we lack comprehensive lists of those who served in the various relevant positions (for example, lists of the county treasurers for all counties in a state for the required bloc of years). Therefore, we must rely on information available in biographies, historical accounts and records, state manuals, newspaper articles, obituaries, campaign materials, and other sources. This means that the relevant experience variable for state auditor and treasurer probably has more measurement error than for the other three offices we study.[28]

[25] We define a major city as one with a population greater than 5 percent of the state's population or 0.2 percent of the national population, or (if no city meets either population requirement) if it is the largest city in the state.

[26] In some states some or all of these offices are appointed. We were able to find information about appointed service in almost all cases, so this service is also included in defining candidates' relevant experience.

[27] Whether or not to include private-sector experience in banking and finance is less clear. On the one hand, working in these industries helps build job-specific human capital. On the other hand, it might also easily lead to conflicts of interest, for example, bias in favor of particular financial firms. The potential conflicts of interest seem especially important for bankers since the office of state treasurer deals directly with banks that hold public funds. Therefore we do not include prior experience as a banker. However, we do include prior experience as a certified or registered accountant.

[28] Missing data and sample selection bias are also potential problems. Most candidates who win office leave a biographical paper trail of some sort. Missing data is more of a problem for those who win nominations but lose in the general election, and most severe for primary losers. However, even for primary losers we are able to find prior experience for all but 17 percent of the cases. To be conservative, in some analyses below regarding the composition of the pool of candidates, we restrict attention to races for which we have information about relevant experience for at least three-quarters of the candidates.

As noted above, the literature from economics and psychology finds that job-specific or task-specific human capital is especially correlated with performance. For the statewide political offices we study, there is a natural distinction between "relevant" and "less-relevant" experience. Since the US Senate is a legislature, prior experience in legislative roles seems more relevant than experience in bureaucratic offices, such as state treasurer or attorney general. Thus, we define less-relevant experience for US Senate candidates as prior experience holding statewide offices or serving as big city mayors.[29] For statewide executive offices the opposite is true, that is, legislative experience is less relevant than experience in executive positions. Thus, we define less-relevant experience for candidates running for governor, state auditor, or state treasurer as prior experience in Congress or a state legislature.

Our measure of relevant experience differs from the more common use of previous officeholder experience as a measure of "candidate quality" in studies of post-World War II US elections.[30] These papers are mainly interested in estimating the impact of candidate attributes on election outcomes. They treat prior officeholder experience as a broad measure of "electability," and include *any* prior elected experience in constructing their measures. We focus on a narrower set of offices that are more clearly associated with the accumulation of relevant job-specific human capital. Also below we will compare the effects of relevant and less-relevant experience on endorsements and election outcomes. This helps us distinguish between electioneering ability and human capital related to performance in office, since experience in less-relevant but elected offices should incorporate the former to a much greater degree than the latter.

5.2.2 Qualifications in Early Primary Campaigns

Here we provide empirical evidence that helps justify our focus on qualifications and relevant experience. In the early days of primaries,

---

[29] The same argument holds for the US House but very few candidates served in these offices prior to running for the House.

[30] Several studies have analyzed post-WWII elections. See for example, Jacobson and Kernell (1983); Bond, Covington and Fleisher (1985); Jacobson (1989, 2009); Lublin (1994); Bond, Fleisher, and Talbert (1997); Cox and Katz (1996); Van Dunk (1997); Goodliffe (2001, 2007). A few studies – for example, Carson and Roberts (2005, 2013) and Carson, Engstrom, and Roberts (2007) – use previous officeholder experience as a measure of quality in the prewar period.

candidates often appealed to voters with the argument that they were particularly well qualified for the office sought. William Davis' campaign advertisement for state auditor discussed above is one example. As another example, consider the 1910 Kansas primary for state treasurer, which was just two years after Kansas had adopted mandatory primaries. The two-term incumbent, Mark Tulley, announced his candidacy for the position by stating: "I assure you that the experience is an advantage and that I feel better qualified to discharge the duties of the office on account of the experience which I have had in conducting the affairs."[31] Tulley's challengers also touted their previous experience, particularly pointing to their service in relevant positions. F. J. Altswager stated, "I am a candidate because I believe I am competent to fill the position. My duties as county treasurer of Reno county for the past four years, and my eight years' service to the State Board of Normal School regents have given me insight to public questions which I feel would greatly aid me in serving the state in the capacity of State Treasurer."[32] A focus on qualifications, often highlighting relevant experience, was a common ingredient in campaign advertisements throughout the pre-1950 period and continues even today.

Another indication that relevant experience may be related to expected future performance is that voters are more likely to support candidates with relevant experience. For example, in primary races for treasurer and auditor, primary voters were more likely to support candidates with prior experience in accounting, auditing, or managing local public funds than those without such experience. We discuss this evidence in more detail in Chapters 6 and 9 below. McDermott (2005) provides some additional evidence that relevant prior experience affected survey respondents' willingness to support particular candidates in the 1994 California general election. Hall and Bonneau (2006) provide evidence that candidates with experience serving on lower courts have greater electoral success when running for higher courts. Thus, irrespective of whether relevant prior experience affects future performance in office, primary voting behavior is consistent with an electorate that believes prior experience matters.

Perhaps even more telling, newspaper editors, publishers, and writers relied heavily on prior experience when assessing candidates' qualifications for a particular office. In their coverage of primary election

---

[31] *The Topeka Daily Capital*, January 30, 1910, page 4.
[32] *Ibid.*

campaigns, newspapers published articles about the candidates, frequently highlighting their previous public and private sector employment, as well as their activities in voluntary associations. When newspapers endorsed candidates, the endorsements would typically include discussions of the candidates' experiences and how these experiences were relevant for performing the tasks of the office being sought. For example in the 1936 race for Illinois Attorney General the *Chicago Daily Tribune* endorsement of Charles W. Hadley stated, "He is a lawyer of proved ability and splendid reputation. To his credit he has 10 years of experience as state's attorney of Du Page county and seven years on the staff of the attorney general. He is fully qualified by experience, ability, and character." In contrast, Hadley's opponent, Berthold Cronson, was described as "a man of excellent character and ability but is lacking in experience."[33]

The significance of relevant experience for newspaper endorsements was evident even more generally. To study this, we collected the *Chicago Daily Tribune*'s endorsements for US Senate, US House, governor, state auditor, and state treasurer for the period 1916 to 1950. The *Tribune* endorsed Republican candidates in all primary elections during this period and Democratic candidates in the 1920, 1924, and 1932 primaries. For non-incumbent candidates, relevant and non-relevant experience are defined as above. We also include a separate variable measuring incumbency status, since incumbents clearly also have relevant experience.

We estimate a linear regression model with newspaper endorsements as the dependent variable, and with incumbency, relevant experience and less-relevant experience as the independent variables.[34] Table 5.1 presents the coefficient estimates and their associated standard errors, clustered by race. The first column presents the estimates including all races, while the second column focuses on non-incumbent primaries. Both incumbency and relevant experience have a statistically significant association with newspaper endorsements. Less-relevant experience has

---

[33] "The Choice Among Republicans," *Chicago Daily Tribune*, April 11, 1936, page 14.

[34] The specification we estimate is: $Endorsement_{ij} = \alpha_j + \beta_1 Incumbency_{ij} + \beta_2 Relevant\ Experience_{ij} + \beta_3 Less\ Relevant\ Experience_{ij} + \epsilon_{ij}$, where i indexes candidates and j indexes races. Race-specific fixed effects are denoted by α_j. $Endorsement_{ij}$ is coded as 1 if candidate i receives a *Tribune* endorsement in race j and 0 otherwise. *Incumbency* is coded as 1 if candidate i in race j is an incumbent and 0 otherwise. $RelevantExperience_{ij}$ is coded as 1 if candidate i in race j has relevant experience for the office being sought. $LessRelevantExperience_{ij}$ is coded as 1 if candidate i in race j has less relevant experience for the office being sought.

TABLE 5.1 *Endorsements and Experience, 1916 to 1950*

Variable	All Primaries	Non-Incumbent Primaries
Incumbency	0.79	–
	(0.12)	
Relevant Experience	0.39	0.40
	(0.12)	(0.12)
Less-Relevant Experience	−0.01	0.13
	(0.16)	(0.15)
Observations	249	159

Table shows OLS regression estimates.

no statistically or substantively significant relationship with newspaper endorsements.

Thus, the editors of the *Chicago Daily Tribune* appeared to place a high value on incumbency and relevant experience and less value on less-relevant experience. This increases our confidence that relevant experience is a reasonable proxy for qualifications.

5.3 CANDIDATE QUALIFICATIONS IN EARLY PRIMARY ELECTIONS

We now use our measures of relevant experience to examine the extent to which the qualifications of candidates and nominees match the theoretical expectations shown above in Figure 5.2. Recall that the figure has four panels, each with the same horizontal axis: whether the primary is for a disadvantaged party, parties-balanced, or advantaged party. The four outcomes of interest are: (i) the percentage of the party nominees who have relevant prior experience; (ii) the average number of candidates; (iii) the average number of candidates with relevant prior experience; and (iv) the average proportion of candidates with relevant prior experience. We examine US House, US Senate, governor, state treasurer, and state auditor for all available cases between 1892 and 1950. For each of the four theoretical variables we use the natural empirical analog.

The results for US House primaries are shown in Figure 5.4. Qualitatively, the patterns clearly match the predictions from our model. The top-left panel of Figure 5.4 illustrates that the probability that a qualified candidate will win a primary for an open-seat race increases from 0.13 in the disadvantaged-party primaries, to 0.33 in

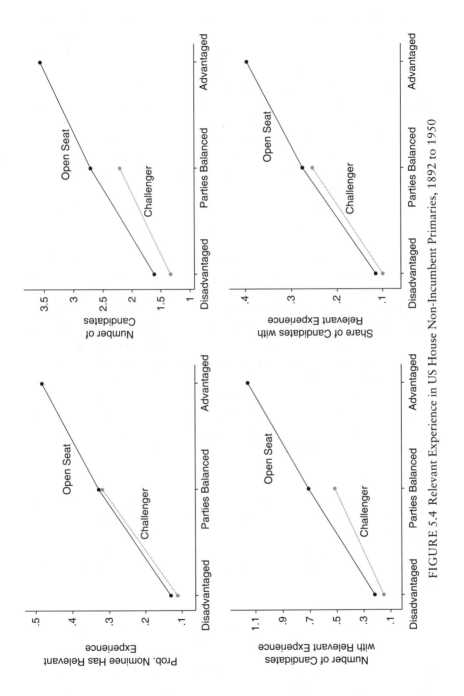

FIGURE 5.4 Relevant Experience in US House Non-Incumbent Primaries, 1892 to 1950

parties-balanced primaries to 0.48 in the advantaged-party primaries. The remaining three panels show that as a constituency becomes safer for a party, the number of candidates entering the party's primary increases, as does the proportion of candidates with relevant experience. The proportion of qualified candidates competing in the primary almost triples as we move from disadvantaged-party primaries to primaries in parties-balanced districts to advantaged-party primaries.

In Figure 5.5 we observe similar relationships for statewide offices – that is, governor, US senator, treasurer, and auditor. The patterns in this figure again show that advantaged-party primaries are more likely to yield nominees with relevant experience than other primaries. The number and proportion of high-quality candidates competing in a party's primary also increases as the party's advantage in the general election increases.

In both figures we separate primaries for open-seat races and primaries with an incumbent in the opposing party's primary. The two types of primaries appear similar, particularly in terms of the probability that the nominee has relevant experience and the share of candidates with relevant experience. This is perhaps not unexpected given the small general election incumbency advantage during the pre-1950 period. As we will see, the differences become more pronounced in the post-1950 period.

Overall, the patterns in these figures are consistent with the predictions of the theoretical model. During their first four or five decades of use, it appears that primaries were contributing to the electoral system where they are most needed – that is, where, in the absence of primaries, candidates might be elected without facing any serious electoral competition. Recall from Chapter 3 that primaries were more competitive in constituencies where a party clearly had a general election advantage. Figures 5.4 and 5.5 show that primaries in these constituencies were also more likely to nominate candidates with relevant experience. However, to properly gauge the contribution of primaries in nominating qualified candidates, we need to compare primaries to another system. In the next section we compare the nomination of qualified candidates under primaries and conventions.

5.4 QUALIFICATIONS IN PRIMARIES VERSUS CONVENTIONS

How did the introduction of primaries affect the probability of nominating qualified candidates? Recall that the theoretical discussion above, in particular 5.1.2, leads to the following hypothesis: relative

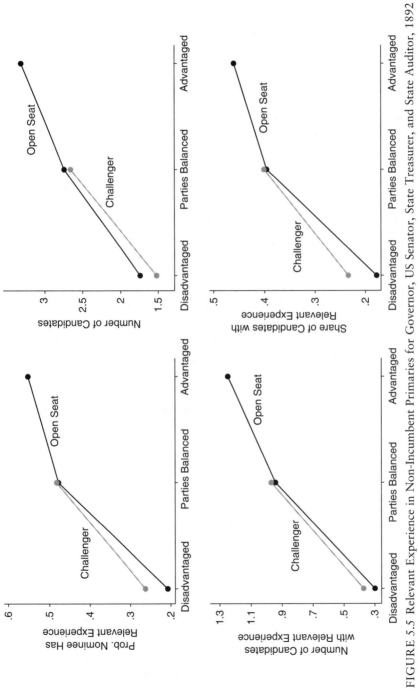

FIGURE 5.5 Relevant Experience in Non-Incumbent Primaries for Governor, US Senator, State Treasurer, and State Auditor, 1892 to 1950

to conventions, under primaries we should expect a party to nominate a higher percentage of qualified candidates in the constituencies where it has an advantage in the general election compared to constituencies where it does not. That is, as illustrated in Figure 5.3, the relationship between the probability that the nominee has qualifications and the expected two-party vote across constituencies should be flatter under conventions than primaries.

We examine the effect of moving from a convention to a primary system on the probability that a nominee has relevant experience during the period 1892 to 1928. As discussed above, this period provides an adequate number of years under each nomination system for the states that adopted mandatory primaries during the progressive era. The main sample consists of races with no incumbent in the party's primary. There might or might not be an incumbent in the opposition party.[35]

We exploit the panel structure of the data, estimating models with both state-specific and year-specific fixed effects, and, in some models, state-specific time trends. Let i index constituencies (which are congressional districts for the US House analyses and states for the analyses of statewide offices) and let t index years. Let $Experienced_{ijt}$ be an indicator variable equal to 1 if party j's nominee in constituency i in year t has the relevant experience for the office they are seeking. Let $Primary_{it}$ be a variable equal to 1 if nominations in the state containing constituency i are made using primary elections in year t. Let $ConstituencyType_{ijt}$ be a trichotomous variable taking on the values +1 if constituency i is "safe" for party j in year t (that is, party j is the advantaged party), -1 if constituency i is "safe" for the opposition

---

[35] One complication is that under the convention system, we only know that the candidate nominated by the convention was not an incumbent. The incumbent might have "run" in the convention but lost. In the primary period we exclude cases without an incumbent in the race. For the analysis of the US House, we analyzed the sample including cases in which an incumbent ran in the primary and lost in order to make the convention and primary samples more comparable. We also analyzed a sample that excludes cases where House incumbents sought renomination but were not nominated by the convention. We used ICPSR 7428 *Biographical Characteristics of Members of the United States Congress, 1789–1979* for information about House incumbents who sought renomination under the convention system. In both of these additional analyses the substantive findings are the same as in Table 5.2. This is perhaps not surprising, since incumbents rarely lose their renomination contests in either system (95.4 percent of House incumbents running for re-election won their primaries, and 95.9 percent of incumbents who sought renomination through the convention succeeded). We do not focus on these results since we are unsure about the sources used to identify cases where an incumbent ran but was not renominated at the convention.

party in year t (that is, party j is the disadvantaged party), and 0 if i is a parties-balanced constituency (safe for neither party). As above, we use a threshold of 15 percentage points to define safe constituencies.

The main specifications are of the form:

$$Experienced_{ijt} = \alpha_k + \theta_t + \beta_1 Primary_{it} + \beta_2 Constituency\,Type_{ijt}$$
$$+ \beta_3 Primary_{it} \times Constituency\,Type_{ijt} + \epsilon_{ijt} \qquad (5.1)$$

The α_k terms are state-specific fixed effects.[36] The θ_t terms are year-fixed effects. The state-specific fixed effects capture factors such as differences in professionalization across state legislatures, as well as differences in size.[37] We might expect the degree to which relevant experience reflects a qualification for a specific office to vary with the exact responsibilities of the various offices in the different states – for example, highly professionalized state legislatures may mean that prior experience is a better reflection of the accumulation of legislative skills, or the state auditor or treasurer position in certain states may encompass additional responsibilities beyond what is expected of local auditors and treasurers. The year effects capture the changes in these factors over time. The state-specific time trends allow these to vary differently across states.[38]

The main variable of interest is *Primary × Constituency Type* and the coefficient of interest is β_3. If the predicted relationships between the probability the nominee has relevant experience and the expected two-party vote under the two nomination systems hold as depicted in Figure 5.3, then β_3 should be positive.

5.4.1 Estimates for the US House

Here we study the US House, focusing on nomination contests without incumbents. In our sample of races, about half of the observations, 46.9 percent, are under the convention system. As discussed above, we define relevant experience for US House candidates as having previously

---

[36] In the analysis of statewide offices, k and i both denote states.

[37] Almost mechanically, the overall fraction of US House nominees with state legislative experience will depend in part on the number of state legislators per US House district, which varies substantially across states.

[38] We also estimated models that included *Opp Pty Incumb* and *Primary × Opp Pty Incumb* as regressors, where *Opp Pty Incumb* is an indicator variable equal to 1 if the opposition party's nominee is the incumbent. This specification allows us to test the hypothesis that the introduction of primary elections led many high-quality candidates to refuse to run against incumbents (Carson and Roberts, 2013). The results are similar to those reported in the table below, and the estimated coefficients on the two additional variables are not statistically significant, so we do not report them separately.

held office in a state legislature or the US Congress. On average, 26.5 percent of non-incumbent nominees had relevant experience under the convention system, and 26.2 percent had relevant experience under the primary system.[39] The distribution of *Constituency Type* is also roughly similar under the two systems, although there are more competitive districts under primaries. Under the convention system, 7.9 percent of the cases are in districts that were safe for the party in question, 31.3 percent are in districts that were safe for the opposition party, and 60.7 percent are in competitive districts. Under the primary system, the corresponding figures are 8.2, 42.9, and 48.9 percent, respectively.[40]

The basic summary statistics demonstrate a relationship between district safety and the relevant experience of each party's nominees. In districts where a party was disadvantaged, the party's nominees were slightly more likely to have relevant experience under the convention system than under the primary system, 15.8 versus 13.2 percent. The corresponding figures for competitive districts are 28.1 and 32.1 percent – a bit higher under the primary system. In districts that are safe for a party, however, there was a larger difference: the party's nominee had relevant experience in 45.2 percent of the races under the convention system compared to 52.6 percent under the primary system.

To examine this relationship more thoroughly, we estimate the parameters in the Equation 5.1. The results, shown in the top panel of Table 5.2, provide clear evidence that the proportion of nominees with relevant experience in safe districts was higher under the primary system compared to the convention system. Consider the simple difference-in-differences estimate in the first column. The estimated coefficient on the interaction term *Primary* × *Constituency Type*, β_3, is positive and statistically significant. Thus, after a state adopted primary elections, the probability that a party's nominee had relevant experience increased by 0.050 more in districts that were safe for the party compared to competitive districts. This is a relatively large difference when we consider that under the convention system the share of nominees with relevant experience was 0.46. Thus, the point estimate corresponds to an increase of 11 percent.

The coefficient estimate on *Constituency Type* is also positive, which suggests that parties were also more likely to have experienced nominees

---

[39] We include cases that are uncontested and consider the opposition nominee as inexperienced. The findings are not affected if we drop them.

[40] The share of safe cases is smaller than the share of unsafe cases, because we are focusing on races without an incumbent. A disproportionate number of incumbents are in safe districts.

TABLE 5.2 *Primaries versus Conventions and Relevant Experience,*
1892 to 1928

US House [N = 5803]				
Primary × Constituency Type	0.050	0.037		
	(0.009)	(0.010)		
Primary	0.036	0.023		
	(0.027)	(0.025)		
Constituency Type	0.143	0.149		
	(0.012)	(0.013)		
Governor [N = 814]				
Primary × Constituency Type	0.121	0.125	0.119	0.121
	(0.043)	(0.043)	(0.041)	(0.041)
Primary	0.011	0.002	0.036	0.030
	(0.041)	(0.046)	(0.041)	(0.051)
Constituency Type	0.098	0.099	0.091	0.093
	(0.029)	(0.030)	(0.026)	(0.026)
Auditor and Treasurer [N = 1242]				
Primary × Constituency Type	0.172	0.168	0.133	0.130
	(0.039)	(0.049)	(0.028)	(0.039)
Primary	0.076	0.077	0.106	0.101
	(0.046)	(0.063)	(0.049)	(0.059)
Constituency Type	0.055	0.056	0.083	0.084
	(0.028)	(0.029)	(0.022)	(0.023)
State and Year FE	Yes	Yes	Yes	Yes
State-Year Trends	No	Yes	No	Yes

Table shows OLS estimates of the parameters in Equation 5.1. Standard errors, clustered
by state, are in parentheses. In Columns 3 and 4, *Constituency Type* is measured just prior
to the introduction of primary elections, and is fixed for the entire period.

in safe districts even under the convention system. This relationship is
not unexpected, given the differences in the pool of potential candidates.
More state legislators are likely to be affiliated with the advantaged party
than the disadvantaged party in safe districts. The coefficient estimate
on *Primary* is also positive, but not statistically significant. Recall from
the theoretical discussion in Section 5.1.2 that we do not have a clear
prediction for this coefficient. Overall, the estimates are similar in the
second column, where the specification includes state-specific time trends.

These patterns are also apparent if we plot the proportion of
US House nominees with relevant experience by district type and

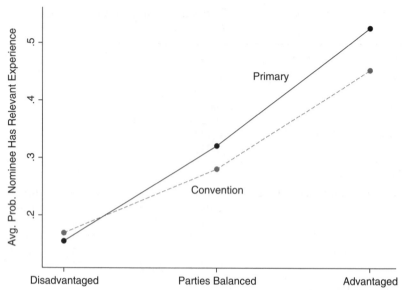

FIGURE 5.6 Convention versus Primaries in the Nomination of Experienced Candidates by Constituency Type, US House

nominating system. Figure 5.6 shows these proportions (after adjusting for differences in the state and year means to account for over-time trends and differences across states). In Figure 5.6 we see that the average probability that the nominee has relevant experience does increase between disadvantaged-party, parties-balanced, and advantaged-party primaries. However, the increase is steeper under the primary system compared to the convention system.[41] This is consistent with the theoretical discussion above, as illustrated in Figure 5.3.

5.4.2 Estimates for Statewide Offices

We use the same difference-in-differences specification in Equation 5.1 to study statewide offices, focusing on governor, state treasurer, and state auditor.[42] We begin with gubernatorial races. In our sample, 57.2 percent of the observations are under the convention system. On average,

---

[41] The slope is slightly different from Figure 5.4, which examines the period 1892 to 1950. Figure 5.6 covers 1892 to 1928; as in the analysis in Table 5.2, we drop states for which we do not have a complete list of state legislators for all years required.

[42] We do not include US senators in this analysis because a large part of the sample covers elections prior to the 17th Amendment, which called for the direct election of senators.

17.6 percent of non-incumbent nominees had relevant experience under the convention system, and 29.0 percent had relevant experience under the primary system. The distribution of *Constituency Type* is somewhat different under the two systems. Under the convention system, 18.5 percent of the cases were in states that were safe for the party in question, 47.9 percent were in states that were safe for the opposition party, and 33.7 percent were in competitive states. Under the primary system, the corresponding figures are 35.3, 30.2, and 34.5 percent, respectively.

The basic summary statistics again show a positive relationship between the relevant experience of nominees and constituency safety. In states where a party was disadvantaged, the party's nominee had relevant experience in 9.0 percent of the races under the convention system and in 9.5 percent of the races under primaries – slightly higher under the primary system. In competitive states, the figures are 21.7 and 31.7 percent, respectively – noticeably higher under the primary system. In states that are safe for a party, the party's nominee had relevant experience in 32.6 percent of the races under the convention system and in 43.1 percent of the races under the primary system – a similarly large difference.

The estimates for gubernatorial nominations are shown in the middle panel of Table 5.2. The point estimate of β_3 is 0.121 in the simple difference-in-differences specification (Column 1). Thus, the change in the probability that the party's nominee had relevant experience after the switch from the convention system to primaries is increasing in the party's expected general election vote share in the state. The estimated effect is large in percentage terms. Under the convention system, the share of nominees with relevant experience in safe states was 0.33. Thus, the estimate of β_3 implies an increase of 37.0 percent relative to the mean under the convention system. Overall, the estimates are similar in the second column, where the specification includes state-specific time trends.

We observe the same overall pattern when we study nominations for state auditor and treasurer. In our sample, 60.0 percent of the observations are under the convention system. On average, 25.7 percent of non-incumbent nominees had relevant experience under the convention system, and 41.5 percent had relevant experience under the primary system. The distribution of *Constituency Type* is again somewhat different under the two systems. Under the convention system, 16.0 percent of the cases were in states that were safe for the party in question, 45.3 percent were in states that were safe for the opposition party, and

38.7 percent were in competitive states. Under the primary system, the corresponding figures are 27.4, 27.6, and 45.0 percent, respectively.

Once again, the basic summary statistics display the positive relationship between the relevant experience of party nominees and constituency safety. In states where a party was disadvantaged, the party's nominee had relevant experience in 15.4 percent of the races under the convention system and in 23.4 percent of the races under primaries. In competitive states, the figures are 35.4 and 41.3 percent, respectively. In states that were safe for a party, there was a more noticeable difference: the party's nominee had relevant experience in 31.1 percent of the races under the convention system and in 60.3 percent of the races under the primary system.

The estimates of Equation 5.1 for state auditor and treasurer nominations are shown in the bottom panel of Table 5.2. The point estimate of β_3 is 0.172 in the simple difference-in-differences specification (Column 1). This reveals that the change in the probability that a party's nominee had relevant experience after switching from the convention system to primaries is increasing in the party's expected general election vote share in the state. Compared to the other offices, the estimated effect is large both nominally and in percentage terms. Under the convention system, the share of nominees with relevant experience in safe states was 0.31. Thus, the estimate of β_3 implies an increase of 55 percent relative to the mean under the convention system. The estimates are quite similar in the second column, where the specification includes state-specific time trends.

For the three statewide offices, we can also address a potential concern about post-treatment bias arising from the fact that the constituency type measure includes state election outcomes after the introduction of primaries. In the third and fourth columns of Table 5.2, we present results in which *Constituency Type* under the primary system is measured using only election returns prior to the adoption of primaries. The estimates are qualitatively similar to those in the first two columns.[43]

Figure 5.7 shows, for the statewide offices, the relationships shown in Figure 5.6 for the US House. We again plot the probabilities that nominees have relevant experience under primaries versus conventions, after adjusting for differences in the state and year means. The upper

---

[43] For these offices we can also investigate alternative measures of constituency type, such as the hybrid measure that incorporates victories in addition to vote shares. The results are again qualitatively similar to those shown in Table 5.2.

panel of Figure 5.7 shows that the probability a party's gubernatorial nominee had relevant prior experience was increasing in the vote share the party was expected to receive in the general election. Moreover, the relationship was much steeper under the primary system compared to the convention system. The graph in the bottom panel of the figure shows the corresponding patterns for state auditor and treasurer. There the pattern is even more pronounced, especially when we compare parties-balanced to advantaged-party primaries. Both plots are consistent with the theoretical discussion above, as illustrated in Figure 5.3.

5.5 DID PRIMARIES FAVOR PARTY INSIDERS?

The results in the previous section show that after primaries were adopted in a state, parties were more likely to nominate candidates with relevant experience in the areas where their nominees were likely to win the general election. All candidates, however, are bundles of attributes. The "new" candidates nominated in these primaries might also have had other attributes that were less admired by progressives. In particular, during the first few years in which primaries were used, many or most of the nominees with prior office-holding experience must have won (and been nominated) under the convention system. Thus, many of these nominees might have been the high-party-service types valued by party elites.

Here we investigate whether primaries appear to have also benefited (or hurt) party insiders. To measure party insider status, we use previous experience as a delegate to a national party convention. We find that after primaries were adopted in a state, the probability that a nominee had experience as a convention delegate *fell* for advantaged parties – the opposite of the pattern we find for relevant experience. These results suggest that most primaries were not controlled by party elites.

Delegates or alternates to a party's national convention, hereafter referred to as simply national party delegates, were often selected for their service to the party. Ray (1924, 143) explains that the delegates were:

[U]sually active party men, politicians in their respective districts who give a good deal of time and attention to politics. They are frequently able and astute managers, frequently, though not always, office-seekers. They are men whose services to the party entitle them to some distinction and recognition. The delegates-at-large are usually men of state or national reputation, the party leaders of the state, the United States senators, or men whose renown or power

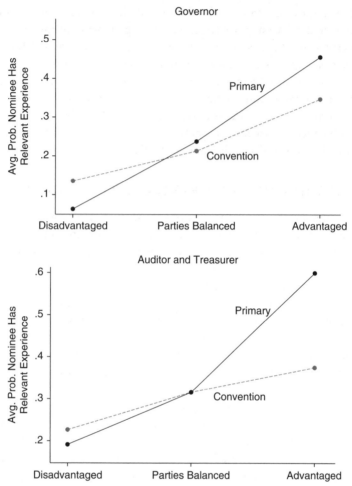

FIGURE 5.7 Convention versus Primaries in Nominating Experienced Candidates for Statewide Office by Constituency Type

as speakers and managers will give the delegation weight and influence in the convention.

Being a national convention delegate was also considered a noteworthy distinction. Delegate names were typically printed in newspapers at the time. Biographical sketches and obituaries of prominent, politically active citizens, such as those found in the *Congressional Biographical Directory*, commonly list participation at national party conventions. Thus, it is likely that most national convention delegates were party insiders. However, not all party insiders served as national convention delegates. As a result, our measure of party insider status probably misses a significant number of actual party insiders – for example, the chairs and other leaders of county and state party committees. Thus, there is measurement error in the dependent variable used below.

We estimate the same specification as in Equation 5.1 above. However, the dependent variable in this case is an indicator variable for whether a party's nominee for a particular office and year had prior experience as a national party delegate. Since we can trace all candidates' prior convention delegate experience, we include all non-incumbent primaries and conventions for all statewide offices – except the US Senate for the reasons given above – and the US House.

The coefficient estimates in Table 5.3 show that the probability that an advantaged-party nominee was also a former national party delegate declined after the introduction of primaries. The coefficient on the interaction between direct primary and constituency safety is negative and statistically significant both when all offices are included together and when we focus only on the US House. The coefficient is also negative when we focus only on statewide offices, but is no longer statistically significant. The pattern is similar if we measure constituency safety excluding the elections after primaries were introduced. These results are the opposite of the patterns we observe for relevant experience in Table 5.2. The positive coefficient on constituency type suggests that advantaged parties under the convention system were more likely to nominate party insiders, particularly for US House elections. These findings are consistent with our expectation that primaries would reduce the likelihood of nominating party insiders in advantaged-party constituencies.

5.6 PRIMARIES AND LESS-RELEVANT EXPERIENCE

It is possible that the primary system disproportionately rewarded candidates with high name recognition or campaign ability, or simply candidates with prior political experience of any sort, whether or not this experience was actually relevant for the office being sought. That is, primaries might have been "beauty contests," which was one of the criticisms by those skeptical of primaries. In our discussion above, we highlighted the distinction between relevant and less-relevant political experience, the former being more closely tied to the desired type of job-specific human capital than the latter.

TABLE 5.3 *Primaries versus Conventions and Party Delegate Experience, 1892 to 1928*

All Offices [N = 14312]		
Primary × Constituency Type	−0.081	−0.070
	(0.026)	(0.027)
Primary	0.018	−0.006
	(0.027)	(0.027)
Constituency Type	0.092	0.092
	(0.025)	(0.024)
US House [N = 8334]		
Primary × Constituency Type	−0.130	−0.118
	(0.040)	(0.040)
Primary	0.036	−0.007
	(0.031)	(0.030)
Constituency Type	0.160	0.158
	(0.036)	(0.035)
All Statewide Offices [N = 5978]		
Primary × Constituency Type	−0.062	−0.067
	(0.038)	(0.041)
Primary	0.048	0.046
	(0.034)	(0.044)
Constituency Type	0.033	0.037
	(0.027)	(0.026)
State and Year FE	Yes	Yes
State-Year Trends	No	Yes

Table shows OLS regression estimates. Standard errors, clustered by state, are in parentheses.

We investigate this hypothesis by estimating Equation 5.1, as in the previous two sections, but with an indicator for less-relevant experience as the dependent variable. The results are shown in Table 5.4. The top panel is for gubernatorial open-seat nominations and the bottom panel is for state auditor and treasurer nominations. For these offices, less-relevant experience refers to prior service in a state legislature or Congress. We find no evidence that primaries increased the probability that a party's nominee had less-relevant experience in constituencies where the party was advantaged more than in other constituencies. That is, the estimates of the coefficient on the interaction variable

TABLE 5.4 *Primaries versus Conventions and Less-Relevant Experience,*
1892 to 1928

Governor [N = 792]		
Primary × Constituency Type	0.006	−0.014
	(0.046)	(0.053)
Primary	0.095	0.137
	(0.047)	(0.062)
Constituency Type	0.148	0.148
	(0.038)	(0.039)
Auditor and Treasurer [N = 1683]		
Primary × Constituency Type	−0.046	−0.057
	(0.041)	(0.040)
Primary	0.003	0.001
	(0.035)	(0.049)
Constituency Type	0.140	0.142
	(0.019)	(0.020)
State and Year FE	Yes	Yes
State-Year Trends	No	Yes

Table shows OLS regression estimates. Standard errors, clustered by state, are in
parentheses.

Primary × Constituency Type are not statistically significant and in three
out of four cases they are negative.[44] This is qualitatively different from
the patterns shown in Table 5.2 for relevant experience. Perhaps not
surprisingly, the positive coefficient on *Constituency Type* suggests that
advantaged-party constituencies under both convention and primary
systems were more likely to have nominees with prior state legislative
experience. This most likely reflects differences in the pool of candidates
under these two systems.

5.7 BOTTOM LINE

How did primary elections contribute to the US system in the early
period? Taken together, the findings in the three previous sections –
that is, Tables 5.2, 5.3, and 5.4 – support the argument that primaries
improved the overall qualifications of advantaged-party nominees.

---

[44] The results are also not statistically significant if we measure constituency safety using
only elections prior to the introduction of primaries.

In this section we evaluate the "bottom line," and explore whether the qualifications of the eventual general election winners for open seats differed between constituencies with competitive and uncompetitive general elections. If primaries in safe constituencies were as effective at selecting qualified candidates as primaries and general elections combined in competitive constituencies, then we would expect the proportion of public officials with relevant prior experience to have been about the same in the two types of constituencies.

We also compare the bottom line under primaries to the bottom line under the convention system for open seats. In Section 5.1 above, we discuss why party elites probably had stronger incentives to nominate more qualified candidates in competitive constituencies than in uncompetitive constituencies, and why these elites might have been in a better position to do this than primary electorates. Thus, we expect that the difference between the average level of qualifications of elected officials in uncompetitive and competitive constituencies should have been lower under the convention system than under primaries.

We present the results in Table 5.5. As in the other analyses that compare primary and convention outcomes, we focus on the period 1892 to 1928.[45] The top panel of the table focuses on gubernatorial races, the middle panel covers state auditors and treasurers, and the bottom panel focuses on US House races. The first row in each panel presents the percentage of open-seat races using primaries in which the elected official has relevant experience. The second row presents the same percentage when candidates are nominated through conventions. The third row of each panel presents the difference-in-differences results between uncompetitive and competitive constituencies under primaries versus the convention system. More specifically, we subtract the percentage of officials with relevant experience elected in competitive constituencies from the percentage elected in uncompetitive constituencies. We then subtract this difference for officials nominated under a convention system from the difference for officials nominated under a primary system.

Table 5.5 shows that under primaries, a higher percentage of officials elected in uncompetitive constituencies had relevant experience compared to those elected in competitive constituencies. This difference is evident in all three panels. This is the pattern we would expect if primaries played an important role in electing public officials with

---

[45] Note that in uncompetitive areas we only examine the advantaged party, since it wins almost all of the offices in these areas.

TABLE 5.5 *Relevant Experience of General Election Winners for Open Seats under Primaries versus Conventions, 1892 to 1928*

	Advantaged Party in Uncompetitive Constituency	Competitive Constituency	Difference
Governors			
Primaries	42.0%	21.6%	20.4%
	[100]	[37]	
Conventions	29.9%	19.6%	10.2%
	[77]	[56]	
Difference-in-Differences			10.2%
Auditors and Treasurers			
Primaries	61.5%	52.4%	9.0%
	[148]	[82]	
Conventions	32.4%	40.4%	-8.0%
	[136]	[151]	
Difference-in-Differences			17.1%
US House Representatives			
Primaries	54.9%	42.4%	12.6%
	[122]	[170]	
Conventions	45.0%	40.2%	4.8%
	[151]	[338]	
Difference-in-Differences			7.8%

Cell entries give the percentage of candidates of each type. Number of observations in brackets.

qualifications in uncompetitive states and districts. If general elections were the only truly effective mechanism for selecting more qualified candidates, then the percentage of winners with relevant experience would have been much higher relative to the pool of primary candidates in competitive areas than in uncompetitive areas.

Under the convention system, a similar pattern exists for elected governors and US House representatives. As shown in the second row, a greater proportion of governors and House members representing uncompetitive constituencies have relevant experience than those representing competitive constituencies. This is not the case for state auditors and treasurers – those elected in uncompetitive states were less likely to have relevant prior experience than those in competitive states.

The third row of each panel shows that, in combination with general elections, primaries were relatively more successful than the convention

TABLE 5.6 *Relevant Experience of General Election Winners versus All Candidates for Open Seats, 1892 to 1950*

	Advantaged Party in Uncompetitive Constituency	Competitive Constituency
Governors and US Senators		
Winners	48.1%	39.5%
	[235]	[119]
All Candidates	34.5%	30.9%
	[916]	[774]
Auditors and Treasurers		
Winners	65.2%	54.7%
	[227]	[170]
All Candidates	52.5%	42.6%
	[526]	[652]
US House Representatives		
Winners	47.9%	40.4%
	[219]	[287]
All Candidates	33.2%	27.2%
	[795]	[1521]

Cell entries give the percentage of candidates of each type. Number of observations in brackets.

system at electing officials with relevant experience in uncompetitive constituencies. Compared to competitive constituencies, the advantaged party in uncompetitive constituencies was 10.2 percentage points more likely to elect a governor with relevant experience under primaries than under the convention system. This difference is 17.1 percentage points for state auditors and treasurers, and 7.8 percentage points for US House members.

We can also compare the qualifications of elected officials to those of the pool of primary entrants, both primary winners and losers.[46] In uncompetitive areas, we only consider the pool of entrants for the advantaged-party primary, since the winner generally comes from this

---

[46] As noted above, we do not include "token" candidates who win less than 1 percent of the vote. If we include these the difference between the winners and pool would be even larger.

group. In competitive areas, the pool consists of entrants from both parties' primaries. If the electoral system as a whole selects qualified officials, then the percentage of general election winners who are qualified should be significantly higher than the percentage of qualified entrants in the overall pool.

Table 5.6 presents the percentage of nominees and primary candidates with relevant experience in advantaged-party primaries and parties-balanced primaries. Since we are not focusing on the change between the convention and primary systems, we examine all races between 1892 and 1950. For all offices, the general election winners under the primary system are more likely to have relevant prior experience compared to the pool of entrants in these primaries. This is true for both advantaged-party primaries and parties-balanced primaries. In five of the six cases, the percentage of elected officials with relevant experience is more than 10 percentage points higher than the pool. The fact that this is true for constituencies where there is an advantaged party, and therefore general elections are typically uncompetitive, suggests that primary voters are not simply selecting a random draw from the pool. The next chapter will focus explicitly on voting behavior in primaries to examine the degree to which voters in primary electorate were supporting candidates with relevant prior experience over other candidates.

5.8 DISCUSSION

Primaries are expected to contribute to the US political system in two ways: (1) by providing an opportunity for voters to weigh candidates' attributes other than partisanship or ideology, such as their qualifications for the office; and (2) introducing competition in constituencies where partisan loyalties make one party safe in the general election. If successful, primaries should facilitate the election of more qualified public officials even in the absence of general election competition. This chapter provides evidence that during the first decades they were used, primaries did in fact contribute in the expected ways. Moreover, primaries might have been an improvement over the old convention system, at least in uncompetitive constituencies.

One potential concern with the above analyses is the use of relevant prior experience as the measure of candidates' qualifications. In later chapters, which analyze primary competition post-1950, we introduce

Republicans of Kansas

A Thirty-Two Million Dollar County Asks Recognition

W. H. CAUBLE
For State Auditor

We, the undersigned citizens of Wilson county, hereby endorse and recommend Willism H. Cauble to the Republicans of Kansas for the nomination of State Auditor.

We ask you to support a man who is a native of this county and has resided in same for the last 35 years, and who has made good in everything he has undertaken. His work in life has been such that he is particularly qualified for the position he now seeks to occupy. His early training on the farm gave him the necessary push and energy for doing things; later his energies have been given to educational pursuits until now he is on his fourth year as county clerk of this county and is regarded as one of the most capable and efficient occupants of that office the county has ever possessed.

Wilson county is one of the best in the State, having an assessed valuation of some 32 million dollars, yet never has had a Republican candidate for a State office. SISTER COUNTIES OF KANSAS, for a half century we have graciously assisted you in electing your citizens to various offices in the State house; now we most earnestly ask you to reciprocate and hereby present for your consideration our FIRST candidate William H. Cauble for State Auditor. Signed.

F. M. Robertson, ex-senator and Pres. Coffeyville State Bank.
F. M. Woodard, County Attorney.
A. F. Squires, County commissioner.
J. F. Clark, County commissioner.
J. L. Rogers, County commissioner.
A. D. Crooks, Pres. State Bank.
T. C. Babb, Postmaster, Fredonia.
J. S. Gilmore, Pub. Citizen.
Jas. W. Finley, Judge 7th District.
Robt. Loofbourrow, Representative.

FIGURE 5.8 Campaign Advertisement for William H. Cauble

two alternative indicators of candidates' qualifications. These measures provide additional confirmation that primaries are contributing to the political system where they are most needed. Thus, we will return to this discussion of how to measure qualifications in those later chapters.

Since this chapter focuses on elite behavior, it provides little direct evidence about the choices made by primary voters and the role primary voters play in selecting qualified public officials. How informed were primary voters during the initial decades after primaries were adopted? Did they identify and support candidates with relevant prior experience? Did they vote on the basis of other dimensions, such factional affiliations or policy issues? We turn to these questions regarding primary voting behavior in the next chapter.

5.9 APPENDIX

Proof of Proposition 1. Denoting cases in which the second candidate does not run as $\emptyset$, there are six possible primary election scenarios. The scenarios, together with their probabilities of occurring, are:

Scenario	Probability Scenario Occurs
(H, H)	$\theta^2 V G_H / 2$
(H, L)	$\theta(1-\theta)V G_L(1-P)$
$(H, \emptyset)$	$\theta 1 - \theta V G_H/2 - (1-\theta)V G_L(1-P)$
(L, H)	$\theta(1-\theta)V G_H P$
(L, L)	$(1-\theta)^2 V G_L/2$
$(L, \emptyset)$	$(1-\theta)1 - \theta V G_H P - (1-\theta)V G_L/2$

Proof of (i). The expected number of candidates is $N = 1 + Prob(N=2)$. Denote $Prob(N=2)$ by N_2. Then $N_2 = \theta^2 V G_H/2 + \theta(1-\theta)V G_L(1-P) + \theta(1-\theta)V G_H P + (1-\theta)^2 V G_L/2$. Thus, $dN/ds = dN_2/ds = (\partial N_2/\partial G_H)(dG_H/ds) + (\partial N_2/\partial G_L)(dG_L/ds) + (\partial N_2/\partial\theta)(d\theta/ds)$. Differentiating, $\partial N_2/\partial G_H = V\theta^2/2 + \theta(1-\theta)P > 0$ and $\partial N_2/\partial G_L = V\theta(1-\theta)(1-P) + (1-\theta)^2/2 > 0$. Also, after canceling some terms and rearranging, $\partial N_2/\partial\theta$ can be written $\partial N_2/\partial\theta = V(G_H - G_L)\theta(1-P) + (1-\theta)P > 0$. Thus, $dN/ds > 0$.

The expected number of high-quality candidates is $N_H = 2Prob(H, H) + Prob(H, L) + Prob(H, \emptyset) + Prob(L, H)$. This can be written $N_H = \theta + \theta V G_H \theta/2 + (1 - \theta)P$. Thus, $dN_H/ds = (\partial N_H/\partial G_H)(dG_H/ds) + (\partial N_H/\partial \theta)(d\theta/ds)$. Differentiating, $\partial N_H/\partial G_H = \theta V \theta/2 + (1 - \theta)P > 0$. Also, after canceling some terms and rearranging, $\partial N_H/\partial \theta$ can be written $\partial N_H/\partial \theta = 1 + VG_H \theta(1 - P) + (1 - \theta)P$. Thus, $dN_H/ds > 0$.

Proof of (ii). The fraction of high-quality candidates is $F_H = Prob(H, H) + Prob(H, \emptyset) + (Prob(H, L) + Prob(L, H))/2$. This can be written $F_H = \theta + \theta(1 - \theta)VG_H P - G_L(1 - P)$. Thus, $dF_H/ds = (\partial F_H/\partial G_H)(dG_H/ds) + (\partial F_H/\partial G_L)(dG_L/ds) + (\partial F_H/\partial \theta)(d\theta/ds)$. Differentiating, $\partial F_H/\partial G_H = \theta(1 - \theta)VP > 0$ and $\partial F_H/\partial G_L = -\theta(1 - \theta)V(1 - P) < 0$. Thus, if $d\theta/ds \approx 0$, $dG_L/ds \approx 0$ and $dG_H/ds > 0$ is "large," then $dF_H/ds > 0$, while if $d\theta/ds \approx 0$, $dG_H/ds \approx 0$ and $dG_L/ds > 0$ is "large," then $dF_H/ds < 0$. So, the sign of dF_H/ds is indeterminate.

The probability that the primary winner is high-quality is $W_H = Prob(H, H) + Prob(H, \emptyset) + (Prob(H, L) + Prob(L, H))P$. This can be written $W_H = \theta + \theta(1 - \theta)VG_H P^2 - G_L(1 - P)^2$. Thus, $dW_H/ds = (\partial W_H/\partial G_H)(dG_H/ds) + (\partial W_H/\partial G_L)(dG_L/ds) + (\partial W_H/\partial \theta)(d\theta/ds)$. Differentiating, $\partial W_H/\partial G_H = \theta(1 - \theta)VP^2 > 0$ and $\partial W_H/\partial G_L = -\theta(1 - \theta)V(1 - P)^2 < 0$. Thus, if $d\theta/ds \approx 0$, $dG_L/ds \approx 0$ and $dG_H/ds > 0$ is "large," then $dW_H/ds > 0$, while if $d\theta/ds \approx 0$, $dG_H/ds \approx 0$ and $dG_L/ds > 0$ is "large," then $dW_H/ds < 0$. So, the sign of dW_H/ds is indeterminate.

Proof of (iii). Recall that $\partial F_H/\partial G_H = \theta(1-\theta)VP > 0$ and $\partial F_H/\partial G_L = -\theta(1 - \theta)V(1 - P) < 0$. Thus, the first two terms of dF_H/ds can be written as $\theta(1-\theta)VP(dG_H/ds) - (1 - P)(dG_L/ds)$. This sum is strictly positive if $dG_H/ds > (dG_L/ds)(1-P)/P$. Regarding the third term of dF_H/ds, differentiate to obtain $\partial F_H/\partial \theta = 1 + (1-2\theta)VG_H P - G_L(1-P)$. This is decreasing in θ, so set $\theta = 1$ (the largest possible value). Then $\partial F_H/\partial \theta = 1 - VG_H P + VG_L(1-P)$. This is positive, since $VG_H P < 1$ (see assumption above regarding the most favorable expected benefit of running). Thus, $\partial F_H/\partial \theta > 0$. Thus, $dF_H/ds > 0$.

Finally, recall that $\partial W_H/\partial G_H = \theta(1-\theta)VP^2 > 0$ and $\partial W_H/\partial G_L = -\theta(1-\theta)V(1 - P)^2 < 0$. Thus, the first two terms of dW_H/ds can be written as $\theta(1-\theta)VP^2(dG_H/ds) - (1 - P)^2(dG_L/ds)$. Since $(1-P)^2/P^2 < (1-P)/P$, this sum is strictly positive if $dG_H/ds > (dG_L/ds)(1-P)/P$.

Regarding the third term of dW_H/ds, differentiate to obtain $\partial W_H/\partial \theta = 1 + (1-2\theta)VG_H P^2 - G_L(1-P)^2$. This is decreasing in θ, so set $\theta = 1$ (the largest possible value). Then $\partial W_H/\partial \theta = 1 - VG_H P^2 + VG_L(1-P)^2$. This is positive, since $VG_H P < 1$ (see assumption above regarding the most favorable expected benefit of running). Thus, $\partial W_H/\partial \theta > 0$. Thus, $dW_H/ds > 0$.

6

Voting Behavior and Primary Elections, 1892 to 1950

"Voters are not fools."

~ V.O. Key, Jr.

A crucial ingredient in Progressive rhetoric about the benefits of primary elections was the virtue of transferring power from corrupt party bosses to a responsible electorate. Senator George W. Norris stated:

> The direct primary system ... gives much more opportunity for intelligent selection. The citizen in his own home has weeks of time to inform himself upon the qualifications of the various candidates seeking the primary nomination ... He decides the question upon what to him seems to be the best evidence. As the citizen becomes used to the direct primary, he takes greater pains to inform himself. The direct primary tends to educate the people. They get together and discuss the qualifications of the various candidates at the meetings of different kinds of clubs and organizations. They do this in no partisan way, but in an honest effort to secure the best nominees.[1]

But did the primary electorate actually behave so responsibly?

With an enlightened electorate, primaries can in theory contribute significantly more to the electoral system than simply adding a second layer of competition. If voters in primary elections evaluate candidates on the basis of issues other than those dividing the major parties, then primaries might help manage intra-party divisions and increase the range of issues voters can consider. In a similar vein if primary election voters evaluate candidates on the basis of attributes and performance, then primaries might help to elect more qualified officials. An article in the

---

[1] Norris (1923, 28).

Altoona Tribune from 1911 stated, "It is almost always easier to frustrate the ambitions of an unfit or incompetent candidate at the primaries than at the regular election."[2]

Whether voters behave "rationally and responsibly" as depicted in V.O. Key, Jr.'s classic work *The Responsible Electorate* is a perennial source of debate among election scholars and observers. The view that voters behave this way forms the basis of many theoretical accounts of representative democracy.[3] Much of the empirical debate centers around whether voters in general elections actually meet these theoretical ideals. For example, recent work by Achen and Bartels (2016) provides a lengthy challenge to the notion that the electorate behaves in a responsible manner.

The obstacles confronting voters are even greater in primaries, so it is no surprise that early skeptics questioned whether the electorate would be up to the task required of it under the new nomination system. According to these skeptics, even the most responsible voters would be hard-pressed to find the time required to cast their primary ballots in an enlightened manner. The substantial costs to becoming informed were caricatured in the following cartoon that appeared in the *Chicago Daily Tribune* on April 5, 1932 (see Figure 6.1).

Even progressive reformers questioned whether enough voters would participate in the primaries to escape the influence of narrow interests – in particular the lingering political machines. If too few citizens vote, then political machines or any narrow interest groups can capture nominations by mobilizing enough of their supporters. In 1924, progressive journalist Oscar K. Davis gave the following description:

We have seen that the bosses easily control the party organization, and get out their vote at the primaries, while the mass of the voters pay no attention to it. Less attention is paid by the people generally to the primaries than used to be paid to the township caucuses. It is rare that a primary polls half the party vote. Even at times of great excitement among the voters, such as the presidential primaries in 1912 when the sharp contest between President Taft and Colonel Roosevelt was on, nowhere is there polled anything like the full party vote. A ridiculous minority, instead of a substantial majority, constantly rules. The total vote in the recent gubernatorial primaries in Louisiana, for instance, was only about 225,000, practically the same as the population of the average congressional district.[4]

[2] August 10, 1911, page 8.
[3] See, for example, Persson and Tabellini (2000); Besley (2006); Dewan and Shepsle (2011); and Achen and Bartels (2016) for discussions and summaries of this literature.
[4] Davis (1924, 9).

HOW TO VOTE INTELLIGENTLY IN THE PRIMARY

FIGURE 6.1 As appeared in the *Chicago Daily Tribune* on April 5, 1932, page 1 (also appeared in Gosnell (1937, 182))

Various empirical accounts document the low level of participation in primaries compared to general elections. These studies have tended to focus on particular offices or narrow time periods. In this chapter, we examine primary turnout across all federal and statewide offices over the entire first half of the twentieth century. We also compare the level of turnout in contexts where we expect primary competition to be the most consequential – non-incumbent primaries for the advantaged party in a safe constituency – with turnout in other contexts.

The other fundamental concern expressed by skeptics of the reform was whether primary voters would be sufficiently informed to select qualified candidates who represent their interests. Unlike general elections, for which the electorate could rely on party cues, primary voters would either need to turn to alternative voting cues, for example, intra-party factional affiliations, or somehow gather relevant information about the multiple candidates competing for nominations to different offices. Under the caucus-convention nomination system, the presumption was that the delegates, or at least the elites influencing them, would be more informed about the attributes of potential nominees. In 1898, Thomas L. Johnson of the Municipal Association of Cleveland wrote:

From our experience in Cleveland, it would seem that the ordinary individual has little fitness to judge of the ability of a candidate for office, or having the ability, little inclination to use it ... In a county having something like four hundred and fifty thousand people, few persons are known to even a small percentage of the whole population, and it seems that almost any sort of publicity given a man, is sufficient to turn a large number towards him when he becomes a candidate for office. The voters have heard his name mentioned, they have seen it in the newspapers, and knowing no other by name, and having no immediate information as to his honesty or ability, or the honesty or ability of any other candidate, they vote for the person whose name they have seen mentioned the greater number of times.[5]

On the other hand, it is possible that over the course of a competitive primary election campaign many voters would be exposed to snippets of useful information – more than just the candidates' names, but far short of comprehensive resumes and policy platforms. Cues and informational shortcuts appeared in a variety of forms. Newspapers, interest groups, and local elites made endorsements, newspapers published articles containing brief summaries of candidates' backgrounds

---

[5] Thomas L. Johnson. 1898. "Crawford County Plan in Cleveland." in the *National Conference on Practical Reform of Primary Elections* (pp. 99–102). Another example is the following quote from Wilson (1916, 398): "Another objection to the primary election system of nominating candidates, and really one of the greatest and most fundamental, is that where the population is large or the territory widely extended the voters in the primary do not know the candidates or their qualifications for office, nor have they any means of finding out what the character of the candidates or these qualifications are ... The convention system is a system by which the final political power is located in that number of the voters who care enough about public affairs to be to some extent informed on the subject. The convention system, therefore, as opposed to the primary election system, has the advantage that the action taken is more intelligent, and in the true sense of the word more honest, since men are not undertaking to act on serious matters in which they take too little interest to be informed."

and positions, and the serious candidates ran extensive campaigns. Even simply knowing a candidate's name might have been a useful cue, if more qualified candidates tended to attract more media attention and campaign resources than less-qualified candidates. In this case, voting on the basis of name recognition would look similar to voting on the basis of actual information about candidates' relative qualifications.

Whether primary voters support qualified candidates or those who share their policy preferences remains an open question. In this chapter, we examine whether the patterns in primary election outcomes are consistent with voting based on qualifications, issue positions, and factional affiliations during the first half of the twentieth century.

In Chapter 5, the theoretical focus was on candidates, political elites, and comparisons across systems. There we assumed that voters favor more qualified candidates. Here, we focus on the primary election system and the degree to which voters actually do support more qualified over less-qualified candidates in the ballot box. This is an important problem because existing studies, especially those associated with the "Michigan School," argue that the average voting-age American is not well informed about politics in general and candidates in particular, which leads voters to rely heavily on partisan cues. In primaries, where voters cannot simply follow partisan cues, existing studies provide little evidence regarding the determinants of voter behavior – particularly with respect to candidate quality.

To our knowledge only one study, Mondak (1995), examines the relationship between voting outcomes and candidate quality in congressional primaries.[6] Lim and Snyder (2012) examine how the relationship between voting and bar association evaluations in judicial elections varies depending on whether or not candidates' party affiliations are listed on the ballot. Their study includes partisan and non-partisan primary and general elections, as well as retention elections. Moreover, little existing research examines whether primary voters consider issues beyond the main partisan cleavages or whether primaries give voters a way to express their support for intra-party factional divisions.

---

[6] Mondak (1995) studies two dimensions of candidate quality, competence and integrity, measured by coding sentences from the *Almanac of American Politics* and *Politics in America*. He finds that competence and integrity are both associated with primary outcomes, but the relationship is stronger for competence. See McCurley and Mondak (1995) for additional information about these measures.

In the next section we provide a simple theoretical framework that highlights the trade-offs voters face between voting on the basis of valence attributes such as candidate qualifications and voting on the basis of ideological or policy cleavages between parties or candidates. The model shows clearly why voters are more likely to vote on the basis of qualifications in primaries compared to general elections. It also illustrates why primary voters may be less likely to vote on the basis of qualifications when there is a salient issue cleavage or factional division within their party. In addition, the model shows one reason why primary elections might be more important in helping select more qualified candidates when the major parties are more polarized.[7]

The bulk of the chapter focuses on the empirical evidence regarding voting behavior in primaries. We begin with a discussion of voter turnout. Although turnout is not explicitly part of the theoretical framework, low-participation elections are particularly susceptible to selecting nominees who do not represent the interests of the broader party or general electorate, but who simply mobilize more primary voters. However, as we will briefly discuss in this section, we do not have clear expectations regarding whether primary turnout will be systematically related to nominees' qualifications.

We then evaluate whether voters tend to support more qualified candidates or those who share their issue positions when given a choice in the primary. We also investigate whether primary voters systematically use factional affiliations to guide their voting behavior across offices in a way analogous to how they use partisan cues in general elections. We assume in part of this analysis that when all else is equal between candidates, voters would prefer to have a nominee who has qualifications that will help her perform the tasks of the office being sought. As long as a sufficient proportion of the electorate is informed about the candidates' qualifications and/or issue positions, primary voters will favor qualified candidates and/or, when issue positions diverge, candidates who share their positions. In the final section, we examine the situation in which voters must choose between more- or less-qualified candidates for an office who also differ on salient issues or who belong to different factions. The theoretical discussion suggests that the presence of significant issue or factional divisions will reduce the likelihood of nominating qualified candidates.

---

[7] Ashworth and Bueno de Mesquita (2008) conduct a more complete equilibrium analysis of a related model and derive similar results.

6.1 THEORETICAL CONSIDERATIONS

Without party labels as the dominant cue dividing the candidates, primaries provide an opportunity for voters to focus on factors other than candidates' partisan affiliations. Here we provide a simple theoretical framework to illustrate why differences between candidates that do not necessarily align with differences between the parties will have a larger impact on primary voting than on general election voting. We focus on the "quality" of the candidates, which simply refers to candidate attributes that voters favor independently of their partisan attachments. For example, having qualifications for office would make a candidate "high-quality."

If voters are strongly attached to parties, then party identification will drive the decisions of most who vote in the general election. Similarly, if the ideological polarization between the parties' candidates is considerable and voters are ideological, then ideology will drive most general election voting. In either case, the relative quality of the nominees will matter little – for example, if a constituency leans Democratic, then the Democrat will win most of the time even if the Republican candidate is of higher quality. Partisan or ideological voting will "crowd out" voting on the basis of candidate quality.[8]

The situation is different in the primary election. Since candidates within a party have the same partisan affiliation, and often have quite similar ideological positions, candidate quality can have a much greater impact on voters' choices. If one candidate in a party's primary is of higher quality than another, then the higher-quality candidate should receive many more votes and win more often than the lower-quality candidate.

These predictions follow from assumptions that are standard in many voting models. For example, suppose there are two candidates, with ideological positions X_1 and X_2 (with $X_2 > X_1$) and quality levels Q_1 and Q_2. Suppose voters have quadratic preferences over ideology and also care about the quality of winning candidates, so a voter with ideal point

---

[8] Ashworth and Bueno de Mesquita (2008) analyze a model of inter-party competition and incumbency advantage that captures the logic clearly. They conclude (p. 1010): "The other component of the policy factor in vote choice is the polarization of the parties. When the parties are highly polarized, voters are more likely to have strong preferences for one party or the other. This diminishes the quality advantage of incumbents, on average, because voters are willing to accept candidates with subpar quality if they are of the favored party and are willing to replace high quality candidates if they are of the wrong party. Thus, a highly polarized party system weakens the incumbency advantage in the quality-difference-based model."

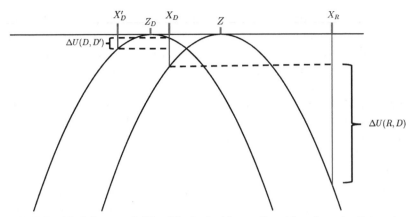

FIGURE 6.2 Salience of Non-Ideological/Issue Considerations in Primaries versus General Elections

Z receives utility $U_i = -(X_i - Z)^2 + Q_i$ if candidate i wins. Then the voter prefers candidate 2 if and only if $U_2 > U_1$, which can be rewritten as

$$\frac{Q_2 - Q_1}{2(X_2 - X_1)} > \frac{X_1 + X_2}{2} - Z \qquad (6.1)$$

The right-hand side is the distance between the voter's ideal point and the midpoint between the candidates' ideological positions. Suppose this is positive, so the voter prefers candidate 1 on the basis of ideology alone (that is, suppose Z is to the left of the midpoint). Then candidate 2 can attract the voter's support only if $Q_2 > Q_1$. Now hold $(X_1 + X_2)/2$ fixed, and consider changing the distance between the candidates' ideological positions, $X_2 - X_1$. Note that if $X_2 - X_1$ is large, then Q_2 must be much larger than Q_1 in order for candidate 2 to attract the voter's vote. However, if $X_2 - X_1$ is small, then candidate 2 can attract the voter's support even if Q_2 is only slightly larger than Q_1. For example, suppose $(X_1 + X_2)/2 - Z = 1$. If $X_2 - X_1 = 5$, then Q_2 must be at least ten units larger than Q_1 in order for candidate 1 to attract the voter's vote. If $X_2 - X_1 = 1$, however, then Q_2 only needs to be two units larger than Q_1 in order for candidate 2 to attract the voter's support.

The first substantive conclusion to draw from Equation 6.1 above is that candidate quality should have a much larger impact in primaries than in general elections. This is illustrated in Figure 6.2 above.

Consider a general election with the Republican candidate's ideological position at X_R, the Democratic candidate at X_D, and a pivotal voter at Z. Figure 6.2 shows the case of a Democratic-leaning constituency. In the absence of any quality differential the pivotal voter will prefer the

128   *Voting Behavior and Primary Elections*

Democratic candidate. As the figure shows, the ideological gap $X_D - X_R$ will typically be quite large. Therefore, a large quality advantage will be required in order for the relative quality of the candidates to affect the election outcome. In the case shown in the figure, the quality differential $Q_R - Q_D$ must be greater than $\Delta U(R, D) = U_R - U_D$ in order for the voter at Z to prefer the Republican candidate. Note that the model assumes voters care explicitly about ideology; however, qualitatively similar predictions can be generated using a simple model in which voters are simply attached to one party or the other.

Next consider a Democratic primary election, with candidates' ideological positions at X_D and X'_D and a pivotal primary voter at Z_D. Figure 6.2 shows the case in which the pivotal Democratic primary voter favors X_D based on ideological positions alone. The ideological gap $X_D - X'_D$ will typically be small compared to the gap between Democrats and Republicans, and the relative quality of the candidates might determine the election outcome even if the quality advantage of the better candidate is small.[9] In the case shown in the figure, the quality differential, $Q_{D'} - Q_D$, must be greater than $\Delta U(D, D')$ in order for the pivotal voter at Z_D to prefer the candidate positioned at $X_{D'}$ to the candidate positioned at X_D. Since $\Delta U(R, D)$ is much larger than $\Delta U(D, D')$, it is clear that differences in quality should tend to have a much larger impact in primaries than in general elections.

The second substantive conclusion to draw from Equation 6.1 is that primary elections become more important – as a device for selecting high-quality candidates – as the two parties become more ideologically polarized. This can be readily seen in Figure 6.3, which depicts two hypothetical general election races – one between X_D and X_R and the other between X'_D and X'_R. In both races, the pivotal voter at Z is ideologically closer to the Democratic candidates than to the Republican candidates. However, the ideological gap between the candidates is much larger in the race with the candidates at X'_D and X'_R. As the gap between the candidates grows from $X_D - X_R$ to $X'_D - X'_R$, we see that the size of the quality differential needed for the pivotal voter at Z to prefer the Republican to the Democrat also grows from $\Delta U(R, D)$ to $\Delta U(R', D')$. Of course the magnitude of the difference depends upon the concavity of the utility function. Nonetheless, the figure illustrates the diminished role that differences in candidates' quality can have in affecting general

[9] Concavity of the voter utility function is necessary for this argument to hold as long as the pivotal voter's position is between the two parties.

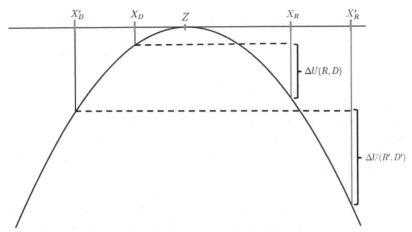

FIGURE 6.3 Salience of Non-Ideological/Issue Considerations with Polarization

election outcomes when the ideological gap is relatively large, which makes the selection of high-quality candidates in the primary (where the ideological gaps are smaller) even more relevant.

An analogous situation may arise in primaries. Candidates or factions within parties might hold different positions on specific issues that matter to voters. If so, these positions may also strongly influence voting in the primaries. This would be analogous to a large ideological gap between primary candidates. In Figure 6.3, we could think of X_D and X_R as two candidates from the same party competing in a primary with different ideological positions. In some cases, these issues or ideological differences might "crowd out" voting on the basis of a quality differential between the candidates, in the same way that partisanship or ideology crowds out quality in the general election. In the past, for example, when Prohibition was a salient issue, this might have been true in Republican or Democratic primaries involving "wet" versus "dry" candidates. In more recent elections, this might be the case in Republican primaries featuring a "Tea Party" candidate running against a "mainstream" Republican. Other candidate attributes – such as race, ethnicity, religion, or gender – might play a role similar to ideological or issue-based cleavages, causing some voters to vote on the basis of attributes other than quality.

6.2 PRIMARY TURNOUT, 1892 TO 1950

Was primary turnout "too low" in the decades after the reform was first introduced? Low primary participation rates *per se* are not problematic for representation, as long as those who turn out represent the interests of the electorate as a whole. In fact, there is at least one argument in favor of a relatively small primary electorate – as the electorate shrinks in size, it is likely that the share of voters that is informed increases. On the other hand, one important concern is that when turnout is low, it becomes more likely that the preferences of primary voters differ systematically from those of primary non-voters. For example, in recent years, observers argue that those who vote in primaries are more ideologically extreme than those who do not and that this exacerbates political polarization (see Chapter 11 for detailed analyses and discussion of this point). Low turnout also leaves the nomination process vulnerable to control by narrow interests that are able to mobilize sufficient voting blocs. In the early days of primary elections, the "narrow interests" of most concern might have been political machines and party bosses. If party machines could control a sufficiently large number of votes, then primary election outcomes might have depended more on candidate attributes such as loyalty to the machine, rather than attributes valued more by the party's rank-and-file.

In this section, we analyze aggregate-level voting data between 1892 to 1950 and ask a simple question: was turnout in primary elections low relative to general election turnout in the early years after the reform was adopted? More importantly, was turnout low even in the constituencies where primary elections were expected to contribute the most to the electoral system – advantaged-party primaries?[10]

A few existing studies investigate aggregate-level turnout in gubernatorial, US Senate, and US House primaries in the second half of the twentieth century. They find that on average, participation in a party's primary was substantially lower than the party's general election support, but that primary participation rates rose as parties' expected general election support increased.[11] Key (1956) examines primary turnout in gubernatorial races during the first half of the twentieth century and finds that primary participation increased as general election support increased. However, he also finds that primary turnout was relatively low even in Democratic-leaning states. Participation in the Democratic primary was only half as large as the support for the Democratic Party in the general election.

[10] We would also like to study the preferences of primary voter and non-voters using survey data. Unfortunately this type of survey data does not exist for the initial decades following the introduction of primaries.
[11] For gubernatorial races see Jewell (1977, 1984a,b). For US Senate races, see, for example, Kenney (1986). For congressional races, see Kenney and Rice (1986).

Here we examine primary turnout for a wider range of offices for this early period. Following previous literature, we study relative turnout. For each party, office, and year, we measure relative turnout as the total votes cast for all candidates competing in a party's primary race for a given office, divided by the votes cast for that party's nominee in the general election.[12] We use the same dataset of statewide and US House races used in previous chapters.

Table 6.1 presents the results. Median relative turnout across all available cases – that is, all primary races for statewide and federal offices during the period 1892 to 1950 – is 49.8 percent.[13] Relative turnout is higher for top of the ticket offices than for lower offices, but the differences are not large. Overall, primary turnout is relatively low compared to general election support.[14]

For advantaged-party primaries, median relative turnout is much higher, 92.0 percent. Thus in these cases the total vote in the primary tended to be nearly as large as the total vote for the party's nominee in the general election. Turnout is arguably most relevant when advantaged-party primaries are contested. For contested advantaged-party primaries, the median relative turnout is 103.6 percent. Median relative turnout is even higher for advantaged-party primaries that are competitive. Thus, even more voters tend to participate in the advantaged party's primary than support that party in the general election.[15]

These high relative turnout rates partly reflect unusually low rates of participation in some general elections, especially in the South. Since the probability that a Republican candidate would win office in the South was essentially zero, there was almost no incentive for voters to turn out for the general election. Thus, for example, median relative turnout in

---

[12] This measure has been widely used in the literature, especially to examine turnout by party (Key (1956); Jewell (1984a,b); Kenney and Rice (1986)). We drop cases for which there are only write-in candidates in the primary. When we have data on the number of votes cast in an uncontested race, we include these observations as well.

[13] We use the median because the distribution of turnout is highly skewed. In particular, general election turnout was very low in many Southern races during this period, leading to extremely high relative turnout. The average relative turnout across all cases would be 74.7 percent.

[14] We also examine how relative turnout changed during this period and find that it was slightly higher in the initial decade after primaries were introduced.

[15] Relative turnout in contested advantaged-party primaries is similar in open-seat and incumbent-contested cases: if we consider all offices the medians are 103.6 and 103.7 percent, respectively. The difference is more pronounced when we include uncontested primaries.

TABLE 6.1 *Relative Turnout in US Primaries, 1892 to 1950*

	All Offices	Governor & US Senate	Statewide Down-Ballot	US House
All Races	49.8%	56.1%	51.1%	48.2%
	[16262]	[1929]	[4896]	[9437]
Advantaged Party	92.0%	111.4%	98.9%	80.0%
	[5380]	[641]	[1811]	[2928]
Contested Primary	103.6%	114.5%	104.1%	98.6%
in Advantaged Party	[3872]	[589]	[1387]	[1896]
Competitive Primary	111.0%	122.2%	104.3%	114.1%
in Advantaged Party	[2029]	[358]	[875]	[796]

Cell entries are medians. Number of cases in square brackets.

contested Southern primaries is 178.9 percent. However, even when we exclude the South, median relative turnout in contested advantaged-party primaries is 78.9 percent, which is still relatively high.[16]

Relative turnout in contested primaries in parties-balanced constituencies is noticeably lower, with a median of 50.4 percent. The median relative turnout is lower still in contested disadvantaged-party primaries – just 33.6 percent. Since the winners of disadvantaged-party primaries are unlikely to win the general election, the low turnout in these primaries probably had less of an impact on representation compared to the turnout in other primaries.

Another concern is that primary turnout may differ significantly across offices. In particular, top-of-the-ticket offices, that is, governor and senator, may draw more primary voters, and voters may be more informed about the candidates in these races. We might expect substantial roll-off for down-ballot offices, since voters may have less information about the candidates in these races.[17] However, the last three columns of Table 6.1 show that roll-off in the primaries was slightly higher than in the general election.[18] Relative turnout for governor and senator primaries (56.1 percent) is similar to the relative turnout

[16] The high relative turnout in advantaged-party primaries might also reflect some "crossover" voting.
[17] Roll-off refers to the presence of voters who cast ballots for top-of-the-ticket races but not for down-ballot races.
[18] Roll-off in contested advantaged-party primaries across statewide offices during this period was quite low. The median was 10.6 percent relative to governor and senator. The roll-off for the general election is 4.9 percent.

for down-ballot offices (51.1 percent). In contested advantaged-party primaries, relative turnout for governor and senator (114.5 percent) is higher than relative turnout for down-ballot offices (104.1 percent).

In the decades immediately following their introduction, turnout in primaries may not have been as low as early political observers had feared. Consider constituencies with uncompetitive general elections, where primaries arguably have the most to contribute to the electoral system. In these constituencies, advantaged parties appear to have been able to attract roughly as many voters to their primary as they did in the general election. This was particularly true when the advantaged-party primary was competitive. Concerns related to low turnout were potentially more justified in parties-balanced constituencies, since in these areas the gap between primary and general election turnout was more pronounced.

6.3 VOTER INFORMATION AND PRIMARY OUTCOMES

Conventional wisdom is that the typical US voter, at least since the middle of the twentieth century, lacks general knowledge about politics.[19] Despite appearing relatively uninformed on various survey questions, in many cases voting outcomes resemble the patterns we would expect if voters were informed. Indeed, scholars have argued that voters are able to rely on various informational shortcuts or cues, although there is some debate over how much information voters glean from these.[20] Some scholars argue that party affiliations serve as an informational shortcut, and there is little question that it exerts tremendous influence over voting behavior.[21]

In the absence of party labels, voters in primary elections clearly face a more challenging decision-making problem than general election voters. This problem is further complicated by the large number of candidates competing in many salient races. In the absence of party cues, do primary voters acquire information about qualifications and go on to support more-qualified over less-qualified candidates (or at least vote as

[19] Berelson, Lazarsfeld, and McPhee (1954); Campbell et al. (1960); Delli Carpini and Keeter (1997).
[20] Alvarez (1997); Lupia (1994); Page and Shapiro (1992); Popkin (1994); Sniderman, Brody, and Tetlock (1991).
[21] On the use of party labels as informational cues, see Downs (1957), Snyder and Ting (2002), and Rahn (1993). Fiorina (1981) argues that party identification incorporates information about incumbent performance.

if they do)? Or do primary voters gravitate toward other cues, such as ballot order, ethnicity, race, and gender?[22] Alternatively, do intra-party factions play a key role, both in providing informational shortcuts and in mobilizing supporters? Or do primary voters appear to vote randomly or on the basis of idiosyncratic factors?

The absence of simple cues raises the costs of voting in an informed manner. Expecting a majority of primary voters to weigh the relative qualifications of candidates within parties seems overly optimistic. However, since primaries are decided by plurality rule, the mapping from votes to victories is highly non-linear, and even a small "informed bloc" can determine which candidates win or lose.[23]

The following simple model shows how this might work. Consider an election between two candidates, one who is qualified and one who is not. Suppose $F_I < 1/2$ of the voters are informed and $1 - F_I$ are not. Suppose the informed voters all vote for the qualified candidate. Assume that uninformed voters vote "randomly" and/or on the basis of factors other than qualifications (race, religion, ethnicity, region, etc.), so that a fraction p vote for the qualified candidate and $1 - p$ vote for the other candidate.[24] For simplicity, suppose p has a symmetric triangular distribution on the interval $0, 1$ with a density of zero at the endpoints of 0 and 1. This captures the idea that p will differ from race to race depending on how qualifications are correlated with issues or other candidate attributes. Then the expected vote share of the qualified candidate is $(1 + F_I)/2$, and the probability that the qualified candidate will win is $1 - 2(.5 - F_I)/(1 - F_I)^2$. So, for example, if only 20 percent of the electorate is informed, then the qualified candidate would be expected to receive 60

[22] This is similar to the problem facing voters in non-partisan elections in which voters have been found to gravitate toward candidate attributes such as race, gender, or religion – see, for example, Pomper (1966); McDermott (1997, 1998). Whether relying on these types of cues improves election outcomes is unknown.

[23] When three or more candidates are running, an additional consideration is the amount of tactical or strategic voting that occurs. Existing theoretical and empirical work on primary elections largely abstracts from this issue and we do as well. For work that does address strategic voting in primaries see Hall and Snyder (2015).

[24] This is obviously related to the law of large numbers. In the classic formulation, the Condorcet Jury Theorem, all the voters are identical and have the same probability $q > 1/2$ of voting for the qualified candidate. Thus, as the electorate grows in size, the probability the qualified candidate wins a majority of the vote goes to 1. Here we are allowing correlated voting by the uninformed voters so that even as the size of the electorate goes to infinity, the choices made by the uninformed voters do not cancel one another. That is, there is "aggregate uncertainty."

percent of the primary vote and win over 70 percent of the time.[25] As the distribution of p becomes more concentrated around 0.5 (holding the share of informed voters fixed), the probability that the qualified candidate wins increases. For example, if p has a truncated normal distribution with a standard deviation of 0.1 then the qualified candidate would still have an expected vote of 60 percent but would win nearly 90 percent of the time.

In the next section we turn to the empirical evidence regarding primary voters' choices when facing candidates with differing levels of qualification for a particular office. We also examine these vote choices when candidates have different issue positions or factional associations.

6.4 DO PRIMARY VOTERS SUPPORT MORE-QUALIFIED CANDIDATES?

In the previous chapter, we find that advantaged parties were more likely to nominate candidates with relevant experience after the introduction of primaries. The theoretical model and discussion there assumes that primary voters favor qualified candidates, and shows how the strategic entry decisions by elites and the pool of available candidates can lead to differences in the probability that qualified candidates are nominated (and elected) in different types of constituencies. The empirical patterns, while consistent with primary voters selecting qualified candidates, do not provide direct evidence that the primary electorate tends to choose the more qualified candidate when given a choice.

Here we investigate whether voters' choices in primaries appeared to depend on candidates' qualifications in the pre-1950 period. Our analysis focuses on five elected offices: US House, governor, US Senate, state treasurer, and state auditor. Qualification for office is again measured using relevant experience as defined in the previous chapter.[26] Incumbents are defined as having relevant experience.

---

[25] This model also highlights the possibility that a political machine or some narrow interest could gain control of a sufficiently large bloc of the "uninformed" voters to defeat the candidate preferred by the "informed bloc." However, unlike qualifications, which we consider to have positive valence, most other interests or machines are likely to have blocs of voters who oppose their candidates.

[26] As discussed in Chapter 5, the samples for the analyses below are not comprehensive for state auditor and treasurer. For the period 1892 to 1950, for the primary races with two to five candidates analyzed below, we were unable to find information on the prior experience of 15.4 percent of the losing candidates and 4.1 percent of the winning candidates. This raises concerns about the sample selection, but depending on

TABLE 6.2 *Voting and Relevant Experience in Two-Candidate Primaries,*
1892 to 1950

Office	Primaries	Experienced Candidate's	
		Win %	Vote %
US House	All	84.9%	67.0%
		[1901]	[1578]
	Non-Incumbent	69.2%	57.3%
		[452]	[382]
Governor & US Senate	All	81.1%	63.6%
		[338]	[335]
	Non-Incumbent	72.3%	57.9%
		[141]	[139]
Auditor & Treasurer	All	78.4%	60.5%
		[231]	[223]
	Non-Incumbent	67.3%	55.3%
		[110]	[107]

Number of observations in square brackets.

The simplest cases to analyze are primaries with two competing candidates, one with relevant experience and one without. Table 6.2 presents the results for these cases, showing the expected vote share and the probability of winning for the candidate with relevant experience. The table shows results for all two-candidate primaries (including races with an incumbent) as well as non-incumbent primaries.

The results in Table 6.2 show that primary candidates with relevant prior experience receive more electoral support than those who do not. In US House primaries, including those that are incumbent contested, the candidate with relevant experience on average receives 67.0 percent of the vote and wins the nomination 84.9 percent of the time. In non-incumbent US House primary races, the experienced candidate on average receives 57.3 percent of the vote and wins 69.2 percent of the races. The fact that the percentages are lower for the non-incumbent primaries could reflect a number of different factors. For example, voters might perceive that experience as an incumbent, that is experience performing the specific tasks of the office sought, is more valuable than experience in a related but different office. Alternatively, voters might

the attributes of the missing candidates, the direction of the bias could be either positive or negative.

have more information about incumbents than non-incumbents. Finally, the differences might reflect other electoral advantages that incumbents have that are unrelated to qualifications.[27] The bottom two panels of the table show the nomination rates and vote shares of candidates with relevant experience running in primaries for the statewide offices – governor, US Senate, state auditor, and state treasurer. These are remarkably similar to those of the US House races. The overall electoral success of experienced candidates for state auditor and treasurer is slightly lower than for the other offices, but the gap mainly reflects differences within the incumbent-contested races.

To examine this relationship more thoroughly and include races with more than two candidates, we regress candidates' primary wins and primary vote shares on relevant prior experience. We focus on primaries with fewer than six candidates. Primaries differ dramatically from race to race in terms of the number of candidates and the distribution of various attributes. Therefore, it seems safest to compare candidates running against each other in the same race. Thus, we include race-specific fixed effects in the regressions.[28]

The coefficient of interest is on the relevant experience variable. This coefficient indicates whether candidates with relevant experience systematically receive higher vote shares than those without relevant experience. Since we are examining races with two to five candidates, the relevant experience variable indicates a candidate's proportion of the relevant experience across all candidates in the primary. For example, if three candidates are competing in a primary and two have relevant experience, then each of the candidates with relevant experience is coded as having half of the experience.[29] The assumption is that the experienced candidates would split the electoral benefits of having experience equally.

---

[27] These percentages are roughly consistent with the simple model in the previous section when 30 percent of the electorate is informed in all races and 20 percent is informed in the non-incumbent races.

[28] More specifically, we use the following specification: $Y_{ij} = \alpha_j + \beta Pct \, of \, Qualifications_{ij} + \epsilon_{ij}$, where α_j is a race-specific fixed effect. The variable $Pct \, of \, Qualifications_{ij}$ measures relevant experience. The standard errors are clustered by race. Since we are missing information about the prior experience of some candidates, we limit the sample to races for which we have information about two or more candidates. Candidates with missing information are dropped.

[29] In other words, $Pct \, of \, Qualifications_{ij}$ would be coded as 0.5 for the two candidates with relevant experience and 0 for the third candidate. If only one candidate has relevant experience, then $Pct \, of \, Qualifications_{ij}$ would be coded as 1 for that candidate and 0 for the other two candidates.

While incumbency is a strong indicator of relevant experience, it may also capture other advantages incumbents have over non-incumbents.[30] Thus, we include separate variables for whether the candidate is an incumbent and whether he or she has other relevant experience.

As discussed in the previous chapter, one concern with using experience to measure qualifications for office is that experience may be correlated with other factors. In particular, if party leaders are able to influence primary outcomes to favor those most loyal to the party, then prior experience may simply indicate that the candidate is a party insider, and favored by the party elites. Alternatively, holding elected office in the past may reflect the candidate's electioneering ability – such as their charisma and access to campaign resources – which could have little to do with their qualifications for office.

To help isolate the effect of relevant experience, we include two additional variables: experience as a national party convention delegate and service in political offices where the experience is less relevant for the particular office being sought. As discussed in the previous chapter, being selected as a delegate to the national party convention was considered a noteworthy indicator of party insider status. Less-relevant experience could be a proxy for either party insider status or electioneering ability, or both. As with relevant prior experience, these variables are measured as shares – so for example, if two candidates are former convention delegates then each of these candidates will be assumed to have half of the benefits of being a party insider. We can then compare the coefficients on these two variables to the coefficient on the share of relevant experience variable. For ease of interpretation, we include only one of these additional variables in each regression.[31]

---

[30] The large literature on the incumbency advantage discusses the various ways, other than having relevant experience, in which incumbency increases a candidate's support in the general election.

[31] In several states, including Maine, New Hampshire, New Jersey, and Tennessee all or most of the statewide down-ballot executive offices – including attorney general, secretary of state, state auditor, and state treasurer – are appointed rather than elected. These appointees probably accumulate a similar amount of job-specific human capital as those elected to these same offices in other states, but they rarely have prior experience winning statewide elections. Thus, at least in principle, one way to help distinguish between actual relevant human capital and simple electioneering ability is compare the electoral outcomes for the appointed versus elected down-ballot officials when they run for higher office, that is, governor. Unfortunately, very few appointed officials run for governor, so we do not have enough power to make a meaningful comparison.

TABLE 6.3 *Voting and Candidate Experience in Primaries, 1900 to 1950*

Office	Depend. Variable	Current Incumb.	Relevant Exper.	Party Insider	p-value for (1)–(3)	p-value for (2)–(3)	Obs.
US House	Win %	80.3 (1.4)	23.0 (2.1)	17.2 (2.5)	0.00	0.09	15490
	Vote %	39.0 (0.7)	13.3 (0.8)	7.9 (1.0)	0.00	0.00	13425
Governor & US Senate	Win %	66.3 (3.8)	24.9 (3.6)	15.6 (3.7)	0.00	0.09	4431
	Vote %	32.6 (1.4)	14.5 (1.3)	9.5 (1.3)	0.00	0.01	4361
Auditor & Treasurer	Win %	83.0 (4.9)	21.5 (5.7)	7.9 (8.5)	0.00	0.18	1883
	Vote %	29.1 (1.8)	8.2 (1.6)	4.8 (2.5)	0.00	0.23	1845

Office	Depend. Variable	Current Incumb.	Relevant Exper.	Less-Rel. Exper.	p-value for (1)–(3)	p-value for (2)–(3)	Obs.
Governor & US Senate	Win %	67.5 (3.7)	23.6 (3.7)	13.4 (3.7)	0.00	0.07	4109
	Vote %	34.0 (1.4)	14.5 (1.4)	7.5 (1.3)	0.00	0.00	4050
Auditor & Treasurer	Win %	83.3 (4.9)	21.5 (5.7)	-2.2 (5.9)	0.00	0.00	1875
	Vote %	29.4 (1.8)	8.5 (1.6)	3.0 (1.8)	0.00	0.02	1837

The columns labelled Current Incumb. (1), Relevant Exper. (2), and Party Insider / Less-Rel. Exper. (3) contain OLS regression estimates. The column labelled p-value for (1)–(3) gives the p-value of the F-test for the hypothesis that the coefficients on Current Incumbency and Party Insider status (or Less-Relevant Experience) are equal. The column labelled p-value for (2)–(3) gives the p-value of the F-test for the hypothesis that the coefficients on Relevant Experience and Party Insider status (or Less-Relevant Experience) are equal.

The results presented in Table 6.3 provide strong evidence that candidates with relevant experience have higher primary election vote shares and are more likely to win nominations than those without relevant experience. Moreover, candidates with relevant experience have more support in primaries than party insiders, and also more support than candidates with less-relevant experience. In most cases, the gap is statistically significant.

In US House primaries, an incumbent is 80.3 percentage points more likely to win the nomination and, on average, has a 39.0-percentage-point higher vote share than a non-incumbent who has neither relevant experience nor experience as a national convention delegate. Non-incumbents with relevant experience are also more likely to win their party's nominations. If there is only one non-incumbent candidate with relevant experience in a race, then that candidate has a 23.0-percentage-point higher likelihood of winning the nomination and a 13.3-percentage-point higher vote share than a candidate without relevant experience or experience as a national convention delegate. If there are two non-incumbent candidates in the primary with relevant experience, then on average this advantage drops by half. The coefficient estimates for non-incumbency-relevant experience reflect a smaller experience advantage for winning the primary but a similar advantage for primary vote share compared to the results for the two-candidate non-incumbent primaries presented in Table 6.2.[32]

Party insiders in US House elections also receive more electoral support than candidates with no relevant experience. However, the electoral benefit is smaller than the electoral benefit associated with incumbency or non-incumbent relevant experience. If there is only one party insider in the primary then that candidate is 17.2 percentage points more likely to win their party's nomination, and has a 7.9-percentage-point higher expected vote share, compared to candidates with no relevant experience. This electoral benefit is not surprising, since those selected as delegates to the national party conventions are likely to have qualities that would make them attractive to primary voters. However, the differences in the electoral benefits between relevant experience and national convention delegate experience are statistically significant for vote shares.

The relationships between primary outcomes, relevant experience, and party insider status are similar for statewide offices. The top panel of Table 6.3 demonstrates that incumbents running in US Senate, gubernatorial, state auditor, and state treasurer primaries are much more likely to win their party's nomination than are candidates without relevant experience or party insiders. Non-incumbent candidates with relevant experience also outperform those who have no relevant experience and have never served as a national convention delegate. As

---

[32] While not shown in the table, the magnitude of the coefficient on non-incumbent relevant experience is roughly the same for open-seat races and incumbent-contested races.

with the US House, the relationship is strongest for incumbents and weakest for former convention delegates. The coefficient estimates follow the same pattern as those in the analysis of the US House. The difference between the coefficients on non-incumbency relevant experience and party insider status is not statistically significant even at the 10-percent level for auditor and treasurer. However, very few candidates running for state auditor or treasurer have experience as former convention delegates, and thus the standard errors on the party insider variable are large. The coefficients on non-incumbency relevant experience are both statistically significant, whereas the coefficients on party insider status are not.

For the statewide offices we also have information about whether the candidates have held other, less-relevant, political offices. As discussed in the previous chapter, experience as a state legislator is likely to be less relevant to performing gubernatorial tasks compared to experience as the executive of a state agency or the mayor of a large city. Similarly, executive experience is likely to be less relevant for US senators compared to experience as a legislator either as a member of Congress or as a state legislator. Relevant experience is more likely to increase a candidate's qualification for a particular type of office than less-relevant experience.

In the bottom panel of Table 6.3 we include a variable for each candidate's share of less-relevant experience. If the electoral benefits of relevant experience mainly reflect a combination of candidates' status as party insiders and their electioneering abilities, then candidates with less-relevant experience should also have similar electoral benefits. However, if primary voters are considering the candidates' qualifications for office, then we would expect primary election outcomes to be more strongly related to relevant experience than to less-relevant experience.

The coefficient estimates at the bottom of Table 6.3 show that non-incumbent candidates with relevant experience are more likely to win primaries than non-incumbent candidates with less-relevant experience, assuming there are the same (or fewer) candidates with relevant versus less-relevant experience in the race. For example, if two non-incumbent candidates are competing in a gubernatorial primary, one with only relevant experience and the other with only less-relevant experience, the candidate with relevant experience is 10.2 percentage points more likely to win than the candidate with less-relevant experience. The vote share of the candidate with relevant experience is also expected to be 6.9 percentage points higher. The difference in the probabilities of winning the nomination between candidates with only relevant versus only less-relevant experience is even more striking for state auditors and treasurers.

While not shown in the table, we also examine whether the coefficient on the non-incumbent relevant experience differs between advantaged-party and parties-balanced primaries. We might expect voters in advantaged-party primaries to have more information or pay greater attention to the qualifications of the primary candidates. However, the coefficient estimates on the share of relevant experience are not larger in the advantaged-party primaries.

6.4.1 Possible Mechanisms

The estimates above indicate that during the period 1892 to 1950, candidates with more qualifications received more votes and had a higher probability of winning – and that primary voters were able to distinguish between candidates with relevant and less-relevant experience. It is less clear how voters acquired this information, or indeed whether they got it at all. Voters might have simply used other cues correlated with qualifications.

One obvious source of information was the mass media. Newspapers increasingly discussed candidates' attributes and qualifications, and even before World War II some newspapers began explicitly endorsing candidates in primaries. These endorsements were often based on qualifications that were highlighted in the endorsement editorials. Much less is known about primary election coverage in radio and television news, but there was definitely some degree of coverage at least in high-profile races. However, we do not know whether voters used information that media sources provided about qualifications when deciding how to vote. Again, the mechanism could have been indirect, for example, voting based on which candidate was endorsed by a trusted newspaper.

The primary election campaigns provided another source of information. Moreover, as the advertisement in Figure 5.1 in the previous chapter illustrates, candidates' campaigns frequently emphasized their experience and qualifications. Yet again, we do not know whether voters used the information provided by campaigns or whether the campaigns had a more indirect effect. For example, voters might simply have supported the candidates whose names they heard most often. Assuming the more qualified candidates tended to have more active campaigns and/or more media coverage, this would again result in higher support for more qualified candidates.

6.5 PRIMARY VOTING AND CANDIDATE ISSUE POSITIONS

If primary voters are casting ballots in an informed way, as the results above suggest, similar voting behavior should occur where candidates clearly differ along some salient issue dimension. Informed primary voters should support candidates who share their position on the issue. To study whether this occurs, we exploit geographic variation in voter preferences on one specific issue, alcohol prohibition, and one more general issue bundle, progressivism. We calculate the correlation between a measure of voter preferences on these issues with the primary vote shares of candidates holding opposite positions on the issues.

6.5.1 Issue Voting: Prohibition

Toward the end of the nineteenth century, groups such as the Women's Christian Temperance Union and the Anti-Saloon League lobbied to limit or abolish the production and sale of alcoholic beverages. They argued that alcohol caused poverty and social vices such as immoral behavior and violence. By 1916, almost half of the states had passed strong anti-liquor legislation, and in that year a large contingent of "dry" members were elected to the US Congress. The 18th Amendment, which prohibited "the manufacture, sale or transportation of intoxicating liquors," was ratified in January 1919 and went into effect in January 1920. In 1919, Congress also passed the National Prohibition Act, more commonly called the Volstead Act, to enforce the 18th Amendment. Over time, bootlegging, corruption, and organized crime arose as by-products of Prohibition, and many state and local governments were lax in their enforcement. With the onset of the Great Depression, many critics argued that the ban on alcohol contributed to unemployment and crime, and that governments desperately needed the tax revenue generated by legal alcohol sales. In December 1933, the 21st Amendment was ratified, repealing the 18th Amendment and ending national prohibition. State prohibition continued in a few states after 1933, with Mississippi being the being last to abandon it in 1966.[33]

Intra-party divisions over Prohibition appeared within both major parties from the 1870s on, especially within the Republican Party in

---

[33] See Pennock and Kerr (2005). For a historical overview, see Aaron and Musto (1981).

the North and the Democratic Party in the South.[34] The powerful Anti-Saloon League was willing to back candidates from either major party as long as they were sufficiently supportive of anti-liquor legislation. The League operated at all levels of government, and pushed hard not only for federal prohibition but also state- and local-level restrictions. During the first two decades of the twentieth century, alcohol prohibition was an important political issue. In 1906 only three states had prohibition laws. This increased to 9 by 1913 and 23 by 1916; 17 of these laws were passed by initiatives or referendums.[35] Prohibition featured heavily in both primary and general election campaigns during this time.

To examine whether primary voters supported candidates who shared their position on Prohibition, we need a measure of voter preferences on the issue and indicators of primary candidates' support for or opposition to Prohibition.

To construct a measure of aggregate county-level voter preferences on this issue, we use the votes on ballot referendums and initiatives. Due to the efforts to restrict or prohibit alcohol consumption at the state level, as well as the national efforts to pass and then repeal the 18th Amendment, ballot measures on Prohibition appeared in most states. We use votes on all available initiatives and referendums that either greatly restricted or expanded access to alcoholic beverages. For each county we define *Pct For Prohibition* as the average percentage of votes cast in favor of restricting access to alcohol, where the average is taken across all ballot measures.

We restrict attention to advantaged-party primaries, since the data on ballot propositions only contains the total vote for and against each measure by county; it is not broken down by voter partisanship. Thus, for example, we do not know how many Republican voters in a county supported or opposed Prohibition. The primary election votes, however, are by definition broken down by voter partisanship (except for crossover voters). By focusing on advantaged-party primaries, we ensure that in most counties there is a high degree of overlap between the types of

---

[34] See Kleppner (1979); Aaron and Musto (1981). Various prohibition parties appeared, but never received strong electoral support. Aaron and Musto (1981, 155) write, "By 1905, the Prohibition Party had surrendered leadership of the movement to the Anti-Saloon League."

[35] Aaron and Musto (1981, 156).

voters included in the ballot proposition data and the types included in the primary election data.[36]

The 1918 California Republican gubernatorial primary between William D. Stephens and James Rolph, Jr. illustrates our approach. Stephens, who was the non-elected incumbent governor, former mayor of Los Angeles, and former member of the US House, favored prohibition and in fact ran uncontested for the Prohibition Party nomination in that same year.[37] Rolph, who was the mayor of San Francisco, was viewed as being more favorable to the "wet" interests. The Committee of Napa Vineyardists placed an advertisement in the *San Francisco Chronicle* that stated in bold letters "ROLPH Must Be Nominated and Elected ... Governor Stephens is a prohibitionist and is the candidate of the prohibition party ... ROLPH IS AGAINST PROHIBITION."[38] Their positions were also discussed widely in various media accounts, especially since ratification of the 18th Amendment was a prominent issue in the upcoming state legislature. Thus, we coded Stephens as the dry candidate and Rolph as the relatively wet candidate. Figure 6.4 presents a scatterplot of the county-level vote for Stephens as a share of the Stephens and Rolph vote against our measure of county-level voter support for Prohibition based on state ballot proposition described above. The figure illustrates the strong correlation between these two variables (the correlation coefficient is 0.86).

To examine whether this pattern appeared more broadly, we identified 31 races in 13 states with one or more "dry" candidates and one or more "wet" candidates. We used a variety of sources including newspapers and publications by temperance groups and opposition groups.[39] For each

---

[36] Thus, the sample of states in our analysis and the years in which the initiatives and referendums occurred are as follows: Alabama: 1909, 1935; California: 1914 (3), 1916 (2), 1918 (2), 1920, 1922, 1926, 1934, 1936 (12 propositions, all in November); Iowa: 1917, 1933; Louisiana: 1932; Maine: 1911, 1934; Maryland: 1933; Michigan: 1909, 1916, 1932; Minnesota: 1918, 1933; North Carolina: 1908, 1933; Oregon: 1904, 1933; Pennsylvania: 1933; Texas: 1919, 1932; Wisconsin: 1920, 1917, 1929, 1933.

[37] Stephens was appointed lieutenant governor in 1916 following the death of John Eshleman, and then became governor in 1917 after Hiram Johnson resigned as governor to begin serving in the US Senate (Melendy, 1964). California allowed cross-filing, so candidates could run in more than one party's primary and receive multiple nominations. Together Stephens and Rolph received nearly 84 percent of the Republican primary vote.

[38] This appeared on page 7 of the *San Francisco Chronicle* on August 26, 1918.

[39] We searched newspapers available online – in particular ProQuest Historical Newspapers and Google News archives – using the keywords ("wet" or "dry") and ("governor" or "senate") and ("primary"). The temperance movement publications include *Home and State* and the *Anti-Saloon League Yearbook*.

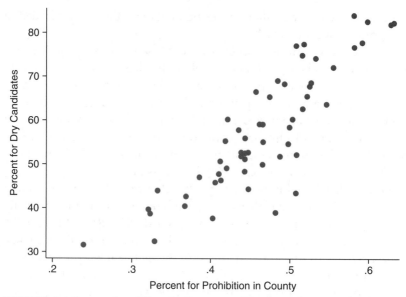

FIGURE 6.4 Scatterplot of Vote for Dry versus Wet Candidates (Stephens versus Rolph) in the 1918 California Republican Gubernatorial Primary against Percent Support for Prohibition, by County

county we aggregate the votes for the dry and wet candidates in each race, and then define *Pct for Dry Cands* as the percentage of votes cast in the county for the dry rather than wet candidates in the race (we drop candidates not classified as either wet or dry).[40]

Table 6.4 displays the correlations between *Pct for Dry Cands* and *Pct for Prohibition* for all 31 races. The correlations are generally high, with an average of 0.57. Although the correlations are based on county-level rather than individual-level data, they are so large, and include so many different states and races, that we doubt they are driven mainly by aggregation bias (ecological inference bias). Instead, the correlations suggest that many voters learned about the candidates' positions on the Prohibition issue and voted accordingly.[41]

We present further evidence that the correlations in Table 6.4 are not spurious factors by examining a set of "placebo" cases, in which both

---

[40] We also drop candidates who received less than 5 percent of the vote. Races with more than five candidates, and races in which the total vote cast for candidates identified as having positions on the Prohibition issue was less than 50 percent of the total votes cast, are excluded from the analysis.

[41] In the 1918 Republican gubernatorial primary discussed above, there was a clear North versus South divide – Rolph was from San Francisco and Stephens was from Los Angeles – that also correlates positively with the county preferences on Prohibition. However,

TABLE 6.4 *Primary Voting and the Prohibition Issue, 1910 to 1934*

State	Year	Office	Party	Correlation
Alabama	1914	Governor	Democratic	0.30
Alabama	1918	Governor	Democratic	0.69
Alabama	1920	US Senator	Democratic	0.44
Alabama	1920	US Senator	Democratic	0.30
Alabama	1932	US Senator	Democratic	0.62
California	1918	Governor	Republican	0.86
California	1926	US Senator	Republican	0.41
California	1930	Governor	Republican	0.65
California	1932	US Senator	Republican	0.81
Iowa	1916	Governor	Republican	0.31
Louisiana	1920	US Senator	Democratic	0.70
Louisiana	1924	US Senator	Democratic	0.77
Louisiana	1926	US Senator	Democratic	0.44
Maine	1930	US Senator	Republican	0.34
Maryland	1934	Governor	Democratic	0.69
Michigan	1924	US Senator	Republican	0.72
Michigan	1930	US Senator	Republican	0.42
Minnesota	1914	Governor	Republican	0.58
North Carolina	1932	US Senator	Democratic	0.35
Oregon	1926	US Senator	Republican	0.22
Pennsylvania	1926	US Senator	Republican	0.50
Pennsylvania	1930	Governor	Republican	0.65
Pennsylvania	1930	US Senator	Republican	0.55
Texas	1910	Governor	Democratic	0.78
Texas	1912	Governor	Democratic	0.81
Texas	1912	US Senator	Democratic	0.82
Texas	1926	Governor	Democratic	0.52
Wisconsin	1920	US Senator	Republican	0.78
Wisconsin	1922	Governor	Republican	0.59
Wisconsin	1926	US Senator	Republican	0.34
Wisconsin	1928	Governor	Republican	0.57
Average				0.57

Cell entries give the county-level correlation coefficients between the vote for dry candidates and the average vote for Prohibition in state ballot propositions.

of the top two candidates are either "wet" or "dry."[42] Unless there is some underlying unmeasured factor driving the correlation, we would

even if we drop the counties adjacent to the candidates' home counties, the correlation remains strong.

[42] We are only looking at the top two candidates, and these candidates have to account for more than 50 percent of the vote with less than five candidates competing in the election.

expect the correlations in these cases to be near zero.[43] Since it is possible that the candidates could have nuanced differences in their positions while still being either both wet or both dry, we take the absolute value of the correlation between the vote shares of the top candidate and *Pct for Prohibition*. Even though this almost surely biases the distribution of correlations upward, the average correlation for the 18 "placebo" cases is still quite low, 0.19. The full set of correlations is presented in Appendix Table 6.10. It is clear even from casual inspection that, overall, the distribution of correlations is closer to zero than the distribution of correlations in Table 6.4.

6.5.2 Issue Voting: Progressive versus Stalwart

Beginning around the turn of the twentieth century, a deep divide opened up between progressives and stalwarts within the Republican Party outside the South. As discussed in Chapter 4, the progressive agenda included items such as lower tariffs, regulation of railroads and monopolies, and political reforms such as women's suffrage, direct election of senators, direct democracy, and primary elections. Fights between progressives and stalwarts frequently dominated primary campaigns, especially in the 1910 election, during which the "insurgents" pushed hard to defeat stalwarts.[44]

Here we conduct an analysis similar to that in the section above on Prohibition but with progressivism as the issue. To measure voter preferences for or against the progressive agenda, we use county-level votes in two presidential elections that featured well-known progressives – Theodore Roosevelt and Robert La Follette. Since both of these candidates were formerly Republicans, we assume that this measure is largely capturing the division within the Republican Party. Thus for primary elections held before 1918, we use the vote for Roosevelt divided by the total vote for Roosevelt and the Republican candidate, William Taft, in 1912. For elections held in 1918 or later, we use the vote for

---

[43] Suppose, for example, that the correlations in Table 6.4 did not really reflect voting on the basis of the Prohibition issue but some other geographically based political division in the state that encompasses multiple issues including Prohibition – for example, urban versus rural or North versus South divisions. If this were the case, we would expect this political division to manifest itself in other races even when there is no "wet" versus "dry" distinction in the primary.

[44] Wyman (1964).

La Follette divided by the total vote for La Follette and the Republican candidate, Calvin Coolidge, in 1924.

To classify primary election candidates for governor or US senator as progressive or stalwart, we use a variety of sources, especially progressive publications such as *The Outlook*, *The Progressive* (formerly *La Follette's Weekly*), and various historical newspapers. As in the previous section, we focus on all Republican primary races where we could identify at least one candidate as a progressive and another candidate as a stalwart.[45]

Analogous to the analysis above, we present simple correlations between the vote shares of progressive candidates and support for the progressive presidential nominees. Table 6.5 shows that the correlations are again quite high, 0.53 on average. Perhaps this is even more surprising since our progressive measure captures preferences on a bundle of issues. There is likely to be some variation in how much voters care about the different elements of the progressive agenda. The measures also incorporate voter preferences regarding the personalities of the presidential nominees. Nonetheless, the bottom line is the same as in the analysis of the Prohibition issue: the correlations are consistent with a significant share of primary election voters casting ballots based on the progressive orientations of the different candidates.

We also analyze a number of "placebo" cases to check whether the correlations we find reflect some other geographically based political division in the state that happens to be correlated with progressivism. The average correlation is again quite low, only 0.21, providing additional assurance that the higher correlations in Table 6.5 likely reflect voters' preferences on progressive issues and are not simply spurious.

6.6 FACTIONAL SLATES AS A SUBSTITUTE FOR PARTY LABELS

If primary voters are grasping for a cue akin to party labels, then intra-party factional slates would be a natural alternative to guide their voting behavior. The informational demands on voters in primary elections most closely resemble what occurs in general elections when there are two stable, competitive factions within a party that each

[45] As above, we drop cases in which the total votes cast for the candidates we could classify was less than 50 percent of the total votes cast in that primary. Note that, unlike the analysis of Prohibition, we do not restrict our attention to advantaged-party primaries, since we have the within Republican Party vote for progressives.

TABLE 6.5 *Voting in Republican Primaries on Progressives versus Stalwarts, 1908 to 1928*

State	Year	Office	Correlation
California	1922	US Senator	0.65
Colorado	1912	Governor	0.75
Colorado	1912	US Senator	0.63
Illinois	1912	US Senator	0.39
Illinois	1916	Governor	0.58
Iowa	1908	Governor	0.66
Iowa	1908	US Senator	0.64
Iowa	1908	US Senator	0.74
Iowa	1910	Governor	0.73
Iowa	1912	Governor	0.41
Iowa	1912	US Senator	0.63
Iowa	1914	US Senator	0.68
Iowa	1922	US Senator	0.38
Iowa	1926	US Senator	0.43
Kansas	1910	Governor	0.48
Kansas	1924	Governor	0.17
Michigan	1910	US Senator	0.34
Montana	1918	US Senator	0.54
New Hampshire	1910	Governor	0.29
New Hampshire	1926	US Senator	0.42
New Jersey	1922	US Senator	0.79
Oregon	1926	Governor	0.48
Washington	1920	Governor	0.41
Washington	1926	US Senator	0.51
Washington	1928	US Senator	0.31
West Virginia	1920	Governor	0.61
Average			0.53

Cell entries give the county-level correlation coefficients between the vote for progressive candidates and Roosevelt's share of the total votes for Roosevelt or Taft in the 1912 presidential general election.

run "slates" of candidates – that is, the factions endorse candidates for each office being contested. There are a few well-known cases of such bi-factionalism in state party organizations during the first half of the twentieth century. These include the Non-Partisan League (NPL) versus the Independent Voters Association (IVA) in North Dakota's Republican Party, the Long versus the Anti-Long factions in the Louisiana Democratic Party, and the Progressives versus Stalwarts in the Wisconsin Republican Party.[46] As discussed in Hansen, Hirano, and Snyder (2016), in these cases the factions actively publicized their slates of candidates.

Finding factional affiliations is more difficult than finding party affiliations. Since the official tabulations of votes in partisan general elections are reported by party, it is easy to find each candidate's party. However, the official tabulations of votes in primary elections are not reported by faction, so identifying candidates' factional affiliations is much more difficult.[47] In some cases we have lists of all of the candidates in each faction's "slate" – we typically found these in newspaper articles or advertisements. In most cases, however, we do not. Fortunately, we can use the pattern of correlations in county-level vote shares to identify many factional slates. The idea is straightforward. If a strong organized faction exists, then we would expect to observe high correlations in the vote shares among the candidates seeking different offices on the faction's slate. In the next section we use the case of the North Dakota Republican Party to illustrate how this works. Then we turn to an examination of factions across the United States during the first half of the twentieth century.

6.6.1 The Case of North Dakota

The most impressive record of longstanding intense bi-factionalism belongs to the Republican Party in North Dakota. For 40 years, from the mid-1910s through the mid-1950s, North Dakota Republicans voted for factional slates with a consistency rivaling voters in partisan general elections. One faction was the NPL, formed in 1915, which had an extensive political program, a monthly newspaper, and a large dues-paying membership.[48] The League held county conferences leading up to statewide nominating conventions, at which it endorsed slates of candidates. Initially the NPL was opposed by the IVA – which closely copied the NPL's structure – and later by the Republican Organizing Committee.

The effects of the NPL's organization and broad appeal were soon felt. The League gained control of the state government in 1919 and passed one of the most radical economic programs ever enacted by an American state, including a state-owned bank, a state-owned mill and

---

[46] See, for example, Key (1956). See Hansen, Hirano, and Snyder (2016) for related literature.
[47] Also, while party labels are by definition listed on the ballot in partisan general elections, factional labels do not appear on the ballot in primaries.
[48] On the history of the Nonpartisan League, see Morlan (1955); Remele (1981).

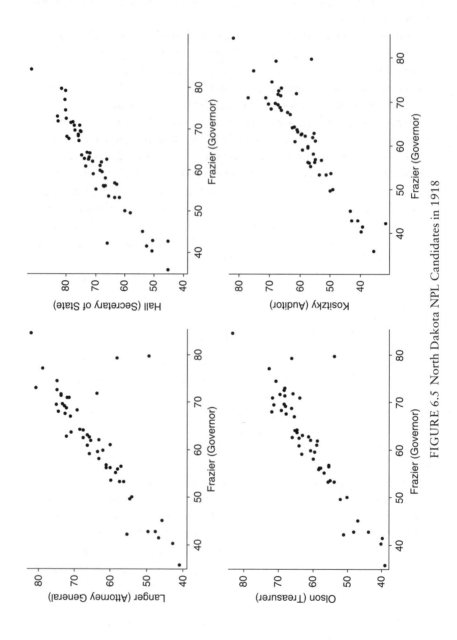

FIGURE 6.5 North Dakota NPL Candidates in 1918

grain elevator, a state home mortgage finance association, and a state hail insurance plan. The NPL was in and out of power during the subsequent four decades, but always had a strong presence in the state's politics.[49]

The relationship between factional slating and county-level primary returns is evident in the 1918 Republican primary, in which Lynn Frazier headed the NPL's slate as its nominee for governor. The other candidates on the NPL slate included William Langer for attorney general, Olbert A. Olson for treasurer, Thomas Hall for secretary of state, and Carl Kositzky for auditor. Figure 6.5 plots the primary vote shares of the four down-ballot NPL candidates against Frazier's primary vote share. The figure illustrates the high correlations among the NPL candidates' votes.

The influence of the NPL's factional slating on voting behavior is further illustrated when we compare the county-level correlations in 1918 and 1920. After the 1918 election the NPL administration broke apart.[50] Secretary of State Thomas Hall and Auditor Carl Kositzky, who were slated as NPL candidates in the 1918 primary, defected from the League and ran as IVA candidates in 1920. As Table 6.6 shows, the correlation in the primary vote share between the incumbent governor and lieutenant governor, who both continued to run as NPL candidates, was positive in both the 1918 and 1920 elections. However, the correlation in the primary vote share between the NPL incumbents and Hall and Kositzky went from being strongly positive in 1918 to strongly negative in 1920. That is, the same counties that supported the NPL candidates in 1918 continued to support NPL incumbents in 1920, but turned against the incumbents who defected from the League. [51]

6.6.2 Factional Slates in Other State Primaries

Was the factional organization in North Dakota primaries an outlier or the norm for elections in the years soon after primaries were

---

[49] In 1956 the League convention voted 173–3 to file its candidates in the Democratic primary. The North Dakota Democratic Party accepted the nominees and a merger, becoming the Democratic-Nonpartisan League Party, still the official name of the Democratic Party in North Dakota. See Talbot (1957); Robinson (1995).

[50] In particular, Treasurer Olbert A. Olson and Secretary of State Thomas Hall resisted the NPL organizer A. C. Townley's direction and criticized the incumbent Governor Lynn Frazier's legislative program. Carl Kositzky's audits found featherbedding, padded expenses, and frivolous spending in League-administered state agencies. Most seriously, Attorney General William Langer upheld the election of an independent as state superintendent of education, exposed financial improprieties in the NPL's acquisition of a bank, and engaged in a war of denunciations with A. C. Townley. See Tweton (1981, 103).

[51] See Hansen, Hirano, and Snyder (2016) for a more extensive analysis of the NPL.

TABLE 6.6 *1918 and 1920 Republican Primaries*

		Lt. Governor	Sec State	Auditor
		Wood	Hall	Kositzky
1918 Primary	Governor Frazier	0.91	0.95	0.92
1920 Primary	Governor Frazier	0.97	−0.96	−0.97

introduced? Unfortunately we do not have comprehensive information about candidates' factional affiliations across all states and years. Instead we use the county-level correlations to assign candidates for different offices to factional slates. We use the following procedure to identify factions.

1. For each state, party and year, find the *highest* positive correlation between any two candidates running for different offices. Call these candidates A_1 and A_2.
2. Find the highest positive correlation involving A_1 or A_2 and some other candidate running for some other office (not sought by A_1 or A_2). Call this candidate A_3.
3. Repeat step 2 until one candidate has been found for *each* of the major statewide offices (governor, US senator, lieutenant governor, attorney general, secretary of state, treasurer, auditor). This will yield candidates A_4, A_5, etc.
4. Repeat the above three steps excluding the "slate A" candidates to identify the "slate B" candidates.

This defines "slate A" and "slate B." We then calculate the *average* correlation among all candidates on the slate. If both slates have the same number of candidates/offices and slate B has a higher average correlation, then we switch the slate names, so that slate A has the highest average correlation. Then, for each party in each state in each year, we use the average correlation inside slate A (after possible renaming) as our measure of factional strength. If there really are two competing factions in a party's primary, then slate A and slate B should identify these factions. Hansen, Hirano, and Snyder (2016) found lists of the candidates on factions' slates for more than a dozen cases, and confirm that the slates identified using the above procedure correspond exactly to the factional affiliations found on the lists. If there is *one* slate – for example, an "organization" slate against an unorganized collection of opponents – then it will be slate A.

TABLE 6.7 *Primary Voting in States with Factions*

State	Party	Years	Average of Correlations	Std. Dev. of Correlations	Number of Cases
Louisiana	Democratic	1928–1948	0.60	0.25	6
Minnesota	Republican	1918–1922	0.80	0.08	3
North Dakota	Republican	1916–1950	0.80	0.11	17
South Dakota	Republican	1908–1914	0.52	0.31	4
Wisconsin	Republican	1914–1932	0.49	0.19	10
All Others		1903–1950	0.28	0.15	367

For each state and party the first column gives the average of $Corr_{jkt}$ across years, and the second column gives the standard deviation of $Corr_{jkt}$ across years.

We analyze the Democratic and Republican Party primaries for all existing states between 1903 and 1950.[52] Since the measure focuses on correlations, we exclude states with fewer than 20 counties and races with fewer than three contested nominations.

We first examine five cases in which the historical literature suggests that two intra-party factions organizations were prominent in state politics: the Louisiana Democratic Party, 1928–1948; the Minnesota Republican Party, 1918–1922; the North Dakota Republican Party, 1916–1950; the South Dakota Republican Party, 1908–1914; and the Wisconsin Republican Party, 1914–1932.[53] In these cases voters were apparently given a clear choice in the factional affiliations of the candidates for each office. Finding high correlations for these cases will provide some confirmation that our measure is identifying factional slates, and that the slates shape electoral outcomes in ways similar to party labels.

Table 6.7 shows the results. The average values of the correlations in primary support across offices in a party's primary provide evidence of slating in the five cases commonly associated with bi-factional competition. The average correlations range from 0.49 to 0.80. This pattern is strongest and most persistent in North Dakota: the mean correlation is quite high, the standard deviation is low, and the time period covered is long. Minnesota Republicans also exhibited strong factionalism, but only briefly. The other cases, Louisiana, South Dakota, and Wisconsin, are more mixed. Moreover, the standard deviations of the correlation

---

[52] We are missing county-level primary election returns for some races, especially in the early years. Also we obviously drop cases where a party did not hold a primary – as was commonly the case for the Republican Party in the South during this period.

[53] See Hansen, Hirano, and Snyder (2016) for a detailed discussion of the factional divisions within these parties.

coefficients are also relatively high, suggesting that in some years slating either did not occur or was not effective at guiding the vote.

Outside these five cases, we find very little evidence of factional slating in primary election voting. The last row of Table 6.7 shows that the average value of the correlations for the remaining cases in our sample is small, only 0.28. Also only 8 percent of these cases have correlations above 0.5. Even among some of the cases that V.O. Key, Jr. identifies as having bi-factional competition in the Democratic Party, such as Georgia and Texas, the average correlations are relatively low. We calculate a similar correlation in the county-level general election vote shares of gubernatorial and US Senate candidates from the same party during this period between 1903 and 1950. The median correlation across years is 0.92, which is significantly higher than the correlations for factional slates within a party's primary. Overall, factional slates were clearly not organizing primary voting in the same way as party labels. The few successful cases of bi-factional slating in primaries, such as the North Dakota Republican Party, raise the possibility that factional slating could be informative voting cues under special circumstances. Even in these special cases, however, it appears that the factional slates were not as effective at organizing the electorate as the political parties.

6.7 QUALIFICATIONS VERSUS PARTY LABELS, ISSUES, AND FACTIONS

The results in the previous sections indicate that primary voting is correlated both with candidates' relevant qualifications and with salient issue positions. The theoretical discussion above suggests that valence considerations, such as qualifications for office, will have a larger impact on primary voting behavior when no other salient attribute or issue division clearly divides the candidates. Also, compared to partisan general elections where there is always a clear party divide between the candidates, primaries often provide a better opportunity to focus on candidates' qualifications when voting. However, even in primary elections there are sometimes significant issues, factions, or other cleavages between the candidates, which may weaken the relative salience of qualifications in voters' choices.

We examine these hypotheses by focusing on two situations. First, we compare the incumbency advantage and the effect of relevant experience in primary versus general elections. Second, we examine the correlation between relevant experience and electoral support in primaries when there is a clear intra-party issue or factional cleavage.

6.7.1 Primaries versus General Elections

Do voters weigh qualifications for office more heavily in primaries than in general elections? As discussed above, there are theoretical reasons why we would expect this to be true. Here we can compare the relationship between relevant experience and electoral support in the two contexts for the pre-1950 period. This gives us a large number of cases and substantial variation in the partisan and ideological divisions across candidates. One caveat in interpreting the results is that the comparisons involve potential selection bias. This is because the candidates in the general election have been through an electoral "filter" – that is, they have won the nomination – while those in the primary election have not.

To estimate the relationship between relevant experience and electoral support, we use a simple regression model. The dependent variable is either vote share or winning, and the two independent variables of interest are incumbency status and relevant experience for non-incumbents. We restrict our attention to two-candidate primaries in order to make the primary elections we study as comparable as possible to two-party general elections.[54] We define the difference in incumbency status as the difference between the incumbency status of the candidate whose name is first alphabetically minus the incumbency status of her opponent – thus, the variable can take on values of 1, 0, or -1. We define the difference in non-incumbent relevant experience analogously. The dependent variable is either the vote share of the candidate whose name is first alphabetically or an indicator variable for whether that candidate won the primary. For general elections, the independent variables are defined similarly. However, the differences are taken between the Democratic and the Republican nominees, and the dependent variable is either the Democratic share of the two-party vote or an indicator for whether the Democrat won the election. For the general elections, we must also control for the normal vote, or else the coefficient estimates on the two variables of interest will be upwardly biased. Thus, for the statewide office general elections we include state-decade fixed effects and also a measure of the normal vote, which is simply the average vote share across all statewide office elections held in the previous eight years. For US House general elections, we include redistricting period fixed effects and a measure of the normal vote, which is the average of all available

---

[54] We drop general election races in which third-party candidates received more than 15 percent of the vote. We also drop general election races in which neither party held a primary.

TABLE 6.8 *Voting and Candidate Experience in Primary versus General Elections, 1900 to 1950*

Office	Depend. Variable	Primary Elections			General Elections		
		Current Incumb.	Relevant Exper.	Obs.	Current Incumb.	Relevant Exper.	Obs.
US House	Win %	41.6	13.0	3452	1.6	1.0	4715
		(0.8)	(1.4)		(1.2)	(1.3)	
	Vote %	20.1	7.4	2885	1.6	0.5	4702
		(0.4)	(0.6)		(0.2)	(0.2)	
Governor & US Senate	Win %	38.6	19.1	685	3.7	-2.0	992
		(2.4)	(2.9)		(2.4)	(2.4)	
	Vote %	17.1	7.8	672	1.4	0.0	983
		(0.9)	(1.1)		(0.4)	(0.4)	
Auditor & Treasurer	Win %	42.2	11.9	430	7.3	-2.5	482
		(2.7)	(3.6)		(3.2)	(2.5)	
	Vote %	15.5	4.8	416	1.6	0.3	475
		(1.0)	(1.0)		(0.4)	(0.4)	

The columns labelled Current Incumb., (1) and (4), and Relevant Exper., (2) and (5), contain OLS regression estimates.

district-level presidential election returns between redistricting periods. To account for partisan tides we also include year fixed effects.

Table 6.8 presents the coefficient estimates for primaries in Columns (1) and (2) and for general elections in Columns (4) and (5). We show the results separately for three groups of offices: (i) US House; (ii) governor and US Senate; and (iii) state auditor and treasurer. The estimates show a much stronger relationship between election outcomes and relevant experience in primaries compared to general elections. For primary elections, the coefficients on the difference in incumbency status and the difference in non-incumbent relevant experience are large and statistically significant in all cases. For general elections, they are not. Less than half of the coefficient estimates are statistically significant and positive, and two are negative. Importantly they are all quite small relative to the corresponding coefficient estimates for primary elections.

A related analysis shows similar differences between primary and general elections. In Figure 6.6, we compare the sophomore surge in primaries and general elections for the US House and top statewide offices for each decade between 1910 and 1949.[55] The sophomore surge

---

[55] As in previous analyses, the top statewide offices include US senator, governor, lieutenant governor, attorney general, state treasurer, and auditor.

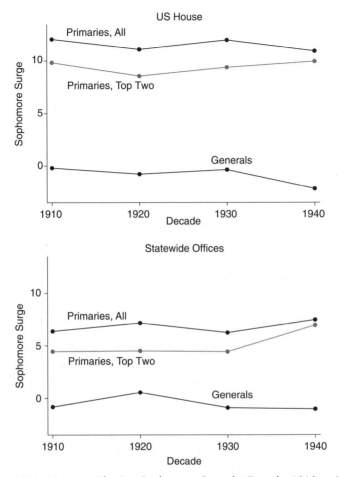

FIGURE 6.6 Primary Election Sophomore Surge by Decade, 1910 to 1949

is simply the difference in a candidate's vote share between her first election as a challenger and her first election as an incumbent. This measure of the incumbency advantage is arguably more comparable across electoral settings than the measure used above.

Figure 6.6 displays the sophomore surge in primaries and general elections by decade.[56] The top panel of the figure plots the average sophomore surge by decade for US House elections. The bottom panel

---

[56] The decades are defined as 1910 to 1919, 1920 to 1929, 1930 to 1939, and 1940 to 1949.

depicts the average sophomore surge by decade for statewide offices.[57] We included primary results using vote share as a percentage of all candidates and vote share as percentage of just the top two candidates. The two estimates are very similar, but the sophomore surge is slightly smaller when we use only the top two.

The panels show that the sophomore surge is noticeably smaller for statewide offices compared to US House elections. More pertinently, for both federal and statewide offices, the sophomore surge is much larger in the primary than in the general election. There is no evidence of a sophomore surge in the general election during the period prior to 1950, which is consistent with existing findings in the literature. The sophomore surge in the primaries for US House races is around 10 percentage points. For statewide offices it is approximately 5 percentage points. Thus, voters appear to be weighing incumbency more in the primaries than in the general elections. This difference in voting behavior is consistent with the predictions from the theoretical model presented above.

6.7.2 Qualifications in Primaries with Issues or Factional Divisions

Intra-party issue and factional cleavages might also have reduced the influence of candidate qualifications on the primary electorates' decisions. As discussed above, voters in primary elections appeared to respond to candidates' positions on Prohibition and progressive issues, as well as factional affiliations when present. Here we investigate the following question: When the candidates differentiated themselves in terms of ideology, issue positions, or factions, did primary voters focus less on the differences in the candidates' qualifications?

---

[57] More specifically, we estimate the primary election sophomore surge using the following equation: $S_{it} = \alpha_d + \beta N_{it} + \epsilon_{it}$. S_{it} is the change in the primary vote share of the candidate in constituency i who was not an incumbent in the previous primary election year $t-1$ but then runs as an incumbent in year t. N_{it} is the change in the number of candidates competing in constituency i between t and $t-1$. α_d is the decade-specific fixed effect. There is a clear selection problem here in that we are only including the sophomore surge estimates for primary races in which the candidates in district i are challenged in years t and $t-1$. A large number of races with incumbents are uncontested. Incumbents with an especially large advantage are probably less likely to be challenged, so the sophomore surge probably understates the true incumbency advantage in primaries. In Ansolabehere et al. (2007) we present estimates using a Heckman selection model using the average number of primaries contested in the previous ten years to help identify the selection effect. The results are very similar to those using simple ordinary least squares regressions. In addition, as is well known, the sophomore surge is a downwardly biased estimate of the incumbency advantage in general elections due to reversion to the mean. A similar downward bias should apply to primary elections as well.

For this analysis, we include three additional intra-party divisions. The first involves another issue, the New Deal. In the 1930s and 1940s, many candidates took strong pro- or anti-New Deal positions in the primaries, especially in the Democratic Party. The second cleavage is between pro- and anti-Ku Klux Klan candidates.[58] The third division involves support or opposition to political organizations. In states with well-known urban machines, for example, Illinois, Missouri, New York, Pennsylvania, New Jersey, and Tennessee, candidates were often portrayed as being pro-organization or anti-organization candidates. The organizations, as well as competing groups, often ran slates similar to the factions discussed above.

The analysis is a straightforward modification of the regression analysis in Section 6.4 above (see Table 6.3). The dependent variable is again either the vote share or winning in the primary. The key independent variables are an indicator for being the current incumbent and the share of non-incumbent relevant experience. We interact these with variables indicating whether the race does or does not involve one of the intra-party cleavages mentioned above. We also include race-specific fixed effects. We run the analysis on all primaries for governor or US senator in which there were two to five candidates.[59]

Table 6.9 presents the results. The columns under the "Different Positions" header show the coefficients for the races for which we have identified an intra-cleavage, while the columns under the "Similar Positions" header show the coefficients for the other races. In many of the races that we place in the Similar Positions category, the candidates might have differed over issues not included in our searches. Thus, this category is clearly a mix, which probably biases the coefficient estimates toward those for the Different Positions category.

The estimates show that incumbency and non-incumbent relevant experience have much stronger relationships with primary election outcomes for the Similar Positions cases than for the Different Positions cases. If only one candidate in an open-seat race has non-incumbent relevant experience, then that candidate can expect a vote share that is 11.8 percentage points higher in primaries without an issue or factional division compared to candidates without such experience. This difference is only 3.7 percentage points when there is such an intra-party cleavage.

---

[58] Although a majority of these cases are in the South, in the 1920s many Klan candidates ran outside the South as well.

[59] We focus on these races because they tend to attract more coverage, making it easier to determine candidates' issue positions and factional associations, and whether or not they were supported by a party organization.

TABLE 6.9 *Voting, Candidate Experience, and Other Issues in Primaries,*
1900 to 1948

Depend. Variable	Similar Positions		Different Positions		p-value for		
	Current Incumb.	Relevant Exper.	Current Incumb.	Relevant Exper.	(1)–(3)	(2)–(4)	Obs.
Win %	74.4 (5.2)	28.2 (5.6)	32.6 (12.3)	10.8 (11.3)	0.00	0.17	2015
Vote %	32.6 (2.1)	11.8 (1.9)	11.4 (2.8)	3.7 (3.0)	0.00	0.02	1972

Columns (3) and (4), under the Different Positions label, show OLS regression coefficients for races where candidates held different ideological/issue positions or were from different factions. Columns (1) and (2), under the Similar Positions label, show regression coefficients for all other races. The column labelled p-value for (1)–(3) gives the p-value of the F-test for the hypothesis that the coefficients on Current Incumbency are equal when candidates share similar positions versus when they do not. The column labelled p-value for (2)–(4) gives the p-value of the F-test for the hypothesis that the coefficients on Relevant Experience are equal when candidates share similar positions versus when they do not.

The results are even more striking for incumbency – an advantage of 32.6 percentage points for Similar Positions cases compared to 11.4 percentage points for Different Positions cases. A qualitatively similar pattern exists when winning the party nomination is the dependent variable.[60]

Overall, these results are consistent with the theoretical hypotheses in Section 6.1. When the candidates competing in primaries differ in terms of issue positions or factional affiliations, their qualifications appear to matter less for the primary election outcomes. We must be cautious in interpreting these results, because the races with and without issue or factional cleavages might also differ on other dimensions – for example, the information available to voters, the balance of partisan loyalties, and the pool of candidates and strategic entry decisions. The findings nonetheless suggest that there is a tradeoff between qualifications and clear intra-party cleavages in voters' decision-making.

6.8 CONCLUSION

One way to summarize the findings above is to amend Key's famous quote that "Not all voters are fools," and add that "elections can work even if some voters are." Overall, during the initial decades after

---

[60] The apparent trade-off between qualifications versus issue or factional divisions in voters' decision-making does not appear to be as strong for down-ballot offices. However, we have been unable to identify candidates' issue positions for many of these down-ballot races.

the introduction of primaries, a reasonable fraction of the primary electorate voted as if it was informed about candidates' qualifications, issue positions, and factional affiliations, at least when there were clear differences between the competing candidates on one or more attributes. Perhaps most importantly, candidates with relevant qualifications for the office they sought – that is, prior experience in related offices for non-incumbents and the experience that comes with incumbency for incumbents – defeated those without such qualifications much more often than we would expect by chance. This suggests that many primary voters were acting responsibly, and that primaries provided clear incentives for elites to act strategically along the lines discussed in Chapter 5. On balance, voter behavior and elite decisions combined to make direct primaries a relatively successful reform – successful enough at least to endure for more than a century.

6.9 APPENDIX

TABLE 6.10 *Primary Voting and the Prohibition Issue, Placebo Cases, 1910 to 1934*

State	Year	Office	Party	Correlation
Alabama	1906	Governor	Democratic	0.24
Alabama	1922	Governor	Democratic	0.08
Alabama	1926	Governor	Democratic	0.18
Alabama	1926	US Senator	Democratic	0.13
Alabama	1930	US Senator	Democratic	0.37
Arkansas	1932	US Senator	Democratic	0.15
Illinois	1920	US Senator	Republican	0.13
Illinois	1926	US Senator	Republican	0.18
Iowa	1920	US Senator	Republican	0.14
Iowa	1926	US Senator	Republican	0.27
Mississippi	1903	Governor	Democratic	0.10
North Carolina	1930	US Senator	Democratic	0.35
Pennsylvania	1922	Governor	Republican	0.17
Texas	1928	Governor	Democratic	0.19
Texas	1930	US Senator	Democratic	0.40
Virginia	1929	Governor	Democratic	0.04
Washington	1922	US Senator	Republican	0.10
Wisconsin	1930	Governor	Republican	0.23
Average				0.19

Cell entries give the absolute value of the county-level correlation coefficients between the vote for the winning candidate and the average vote for Prohibition on state ballot propositions.

TABLE 6.11 *Voting in Republican Primaries on Progressives versus Stalwarts, Placebo Cases, 1908 to 1928*

State	Year	Office	Correlation
California	1914	US Senator	0.08
California	1918	Governor	0.27
California	1922	Governor	0.24
Illinois	1924	US Senator	0.14
Illinois	1926	US Senator	0.23
Kansas	1924	US Senator	0.05
Kansas	1928	Governor	0.14
Michigan	1914	Governor	0.33
Michigan	1918	US Senator	0.17
Michigan	1922	US Senator	0.40
Michigan	1928	Governor	0.19
Nebraska	1916	US Senator	0.15
Nebraska	1924	US Senator	0.28
Nebraska	1928	US Senator	0.09
Ohio	1922	US Senator	0.21
Ohio	1928	US Senator	0.42
Washington	1922	US Senator	0.25
Average			0.21

Cell entries give the absolute value of the county-level correlation coefficients between the vote for winning candidates and Roosevelt's share of the total votes for Roosevelt or Taft in the 1912 presidential general election.

7

Primaries in a Changing Electoral Environment, 1950 to 2016

On November 7, 2000, the Pennsylvania Republican nominees for state treasurer and auditor, Barbara Hafer and Katie True, both faced competitive general elections. Hafer, who was an incumbent, was elected to office with a 2-percentage-point margin. True, who was challenging an incumbent, was defeated by more than a 15-percentage-point margin. All of the Pennsylvania statewide elections were won by incumbents. The Republican Party no longer dominated Pennsylvania's general elections as it did a century ago. Over the previous two decades there were five changes in partisan control of the state treasurer and auditor offices.[1] During this period, neither party won control over both offices in the same election. The average margin of victory in open-seat races for major statewide offices during this period was slightly more than 5 percentage points.

The 2000 election reflected the changes in the US electoral landscape that coincided with the social, economic, and technological shifts that took place during the twentieth century. Partisan control of all state executive offices was less common during this period. The geographic partisan divides were much less stark than in previous periods of US history. Party attachments in the electorate had also been weakening for decades, as more and more voters began viewing themselves as independents.[2] Incumbents, like those in the 2000 Pennsylvania statewide races,

---

[1] The state auditor changed from Democrat to Republican in 1988 and back to Democrat in 1996. The state treasurer changed from Democrat to Republican in 1980, a Democrat was appointed in 1987, and the Republicans regained control in 1996.

[2] The fraction of independents in the American National Election Studies rose from 23 percent in 1952 to 37 percent in 1976 to 39 percent in 2008. See Hershey (2006) for more discussion.

appear to have been beneficiaries of the general electorates' willingness to vote for specific candidates rather than a straight party ticket. Incumbents were winning with larger margins than in previous decades.[3]

In this new political environment, did primaries continue to contribute to the electoral system as they did at the turn of the twentieth century? Are primaries still an important "escape from one-partyism?" Do they function as they did when they were first introduced? Have primaries themselves contributed to the changes in the electoral landscape? The next five chapters examine these issues.

We begin by discussing four aspects of the electoral environment that are widely acknowledged to have changed during the post-World War II period: (i) the balance of partisan loyalties within and across constituencies; (ii) the salience of candidate-specific attributes in general elections; (iii) the incumbency advantage; and (iv) the polarization of the two major parties. While many other changes occurred in the electoral environment, these four are well-documented, and also broad changes that clearly differed between the two periods. Moreover, there are good reasons to believe that these characteristics may have changed the way primaries function compared to the pre-1950 period, and may have affected how much primaries contribute to the US electoral system.[4]

The second half of this chapter examines how the basic patterns of primary competition for the post-1950 period compare to those we identified for the earlier period in previous chapters. We again show how primary competition varies across constituency types, competitive versus uncompetitive general elections, and incumbent-contested versus open-seat races. We also show how the level of primary competition has evolved over time, as well as the extent to which primaries continue to contribute to the overall competitiveness of the electoral system.

7.1 RISE OF COMPETITIVE CONSTITUENCIES?

Our discussion of electoral competition in the 1892-to-1950 period highlighted the prevalence of constituencies expected to have uncompetitive general elections, and the potential connection to not only the decisions to adopt primaries but also to the way nomination systems function.

---

[3] See, for example, Ansolabehere and Snyder (2002).

[4] The choice of 1950 as the dividing year is of course arbitrary, but this would be the case for any year. We chose 1950 because it is a round number that puts the Sixth Party System era of candidate-centered politics all in one period.

Primaries spread most rapidly in states where one party had an electoral advantage and controlled the state governments, which provided voters in these states an intra-party electoral alternative to competitive general elections. In the absence of general election competition, primaries provided the only competition elected public officials would face on their way to office. These constituencies with uncompetitive general elections stood to benefit the most from the nomination reform, and the evidence presented above suggests that this was largely the case.

Overall, states exhibited higher levels of two-party electoral competition during the post-1950 period than they had previously. Primaries would conceivably have less to contribute to the post-1950 electoral system if vibrant two-party competition was widespread across constituencies. However, many of the forces identified in Chapter 2 that lead to one-party-dominated areas continued to influence the US political landscape, especially in constituencies below the state level.

In this section, we document the average levels of competitiveness in general elections at the state, county, and congressional district levels since 1950, and compare them to pre-1950 levels. We employ the same measures we used in Chapter 2 to examine the pre-1950 period. As in Chapter 2, competitive and uncompetitive constituencies refer to the competitiveness of the general election.[5] A constituency is considered to be competitive (or parties-balanced) if the Democratic normal vote is between 42.5 and 57.5 percent. In such constituencies candidates from either of the major parties have a reasonable chance of winning the general election at least in open-seat races. Otherwise, a constituency is considered uncompetitive, since one party has a seemingly insurmountable advantage in the general election. We also examine a hybrid measure of competitiveness that takes into account win percentages in addition to vote shares (again, see Chapter 2 for more details).

Figure 7.1 shows the over-time trends in the percentage of uncompetitive constituencies for the period 1900 to 2016. At the state level there

---

[5] At the state level, we use all available electoral returns for statewide offices. The competitiveness for any year t is measured using a nine-year moving average, from $t-4$ to $t+4$. For the elections between 2013 and 2016 the moving average for each year only includes the available elections after that year – for example, 2014 includes elections between 2010 and 2016. At the county level, we construct a similar measure but only include elections for president, governor, and US senator. At the congressional district level, we have data on the presidential vote at the district level, but we must break the data up by redistricting period. For the US House, the measure for the 2010s only includes the 2012–2016 results. See Chapter 2 for the details about the data and measures.

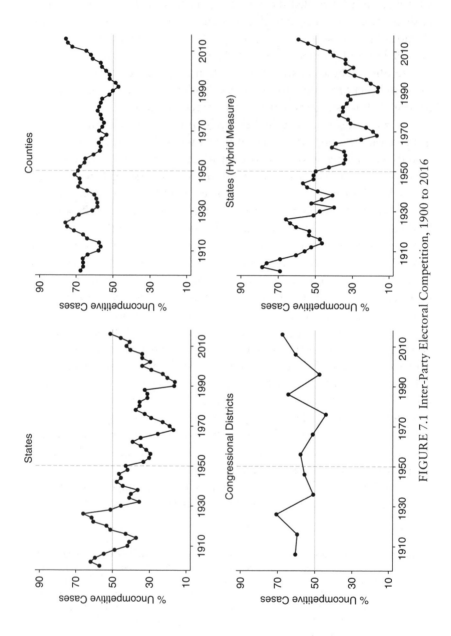

FIGURE 7.1 Inter-Party Electoral Competition, 1900 to 2016

was a drop in the proportion of uncompetitive constituencies starting in the early 1950s. This is evident in both the vote-share and hybrid measures of competitiveness. Over half of all states were uncompetitive for several decades during the first half of the twentieth century, while less than a third fell into this category for extended periods during the second half of the century.

The increasing competitiveness of state general elections is likely the result of at least four different trends. One is the solidification of Democratic Party support in industrial areas that traditionally supported the Republican Party. Second, the Democratic Party's hegemony eroded in the South due to increasing support for civil rights reforms among non-Southern Democratic elites.[6] Third, several cross-cutting issues related to fighting the Cold War, the Vietnam War, and women's rights contributed to the dealignment. Finally, the long shadow of the Civil War was probably fading with time.

Counties were also becoming more competitive in terms of two-party competition. However, the change in partisan balance at the county level was more gradual than at the state level. The percentage of counties considered to be competitive declined by about 20 percentage points between 1950 and 1992. However, more than half of the counties were considered uncompetitive for the entire period, aside from a brief dip below 50 percent in 1992 and 1994. Therefore, much of the time, candidates running in constituencies below the state level could still expect an uncompetitive general election.

The patterns for congressional districts are somewhat different. There was a modest decline in the proportion of districts considered uncompetitive during the first three redistricting periods after 1952. However, in the 1980s there was a sharp 20-percentage-point increase in this proportion, before declining again in 1990s, and then increasing again in the 2000s and 2010s. The differences in the patterns for congressional districts compared to states and counties probably reflects gerrymandering, as well as shifting urban versus rural demographics and partisanship. Also, since this measure is based only on presidential elections, it is subject to more variation due to factors specific to each presidential race. The bottom line is that for most of post-1950 period more than half of congressional districts were not competitive.

Figure 7.1 also indicates that the trend towards more competitive constituencies started to reverse around 1990, particularly at the state and county levels. In 1992 about 16 percent of states were uncompetitive.

---

[6] See, for example, Sundquist (1983).

By 2012, this proportion had increased to 42 percent, which is close to the levels we observed six decades earlier. For the hybrid measure the trend is even more apparent, with over 50 percent of states being classified as uncompetitive. Similarly, the share of uncompetitive counties dipped just below 50 percent in 1992 and rose to over 70 percent by 2012. As discussed below, other features of the electoral environment also appear to have changed during and after the early 1990s.

For most of the post-1950 period a larger percentage of states and counties were competitive relative to 1950 and the preceding decades. Thus, primaries might have been needed less often to provide relief from one-partyism after 1950 compared to the decades immediately following the introduction of the reforms. Of course they continued to serve this function in the constituencies that remained uncompetitive, which was true in a majority of counties and congressional districts. The recent trends indicate that one-party dominance may be making a reappearance even at the state level. Thus, there is more potential for primaries to increase the overall competitiveness of the electoral system.

7.2 CANDIDATE-CENTERED POLITICS

In Chapter 6 we argued that primary election outcomes are more likely than general elections to be influenced by differences in candidates' relative qualifications. General election voters are more likely to focus on the policy or ideological differences between candidates from different parties than on the qualifications. However, if general election outcomes become increasingly influenced by candidate attributes, in particular qualifications, then primaries could become less crucial for ensuring that qualified officials are ultimately elected. This section documents the dramatic rise in candidate-centered voting between the 1950s and the 1980s. It also highlights a noticeable change in candidate-centered voting that started in the 1990s and continues still.

Conventional wisdom is that the early shifts towards candidate-centered politics that we identified in Chapter 3 pale in comparison to the changes in voting behavior that occurred around the 1960s. Many scholars have documented the weakening of partisanship in voting in the post-1960 era.[7] Aldrich (1995, 253) summarizes the literature as follows: "Together these studies show that there was an important shift

---

[7] See, for example, Nie, Petrocik, and Verba (1979), Alford and Brady (1989), Wattenberg (1990, 1991), Jacobson (1992), Shively (1992), and Aldrich (1995).

in elections to all national offices in or about 1960, demonstrating that voters respond to candidates far more than previously. Voting became candidate centered, and so parties as mechanisms for understanding candidates, campaigns, and election became less relevant." Aldrich and Niemi (1990) refer to this period as the "sixth party system."

The rise in candidate-centered elections is often attributed to changes in the political environment that increased the salience of politicians' personal attributes and weakened traditional party organizations – for example, changes in campaign advertising technologies such as the rise of television, the replacement of patronage with civil service employment, and an increase in the personal resources available to elected officials for constituency services. This period coincided with a weakening of voters' partisan attachments.[8] While the literature has focused on general elections, some of these forces might also have affected primaries. For example, the changing media environment might have facilitated the nomination of qualified candidates by providing primary election voters with easier access to information. Moreover, if qualifications matter more for winning general elections, primary voters have stronger incentives to nominate more highly qualified candidates.

We document the changes in candidate-centered voting using the same split-ticket voting measure introduced in Chapter 3.[9] Figure 7.2 displays changes in the split-ticket voting measure for the years 1896 to 2016. We plot split-ticket voting across only open-seat races as well as across all races including incumbent-contested races. The measures are averages – for example, 2010 is the average standard deviation during the period 2006 to 2016. The measure using only open-seat races provides a measure of candidate-centered voting that is not directly due to the incumbency advantage.

Figure 7.2 shows the dramatic increase in split-ticket voting that was apparent in the 1960s and continued through the 1980s. The pattern is evident both for the curve that includes all races and the curve that

---

[8] Campbell (2007, 68) describes the process as follows: "Since the 1960s the role of the political parties in American politics has fundamentally changed. A series of technological, institutional, legal, and cultural shifts diminished their once central function as the organizers and inclusive mobilizers of American elections. They ceded control over nominations and were pushed aside by new candidate-centered campaigns. Technological advances allowed candidates to speak directly to the people, and the parties lost their monopoly."

[9] The measure is simply the standard deviation of the general election vote shares across all statewide races and the state-level presidential vote for a given electoral cycle.

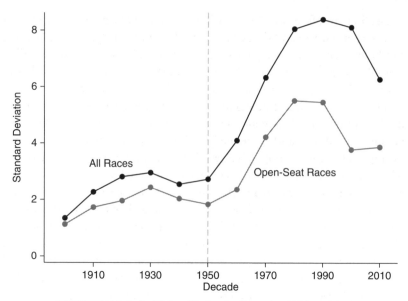

FIGURE 7.2 Split-Ticket Voting by Decade, 1900 to 2010

excludes incumbent-contested races. This suggests that the change is not simply reflecting the growing incumbency advantage, but is instead connected to a shift towards the greater incorporation of candidate attributes into voting decisions.

The rapid increase in split-ticket voting came to a halt around 1990. The curve including all races fell slightly in the next period but then fell sharply between the 2000 and 2010 periods. In the open-seat races the steep decline came earlier, between the 1990 and 2000 periods. Other measures of split-ticket voting also show a rise and decline over the post-1950 period, including split-ticket voting between presidential and US House races and self-reports of split-ticket voting in surveys.[10]

The reasons underlying the recent decline in split-ticket voting are a matter of debate. The drop in candidate-centered voting coincides with the often-discussed increase in the influence of national party leaders in Congress, and with the rise in partisan polarization in Congress, which we discuss below.[11]

---

[10] Jacobson (2015).

[11] On the increasing influence of national party leaders see, for example, Lee (2016); Cox and McCubbins (1993); Rohde (1991).

Did these shifts in candidate-centered voting affect the relative importance of qualifications in primary versus general elections? We examine the relationship between relevant experience and voting behavior in both primaries and general elections in Chapter 9.

7.3 INCUMBENCY ADVANTAGE

The rising general election incumbency advantage is a well-documented feature of US electoral politics in the second half of the twentieth century.[12] Sometime in the 1960s, candidates elected in open seats observed a significant increase in their general election vote shares in their re-election bids. This pattern has been observed for a wide range of offices, including the US House, US Senate, statewide offices, and state legislatures.

How does the large general election incumbency advantage affect our arguments about primaries? Consider races where the incumbent is running for re-election. There are two potential forces. First, the incumbency advantage turns some competitive constituencies into safe constituencies, at least for the incumbent. In these constituencies, when an open-seat election produces a poorly qualified winner, who also under-performs while in office, we cannot rely on subsequent general elections to remove him or her. Second, the general election incumbency advantage gives party elites and rank-and-file supporters incentives to renominate their incumbents. This is because the incumbency advantage does not adhere to the party, but is personal, and will be lost if the incumbent is not renominated.

The extent to which these two forces matter depends crucially on the degree to which the incumbency advantage is conditional. For example, if incumbents who remain unqualified for their office – that is, incumbents who were initially not well-qualified for the office and also fail to take advantage of on-the-job learning – have the same electoral advantage as other incumbents in the general election, then these forces will simply insulate less-qualified incumbents from electoral pressures. On the other hand, if the advantage mainly accrues to incumbents whose performance indicates that they are well qualified to continue in office, then these forces will be less of a concern. Therefore if the general election incumbency advantage is largely unconditional, then our previous

---

[12] The literature is enormous; see Ansolabehere and Snyder (2002) for a review.

arguments about the importance of primaries in open-seat elections hold with even more force, especially in parties-balanced constituencies.[13]

Another factor we must consider is the prevalence of candidate-centered voting in general elections for open seats. As noted in the previous section, candidate-centered voting was much higher in the post-1950 period than previously. However, even when candidate-centered voting reached its peak, partisanship continued to be an important determinant of general election outcomes. Moreover, candidate attributes other than qualifications, such as race, gender, and issue positions, likely influenced voting as well. As a result, in competitive constituencies, when a more qualified candidate faced a less-qualified one in the general election, the less-qualified candidate would still win much of the time. In order to reliably elect a highly qualified candidate in these constituencies, we would need both parties to select highly qualified nominees.

On the positive side, by insulating incumbents from electoral pressure, the general election incumbency advantage also increased the expected future returns to winning open-seat elections. This in turn increased the incentives for qualified candidates, at least those with future career concerns, to enter the primaries in competitive constituencies. Thus, the general election incumbency advantage might have increased the likelihood that both parties would nominate highly qualified candidates in competitive constituencies.

7.4 POLARIZATION

There is widespread agreement that US politics has become increasingly polarized since the late 1970s. Perhaps the most visually striking evidence of partisan polarization is the growing gap in congressional roll-call voting behavior between Democrats and Republicans, as exemplified by the well-known DW-NOMINATE scores.[14] This gap was large at the end of the nineteenth century but then declined during the first decades of the twentieth century and remained relatively small for close to half-a-century between the 1930s and the 1970s. Since the late 1970s the partisan gap in roll-call voting has risen to levels higher than at any other point during the post-Reconstruction period.[15]

---

[13] If factors increasing the unconditional part of the general election incumbency advantage had similar pro-incumbent effects in primaries – for example, simple name recognition – then primaries in open-seat races become even more important in parties-balanced constituencies.

[14] McCarty, Poole, and Rosenthal (2006).

[15] Some observers view the period since the early 1990s as being particularly polarized (Lee, 2016; Gentzkow, Shapiro, and Taddy, 2019).

The causes of this polarization continue to be debated. A popular claim that often appears in the media is that primaries are causing, or at least contributing to, the increase in polarization. One way this might be occurring is through "partisan sorting" of the electorate – liberals becoming steadily more affiliated with the Democratic Party and conservatives moving steadily into the Republican Party – causing the Democratic primary electorate to become more liberal and the Republican primary electorate to become more conservative. We examine the hypothesis that primaries cause polarization in Chapter 11. In this section, we discuss how polarization might be affecting the way primaries function.

In Chapter 6 we provided a theoretical discussion about the way issue-based, ideological, or simple partisan divisions could reduce the importance of candidates' attributes, such as incumbency or qualifications for office, in voters' decision-making. With this logic in mind we would expect incumbency and relevant experience to become less salient in general elections during periods of increasing polarization. The pattern of split-ticket voting depicted in Figure 7.2 above roughly matches these expectations. The sharp rise in split-ticket voting ends in the 1990s and even declines afterwards. This pattern is consistent with partisanship having a greater impact on voting behavior.

As argued above, in parties-balanced constituencies it was not necessary for both parties to nominate highly qualified candidates in order for the winner to be highly qualified, because in the general election voters would tend to select the more qualified candidate. Unless there are sufficient numbers of independent or moderate voters supporting the more qualified candidate, this candidate is certain to win the general election if enough voters cross party lines to vote for him or her. However, this is less likely in a highly polarized environment.[16] Thus, as voting behavior in general elections becomes more partisan, primaries become increasingly important for electing qualified officials. In Chapter 9 we examine whether the association between relevant experience and election outcomes differs between periods of high partisan polarization and other periods in both primaries and general elections.

Whether partisan polarization weakens the relationship between candidate qualifications and primary election outcomes in part depends upon whether this polarization coincides with greater differentiation between candidates within primaries based on attributes other than qualifications. If polarization mainly affects voters' perceptions of the *parties*, then it is unlikely to have a significant impact on voting behavior

---

[16] Ashworth and Bueno de Mesquita (2008) also make this theoretical point.

within primaries. On the other hand, since the partisan sorting mentioned above produces more ideologically homogeneous primary electorates, we might expect the pool of candidates to also become more ideologically homogeneous. In this case we would expect primary election outcomes to depend even more on candidate qualifications. Finally, if ideological polarization has been occurring – that is, elites and voters are actually moving further apart – then candidates within primaries might also be adopting more distinct ideological or issue positions. In such an environment candidate qualifications might have less impact on primary election outcomes.

We do not have measures of the ideological or issue positions of primary election candidates for the entire period during which partisan polarization occurred. However, we do have such a measure for the past 20 years. As discussed in detail in Chapter 11 below, we can use candidate surveys and roll-call voting records in Congress and state legislatures to construct ideological scores for a large number of primary candidates. Interestingly, during this period, the candidates running in US House primaries have not on average become increasingly distinct in their ideological positions. Consider, for example, the average difference between the nominee and the runner-up. In the US House primaries of 1994 and 1996 the average absolute difference between the two candidates' ideological scores was 0.16, and in the primaries of 2012 and 2014 the difference was again 0.16. In contrast, during this same period the average difference in ideological scores between Democratic and Republican members of Congress continued to grow rapidly, from 0.72 to 0.84. Assuming that the ideological differentiation between candidates within primaries was also similar pre-1990, we would not expect to observe a change in the relationship between candidate qualifications and primary election outcomes due to polarization.

Perhaps most importantly, these numbers clearly show what we assumed above – that the typical ideological gap between primary election candidates is much smaller than the gap between candidates from different parties. Over the period 1994 to 2014, the average difference between the opposing major party candidates in each general election contest was 0.76.[17] Given the large ideological gap between the parties' general election nominees over the past 20 years, and the small ideological cleavage among the candidates running within each party's primaries, it seems likely that primaries have been as important

---

[17] For the within-race calculation we are limited to the sample for which we have an ideological score for the losing candidate (see Chapter 11).

as general elections in helping to elect more qualified candidates, even in parties-balanced constituencies.

7.5 PRIMARY COMPETITION, 1950 TO 2016

The introduction of primaries had an important role in injecting competition into constituencies that otherwise elected officials who never faced serious electoral competition. As we demonstrated in the first half of the book, primary competition in the early decades of the twentieth century was particularly relevant for advantaged parties in open-seat races. Advantaged-party primaries in open-seat races were considerably more competitive than parties-balanced and especially disadvantaged-party primaries during this period.

In this section, we investigate whether the patterns of primary competition continue to hold in the post-1950 period. The discussion above gives us little reason to expect that changes in the electoral environment during this period should have a significant impact on competition within advantaged-party primaries. These changes in the electoral environment, however, are more likely to affect competition in other types of primaries. For example, the incumbency advantage may lead to more primary competition in open-seat races in parties-balanced constituencies, but less competition in incumbent-contested primaries.

We examine the same four measures of primary competition that we used for the early period: the percentage of races that were contested, the percentage of races that were competitive (that is, the winner received less than 57.5 percent of the total votes cast), the number of candidates running, and the total vote percentage won by the losing candidates.[18] Figures 7.3 and 7.4 plot the average level of competition in the three types of primaries – advantaged, parties-balanced, disadvantaged – over the 1950-to-2016 period for all statewide and US House offices, respectively. The panels in each correspond to the four measures of competition, and each panel plots the three types of races: incumbent-contested, challenger-party (that is, an incumbent is contesting the opposition's primary), and open-seat.

Figure 7.3 shows the continued high level of electoral competition in advantaged-party primaries for open-seat races for statewide offices during this later period. As expected, the levels of primary competition for incumbent-contested and challenger-party races are noticeably

---

[18] Candidates who receive less than 1 percent of the vote are not included.

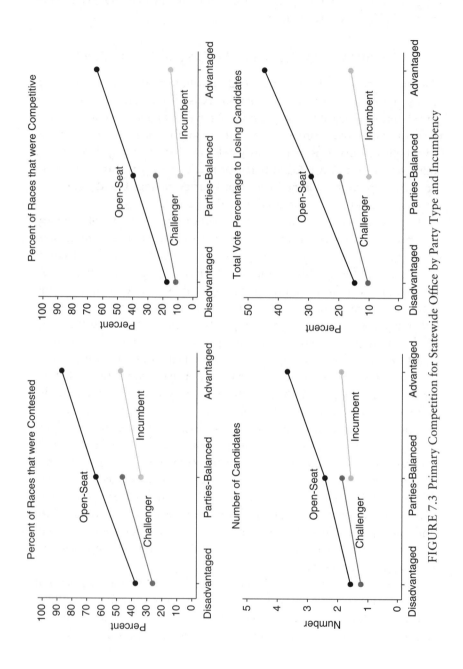

FIGURE 7.3 Primary Competition for Statewide Office by Party Type and Incumbency

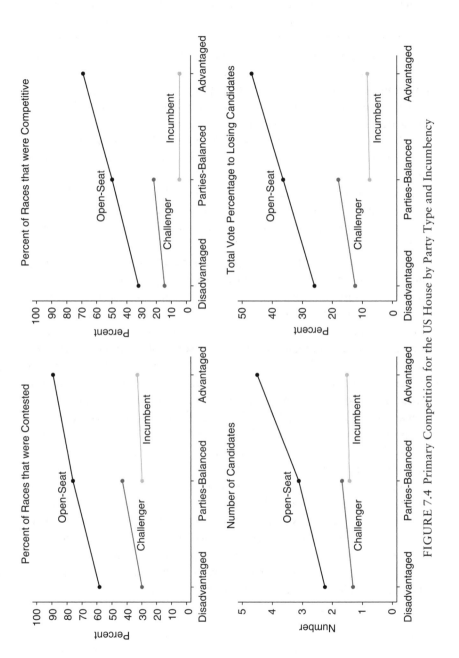

FIGURE 7.4 Primary Competition for the US House by Party Type and Incumbency

179

lower for both parties-balanced and advantaged-party primaries during this period.[19] The lower level of competition in incumbent-contested primaries suggests a growing primary election incumbency advantage, while the drop in competition in challenger-party primaries is consistent with the general election incumbency advantage deterring entrants by lowering the likelihood of being elected.

The level of competition for open-seat races is noticeably lower in parties-balanced primaries than in advantaged-party primaries. This could be interpreted as evidence that the potential entrants in the overall pool are not responding to higher expected future returns to winning office – in terms of the probability of being re-elected – associated with a growing incumbency advantage. However, as we show in the next chapter, the patterns are different when we distinguish between those with and without relevant experience, which is consistent with strategic entry behavior.

Figure 7.4 displays the patterns of primary competition for US House races. Again, advantaged-party primaries for open-seat races continue to be the most competitive, on average. The low level of primary competition in incumbent-contested races is even more striking for the US House than for statewide offices in all three types of primary constituencies. The larger gap between open-seat and incumbent-contested races may reflect the larger general election incumbency advantage in US House races compared to those for statewide offices further down the ballot. Interestingly, for open-seat races the level of competition in US House primaries increased for all types of constituencies compared to the pre-1950 period. This pattern is consistent with entrants responding to the higher future expected returns from winning open seats due to the incumbency advantage.

Overall, Figures 7.3 and 7.4 show that primaries are continuing to inject competition into the areas where they can make a significant contribution to the electoral system. The changes in the electoral environment that have occurred in the last half-century appear to have had the most noticeable impact in races in which an incumbent is seeking re-election. In the next section, we examine the over-time trends in competition for open-seat, challenger-party, and incumbent-contested primaries.

---

[19] We do not plot the level of competition for incumbent-contested races in disadvantaged-party primaries, as these are relatively rare and unusual events. For a similar reason we do not plot the level of competition for challenger-party races for advantaged-party primaries.

7.5.1 Over-Time Trends

How has the level of primary competition evolved over time? Figures 7.5 and 7.6 plot the decade averages of primary competition for statewide and US House offices, respectively, using the same four measures of primary competition as the previous two figures. We focus on competition in advantaged-party and parties-balanced primaries, as elected officials are most likely to come from these races.

Figure 7.5 illustrates that there was a noticeable decline in primary competition in statewide races for all four measures of competition from the high levels of the 1930s through the 1950s. This drop was most pronounced for incumbent-contested races. There was also a noticeable but less significant decline in competition in open-seat races, which may partly reflect the changing competitiveness of general elections for statewide offices during this period. Figure 7.1 highlights the relatively low number of states with uncompetitive general elections during most of the post-1950 period.

While competition in open-seat races has remained relatively stable since the 1960s, the competitiveness of incumbent-contested primaries continued to decline in the second half of the twentieth century. This may reflect a response to some of the changes in the electoral environment discussed above, or simply the rise of the incumbency advantage in the primaries themselves. It is perhaps not surprising that incumbent-contested primaries appear to have become more competitive in the most recent decade, given that general election competition, the incumbency advantage, and the amount of candidate-centered voting have all declined since the turn of the century. This uptick might also reflect the emergence of issue or factional divisions within the parties.

Figure 7.6 shows that, overall, the trends in primary competition for statewide offices also hold in US House races. However, there is one notable difference. In US House primaries for open seats the level of competition has been generally increasing rather than decreasing since the 1940s. This may be because the share of US House districts expected to have competitive general elections was relatively constant during this period. As a result of this, the gap in competitiveness between open-seat and incumbent-contested races has been noticeably larger in US House races than in statewide races throughout most of the twentieth century.

Interestingly, the downward trend in primary competition for incumbent-contested races reversed in the last decade. While incumbents still almost never lose in primary elections, during the 2010s there was

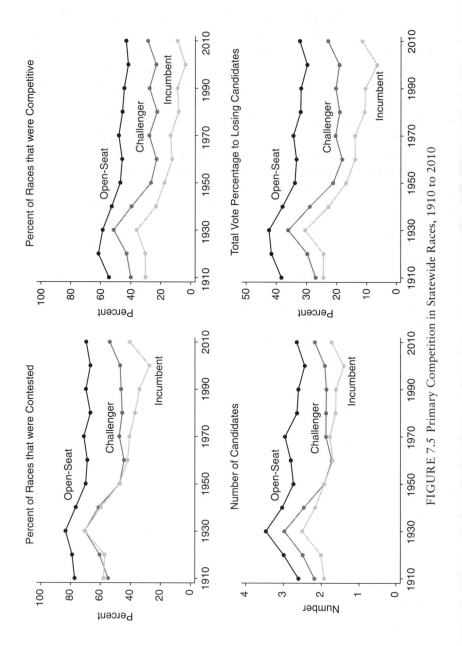

FIGURE 7.5 Primary Competition in Statewide Races, 1910 to 2010

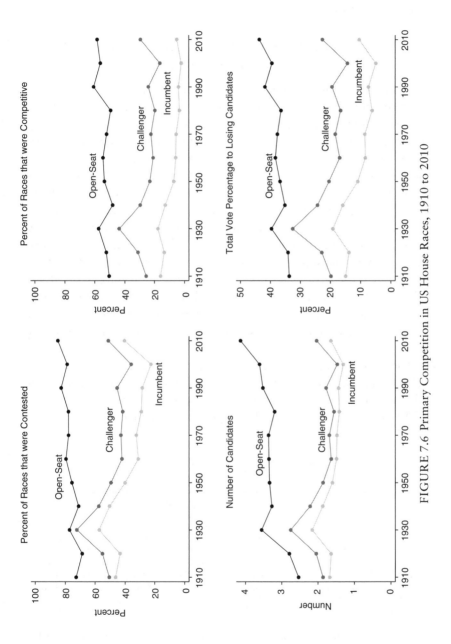

FIGURE 7.6 Primary Competition in US House Races, 1910 to 2010

an uptick in competition for all measures. This reversal is apparent in both parties' primaries.

7.6 CONTRIBUTION OF PRIMARY ELECTORAL COMPETITION

How much are primaries contributing to the overall level of competition in the electoral system? In this section we examine the extent to which primaries are forcing elected officials to face competition that they might not face if they only competed in the general election. As in our analysis of the pre-1950 period, we focus on whether the ultimate winner of the election faced competition on their way to winning, and whether this competition arose in the primary election, the general election, or in both.

Table 7.1 below shows the results, that is the percentage of statewide and US House races that were competitive in the primary only, general election only, both elections, or neither. The races are also divided between those that were open seats and those with an incumbent present. Again, we consider a race to be competitive if the winner received less than 57.5 percent of the total votes cast. The proportion of officials who face competition only in their primary election is an indicator of the degree to which primaries are contributing to the competitiveness of the system.

The table highlights the dearth of competition faced by elected officials in either primary or general elections between 1950 and 2016. Across all races, only 57.4 percent of statewide officials and 28.9 percent of US House members faced competition in either the primary or

TABLE 7.1 *Competition in Primary versus General Elections, 1950 to 2016*

	Election that is Competitive				
	Primary Only	General Only	Both	Neither	Number of Cases
Statewide, All Positions	11.5%	33.4%	12.5%	42.6%	6270
Statewide, Open Seat	23.4%	32.6%	25.3%	18.8%	1987
Statewide, Incumbent Present	6.0%	33.8%	6.6%	53.6%	4283
US House, All Seats	5.9%	18.3%	4.7%	71.1%	14311
US House, Open Seat	33.1%	21.3%	27.3%	18.3%	1368
US House, Incumbent Present	3.0%	18.0%	2.3%	76.7%	12943

Cell entries give the percentage of cases of each type.

general election. Of course most of the uncompetitive elections were incumbent-contested races. Only 46.4 percent of statewide officials and 23.3 percent of US House members elected in an incumbent-contested race faced either a competitive primary or general election. This low level of competition in incumbent-contested races does not simply reflect the absence of general election competition. Primaries make a very small independent contribution to the overall competition in these races. Only a single-digit percentage of statewide officials or US House members faced competition only in the primaries.

Officials elected in open-seat races continue to face the most significant competition. More than 80 percent of officials elected in either statewide or US House races for an open seat faced electoral competition in either the primary or general election. Regarding primary competition, 23.4 percent of statewide officials and 33.1 percent of US House members only faced electoral competition in their primary. Primaries in the modern period are contributing slightly less to the competition elected officials face in open-seat races compared to the early decades of the twentieth century. The drop is more pronounced for statewide races, which is likely to be related to the increase in inter-party competition in these races.

7.7 CONCLUSION

The results above indicate that primary elections continue to play a significant role in injecting competition into open-seat races, especially in constituencies with uncompetitive general elections. However, the results do not tell us whether primaries continue to facilitate the election of qualified officials. Moreover, in the rare instances of primary competition in incumbent-contested races, we do not know whether primaries are helping to hold elected officials accountable for their actions in office. Changes in the nature of general elections during the post-1950 period – increased two-party competition at the state level, the rise of candidate-centered voting, the increase in the incumbency advantage, and growing partisan polarization – might also have affected the role primaries play in electing and retaining qualified officials. We turn to these questions regarding electoral selection and accountability in the next three chapters.

8

Primaries and Candidate Selection in the Modern Era

In 1952, John Fitzgerald Kennedy vacated the 11th Congressional District of Massachusetts to run for the US Senate. Seven candidates ran in the Democratic primary in this district, which is a Democratic stronghold covering parts of Boston and Cambridge. By the end of a tough campaign there were only two real contenders, Thomas P. "Tip" O'Neill and Michael LoPresti. Both were strong candidates with many years of legislative experience: O'Neill was at that time the Speaker of the Massachusetts House of Representatives, and LoPresti was a state senator. The other five candidates were relatively unremarkable. O'Neill and LoPresti had no major policy differences between them, but there was an ethnic cleavage: O'Neill was supported by most of the Irish community (though not the Kennedy clan), while LoPresti was backed by the Italians. When the smoke cleared – after recounts and claims of vote fraud – O'Neill won by fewer than 3,300 votes out of nearly 53,000 cast. Since the Democrats were the advantaged party in that district, O'Neill was elected to office with little general election competition.

Thus began O'Neill's long and distinguished career in the US House, which ended more than three decades later as Speaker. None of his subsequent elections was nearly as hard-fought or close. In 6 general elections and 11 primaries he was uncontested. His toughest races continued to be primaries: in 1954 he defeated LoPresti in a rematch, 64 to 36 percent, and in 1976 he won his primary with 70 percent of the vote. In the general elections he crushed his Republican opponents, winning more than 70 percent of the vote in every election – on average, he received three votes for every vote for his Republican challengers.

186

While Tip O'Neill was not a typical member of Congress, in 1952 – or even 1962 – few would have guessed that he would become Speaker of the US House of Representatives. Although it is unclear whether LoPresti or any of the other challengers in the 1952 primary would have revealed themselves to be an even more successful member of the US House than O'Neill, the primary in this case clearly nominated an unusually high-quality politician. LoPresti went on to become a leader in the Massachusetts State Senate. The second runner-up, Francis X. McCann, was elected to the state senate in 1954 and served for more than a quarter-of-a-century. As we would expect, the open seat in the advantaged-party primary attracted a large number of high-quality challengers, one of whom was eventually elected.

In this chapter, we again examine the effectiveness of primaries in nominating qualified candidates across different types of constituencies. Recall that in Chapter 5, we provided evidence that the advantaged party is more likely to nominate candidates with relevant experience for open-seat races under the primary system than under the prior convention system. In this earlier period from 1892 to 1950, those elected in open-seat races to represent safe constituencies were more likely to have relevant experience than those elected in open-seat races for parties-balanced constituencies.

The changes in the electoral environment discussed in Chapter 7 provide two reasons to expect qualified candidates to have stronger incentives to run in parties-balanced primaries than they did in the earlier period. First, the increase in candidate-centered voting in general elections means that qualifications can matter more for winning. Second, the larger incumbency advantage means that even constituencies that are competitive in open-seat elections are relatively safe for whoever becomes the incumbent – thus, winning open-seat elections is more valuable for career-oriented politicians.

Additionally, for this later period we can partially validate our experienced-based measure of relevant qualifications by comparing it with newspaper endorsements. We can also study more comprehensive measures of candidates' qualifications and prior performance. These are based on expert evaluations and are available for two offices: state legislators in North Carolina and circuit court judges in Illinois.

8.1 QUALIFICATIONS FOR OFFICE

How do we measure candidates' qualifications for a particular office? For incumbents the task is somewhat easier, because there are various policy-related outcomes that are at least partly attributable to their actions. For non-incumbents, we need measures of future expected performance, which are more difficult to quantify. For the earlier period we relied on a measure of prior experience performing tasks similar to those expected to be performed in the office being sought. In Chapter 5, we mainly offered theoretical arguments and evidence from psychology, labor economics, and personnel management, to justify this measure as a proxy for qualifications. We offered some evidence for the validity of the measure by examining the relationship between prior experience and the endorsements of one newspaper in the pre-1950 period. In this section, we provide more comprehensive empirical evidence that relevant experience in recent decades is likely capturing candidates' qualifications for particular offices.

We also introduce another measure of candidate qualifications, state bar association evaluations. These evaluations only cover judicial offices, but they are more comprehensive than measures based solely on prior experience, because they incorporate a variety of additional performance information. If the analyses using this measure produce results similar to those found in analyses using measures based only on relevant experience, then we can be more confident in our interpretation of the findings.[1]

8.1.1 Relevant Experience as a Measure of Qualification

For five major offices – governor, US senator, state auditor, state treasurer and US House representative – we define relevant experience using prior political office holding, as above. For gubernatorial candidates, the offices that constitute relevant experience are statewide executive offices and mayors of major cities. For US Senate candidates, the offices are the US House and state legislative seats. For state auditor and treasurer candidates we consider previously holding a local office that involves auditing or managing state funds – for example, county auditor or county treasurer – as relevant experience. We also include being a certified public accountant as an indicator of relevant experience. Finally, for US House candidates, relevant experience includes service as a state legislator or prior, but not current, service as a member of Congress. For all five offices, incumbents are also considered to have relevant experience.

---

[1] Some of the analyses and background material presented in this chapter draw on Hirano and Snyder (2014) and Lim and Snyder (2012).

As in the pre-1950 period, primary candidates often promote their relevant experience as evidence of their qualifications for a particular office. For example, in the 1962 primary for New Mexico state auditor, the candidates featured their previous experiences in campaign advertisements. The header of one candidate's advertisement read "ELECT A CPA!" Another highlighted his experience as a state budget auditor and state treasurer, and stated "Your state needs a qualified, honest and experienced State Auditor." The one candidate who did not obviously have any relevant experience asserted in his campaign advertisement that he was "EXPERIENCED AND QUALIFIED."[2] The voters nominated the candidate who was described in the *Albuquerque Journal* endorsement as "experienced in the work connected with this office."[3] In Chapter 9, we also find that voters appear to value candidates' relevant experience.

What is the empirical evidence that candidates who have experience relevant to the office they are seeking are actually more qualified? We use two additional measures to examine this link – legislative effectiveness scores for the North Carolina state legislature and newspaper endorsements. We discuss the construction of these measures in some detail and also provide some necessary background information. These measures will appear again in Chapters 9 and 10.

Effectiveness Scores for the North Carolina Legislature

The North Carolina state legislature is one of the few settings for which we have expert evaluations of elected officials' performance in office. These scores allow us to test our assumption that candidates with prior experience in positions that involve similar tasks as the office being sought will perform better in that office than those without such experience. More specifically, we can test whether state senators elected to open seats who previously served as state representatives have higher effectiveness scores than newly elected senators without prior experience as a representative.

Another advantage of studying the North Carolina legislature, called the General Assembly, is that it is a hybrid legislature – an amateur, citizens' legislature with some professional characteristics. It consists of two chambers, a House of Representatives with 120 members and a Senate with 50 members. All members are elected every two years for

[2] The advertisements appeared in *The Santa Fe New Mexican* on May 6, 1962, pages 3 and 6.
[3] *Albuquerque Journal*, May 6, 1962, page 4.

two-year terms. In 1986–1988 it was ranked 22nd by the Squire (1992) index of legislative professionalism. Thus, there is substantial variation in legislators' workload, which should make it easier for journalists, lobbyists, and legislators to identify the less-effective legislators.[4]

The Democratic Party dominated the North Carolina General Assembly until very recently. Democrats held 86 percent of all state legislative seats during the period 1971–1980, 75 percent during 1981–1990, and 59 percent during 1991–2000. In 1994, Republicans won control of the state House for the first time in 100 years. They won again in 1996, but then lost in 1998.[5] In the most recent sessions, 2007–2016, the Democrats held only 46 percent of the seats. Internally, the legislature is organized mainly along party lines. The majority party controls all committee chairs, but some vice-chairs and subcommittee chairs go to the minority. Electorally, party organizations in North Carolina are stronger than in most other Southern states, but typically rank just below the US average.[6] Morehouse (1981) classified North Carolina as a state in which pressure groups are strong.

The legislative effectiveness measure for the North Carolina state legislature comes from the North Carolina Center for Public Policy Research (NCCPPR).[7] The NCCPPR is an independent non-partisan organization that ranks the effectiveness of each state legislator after each regular legislative session based on a survey that asks experts to rate each representative's "participation in committee work, their skill at guiding bills through floor debate, their general knowledge and expertise in special fields, the respect they command from their peers, the enthusiasm with which they execute various legislative responsibilities, the political power they hold (either by virtue of office, longevity, or personal attributes), their ability to sway the opinion of fellow legislators, and their aptitude for the overall legislative process."[8]

---

[4] Regular legislative sessions are biennial, convening in January following each election, although there have been special sessions in almost every even-numbered year since 1974. Despite being a hybrid legislature, some observers argue that until recently the North Carolina General Assembly was one of the most powerful legislative bodies in the nation since the state's governor had no veto until 1996.

[5] The 2002 elections produced an exact 50–50 split in the House, resulting in a unique system of shared control. Democrats controlled the state Senate throughout the period under study, but with a narrow 26–24 margin during 1995–1996.

[6] See, for example, Cotter et al. (1984).

[7] The NCCPPR was created in 1977. It is "an independent, nonprofit organization dedicated to the goals of a better-informed public and more effective, accountable, and responsive government" (www.nccppr.org/mission.html#mission).

[8] From *Article II: A Guide to the 1991-1992 N.C. Legislature*, p. 212.

The *Effectiveness* rankings are based on subjective evaluations. However, the number of evaluations is large, the evaluators are all legislative "specialists" of some sort, and the rankings have been constructed in a consistent manner over a long period of time. The NCCPPR surveys all 170 legislators, lobbyists registered in the state capital who reside in North Carolina (250–325 lobbyists), and journalists who regularly cover the state General Assembly (35–45 journalists), for a total sample size of 475–550.[9] The NCCPPR publishes these ratings in its biennial handbooks, *Article II: A Guide to the N.C. Legislature.*

Two other facts about the rankings provide evidence that the measure is capturing actual legislative effectiveness rather than the biases of particular specialists. First, between 1977 and 1992 the NCCPPR reported the average evaluation that each representative received from each of the three types of respondents – legislators, lobbyists, and journalists – in addition to the overall evaluation and ranking. The correlations across the three separate scores are quite high: the correlation between the average rating by legislators and the average rating by lobbyists is 0.93, 0.89 between legislators and journalists, and 0.91 between lobbyists and journalists. Thus, various biases that we might imagine in the responses – for example, lobbyists might systematically underrate legislators who oppose their positions, and legislators might systematically underrate members of the opposing party – do not appear to be a problem. Second, NCCPPR's *Article II* guides also contain information on the number of bills each member introduced, and how many of these became law. For representatives serving during the period 1981–2000, the correlation between *Effectiveness* and the number of bills introduced is 0.51, and the correlation between *Effectiveness* and the number of bills ratified is 0.50. Thus, the more objective measures of activity are strongly and positively related to *Effectiveness*. Yet the correlation is far from 1, indicating that *Effectiveness* measures something other than simply introducing and passing bills.[10]

Padró i Miguel and Snyder (2006) examine the NCCPPR's effectiveness ranking and find that state legislators become more effective over the course of their tenure. This provides some indication that

[9] Response rates were only about 33 percent for the period 1977–1981, but have been over 50 percent in later years. For more information, see the North Carolina Political Review's August 2002 interview with Ran Coble, executive director of the NCCPPR, www.ncpoliticalreview.com/0702/coble1.htm.

[10] See Padró i Miguel and Snyder (2006) for additional checks regarding the validity of this measure.

legislative experience is related to legislators' future expected performance. However, we are also interested in the relevant experience of non-incumbents. We might expect that newly elected legislators with prior experience as a representative in another legislative setting (for example, a senator elected with experience as a representative) will bring with them knowledge about the legislative process that they acquired from their previous position. If this is true, then legislators with relevant experience will be more effective than those without such experience.

We test this hypothesis using the same North Carolina legislative effectiveness ratings.[11] If state senate candidates with experience in the state lower house are more qualified than those without this experience, then North Carolina state senators with relevant experience in the state lower house should have a higher effectiveness ranking compared to those without relevant experience. Indeed, we find a fairly large and statistically significant difference: state senators with relevant experience rank about 3.1 places higher (the scale ranges from 1 to 50) after controlling for membership in the majority party and accounting for year effects. By comparison, the estimated difference in ranking between majority- and minority-party freshman senators in this specification is 10.0 places.

Newspaper Endorsements

US newspapers routinely endorse candidates running for office, both in primary and general elections.[12] These endorsements provide another indicator of the relative qualifications of candidates. Journalists and newspaper editors have much more information than others about the candidates, because they collect this information as a routine matter in the course of reporting the news. In addition, most newspaper staffs interview candidates before making their endorsements.

We have not attempted to construct a comprehensive catalogue of the criteria newspapers use to make their endorsements. After reading hundreds of endorsement editorials, however, the dominant criteria in primary election endorsements appear to be previous experience, accomplishments, and qualifications relevant for the office sought. Relevant experience would include prior state legislative experience for

---

[11] The number of newly elected state senators in the 1978–2014 period was 228.

[12] Some newspapers, such as the *Los Angeles Times*, have a policy of endorsing candidates in the general election but not in the primary election, or of endorsing in the primary election mainly in one-party areas where the primary is likely to determine the final winner.

candidates running for Congress or the other state legislative chamber, prior public-sector or private-sector auditing experience for candidates running for state auditor, and prior experience as a district attorney, US attorney, or prosecutor in the state attorney general's office when running for state attorney general. Newspapers often cite experience running a large bureaucratic organization – for example, as mayor of a large city, statewide executive officer, or civic association leader – for candidates running for governor or other executive office. They also often cite the opinions of other experts – for example, legislative colleagues who attest to how hardworking, responsible, and intelligent a candidate is. Newspapers overwhelmingly endorse incumbents running for re-election, usually citing their performance and effort in office. The rare instances in which the incumbent is not endorsed are generally cases where he or she has been involved in a scandal or has been obviously underperforming.[13]

We have collected thousands of primary election endorsements, mainly for the period 1990–2014 but in some cases for earlier years.[14] These endorsements can be used to construct a measure of the relative qualifications of the candidates running for a particular office. Since endorsements indicate relative qualifications within a primary, they are not as appropriate for examining our main question of interest for this chapter – whether advantaged-party primaries are more likely to nominate qualified candidates than parties-balanced or disadvantaged-party primaries. However, the endorsements allow us to check the validity of relevant experience as a measure of candidate qualification.

The following endorsement by *The Charlotte Observer* for the 2008 North Carolina state auditor race exemplifies how prominent a role previous experience plays when explaining their decisions:

Two Democrats are seeking their party's nomination to face State Auditor Les Merritt, a Republican, this fall ...

Mr. Aikens, a retired Army National Guard colonel with more than 30 years of service who served in Kuwait, has been a senior fiscal analyst at the legislature, deputy secretary of the N.C. Department of Correction and chief deputy secretary of the N.C. Department of Transportation. His considerable

---

[13] Gordon and Landa (2009) provide a theoretical model that highlights how the rare situation where incumbents are not endorsed sends a strong signal about incumbent quality to voters.

[14] We have collected a total of 7,028 endorsements, covering 3,590 races for US House and statewide offices. We collected them from online archives as well as microfilm at libraries around the country.

management experience in the military and in state government posts would be an asset in the auditor's office.

But Beth Wood exemplifies the background, training, energy and leadership most needed in the auditor's office. She has 15 years of auditing experience and has worked in both the state treasurer's and the state auditor's offices. While in the auditor's office she redesigned the agency's internal training program, worked to make employee evaluations meaningful rather than pro forma and has good ideas for monitoring taxpayers' money and examining how state agencies spend it. We recommend Beth Wood for state auditor.[15]

One potential concern is that some newspapers have partisan or ideological biases. Even if a newspaper has such a bias, however, it is much less likely to matter for the endorsements the newspaper makes in primary elections compared to those it makes in general elections. This is because all of the candidates in a given party's primary are affiliated with the same party, and the ideological differences between the candidates tend to be small.[16] Thus, if relevant experience is capturing a candidate's qualification for a particular office, then the measure should also be correlated with newspaper endorsements.

How often do newspapers endorse candidates with relevant prior experience? There is a strong, positive correlation between newspaper endorsements in US House primaries and candidates' previous legislative experience. We consider a candidate to be "highly endorsed" if he or she received at least 75 percent of the newspaper endorsements in a race.[17] We examine all open-seat races in which at least one candidate has previous legislative experience and at least one candidate does not.[18] There are 236 such races, involving 765 candidates, for which we also have a highly endorsed candidate. In these cases, 70.8 percent of the highly endorsed candidates have previous state legislative experience, compared to only 23.4 percent of those opposing a highly endorsed candidate.

A similar pattern emerges when we examine primary races for statewide office. We again focus on open-seat races for which we have endorsement information and there is at least one candidate with relevant

---

[15] *The Charlotte Observer*, April 25, 2008.
[16] It is possible that an extremely partisan newspaper might try to sabotage the nomination of the party it opposes, and endorse weak candidates in that party's primaries. However, such behavior would be so outrageously unprofessional by today's journalistic standards that it must occur rarely if ever.
[17] To increase the sample size, in the analysis we include all races with at least one endorsement.
[18] We only include races with five or fewer candidates.

experience and one candidate without such experience. We have 221 gubernatorial or US Senate races in our sample, involving 755 candidates, in which one candidate is highly endorsed. In these cases, 72.2 percent of the highly endorsed candidates have relevant prior experience, compared to 24.2 percent of the non-highly endorsed candidates. We also have 72 state auditor and treasurer races, involving 204 candidates, in which one candidate is highly endorsed. In these cases, 51.4 percent of the highly endorsed candidates have relevant prior experience, compared to only 35.6 percent of those opposing a highly endorsed candidate.[19]

Newspaper endorsements also differentiate between relevant and less-relevant prior experience in open-seat races. As discussed above, experiences that are relevant for performing the tasks of a particular office may be less relevant for performing the tasks of other offices. Here, we consider previous legislative service in the US Congress or a state legislature as less-relevant experience for governor, state auditor, and state treasurer. We consider previous service in executive offices viewed as relevant for governor – that is, statewide down-ballot offices and big city mayors – as less relevant experience for US senator. We find that being the highly endorsed candidate in a primary is more strongly correlated with the candidate's share of relevant experience than with her share of less-relevant experience. More specifically, we regress an indicator for whether a candidate is highly endorsed on the share of relevant experience, the share of less-relevant experience and race-specific fixed effects (for races for governor, US senator, state auditor, and state treasurer). The estimated coefficient on the share of relevant experience is 0.41, while the coefficient on the share of less-relevant experience is 0.26. The difference is statistically significant.

8.1.2 Judicial Evaluations

Judicial evaluations provide another measure of qualifications. We focus on evaluations of candidates for the Illinois circuit and appellate courts. We study these cases because they involve partisan primaries, and we have comparable evaluations for races throughout the state.[20]

Prior to each election, the Illinois State Bar Association (ISBA) and various Chicago area (Cook County) bar associations evaluate judicial

---

[19] As discussed below, our measure of relevant experience for state auditor and treasure may include more measurement error in the post-1950 period compared to the pre-1950 period.

[20] See Lim and Snyder (2012) for related analyses of judicial elections in other states.

candidates. The ISBA Judicial Evaluations Committee issues ratings of Highly Qualified, Qualified, or Not Qualified based on questionnaires and interviews. The ISBA also gives ratings of Recommended or Not Recommended based on surveys of ISBA members. The largest bar association in the Chicago area is the Chicago Bar Association (CBA). Similar to the ISBA, the CBA's Judicial Evaluation Committee gives ratings of Highly Qualified, Qualified, or Not Recommended based on questionnaires and interviews.[21] Like newspaper endorsements, these bar association evaluations are based on a more comprehensive set of considerations than simply the prior offices listed on candidates' resumes (see the appendix for more details). We have ratings for almost all circuit and appellate court candidates from 1986 to 2010.

Bar associations claim that one of the main reasons they evaluate judges and judicial candidates is to inform voters. The surveys are conducted during the months preceding elections, and the evaluations are released within a few weeks of election day. The evaluations also tend to receive a non-trivial amount of newspaper coverage when they are released. As usual, bad news is good news when it comes to generating eye-catching headlines: "Lawyers Rank 9 Judges 'Unqualified,'" "Lawyers Rate PA Judge Unfit," "Bar Association Rates Two Judicial Candidates as Unqualified," and "Democrat Gets Negative Rating from Bar in County Court Race" are examples. Sometimes, however, good news prevails: "Bar Group Rates Court Candidates – 6 in Appellate Race Given Top Marks."[22]

To assess whether bar association ratings are a good measure of candidate qualifications, Lim and Snyder (2012) check whether the evaluations from bar associations and state commissions appear to signal candidates' ideological positions rather than qualifications. Although the items on the surveys sent out by the bar associations are not explicitly

---

[21] The other Chicago area bar associations that rate candidates are the Chicago Council of Lawyers, the Cook County Bar Association, the Women's Bar Association of Illinois, the Asian American Bar Association of the Greater Chicago Area, the Hellenic Bar Association, the Black Women's Lawyers Association of Greater Chicago, the Hispanic Lawyers Association of Illinois, the Lesbian and Gay Bar Association of Chicago, the Puerto Rican Bar Association of Illinois, the Decalogue Society of Lawyers, and the Northwest Suburban Bar Association. See Lim and Snyder (2012) for more details about the judicial ratings data, including information about the criteria used and checks on the validity of the ratings, such as evidence that the ratings do not exhibit a partisan bias.

[22] In order, these headlines are from: *Chicago Tribune*, October 12, 1988; *Philadelphia Inquirer*, May 14, 2010; *Ventura County Star*; October 19, 1993; *Syracuse Post-Standard*, October 9, 2009; *Chicago Tribune*, March 2, 1990.

ideological or partisan, it is possible that the responses and resulting evaluations exhibit an ideological or partisan bias. Many conservative commentators argue that lawyers in general, and bar associations in particular, are more liberal than the overall population. Thus, we might worry that evaluations are correlated with judges' ideologies or party affiliations. Even if they are not, voters might believe they are, and assess them accordingly. Lim and Snyder (2012) find no consistent evidence that this is the case. First, they find that the correlation between evaluations and judges' party affiliation is small. Second, the correlation between judicial evaluations and the normal vote across precincts is also small – that is, it is not the case that judges with higher evaluations receive a larger share of votes in Democratic precincts than in Republican precincts. Finally, we are less concerned about ideological biases because we are studying primaries, and the candidates competing in the same party's primary generally share similar ideological positions.

We can also examine the relationship between endorsements and judicial evaluations. We have both primary election endorsements and bar association evaluations for a large number of judicial candidates for Illinois and five other states (CA, OH, PA, TX, and WA). In these cases, the newspaper endorsements are highly correlated with bar association evaluations. We define candidates who received at least two newspaper endorsements, and for whom we have at least one bar association evaluation, as "highly endorsed."[23] In 247 of 251 cases (98.4 percent), the highly endorsed candidate received a bar association evaluation of Qualified or better. That is, a highly endorsed candidate received an Unqualified or Not Recommended evaluation in only four cases (1.6 percent).[24] Moreover, in these four cases *all* of the candidates in these races received Unqualified or Not Recommended evaluations. Even the candidates with just one newspaper endorsement were rated as Qualified or better in 97.2 percent of the cases (out of 1,111). By comparison, the candidates who received no newspaper endorsements were rated as Qualified or better in only 63.8 percent of the cases (out of 2,013).

In the analyses below, we consider a candidate to be qualified if the candidate received a rating of Qualified or better from more than half

---

[23] We include non-partisan general election races, in addition to primary races, to increase the sample size.

[24] We also classify candidates as unqualified if they are rated as "lacking qualifications" or if they refused to participate in the review process.

of the bar associations that rated him or her. Note that the Chicago area bar associations only evaluate candidates running for Cook County judgeships, so outside Cook County we use only the ISBA ratings.[25]

8.2 QUALIFICATIONS AND CONSTITUENCY TYPE

We have argued at numerous points in this book that if elections are mainly about selection, then nominating qualified candidates is more important in advantaged-party primaries for open-seat races and least important in disadvantaged-party primaries. Of course, primaries in parties-balanced areas also have an important role in selecting qualified officials. However, since the general election provides an additional competitive hurdle that allows voters to evaluate candidates from both parties, as long as one party nominates a qualified candidate then the voters have a good chance of electing a qualified representative. As noted in Chapter 7, the post-1950 period saw an increase in the fraction of parties-balanced constituencies, a sharp increase in the general election incumbency advantage, and also (later) an increase in inter-party polarization. Thus, during this period it might have become even more consequential for both parties to nominate qualified candidates in open-seat, parties-balanced cases.

In Chapter 5, we provided a simple theoretical model regarding the conditions under which entrants' strategic behavior would lead to a positive correlation between a party's likelihood of nominating a qualified candidate and the extent to which a constituency's partisan balance favors candidates from that party. The model predicts that the number of candidates, the number of qualified candidates and the fraction of qualified candidates will increase between disadvantaged-party, parties-balanced, and advantaged-party primaries. Thus, even randomly drawing from the pool of primary candidates should lead to relatively more qualified candidates being nominated in advantaged-party primaries.

For the pre-1950 period, we studied primary elections for four statewide offices and the US House, and relied exclusively on our relevant experience measure of qualifications. Here, for the post-1950 period, we first study those same five offices again using relevant experience to

---

[25] We also conducted an analysis that relies exclusively on the ISBA evaluations even inside Cook County, and the results are quite similar to those reported here. We are missing ISBA evaluations for Cook County candidates before 1998.

measure qualifications. We then conduct additional analyses for judicial primaries, measuring qualifications using the more comprehensive bar association evaluations.

8.2.1 Relevant Experience

We now consider the US House and the four statewide offices analyzed throughout the book – governor, US senator, state treasurer, and state auditor. Our four outcomes of interest are: (i) probability that the nominee has relevant experience; (ii) average number of candidates competing in a primary; (iii) average number of candidates in a primary with relevant experience; and (iv) average share of candidates in a primary with relevant experience. We plot these outcomes against the three types of primaries: (i) advantaged-party; (ii) parties-balanced; and (iii) disadvantaged-party. The primaries are classified using the measures of constituency partisanship described earlier.[26]

Figure 8.1 presents the results for non-incumbent US House primaries between 1950 and 2016. The top-left panel presents the main outcome of interest – the probability that the primary winner has relevant prior experience. We find a positive relationship between winners' relevant prior experience and the division of partisan loyalties within constituencies. The probability that the nominee has relevant experience is highest in advantaged-party primaries, 0.15 lower in parties-balanced primaries, and lowest in disadvantaged-party primaries.

The other panels reveal similar patterns for the three outcomes related to the pool of primary candidates. Consistent with our theoretical predictions, as a party is expected to have less general election competition, it is expected to draw not only more candidates but also more candidates with relevant experience. The bottom-right panel illustrates that the share of candidates with relevant experience is higher in advantaged-party compared to parties-balanced primaries – a difference of 0.06 – but again the gap is not as substantial as the difference between the parties-balanced and disadvantaged-party primaries. This is similar to the patterns we observe for US House primaries in the pre-1950 period.

Figure 8.1 also shows what happens in primaries to nominate challengers to US House incumbents. The nominees in these cases are much less likely to have relevant experience than when the seats are

---

[26] The patterns are also evident in simple regressions of the various outcomes on primary type.

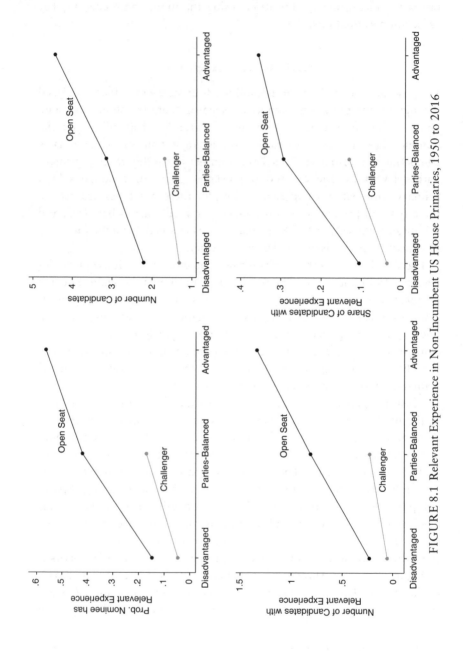

FIGURE 8.1 Relevant Experience in Non-Incumbent US House Primaries, 1950 to 2016

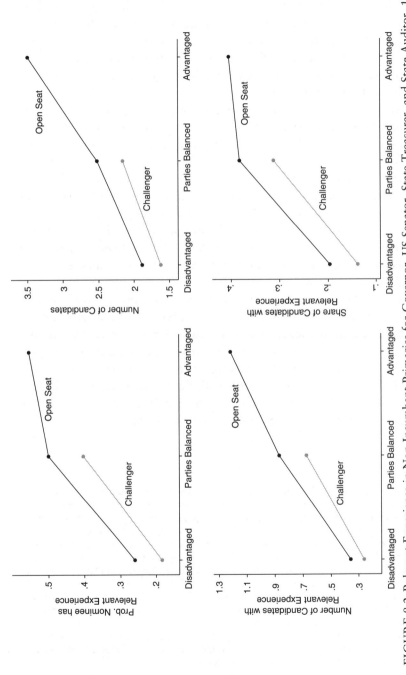

FIGURE 8.2 Relevant Experience in Non-Incumbent Primaries for Governor, US Senator, State Treasurer, and State Auditor, 1950 to 2016

open. This is true for both parties-balanced and disadvantaged-party constituencies. The differences are also evident in the other three panels. Also, all of the differences are more substantial than what we observed for the pre-1950 period in Figure 5.4. This is what we expect: after the large increase in the general election incumbency advantage, both qualified and less-qualified candidates had less incentive to enter primaries to face incumbents.[27]

Figure 8.2 plots the outcome variables of interest against primary type for the four statewide offices. The patterns of candidate qualification and entry decisions in primary races for these offices are consistent with the predictions of our model, and resemble the patterns for the US House. The top-left panel of Figure 8.2 shows that the probability that a nominee for statewide office has relevant qualifications is highest for advantaged-party primaries, slightly lower for parties-balanced primaries (difference of 0.05), and lowest for disadvantaged-party primaries. In the bottom-right panel, we see that the share of candidates with relevant experience in parties-balanced and advantaged-party primaries is very similar, with a difference of only 0.02.

As in US House races, primaries to nominate general election challengers for the statewide offices are noticeably less likely to attract entrants and to nominate candidates with relevant experience than are primaries for open seats. The gaps between primaries in the challenging party and primaries for open seats are much larger than they were in the pre-1950 period. This is consistent with the hypothesis that candidates' entry decisions should respond to the electoral incentives created by the large incumbency advantage in the post-1950 period.[28]

---

[27] Note also that the share of candidates with relevant experience is noticeably lower in primaries to nominate challengers than in primaries for open seats. One possible reason is that the candidates with relevant experience are almost all state legislators. The incumbency advantage also increased for state legislators during the post-1950 period. Since in order to challenge an incumbent these candidates would have to give up their state legislative seats and the accompanying incumbency advantage, many of them may have decided not to run against incumbents. Other candidates did not face this additional cost.

[28] There is another intriguing pattern in Figure 8.2. Compared to the pre-1950, there is relatively little difference in the probability that the nominee has relevant experience in parties-balanced and advantaged-party primaries. This is also true for the share of candidates running with relevant experience. This is also consistent with strategic candidate entry, since the incumbency advantage turns parties-balanced constituencies into safe constituencies, at least for incumbents.

8.2.2 Judicial Evaluations in Illinois

As discussed above, bar association evaluations provide a measure of candidate qualification that is even more comprehensive than the relevant experience measure used for US House and statewide offices. Here we present results for Illinois circuit and appellate court primaries analogous to those in Figures 8.1 and 8.2. Recall that we classify a candidate as qualified if he or she received a rating of Qualified or better from more than half of the available bar association ratings.

The circuit courts are the general jurisdiction trial courts in the state. Circuit court judges are initially elected in partisan elections, and incumbent judges face a retention election every six years. There are 22 circuits, and many vacancies are filled in elections where voting is restricted to a single county or sub-circuit. The appellate courts have a similar election process, but serve ten-year terms. Election data are from the *Official Vote* booklets published by the Illinois State Board of Elections. We construct the normal vote for each judicial district using the average vote for president, governor, and senator. As above, we classify a judicial district as safe for an incumbent if the normal vote for the incumbent's party exceeds 57.5 percent. We have ratings, primary election information, and normal vote data for over 1,460 judicial candidates from 1986 to 2010.[29]

The results for open-seat Illinois judicial primary elections are presented in Figure 8.3. The top-left panel shows that the winners of advantaged-party primaries are more likely to be qualified than the winners of parties-balanced or disadvantaged-party primaries – the probability is over 0.9, compared to about 0.85 and about 0.75, respectively. The top-right panel illustrates that, on average, advantaged-party primaries have close to three primary candidates, while parties-balanced primaries average slightly fewer than two candidates per race and disadvantaged-party primaries have fewer than 1.5 candidates per primary. The bottom panels of the figure indicate that candidates in advantaged-party primaries also tend to be of higher quality than those in parties-balanced or disadvantaged-party primaries.

The patterns in Figure 8.3 for Illinois judicial primaries are similar to those in Figures 8.1 and 8.2 for US House and statewide office primaries for open-seat races. This gives us greater confidence that the patterns we

---

[29] We have ratings and primary election information for many other candidates running in sub-circuits inside Cook County, but we do not have the normal vote data at the sub-circuit level.

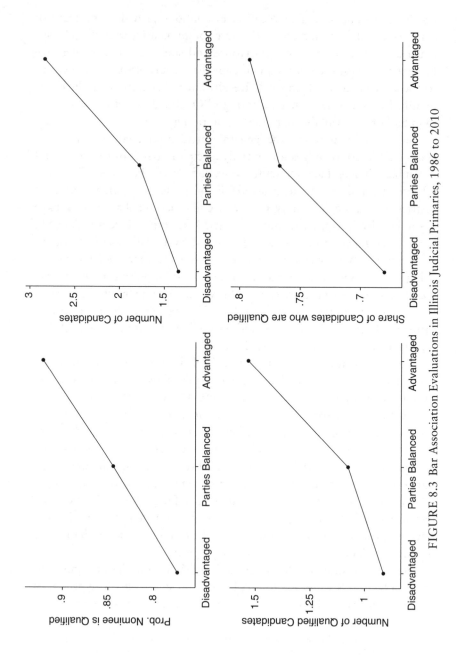

FIGURE 8.3 Bar Association Evaluations in Illinois Judicial Primaries, 1986 to 2010

observe for the US House and statewide offices are not simply reflecting something particular about our relevant experience measure.

8.3 QUALIFICATIONS OF OPEN-SEAT WINNERS

The analyses above suggest that open-seat primaries for advantaged parties nominate candidates who are at least as qualified as those nominated in parties-balanced primaries. If candidate qualifications are also important for winning general elections for open seats, then we might expect the officials serving in parties-balanced constituencies to be qualified with higher probability, since they usually face two serious elections. With the post-1950 increase in candidate-centered electoral politics, general elections in parties-balanced constituencies may be even more relevant as an additional screening mechanism that facilitates the election of qualified representatives. On the other hand, if primaries in advantaged-party constituencies are as effective at nominating qualified candidates as those in parties-balanced constituencies, then the proportion of qualified elected officials might be similar in the two types of constituencies. In this section, we evaluate whether the qualifications of the eventual winners of general election open-seat races differ between constituencies with competitive and uncompetitive general elections.[30]

Table 8.1 shows the bottom line for the six offices grouped in four panels – governor and US senator in the top panel; state auditor and treasurer in the second panel; US House in the third panel; and Illinois circuit court judges in the bottom panel. In each panel, the first row shows the percentage of general election winners who are qualified. The second row shows the percentage of all candidates competing in the primary – that is, the "pool" of entrants – who are qualified.[31] The percentages for competitive and uncompetitive constituencies are presented in separate columns. In uncompetitive states or districts, the percentages are only for the advantaged party, since this party wins most of the offices in these areas. For each type of area, the percentage of qualified elected officials is higher than the percentage of qualified candidates in the pool, which is consistent with an electoral system that

---

[30] As above, the competitive and uncompetitive refers to the expected competitiveness of the general election based on the partisan loyalties in that constituency. An additional complication is the re-emergence of partisan voting and decline of candidate-centered voting, which has accompanied the rising polarization of the past few decades.

[31] We do not include token candidates who win less than 1 percent of the vote.

TABLE 8.1 *Qualifications of General Election Winners versus All Candidates for Open Seats*

	Advantaged Party in Uncompetitive Constituency	Competitive Constituency
Governors and US Senators, 1950–2016		
Winners with	59.2%	62.3%
Relevant Experience	[130]	[244]
All Candidates with	32.8%	32.1%
Relevant Experience	[644]	[1578]
Auditors and Treasurers, 1950–2016		
Winners with	45.7%	45.1%
Relevant Experience	[129]	[284]
All Candidates with	37.7%	37.2%
Relevant Experience	[355]	[1047]
US House Representatives, 1950–2016		
Winners with	55.8%	53.3%
Relevant Experience	[538]	[775]
All Candidates with	31.1%	26.7%
Relevant Experience	[2327]	[4720]
Illinois Judges, 1986–2010		
Winners with	93.3%	91.7%
Qualified Bar Rating	[149]	[230]
All Candidates with	73.6%	70.3%
Qualified Bar Rating	[303]	[536]

Cell entries give the percentage of candidates of each type. Number of observations in brackets.

selects qualified candidates more often than a random draw from the pool of candidates.

There are two clear patterns in Table 8.1. First, in all four panels the percentage of qualified general election winners is similar in both competitive and uncompetitive constituencies. Even in the recent candidate-centered electoral environment, the effectiveness of advantaged-party primaries at nominating qualified candidates does not lead to a significant gap in the qualifications of elected officials across these two constituency types. A similar bottom line table in Chapter 5 suggested that officials elected in competitive constituencies were on average less qualified than those elected in uncompetitive constituencies in the pre-1950 period. The increasing similarity in the qualifications of elected officials in the two types of constituencies is consistent with general elections becoming more candidate-centered and general election voters giving greater weight to qualifications in their voting decisions. Strategic candidate entry, together with primary election outcomes, may also be playing a role. As noted above, the differences between parties-balanced and advantaged-party primaries – in terms of the share of qualified candidates running and winning – are noticeably smaller in the post-1950 compared to pre-1950 period.

Second, the percentage of those elected who are qualified is higher than the corresponding percentage in the pool of candidates who run. Thus, elections appear to matter, and in particular voters appear to systematically favor more qualified candidates. Since we find this difference in both competitive and uncompetitive constituencies, the voting behavior of the primary electorate is very likely to be contributing to the pattern. Chapter 9 will investigate the conditions under which primary voters in the post-1950 period have favored qualified candidates.

8.4 WOULD CONVENTIONS DO JUST AS WELL?

The above analyses suggest that primaries are contributing to the electoral system in a manner consistent with our theoretical predictions. However, to fully assess their impact we need to compare them to alternative nomination systems. In Chapter 5, we compared primaries to conventions by exploiting the nomination reforms that occurred at the turn of the twentieth century. We found that switching from conventions to primaries led to an increase in the qualifications of advantaged-party nominees. Unfortunately, we cannot conduct the analogous analysis in reverse for the post-1950 period, because no states have switched back to conventions.[32] We can, however, conduct more limited analyses that focus on three sets of special cases in which nomination methods other than primaries were used.

Our first analysis examines the four states that used conventions rather than primaries to nominate candidates for governor and US senator, for at least some years in the post-1950 period – Connecticut until 1956, Delaware until 1970, Indiana until 1976, and New York until

---

[32] If anything, the tendency in recent years has been toward more inclusiveness – open primaries, blanket primaries, and top-two systems.

1968. A simple before-and-after analysis indicates that the change in nomination system did not significantly reduce the relevant experience of the major party nominees, and might have even increased it. For each state, we consider an eight-year window around the year of the switch.[33] Within this window, 56 percent of the open-seat candidates nominated under primaries had relevant experience, compared to only 43 percent of those nominated under the convention system. Although the difference is substantial, given the small number of observations it is not statistically significant. We also compare the four states to their neighbors – Illinois, Kentucky, Maryland, Massachusetts, Michigan, New Hampshire, New Jersey, Ohio, Pennsylvania, Rhode Island, and Vermont. We estimate a standard difference-in-differences regression model for the period 1948–1982 with *Relevant Experience* as the dependent variable and the following independent variables: state-specific fixed effects, year-specific fixed effects, and a variable, *Primary Election*, indicating whether the nominee was chosen by primary election or convention.[34] The estimated coefficient on *Primary Election* is small and not statistically significant.

For the second analysis, we examine three states – Indiana, Michigan, and South Dakota – that use conventions to nominate candidates for statewide down-ballot offices, but use primary elections for governor and US senator. We again compare these states with their neighbors, in this case Illinois, Iowa, Kentucky, Minnesota, Montana, Nebraska, North Dakota, Ohio, Wisconsin, and Wyoming. A simple comparison of the nominees for open-seat races for state auditor and treasurer shows no substantively meaningful or statistically significant differences: 44 percent of those nominated by convention had relevant experience, compared to 42 percent of those nominated in primary elections. We can also compare these states using a difference-in-differences analysis (exploiting the fact that, except for Indiana before 1976, all of the states used primaries to nominate candidates for governor and US senator). More specifically, we estimate a model with *Relevant Experience* as the dependent variable and with the following independent variables: state-specific fixed-effects, year-specific fixed-effects, indicator variables for each office (auditor, treasurer, governor, US senator), and a variable, *Primary Election*, indicating whether the nominee was chosen by primary election or convention. The estimated coefficient on *Primary Election* is close to zero and not statistically significant.

---

[33] For Connecticut we include elections in 1946 and 1948.

[34] We chose this window 1948–1982 because it gives each of the four states that changed nomination systems at least eight years of observations under each system.

Finally, we examine cases where the parties nominated their candidate for the US House by a convention, caucus or party committee (for simplicity we use the term "convention" to refer to all the methods other than primaries). There are five situations in our sample from 1950 to 2016 where this occurs: (1) states that adopted primaries after 1950, that is, Connecticut and Delaware; (2) in the 1950s and 1960s the Republican Party in states such as Alabama, Georgia, Mississippi, South Carolina, and Texas did not garner enough support statewide to be required to use primaries; (3) in Virginia the primary is optional and congressional district committees choose whether to nominate candidates through primaries or conventions; (4) in several states, for example, New York, Pennsylvania, Kentucky, and Indiana, conventions, caucuses, or party committees are generally used to nominate candidates for special elections; and (5) to select replacements for nominees chosen in primaries who withdrew before the general election. For all states that had at least one congressional candidate not nominated by a primary, we can compare the relevant experience of those nominated by primaries to those nominated by the other methods. We focus on open-seat races.

Overall, primaries are 3.8 percentage points more likely to nominate a US House candidate with relevant experience than the alternative methods, a modest difference. We also have enough observations and enough variation in the partisanship of districts to also compare districts expected to have uncompetitive general elections with those that are expected to have competitive general elections, under both the primary and the convention systems. In uncompetitive districts, the percentage of advantaged-party nominees with relevant experience is 16.5 percentage points higher under primaries compared to alternative nomination mechanisms. In competitive districts the difference is 4.1 percentage points. A simple difference-in-differences estimate, which is shown in Table 8.2, provides evidence that primaries in uncompetitive districts are more likely to nominate candidates with relevant experience than conventions, even relative to the difference in the competitive districts. We can also run a regression analysis that includes state-specific and year-specific fixed effects, as well as a variable indicating whether the nominee is chosen by primary or convention. The point estimate on the primary election indicator variable is even larger than the difference shown in Table 8.2 and statistically significant. Thus, the evidence from the US House is consistent with patterns we observed in the pre-1950 period: primaries are more effective at selecting nominees with relevant experience in uncompetitive districts. Combined with the two previous

TABLE 8.2 *Relevant Experience of Nominees Under Primaries versus Conventions, US House Open-Seat Races, 1950 to 2016*

	Advantaged Party in Uncompetitive District	Competitive District	Difference
Primaries	50.9%	20.4%	30.5%
	[527]	[5496]	
Conventions	34.3%	16.3%	18.0%
	[67]	[306]	
Difference-in-Differences			12.5%

Cell entries give the percentage of candidates with prior legislative experience. Number of observations in brackets.

analyses, the evidence suggests that conventions would not lead to significantly more qualified nominees than primaries.

8.5 CONCLUSION

Despite the significant changes in the electoral environment highlighted in Chapter 7, primaries in the post-1950 period continue to contribute to the election of qualified candidates, especially in uncompetitive constituencies. However, the discussion in Chapter 7 suggests that the growth of constituencies with competitive general elections, the incumbency advantage, and partisan polarization may magnify the importance of primaries in competitive areas. The significant drop in the entry and nomination of qualified candidates to challenge incumbents implies that the outcomes of open-seat primaries in competitive areas are even more consequential than before. The bottom line results regarding the qualifications of officials elected in open-seat races provide some assurance that the differences between competitive and uncompetitive constituencies are not particularly substantial.

8.6 APPENDIX

The Illinois State Bar Association webpage gives the following description of how the advisory polls work:[35]

---

[35] This information is from www.isba.org/judicialevaluations/howitworks.

In counties outside of Cook, ISBA conducts an advisory poll. The poll is conducted by mail and is sent to all ISBA members in the circuit or district from which a candidate seeks election or a judge seeks retention. Licensed attorneys who are not members of ISBA, or any attorney outside the circuit or district may request a ballot. Participants of the poll are asked to evaluate each candidate only if they have professional knowledge of the candidate(s) that enables them to make an informed evaluation. Ballots are confidential and returned inside a ballot envelope which is mailed in a Teller envelope. A certification slip stating that the participant read and understood the instructions of the poll is signed in order for the ballot to be counted. Candidates and judges are rated "recommended" or "not recommended" based on whether respondents agree that the candidate "meets acceptable requirements for the office". Those receiving 65 percent or more "yes" responses to that question are rated "recommended" and those receiving less than 65 percent are rated "not recommended." Opinions expressed in the poll are of those attorneys who chose to respond and do not reflect the opinion of the Illinois State Bar Association or the opinion of all Illinois attorneys.

For open-seat elections, the following questions are asked on the poll.

- Considering the qualifications of the candidate, do you believe this candidate meets acceptable requirements for the office?
- Adheres to the high standards of integrity and ethical conduct required of the office?
- Acts and rules impartially and free of any predisposition or improper influence?
- Has adequate legal experience, knowledge, and ability?
- Exercises appropriate temperament with courtesy, consideration, firmness, fairness, patience and dignity?
- Attends to all professional responsibilities including the management of cases/clients, and completes work in a prompt and skillful manner?
- Has the physical, mental and emotional health, stamina and stability needed to perform judicial duties?
- Conducts self and deals with others appropriately to reduce or eliminate conduct or words which manifest bias based on race, gender, national origin, religion, disability, age, sexual orientation or socio-economic status against parties, witnesses, counsel or others?

9

Voting Behavior and Primary Elections, 1950 to 2016

More than a century after the introduction of the direct primary, skeptics of the system continue to raise concerns about voter behavior – in particular, low turnout and low voter information. Political participation in general has been declining in the last few decades, and there is little evidence that voters are more informed about politics today than they were in the past, despite the technological changes in the media and campaign communications.

As we showed in the analysis of the early period, these concerns, at least in the first few decades after primaries were adopted, did not turn out to be as deeply problematic as initial skeptics had feared. Turnout was relatively high in the advantaged-party cases where primaries theoretically have the most to contribute. Moreover, a significant portion of those who voted appeared to vote as if they were informed about the qualifications and policy positions of the primary election candidates.

In this chapter we examine voter behavior after primaries had been in use for decades and had become an established part of the electoral system. Are voters in advantaged-party primaries continuing to turn out at relatively high rates compared to voters who support the advantaged party in the general election? Are primary voters still supporting qualified candidates and candidates with shared issue or ideological positions?

For the modern period, we can draw on additional measures due to data availability, as well as institutional variation produced by reformers' attempts to improve the primary system, to investigate voter behavior in more detail than we could for the earlier period. For example, in some cases we have expert evaluations of candidates' qualifications, which incorporate more information than simply a resumé of previous offices. We can also investigate more directly the trade-off between qualifications and partisanship/ideology by exploiting variation in the information available to voters on the primary election ballot when candidates are allowed to compete in more than one primary (that is, under cross-filing). With modern survey data we are also able to study voters at the individual level, or at higher frequencies. This allows us to examine questions such as: are voters actually learning about the candidates over the course of the campaign?

9.1 PRIMARY ELECTION TURNOUT

Similar to the analysis for the early period, we study turnout using a dataset of election returns for statewide and US House races. For each party, office, and year, we measure relative turnout in primaries, which we refer to simply as relative turnout, as the total votes cast for all candidates competing in the given party's primary for a specific office and year, divided by the votes cast for that party's nominee in the general election. We focus on the period 1950 to 2016.[1]

Table 9.1 presents the median relative turnout for the different types of offices and races; for all available cases it is 40.4 percent. In the advantaged-party primaries, median relative turnout is still rather low,

TABLE 9.1 *Relative Turnout in US Primaries, 1950–2016*

	All Offices	Governor & US Senate	Statewide Down-Ballot	US House
All Races	40.4%	43.5%	42.9%	39.2%
	[26135]	[3227]	[5642]	[17266]
Advantaged Party	48.1%	75.1%	73.0%	42.7%
	[5686]	[549]	[1042]	[4095]
Contested Primary	57.4%	81.1%	84.6%	49.5%
in Advantaged Party	[3455]	[480]	[723]	[2252]
Competitive Primary	69.4%	101.4%	86.9%	56.1%
in Advantaged Party	[1233]	[215]	[422]	[596]
Parties Balanced	40.1%	41.5%	40.1%	39.8%
	[15390]	[2277]	[4052]	[9061]

Cell entries are medians. Number of cases in square brackets.

---

[1] In Chapter 6 we discussed some of the challenges associated with measuring primary election turnout and some of the alternative measures scholars have proposed.

48.1 percent, which is substantially lower than the turnout for these types of races in the pre-1950 period.[2] This in part reflects the low turnout in advantaged-party primaries that are incumbent-contested, which is only 45.7 percent. When the advantaged-party primary is competitive, that is, the winner receives less than 57.5 percent of the total primary vote, and the general election is contested, the median relative turnout rises to 69.4 percent. Relative turnout levels in primaries in parties-balanced and disadvantaged-party primaries are noticeably lower, 40.1 and 30.7 percent, respectively. The low turnout levels for disadvantaged-party primaries are perhaps not too surprising, as they are often uncompetitive and the nominees rarely win the general election.

Overall, relative turnout is substantially lower in the modern era compared to the early period.[3] Similar to the pre-1950 period, however, relative turnout varies by office. For governor and US Senate races, median relative turnout in advantaged-party primaries has declined by over 30 percentage points, but the size of the primary electorate is still about three-quarters as large as the party's general election support. When the primary is competitive, there is a negligible difference between a party's primary turnout and general election support. Somewhat surprisingly, the relative roll-off between top-of-the-ticket and statewide down-ballot offices is not particularly large.

The most striking decline in relative turnout appears in advantaged-party primaries for the US House. Even in competitive primaries for advantaged parties, relative turnout after 1950 is only about half that of the pre-1950 period. Surprisingly, relative turnout for US House primaries is still low even when the top-of-the-ticket races are competitive.

What does the low primary turnout for the US House mean for the impact of primaries? As discussed in Chapter 6, the early skeptics of primaries were often concerned that the small primary electorates could be captured by narrow interests or political elites, who place less value on qualifications or who have different issue preferences than the typical partisan. However, the findings in Chapter 8 suggest that primaries for open-seat US House races continue to facilitate the election of qualified candidates in advantaged-party constituencies,

---

[2] We use the median because the distribution of turnout is highly skewed.

[3] Primary turnout has been declining since the 1970s. We examine the variation in turnout with respect to partisan polarization in Chapter 11. This decline may in part reflect the growing general election support for the Republican Party in the South, while the Southern Republican primaries continue to attract relatively few voters.

and that they are more successful at producing qualified nominees in these areas compared to conventions, caucuses, or party elite meetings. Perhaps this is not surprising, since the size of the electorate does not necessarily indicate whether the electorate is more or less informed. From a voter information perspective, small primary electorates are likely to contain a larger percentage of strong partisans, who tend to be more informed than average in surveys such as the *American National Election Studies*.

In recent years, political observers have been more vocal in their concerns that low turnout in US House primaries is contributing to partisan polarization. The small primary electorates are perceived to have issue and ideological preferences that do not reflect the preferences of the median voter in the electorate as a whole or even among partisans. We will return to this connection between primary turnout and partisan polarization in Chapter 11.

9.2 PRIMARY VOTING AND CANDIDATE QUALIFICATIONS

In the next two sections, we examine whether a sufficient number of primary voters appear to be voting as if they are informed about the candidates. As we discussed in Chapter 6, the electorate as a whole does not have to vote in an informed manner in order for the election outcome to reflect the preferences of those who *are* informed. In that chapter we provided evidence that the primary electorate was more likely to support more qualified candidates, and to vote for candidates who shared their positions on salient issues that divided the parties internally.

We begin by asking the same question we asked about voters in the early period: when faced with the choice between a more qualified and a less-qualified primary candidate, do primary voters tend to support the more qualified candidate? Because of data availability for the modern period, we are able to exploit more measures of candidate qualifications, which are based on more comprehensive assessments than those available for the early period. More specifically, we focus on the three measures discussed in the previous chapter: relevant experience, judicial evaluations, and newspaper endorsements. If the relationship between voting and qualifications is consistent across these three measures, then that will provide some additional assurance that primary voters are assessing candidates' relative qualifications.

TABLE 9.2 *Voting and Relevant Experience in Two-Candidate Primaries, 1950 to 2016*

Office	Primaries	Experienced Candidate's:	
		Win %	Vote %
US House	All	92.3%	75.5%
		[3079]	[3068]
	Non-Incumbent	79.0%	63.0%
		[619]	[617]
Governor & US Senate	All	88.8%	73.4%
		[616]	[616]
	Non-Incumbent	79.2%	65.5%
		[264]	[264]
Auditor & Treasurer	All	76.7%	60.4%
		[236]	[235]
	Non-Incumbent	66.4%	54.7%
		[137]	[137]

Number of observations in square brackets.

9.2.1 Relevant Prior Experience

In the previous chapters, we argued that experience in positions that required the candidate to perform tasks similar to the ones conducted in the office being sought provide the candidate with some qualification for the office. Voters, at least in the decades immediately following the adoption of primaries, were more likely to support candidates with such relevant experience over those without it. First, we examine the least complicated cases: two candidates competing in a primary, only one of whom has relevant experience. Table 9.2 presents the results. There are three panels, for different offices – US House, governor, and US Senate, and state auditor and state treasurer. Each panel has two rows. The top row presents the results for all primaries, and the bottom row presents the results for non-incumbent primaries. The results in the table show that when primary voters are given the simple choice between candidates with or without relevant experience, they are more likely to support the experienced candidate. The third column of the table displays the percentage of races that the experienced candidate wins. The fourth column displays the average vote share of the experienced candidate.

When we examine all races, including incumbent-contested races, the candidate with relevant experience is nominated in close to 90 percent of the primaries for governor, US Senate, and US House, and more than three-quarters of the primaries for state auditor and treasurer. The experienced candidates' average vote share percentages are also quite high, especially in gubernatorial, US Senate, and US House primaries. Primary electorates are clearly favoring candidates with relevant experience. Candidates with relevant experience running in US House, US Senate, and gubernatorial primaries have even more electoral success in the post-1950 period than in the earlier period. Support for state auditors and treasurers is similar in the two periods. These patterns may reflect the growing incumbency advantage in primary elections that is due to factors other than voters' attention to candidate qualifications.

Electoral support for the candidate with relevant experience is slightly lower in non-incumbent primaries. The win percentage for candidates with relevant experience declines close to 10 percentage points for each of the offices; experienced candidates for governor, US Senate, and US House still win close to 80 percent of the primaries, and experienced candidates win almost two-thirds of the state auditor and treasurer primaries. The primary races for governor, US Senate, and US House also remained uncompetitive on average in terms of vote shares, and experienced state auditors and treasurers had average vote shares close to 55 percent. Even in these non-incumbent primaries, the win and vote percentages for the US House, governor, and US Senate are higher in the modern period than in the pre-1950 period. Thus, some of the decline in primary competition after 1950 discussed earlier could be a result of voters focusing more on relevant experience than they did in the earlier period.

While Table 9.2 provides some evidence that is consistent with voters favoring candidates with relevant prior experience, the patterns are also consistent with other explanations – for example, that congressional candidates with state legislative experience are better at campaigning. To examine whether primary voters are voting for candidates with *relevant* prior experience, rather than simply selecting those with *any* prior office-holding experience, we focused on the nuanced differences in the relevance of various prior experience for the office being sought. In the early period voters appeared to be distinguishing between candidates' relevant and less-relevant experience in primaries for statewide office. If relevant experience is a qualification for office that voters favor, then we would expect to observe a stronger relationship between this variable

TABLE 9.3 *Voting and Candidate Experience in Primaries, 1950 to 2016*

Office	Depend. Variable	Current Incumb.	Relevant Exper.	Less-Rel. Exper.	p-value for (1)–(3)	(2)–(3)	Obs.
US House	Win %	92.6	42.2				25535
		(0.9)	(2.0)				
	Vote %	55.7	24.3				25458
		(0.6)	(0.8)				
Governor &	Win %	86.3	40.9	23.4	0.00	0.00	6950
US Senate		(2.3)	(2.8)	(3.0)			
	Vote %	54.7	27.7	18.0	0.00	0.00	6950
		(1.2)	(1.2)	(1.3)			
Auditor &	Win %	76.9	27.6	18.4	0.00	0.27	1882
Treasurer		(6.5)	(6.0)	(6.1)			
	Vote %	33.6	8.7	8.8	0.00	0.98	1875
		(2.7)	(1.8)	(1.8)			

The columns labelled Current Incumb. (1), Relevant Exper. (2), and Less-Rel. Exper. (3) contain OLS regression estimates. The column labeled p-value for (1)–(3) gives the p-value of the F-test for the hypothesis that the coefficients on Current Incumbency are equal when candidates share similar positions versus when they do not. The column labeled p-value for (2)–(3) gives the p-value of the F-test for the hypothesis that the coefficients on Relevant Experience are equal when candidates share similar positions versus when they do not.

and winning or vote shares in the primary. For the modern era, we run the same regression of primary win or vote share on prior relevant experience and prior less-relevant experience as we did for the early period. We include primary races with two to five candidates. To account for the different numbers of candidates and other race-specific factors, we include race-specific fixed effects and cluster the standard errors by race. The relevant (less-relevant) experience variable is the candidate's share of total relevant (less-relevant) experience summed across all candidates in the primary. See Chapter 6 for more details about the specification and measures.

The coefficient estimates in Table 9.3 show that both incumbency and non-incumbent-relevant experience have a significant effect on the probability of winning and vote share in the primaries. The coefficient on incumbency is much larger than the coefficient on non-incumbency relevant experience. This may reflect a number of different factors, such as measurement error in relevant experience, incumbency being a more significant qualification, or incumbency providing non-qualification-related electoral benefits. For governor and

US Senate races, the coefficient on less-relevant experience is even smaller than the one on relevant experience. This difference is large in magnitude, over 15 percentage points for the probability of winning and close to 10 percentage points for vote share, and statistically significant. For state auditor and treasurer, the differences in the coefficient estimates on relevant and less-relevant experience are not statistically significant, and for vote percentage the size of the difference is negligible. These patterns may reflect changes in the types of experience that voters consider relevant for state auditors and treasurers in the modern period. For example, with the growth of state bureaucracies, management experience may be more relevant for these offices, or the professionalization of legislatures and the specialization of committees may make certain legislative experience more relevant.

Additional evidence that voters favor candidates with relevant experience is that voters appear to offer even more support for these candidates when this information is readily available. As discussed in Chapter 6, the win and vote shares of qualified candidates will be lower when a larger share of the electorate is uninformed when they vote. Thus, we might expect these percentages to be higher in races where voters have information about the candidates' experience. This is the case in California, where occupations are listed on the ballot, giving California primary voters easy access to certain information about the candidates' relevant experience. In non-incumbent two-candidate US House primary races in which only one candidate has relevant experience, the candidate with relevant experience on average wins 87.0 percent of the races and has an average vote share of 70.3 percent.[4] These averages are higher than the win and vote percentages for non-incumbent two-candidate primaries across all states presented in Table 9.2. Thus, California primary voters are even more likely to nominate US House candidates with prior state legislative experience than are voters in other states.[5] The importance of these ballot designations to inform voters about relevant experience is evident in the numerous court cases challenging the designations. Candidates have been ordered to change their ballot designations to prevent them from listing occupations that could appear

---

[4] This is based on 23 California House races between 1950 and 2016.

[5] One concern about interpreting these patterns is that they may simply be reflecting the high level of professionalization of the California state legislature rather than the ballot designations. However, the pattern of primary voting behavior in California stands out even among the most professionalized state legislatures.

to indicate relevant prior experience when the candidates did not have such experience.

Another consideration is the number of candidates. Voters face a more difficult task when there are many candidates on the ballot, since in principle they must collect information about all of them in order to assess which candidate is best for them. If voters collect only partial information, then there might be a higher probability of "mistakes." In fact, at least when the numbers of candidates is not too large and when we focus on candidate qualifications, this does not appear to be the case. Consider for example, races for US House, US Senate, or governor in which there are two, four, or six candidates and exactly half of those running have relevant experience and half do not. In these cases, the percentage of winners with relevant experience is 76 percent when there are two candidates, 75 percent when there are four, and 75 percent when there are six. When there are three candidates and only one has relevant experience, then the probability that the winner has relevant experience is 60 percent; and when there are six candidates and only two have relevant experience, then the corresponding probability is 65 percent. Finally, when there are three candidates and two have relevant experience, then the probability that the winner has relevant experience is 85 percent; and when are six candidates and four have relevant experience, then the corresponding probability is 80 percent. Thus, holding fixed the fraction of candidates who have relevant experience – and thus holding fixed the probability that random voting would lead to an experienced nominee – the probability that voters choose an experienced nominee does not fall consistently as the number of candidates increases.

9.2.2 Bar Association Evaluations

The judicial evaluations introduced in Chapter 8 provide an additional measure of candidate qualifications that involves expert evaluations of candidates' expected performance as Illinois circuit and appellate court judges. Table 9.4 displays the win and vote percentages of qualified versus unqualified judges. It shows that in two-candidate races in which one candidate is evaluated to be qualified and the other is not, the qualified candidate is about four times more likely to be nominated and is expected to have a 20-percentage-point higher vote share compared to the unqualified candidate.

For races with three to five candidates, we can examine the win and vote percentages of qualified and unqualified candidates at both the race and candidate levels. The race level, that is, summing the vote and

TABLE 9.4 *Voting and Candidate Valence in IL Judicial Primaries,*
1986 to 2010

	Win %		Vote %	
	Qualified Candidate	Unqualified Candidate	Qualified Candidates	Unqualified Candidates
2 Candidate Races	82.3%	17.7%	59.6%	40.4%
	[96]	[96]	[96]	[96]
3–5 Candidate Races, Totals	82.6%	16.7%	64.0%	36.0%
	[132]	[132]	[132]	[132]
3–5 Candidate Races, Per Candidate	38.9%	10.3%	30.2%	22.2%
	[280]	[214]	[280]	[214]

Number of observations in square brackets.

nomination outcomes for all qualified and unqualified candidates, shows win and vote percentages that are very similar to the two-candidate races. For example, the probability that the winner is a qualified candidate is 82.6. However, this may reflect something about the composition of the candidate pool – that is, there may simply be more-qualified candidates seeking the office. At the candidate level, we still see that qualified candidates are much more likely to win the nomination, and have a higher expected vote share than unqualified candidates. This suggests that primary voters, even for offices that are very low on the ballot, cast ballots "as if" they knew about the candidates' relative qualifications.

9.2.3 Newspaper Endorsements

Newspaper endorsements in primaries are the third measure of candidate qualifications introduced in Chapter 8. As discussed there, these endorsements are based on a relatively comprehensive assessment of candidates' qualifications. They are therefore similar to the judicial evaluations studied in the previous section, but are available for a much wider range of offices. They are particularly useful for analyzing voting behavior, since they provide an assessment of the candidates' qualifications relative to one another. Thus, even if two candidates have relevant experience by our definition, typically only one receives a newspaper endorsement.

We focus on races where we have endorsements from at least two newspapers. If we have endorsements from several newspapers for the same race, and one candidate receives most or all of these endorsements, then we can be relatively certain that this candidate is more qualified for the office than his or her competitors. It is less clear what newspaper endorsements mean when they are split relatively evenly across two or

TABLE 9.5 *Primary Outcomes and Endorsements,*
1990 to 2014

Definition of Highly Endorsed Candidate	2 Cands in Primary	3+ Cands in Primary
At Least 3 Endorsements and 75% of Total	86.7% [120]	68.3% [164]
At Least 2 Endorsements and 75% of Total	80.4% [250]	64.2% [285]
At Least 3 Endorsements and 67% of Total	84.5% [129]	65.9% [182]
At Least 2 Endorsements and 67% of Total	78.8% [269]	60.2% [344]

Cell entries give the percentage of highly endorsed candidates who won primaries. Number of observations in brackets.

more candidates. If a candidate receives multiple endorsements, then he or she is likely to be relatively qualified, even if another candidate also received one or more endorsements. We are not as certain that this is the case when a candidate receives just one endorsement, since, for example, even relatively weak candidates might sometimes be endorsed by their "hometown" newspaper. Thus, we consider candidates to be "highly endorsed" when they receive a large share of multiple newspaper endorsements.

Table 9.5 shows the results of our analysis of how often "highly endorsed" candidates, compared to other candidates, win in non-incumbent primary elections for statewide office – including governor, US Senate, and major statewide down-ballot offices – or the US House during the period 1990 to 2014 for which we have two or more endorsements. The table is divided into several panels, in which we vary the definition of a "highly endorsed" candidate (rows) and consider primaries with different numbers of candidates (columns). For example, in the top panel, a candidate is classified as highly endorsed if and only if he or she received at least three endorsements and also received at least three-quarters of the total number of endorsements in our sample. The first column shows the results for races with exactly two candidates, and the second column covers races with three or more candidates.

First consider the two-candidate contests. If endorsements do not influence voters' choices, and the primary electorate simply nominates candidates based on a "coin flip," then the highly endorsed candidates should be winning primaries about 50 percent of the time. However, Table 9.5 shows that highly endorsed candidates win the primary over 80 percent of the time, and that this advantage is not sensitive to the different definitions of highly endorsed.

Next, consider the races with three or more candidates. In our sample, the multi-candidate races involve an average of slightly more than four candidates, so if voting were random then we would expect each candidate to win about 25 percent of the time.[6] However, the table shows that the highly endorsed candidate wins more than 60 percent of these races. The lower percentage compared to two-candidate races may reflect voter confusion when there are more than two candidates, or perhaps the presence of other factors that lead to the entry of more candidates. Nonetheless, the percentage of highly endorsed candidates winning primaries is much higher than what we would expect under random voting.

We do not present results comparing advantaged-party, disadvantaged-party, and parties-balanced primaries using the endorsements measure of qualification, but the differences are small and statistically insignificant. More precisely, the probability that the winner in a given party's primary is a highly endorsed candidate is approximately the same in constituencies that are safe for that party and those that are not safe. The reason, most likely, is that endorsements only provide a measure of the relative qualification conditional on the candidates who run, because newspapers almost always endorse only one candidate.[7] For example, advantaged-party primaries probably involve two highly qualified candidates, where one candidate is only slightly more qualified than the other, much more often than disadvantaged-party primaries. In such cases, newspapers may endorse the slightly better candidate, but voters might sometimes choose the other one.[8]

However, the bottom line from Table 9.5 is clear. Assuming that the highly endorsed candidates are more qualified than their competitors, the results show that the winners of non-incumbent primaries are much more likely to be highly qualified winners than "random draws" from

---

[6] The average of the inverse of the number of candidates is also about 1/4.

[7] Occasionally, a newspaper will decline to make an endorsement or will endorse multiple candidates, but such cases are rare.

[8] By contrast, we might expect to see cases involving a clearly qualified candidate and a clearly unqualified candidate more often in disadvantaged-party primaries. And these are the "easy" cases, in which newspaper endorsements and voters are most likely to agree on which candidate is more qualified.

the parties' pools. Of course the newspaper endorsements themselves may be affecting voting behavior in primaries, but that does not affect our conclusions as long as these endorsements themselves reflect actual differences in candidates' qualifications.

9.3 PRIMARY VOTING AND CANDIDATE POLICY POSITIONS

Although we have focused on voting behavior with respect to candidate qualifications, we are also interested in other types of information voters appear to be using more generally when voting in primaries. In this section, we examine whether primary voters in the modern period differentiate between candidates based on their issue or ideological positions. If primary voters behave as if they are informed about candidates' policy positions and ideology, then this will also give us more confidence in our finding that they appear to differentiate between more-qualified and less-qualified candidates.

We begin with a study that parallels the analyses above regarding primary voting and candidates' positions on Prohibition and progressivism in the early period. We use voting data aggregated at the municipal level to examine the correlation between the geographic distribution of preferences on regulating abortion and electoral support for candidates with "pro-choice" versus "pro-life" positions running in the advantaged party's primaries. We then move to a study that exploits the survey data available in the modern period that allows us to track the correlations between voters' ideological positions and their intention to support candidates with similar positions in primary campaigns.

9.3.1 Issue Voting: Abortion

By the end of the twentieth century, positions on the abortion issue divided along partisan lines – "pro-choice" Democrats and "pro-life" Republicans. However, a few decades earlier both parties were more internally divided on this issue. We examine whether areas that voted for "pro-choice" ("pro-life") policies in a referendum tended to support "pro-choice" ("pro-life") candidates in the primary. We examine how the aggregate municipal-level votes on a Massachusetts constitutional amendment to allow the state legislature the right to prohibit or regulate abortions is correlated with the votes cast for primary candidates for

TABLE 9.6 *Voting in Democratic Primaries and the Abortion Issue in Massachusetts, 1974 to 1984*

Year	Office	Pro-Choice	Pro-Life	Correlation
1974	Governor	Dukakis	Quinn	0.59
1976	Senate	Kennedy*	Dinsmore, Langone	0.21
1978	Governor	Dukakis*, Ackermann	King	0.64
1982	Governor	Dukakis*	King	0.69
1984	Senate	Kerry, Shannon	Bartley, Connolly	0.33
Average Correlation				0.49

An asterisk indicates that the candidate was an incumbent.

governor or US Senate with "pro-life" or "pro-choice" positions.[9] The ballot proposition vote was held on November 4, 1986. As in the analysis from the earlier period, we focus on the advantaged-party primary, which in Massachusetts during this period is the Democratic primary. Since the ballot proposition data only contains the total vote for and against the amendment and is not separated by voter partisanship, the advantaged party provides greater overlap between the types of voters included in the proposition data and the types included in the primary data.[10]

The results in Table 9.6 show a clear positive correlation between the "pro-choice" vote on the amendment and the vote for "pro-choice" candidates in the primary. The positive correlation is consistent with a segment of the primary electorate voting "as if" they are informed about the candidates' issue positions. The average correlation is not as strong as the findings in Chapter 6 regarding voting in primaries over

[9] The amendment was summarized as: "The proposed constitutional amendment would allow the legislature to prohibit or regulate abortions to the extent permitted by the United States Constitution. It would also provide that the state constitution does not require public or private funding of abortions, or the provision of services or facilities for performing abortions, beyond what is required by the United States Constitution. The provisions of this amendment would not apply to abortions required to prevent the death of the mother." (From Massachusetts Secretary of State's webpage: http://electionstats. state.ma.us/ballot_questions/view/5508/.)

[10] We drop races where the "pro-life" or "pro-choice" candidates received less than 20 percent of the vote. In all of the Democratic primaries for governor and US senator between 1986 and 1996, either the primary was not contested, or the candidates did not clearly take opposing positions on the abortion issue. In the 1998 gubernatorial primary, Brian J. Donnelly had a more "pro-life" record compared to his opponents. Even though he received less than 20 percent of the vote, the correlation is still 0.40.

Prohibition and progressive policy positions.[11] Of course, other issues were also salient in Massachusetts during the period under investigation, such as desegregation busing.

9.3.2 Voter Learning About Ideology

The analyses above suggest that an influential portion of the primary electorate vote as if they are informed about the candidates. These findings suggest that voters learn about the candidates before the elections. In a previous article with Gabriel Lenz and Maksim Pinkovskiy, we exploit variation over time within a campaign to examine whether voter knowledge appears to be growing. More specifically we study whether voters are increasingly likely to support primary candidates who share their ideological positions. We use responses to surveys conducted at different dates during the months leading up to the primary election. Here we summarize the hypotheses, research design, and key findings from the article, and tie these findings to the main argument of this chapter.[12]

The following example illustrates our approach. In the 2006 Florida Republican primary, the state attorney general, Charlie Crist, and the state chief financial officer, Tom Gallagher, competed to replace the term-limited governor, Jeb Bush.[13] Crist was considered more moderate, with a wide base of support, while Gallagher was evidently perceived as more socially conservative.[14] In the three months prior to the election Survey USA (hereafter, SUSA) released polls of likely Republican primary voters at four different points in time (June 12, July 11, August 24, and August 31). In the first poll Crist had more support among ideological conservative respondents than among moderate respondents (54 to 49 percent) and the opposite was the case for Gallagher (18 to 28 percent). These gaps narrowed in July and reversed for both candidates by August. In the last poll Crist had less support among conservatives than among

---

[11] The average correlation might overstate the underlying relationship if the gubernatorial voting patterns reflect something particular about the support for Dukakis that is not related to his position on abortion.

[12] See Hirano et al. (2015) for more details about the data, measurement, and analysis as well as some additional tests.

[13] Gallagher was the first person to hold this office, which combined the responsibilities of state treasurer and comptroller. Two additional candidates were also on the primary ballot but they received less than 2 percent of the vote.

[14] Gallagher was much more active in courting the socially conservative wing of the party. He was endorsed by the Florida Right to Life PAC and the head of the Florida Family Policy Council, and supported by the founder of Focus on the Family.

moderates (52 to 71 percent) and the opposite was the case for Gallagher (42 to 20 percent). Thus, in relative terms, over the course of the primary campaign conservative respondents shifted toward Gallagher while moderates shifted toward Crist.

We want to know whether similar patterns hold more generally. To conduct this analysis we must first identify a number of contested primary elections in which there is a clear ideological difference between the candidates. We do this for gubernatorial and US Senate primaries for which we have at least one poll conducted "early" in the campaign and at least one taken "late" in the campaign. For each race, we classify candidates as relatively liberal or conservative using information from newspaper articles and interest group endorsements.[15] In most of the races, this distinction is relatively clear; we use races with no distinction in placebo tests. In races with more than two candidates, we focus on the two with the largest ideological differences who are also among the top three vote-getters.

The other key pieces of information we need for our analysis are the ideological position of the survey respondents and their vote intentions. We gathered this information from two types of surveys. First, we use data from the California/Field Poll for Democratic and Republican primaries in California between 1966 and 2006. Second, we use data from SUSA. We use the publicly available summary information for primary elections available since 2005. The publicly available data consists of cross-tabulations of ideology and voter preferences across the candidates. The sample frame is likely voters. For each race, we have Field Poll or SUSA responses that were taken early in the primary campaign as well as survey responses taken toward the end of the campaign. If the electorate is learning about the candidates during the campaign, then we would expect the correlation between the ideological positions of voters and the candidates they support to be stronger in the late surveys compared to the early surveys. We focus on non-incumbent races. Incumbent-contested races are typically not competitive enough to motivate the collection of individual-level polling data. Moreover, in these cases we might not expect much learning to occur, at least about the incumbent.

---

[15] Each candidate is given a score based on their policy positions and statements made in various media outlets that was independently coded by multiple students. See Hirano et al. (2015) for more details.

To test whether voters appear to be learning about the candidates' ideological positions, we use the following simple model. Consider a primary election with only two candidates: one who is more conservative and one who is more liberal. Also suppose that there are only two types of voters in the primary electorate: relatively conservative and relatively liberal. Finally, assume that two polls were taken during the primary: an early poll ($t = 0$) and a late poll ($t = 1$). Let L_{it} be the indicator for the late poll ($t = 1$). Let V_{it} be the preference of respondent i at time t, with $V_{it} = 1$ if respondent i prefers the more conservative candidate and $V_{it} = 0$ if respondent i prefers the more liberal candidate. Let C_{it} be the respondent's ideology, with $C_{it} = 1$ if the respondent is relatively conservative and $C_{it} = 0$ if the respondent is relatively liberal. To determine the relative change in support for the conservative candidate among conservatives, we estimate the following regression model:

$$V_{it} = \alpha + \beta_C C_{it} + \beta_L L_{it} + \gamma\, C_{it} L_{it} + \epsilon_{it} \qquad (9.1)$$

Each coefficient has an intuitive interpretation. The intercept α is the fraction of liberal voters intending to vote for the conservative candidate in the early poll. The coefficient on ideology, β_C, is the amount by which the conservative voters' support for the conservative candidate in the early poll is greater than the liberal voters' support for this candidate. The coefficient on the late indicator, β_L, is the amount by which liberal voters increase their support for the conservative candidate between the early and the late polls. Finally, the interaction coefficient γ is the amount by which conservative voters increase their support for the conservative candidate over the course of the campaign *over and above* the amount by which liberal voters increase their support for the conservative candidate – as a shorthand we refer to this as the change in congruence.

Since we are mainly interested in whether voters acquire information during the primary campaign, we focus on our estimates of the change in congruence. Assuming that the only differential trends in support for the conservative candidate among conservatives and liberals arise from voter learning, the change in congruence also measures how much voters' voting intentions change because of information they learn during the campaign. If campaigns inform voters about candidates' positions and voters incorporate that information into their voting decisions, then we should observe an increase in congruence ($\gamma > 0$); that is, conservatives should increase their support for the conservative candidate over the course of the campaign more than liberals do for that same candidate.

TABLE 9.7 *Gubernatorial and Senate Races*

	Baseline	Placebo	Incumbents
Δ Voter-Cand. Ideological	0.100**	−0.036	0.022
Congruence (γ_{avg})	(0.021)	(0.034)	(0.044)
Observations	12099	4723	2894
Number of Primaries	28	9	5
p-value	3.39e-08	0.774	0.199

Notes: robust standard errors in parentheses; The p-value is for the test of the null hypothesis that all interaction coefficients are zero. The dependent variable is support for the conservative candidate. Δ Voter–Candidate Ideological Congruence is the average interaction coefficient, γ. This estimates the amount by which conservative voters increase their support for the conservative candidate over the course of the campaign over and above the amount by which liberal voters increase their support for the conservative candidate. ** p<0.01, * p<0.05

Across all open-seat races, the average estimate of the change in congruence is 0.10 and the point estimate is statistically significant. Conservatives increase their support for conservative candidates over the course of the campaign by an average of 10 percentage points more than liberals do. Thus by the end of the campaign, there is substantially more congruence between the ideological position of the voters and the candidates they support.

When we focus on the handful of cases for which we found little or no difference in the candidates' ideological positions, the average estimate of the change in congruence is -0.04 and not statistically significant. Similarly there appears to be little learning in the incumbent-contested cases.

In Hirano et al. (2015) we also present a number of additional results. First, we might also expect the increase in conservative voter support for conservative candidates to be small when a large number of conservative voters already supported the conservative candidate in the early survey – that is, when β_C is large. Figure 9.1 plots the change in congruence on the y-axis and the initial level of congruence on the x-axis for all the races in our sample. The figure illustrates the negative relationship between how much conservative voters moved their support toward the conservative primary candidate over the course of the campaign and the degree to which conservative voters were already supporting the conservative (less conservative) candidate at the beginning of the campaign.[16]

---

[16] We also examined whether the size of the ideological gap between the primary candidates also influenced the extent to which voters learned about the candidates'

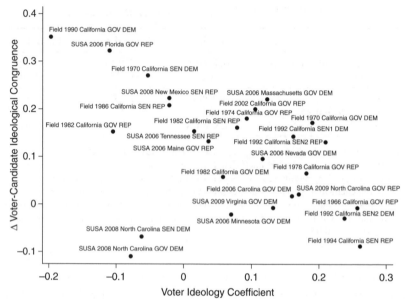

FIGURE 9.1 Scatterplot of Δ Voter-Candidate Ideological Congruence versus Ideology Coefficient in Early Poll

Second, we provide additional evidence from an internet panel survey of likely voters we conducted in Michigan, New Hampshire, and Pennsylvania during the 2012 gubernatorial and US Senate primaries in those states.[17] The panel analyses give us more confidence that respondents are learning, since we observe the same individuals during the primary campaign and then again shortly after the election. In addition to asking respondents about their ideological positions and vote intentions, we also asked them to give their assessment of the candidates' ideological positions. This provides an even more direct measure of voters' beliefs and how these beliefs changed over the course of the campaign. It also allows us to determine whether the respondents who learned about the candidates were more likely to adjust their vote

ideologies. The size of the ideological gap between candidates is positively correlated with the change in congruence. Thus, there appears to be more learning when there is a larger ideological difference between the candidates.

17 We studied the following races: Democratic and Republican primaries for governor in Michigan and Pennsylvania and Republican primaries for US Senate in New Hampshire. In the New Hampshire Republican primary for governor and the Pennsylvania Republican primary for US senator, the candidates' ideological positions were not particularly distinct, so we considered these to be placebo races.

intentions during the campaign. The results of the analysis confirm the findings from the Field and SUSA polls and provide additional evidence that the change in voter behavior is a result of what voters learned during the primary campaign.

9.3.3 The Role of Factions and Slates

As we discussed in Chapter 6, Key (1956) and others argued that factional politics would become more prevalent in elections after the introduction of primaries. Our examination of the pre-1950 period revealed several instances, most notably in Louisiana, Minnesota, North Dakota, and Wisconsin, where factional slating played a significant role in organizing support for particular candidates. It is plausible that this slating activity helped to reduce the informational hurdles facing primary election voters, similar to one of the roles party labels play in general elections.

In Chapter 6, we measured the strength of faction slating using the patterns in the county-level primary vote shares across major statewide offices (see Section 6.6.2 above for details, including the exact procedure used). Using this same measure we can examine whether factional divisions, similar to those we identified in the early period, also appeared during the post-1950 period.

Figure 9.2 shows our measure, which we call Average Correlation, for all years from 1903 to 2006. Higher values of Average Correlation indicate stronger factional slating. Evidently, aside from the continuing factional divisions in Louisiana and North Dakota that persisted into the mid-1950s, factional slating did not have a prolonged impact on primary election voting across states in the post-1950 period. Patterns resembling factional slating appear to have been short-lived, with the potential exception of the factional divisions within the New Mexico Democratic Party.[18] For the most part, the strong persistent factional organization that appeared in the electorate in the early period largely disappeared a few decades later.

We still do not know why factions no longer organize the primary electorate for statewide races in the modern era as they occasionally did in the early period. A number of factors could be contributing to this change, including the decline of one-party-dominant states, the rise of personalistic politics, changing demographics, and the increasing

---

[18] The Hispanic population may have formed a type of faction within the Democratic Party in New Mexico. See Hansen, Hirano, and Snyder (2016) for a discussion of this point.

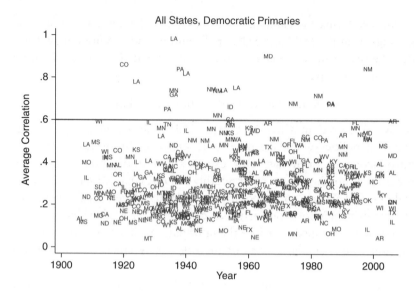

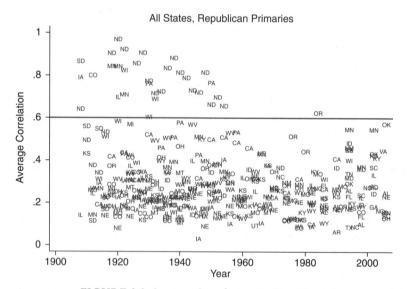

FIGURE 9.2 Average Correlations in Top Slates

role of the federal government. Of course, it is very possible that factions may continue to organize primary voting more locally, as one-party dominance remains prevalent in these areas. Also, the average correlations within the Republican primary electorates appear to be increasing slightly since the late 1970s, but they are still relatively low.

9.4 QUALIFICATIONS AND PARTY LABELS

The theoretical discussion in Chapter 6 highlighted the trade-off voters face when evaluating the valence characteristics of candidates (for example, qualifications) versus the partisan, issue, ideological, or factional differences between candidates. The simple prediction is that candidate attributes such as qualifications are less likely to influence electoral behavior when voters are facing choices between candidates from different parties or who have different positions on a highly salient issue, or where there is a clear factional division. Our analysis of voting behavior in the first half of the twentieth century provides evidence that voters, at least in the early period, were less likely to support candidates with relevant experience when there was a partisan, issue, or factional divide among the candidates.

Here we focus on what is likely the most salient cleavage, partisanship. We begin with a simple comparison of the effect of qualifications in primaries and general elections. This gives us a large number of cases and substantial variation in the partisan and ideological divisions across candidates. As noted in Chapter 6, these comparisons must be treated with caution due to potential selection bias problems – the candidates in the general election have been through the nomination "filter," while those in the primary election have not.

Thus, we include three additional analyses. The first compares the effect of qualifications in polarized versus less-polarized periods in both primary and general elections. The second examines the first round of the top-two system and compares the effect of qualifications on vote shares in races where all the candidates share the same party label with races where both Democratic and Republican candidates were on the ballot. The third exploits the change in cross-filing rules in California primaries in the 1950s to examine whether the introduction of party labels on the primary ballot affected the degree to which qualifications influenced voter support for cross-filing candidates. All of these involve comparisons of candidates at the same electoral stage. The second and third analyses have an additional advantage for drawing inferences about primaries, because they examine the effects of partisan and ideological differences at the nomination stage.

9.4.1 Qualifications in Primaries versus General Elections

Our first analysis compares the relationship between election outcomes and candidates' relevant experience in primaries versus general elections. Recall that for elections in the pre-1950 period, voters appear to have weighed qualifications for office, both incumbency and other relevant experience, more heavily in the primary compared to the general election. This is consistent with the simple predictions from our theoretical considerations.

Here we conduct an analogous analysis for the post-1950 period. That is we regress election outcomes on variables measuring incumbency status and non-incumbent-relevant experience. All of the variables are constructed in the same manner as in Section 6.7.1 of Chapter 6. We present separate coefficient estimates for three groups of offices: (i) US House; (ii) governor and US Senate; and (iii) state auditor and treasurer.

Table 9.8 presents the results. Across all three office groupings, the coefficient estimate on incumbency status in the primary is noticeably larger than in the general elections. In terms of winning, the coefficient estimate on incumbency for primaries is much larger than the coefficient estimate for general elections. For US House and governor and US Senate, incumbents are almost 50 percentage points more likely than non-incumbents without relevant experience to win their primary. In terms of vote shares, the coefficient estimates on incumbency are more than four times larger for primaries than for general elections. In US House and governor and US Senate primaries, the incumbent vote share is noticeably higher in the primary compared to the general election.

Overall, the patterns are similar for relevant experience. The coefficient estimates on relevant experience for primaries are large and statistically significant for winning and vote share across all three office categories, while the coefficient estimates for general elections are much smaller and not consistently statistically significant.[19] Interestingly, in percentage terms the differences between the coefficient estimates on non-incumbent-relevant experience in primaries versus general elections

---

[19] The coefficient estimates in Table 9.8 are, for the most part, larger than the corresponding coefficient estimates for the same variables and outcomes from the pre-1950 period. The difference is particularly noticeable for US House, governor, and US Senate primary races. Not surprisingly, the coefficient estimate on incumbency is significantly larger for general elections, which is consistent with the well-documented pattern discussed in Chapter 7.

TABLE 9.8 *Voting and Candidate Experience in Primary versus General Elections, 1950 to 2016*

Office	Depend. Variable	Primary Elections			General Elections		
		Current Incumb.	Relevant Exper.	Obs.	Current Incumb.	Relevant Exper.	Obs.
US House	Win %	47.1	22.9	5899	16.1	4.4	12057
		(0.4)	(1.3)		(0.9)	(1.0)	
	Vote %	28.6	13.1	5877	7.1	2.4	12040
		(0.3)	(0.5)		(0.2)	(0.2)	
Governor & US Senate	Win %	47.6	25.2	1066	23.9	3.2	1900
		(1.2)	(2.2)		(1.7)	(2.0)	
	Vote %	28.8	15.2	1066	6.7	1.5	1899
		(0.7)	(1.0)		(0.3)	(0.3)	
Auditor & Treasurer	Win %	41.9	14.7	479	12.5	-1.7	639
		(3.0)	(3.5)		(3.9)	(3.8)	
	Vote %	17.8	4.4	476	4.3	0.4	639
		(1.3)	(1.0)		(0.5)	(0.5)	

The columns labelled Current Incumb. and Relevant Exper. contain OLS regression estimates. For the US House general elections, 1950 is dropped due to redistricting.

are even larger than the differences between the coefficient estimates on incumbency.

Since the models used to estimate the coefficients for primaries and general elections differ, the comparisons between them must be treated with caution. However, since the models are linear and the variables are all measured on comparable scales, the estimates provide some general indication of the relative importance of incumbency and relevant experience in the two types of elections. As Table 9.8 shows, the differences appear to be quite large.

As we discussed in Chapter 7, one of the significant changes in US elections that occurred during the post-1950 period is the increasing partisan polarization since the late 1970s, with a noticeable surge in the 1990s and 2010s. The theoretical discussion above suggests that with more polarized choices, the partisan differences between the candidates are expected to have a larger impact than qualifications on voter decisions. Therefore, in general elections the coefficient estimates on incumbency status and relevant experience should be smaller in the most recent decades.

We use the same specifications as those in Table 9.8, but we
estimate separate coefficients for four different periods: (i) 1952 to
1970; (ii) 1972 to 1990; (iii) 1992 to 2010; and (iv) 2012 to 2016.
The coefficient estimates for the US House are presented in Table 9.9.
For general elections, the estimated coefficients on both incumbency
status and relevant experience peak during the second period and
are smallest in the last period. Although the coefficients for primaries
show a similar pattern, in percentage terms the decline is not as large.
Moreover, for both types of elections, the coefficient estimates on
relevant experience in the last period are similar in magnitude to those
for the 1952-to-1970 period; and the coefficient on incumbency for the
general election is particularly small compared to other periods.[20] We
observe a qualitatively similar up-and-down pattern for the coefficient
estimates on incumbency and relevant experience for governors and US
senators (estimates not shown). In particular, the point estimates fall
sharply between the 1992-to-2010 period and the most recent period.
Overall, these results suggest that the current high level of partisan
polarization is affecting the relationship between qualifications and
general election outcomes.

9.4.2 Qualifications in Top-Two Systems

The top-two system provides an opportunity to examine whether the
presence of party labels in nomination contests affects the relationship
between qualifications and vote shares. In this type of system there are
two rounds of elections. In the first round, all candidates regardless of
party compete in the same election. The candidates with highest and
second highest vote totals go on to compete in the second round. For
US House races the system was first used in Louisiana in 1978, in
Washington in 2008, and in California in 2012.[21]

---

[20] We might expect the coefficients on qualifications in the primaries to also reflect the
importance of qualifications in the general elections. If primary voters do not expect
qualifications to affect general election outcomes, then they will have less of an incentive
to support qualified candidates.
[21] Some observers refer to this as the top-two primary or the "jungle" primary. We refer
to this as the top-two system since both the first- and second-round elections are
often qualitatively different from what happens with partisan primaries. In partisan
first-past-the-post electoral systems, each party gets to nominate one candidate for the
office sought. Under the top-two system both candidates that proceed to the second
round can be from the same party, in which case all other parties are deprived of
nominees. In Louisiana the second-round election is not held if the first-round winner

TABLE 9.9 *Voting and Candidate Experience in Primary versus General Elections, US House 1952 to 2016*

Period	Primary Elections		General Elections	
	Current Incumb.	Relevant Exper.	Current Incumb.	Relevant Exper.
1952–1970	25.5	11.2	4.5	1.3
	(0.7)	(0.9)	(0.3)	(0.3)
1972–1990	31.5	14.3	9.4	3.2
	(0.4)	(0.9)	(0.3)	(0.4)
1992–2010	29.6	14.4	7.5	2.5
	(0.4)	(1.0)	(0.3)	(0.3)
2012–2016	27.1	10.7	2.9	1.0
	(0.7)	(1.8)	(0.4)	(0.5)
p-value 1	0.00	0.02	0.00	0.00
p-value 2	0.00	0.99	0.00	0.17
p-value 3	0.00	0.08	0.00	0.02

The columns labelled Current Incumb. and Relevant Exper. contain OLS regression estimates. Number of primary election observations = 5877. Number of general election observations = 12,510. For general elections 1950 is dropped due to redistricting. The p-values are for the following hypothesis tests: p-value 1 is for the differences between 1952–1970 and 1972–1990, p-value 2 is for the differences between 1972–1990 and 1992–2010, p-value 3 is for the differences between 1992–2010 and 2012–2016.

In more than 10 percent of the first-round races under the top-two system all of the major party candidates are from the same party, while in the remaining cases there is at least one candidate from each major party. According to the model above, qualifications should have a larger effect on the first-round vote shares when there is no inter-party competition. The former cases are akin to within-party primaries, in which the ideological variation across candidates is relatively small and there are no differences in candidates' party affiliations.[22] The latter cases have elements of general elections, in which there are candidates from

receives more than 50 percent of the total vote. For simplicity we will refer to this as a top-two system. See Chapter 11 for more details about this system.

[22] One difference is that in these cases, the voters who are co-partisans of the candidates do not have to worry about defeating the other party in the second round (general) election. This might reduce the incentive to vote on the basis of qualifications, if part of the reason to vote based on qualifications is strategic – that is, the desire to nominate a more highly qualified candidate in order to defeat the other party's candidate in the general election.

each major party and the ideological variation across these candidates is relatively large. We refer to the first type as "one-party races" and the second type as "two-party races."

We estimate the effect of qualifications on the vote percentage of candidates in the first round allowing for the effect of qualifications to differ between one-party races and two-party races.[23] We focus on US House races and include both open-seat and incumbent-contested races. As in previous analyses, qualifications are measured by the share of relevant experience.

The estimated effect of qualifications on vote percentage for the one-party cases is 62.8, while the coefficient estimate for the two-party cases is noticeably lower, 45.2. The difference between these two estimates is statistically significant.[24] Thus, as predicted, qualifications have a larger effect on vote choice when all candidates running are from the same party.

One potential concern with this analysis is that one-party races occur more often in districts with an advantaged party. However, there is no obvious reason why voters in such districts should care more or less about qualifications than voters in parties-balanced districts.[25] Moreover, including a variable that interacts *Pct of Qualifications* and district safety does not affect the findings. The findings are also qualitatively similar if we split the sample, restricting attention only to parties-balanced districts or only to safe districts. In both cases, the estimated effect of qualifications is substantially higher in the one-party races, and the difference between the two types of races is statistically significant. The total number of candidates running is slightly higher in the two-party races – 3.4 to 2.8. However, including the number of candidates interacted with *Pct of Qualifications* does not affect the

---

[23] We estimated the following regression model for each race i:

$$VotePct_{ij} = \alpha_i + \beta_1 Pct\,of\,Qualifications_{ij} \times One\text{-}Party\,Race_i +$$
$$\beta_2 Pct\,of\,Qualifications_{ij} \times Two\text{-}Party\,Race_i + \epsilon_{ij}$$

where j is used to index the candidates running in race i. Standard errors are clustered by race. We include only races with two to five candidates. The total number of observations is 764, and of these 11.9 percent occur in races where all candidates share the same party label.

[24] The F-statistic is 16.0 with a p-value of 0.001.

[25] As noted above, we did not find evidence that qualifications have a stronger relationship with electoral support in advantaged-party versus parties-balanced districts. We have even less reason to suspect that this relationship should exist in the top-two system.

findings. The total number of qualified candidates is essentially the same in the two types of races.

9.4.3 Qualifications in California Primaries Under Cross-Filing

Variation in ballot forms and cross-filing in California primaries provides another, even more direct, setting for estimating whether party labels influence the effect of candidate qualifications on voting behavior in primaries. Before 1960 it was legal for candidates in California to run in more than one party's primary, that is, to "cross-file." The practice became quite common, especially among popular incumbents who often won both major party nominations and thereby faced no serious general election competition. In 1952 voters adopted an initiative that required candidates to list their party affiliation on the primary election ballots, and in 1959 cross-filing was abolished entirely.[26] Thus, from 1954 to 1958 cross-filing was still allowed and still common, but cross-filing candidates – that is, Republicans running in the Democratic primary and Democrats running in the Republican primary – were at a distinct disadvantage relative to 1952 and prior years. Comparing the voting patterns in these years with the elections held just prior to the change provides a good opportunity to test the hypothesis that partisanship and/or ideology "crowds out" voting on the basis of qualifications.

We estimated the effect of qualifications on vote percentage for cross-filing candidates over the period 1946–1958, allowing the effect of qualifications to vary depending on whether party affiliations were listed on the ballot.[27] We focus on US House and California State Senate elections, including both non-incumbent and incumbent-contested races. For both offices, candidates with prior state legislative or congressional experience, as well as incumbents running for re-election, are coded as

---

[26] Democrats wanted to abolish cross-filing even in 1952, and put an initiative on the ballot to do this. Republicans countered with an initiative that kept cross-filing but required candidates to list their party affiliations on the primary election ballots. The Democratic initiative failed and the Republican initiative passed. In 1958 Democrats won the governorship and majorities in both chambers of the state legislature, and the government passed a law that abolished cross-filing.

[27] We estimated the following regression model, for cross-filing candidates only:

$$Vote\,Pct_{it} = \beta_0 + \beta_1 Pct\,of\,Qualifications_{it} \times Party\,Not\,On\,Ballot_t +$$
$$\beta_2 Pct\,of\,Qualifications_{it} \times Party\,On\,Ballot_t + \beta_3 Party\,On\,Ballot + \epsilon_{it}$$

We also include indicator variables indicating whether the total number of candidates running was two, three, four, or five. Standard errors are clustered by candidate.

having relevant qualifications. The total number of observations in the sample is therefore 538.[28]

For the period during which party affiliations were not on the ballot, the estimated effect of qualifications is 33.0 (standard error = 2.0). After party affiliations were put on the ballot the estimated effect of qualifications fell to 25.5 (standard error = 1.6). This difference is statistically significant with a p-value of 0.002 based on the usual F-test. This is consistent with the theoretical prediction.

As a comparison, we conducted a similar analysis for non-cross-filers, restricting our attention to races in which no candidates cross-filed (n = 98). Here we do not expect to find an effect of putting party labels on the ballot. In fact, in these cases the estimated effect of relevant qualifications on vote share is essentially unchanged when party affiliations are on the ballot. For the period during which party affiliations were *not* on the ballot, the estimated effect of qualifications is 48.7 (standard error = 3.3), and for the period *with* party affiliations on the ballot the estimated effect of qualifications is 50.5 (standard error = 7.8). The difference is not statistically significant, with a p-value of 0.828.

9.5 CONCLUSION

Overall, the analyses above show that voting behavior in primaries in the post-1950 period is not dramatically different from that in the earlier period, except regarding turnout. We care especially about the ability of voters to distinguish between more- and less-qualified candidates. Encouragingly, we find that across all of the offices studied, more-qualified candidates win in the primaries significantly more often than less-qualified candidates. This appears to hold even for offices towards the bottom of the ballot, as shown in the analysis of Illinois circuit court judges.

The judicial analysis also gives us more confidence that the correlations we document for other offices, such as US House and state treasurer and auditor, are actually tied to qualifications. In those analyses, the measure of qualifications for each candidate is crude and based solely on a list of previous offices held. The measure we use in the judicial

---

[28] If the types of candidates who ran for office changed after party labels were put on the ballot, this may lead us to underestimate the effect of party labels on the relationship between election outcomes and qualifications. Cross-filing candidates when party labels are on the ballot may be more likely to be moderates or those who believe their attributes, such as qualifications, will have significant weight relative to party labels.

analysis, by contrast, is based on expert evaluations of a much more comprehensive and nuanced set of performance indicators relevant for the office.

Finally, as shown above and argued by other scholars, voting in general elections in the current highly polarized environment seems to be driven largely by party and ideology. Our studies of the top-two system, and of cross-filing in California, further highlight the tension between voting on the basis of partisanship or ideology and voting on the basis of qualifications. Thus, if current trends in polarization continue, primaries may play an even larger role than they have in the past in helping to elect qualified candidates.

10

Primaries and Accountability in the Modern Era

In 1992, Mickey Edwards was an eight-term US House member representing the Oklahoma 5th district, and chairman of the House Republican Policy Committee, the party's fourth-ranked leadership position. At the time, his district was safely Republican. He had won the previous seven general elections with an average of 73 percent of the two-party vote. In the 1992 presidential election, the Republicans polled more than twice as many votes as the Democrats in the district. There appeared to be little chance Edwards would lose the general election.

In March of 1992, Edwards found himself on the House Ethics Committee's list of the 22 worst offenders in the House banking scandal, also known as the "check kiting scandal."[1] He had written more than 386 overdrawn checks from the House bank. Although he faced almost no primary competition in his previous re-election bids, in this primary Edwards attracted four challengers and finished third with only 26 percent of the primary vote.[2] The nominee and eventual general election

---

[1] The House bank had allowed members to overdraw their accounts without penalties, provided that the overdraft did not exceed the representative's next paycheck. Many members exploited this practice, routinely taking advances on their paychecks and repaying them later. Overall, more than 300 members of the House kited over 22,000 checks; 25 members kited 300 or more checks each. Three House members were convicted of felonies and a fourth pleaded guilty to a misdemeanor charge, and the manager of the bank was convicted of embezzlement and other crimes. The House bank was closed in December 1991, before the scandal broke. See Alford et al. (1994), Groseclose and Krehbiel (1994), Jacobson and Dimock (1994), Stewart (1994), and Dimock and Jacobson (1995) for more details and analyses.

[2] Edwards faced no primary challengers in five of his previous seven re-election bids. In the two primaries where Edwards faced competition he won with 89 percent and 83 percent of the vote.

winner was Ernest Istook, who had served in the Oklahoma state legislature since 1987. Without a primary, it is unlikely that Edwards would have been ousted from office.

Adam Clayton Powell, Jr. provides another example of how primary elections can hold incumbents accountable in constituencies where the general elections are safe for one party. Powell, who was first elected to Congress 1944 and became one of the most powerful members of Congress, represented a solidly Democratic district in New York City.[3] There was little chance Powell would be defeated in a general election. In the two-and-a-half decades Powell was in office, he won every general election by over 60 percent of the vote.

The extent of Powell's general election security was highlighted in the late 1960s. Although he continued to be an influential and important member of Congress, he was also gaining a reputation for his poor attendance in Congress, in some years participating in only about half of the roll-call votes. In 1967, a House ethics investigation led to Powell being stripped of his committee chairmanship and forced to leave Congress; the members voted to exclude him from the current session. Nonetheless, Powell was returned to office later that year in a special election to fill his vacant seat, garnering close to seven votes for every vote received by his Republican challenger. Powell's claim that "My people would elect me ... even if I had to be propped up in my casket" appears to be an accurate reflection of his secure position.[4]

Although Powell had rarely faced a serious primary challenge since winning office, he faced four challengers in the 1970 Democratic primary, only one of whom, Charles B. Rangel, had prior legislative experience.[5] He was a state assemblyman. Rangel's campaign highlighted Powell's poor performance while in office, emphasizing his absence on key roll-call votes. Rangel received endorsements from several prominent Democratic leaders in the city, as well as *The New York Times*. Rangel won the primary with 32.8 percent of the vote, edging out Powell by just 0.6 percent of the vote.

These two examples highlight the potential role primaries can play in holding representatives accountable when the general elections are

---

[3] As chairman of the House Education and Labor Committees, he helped shape and pass landmark civil rights legislation in the 1960s.

[4] *Adam Clayton Powell, Jr.* (1992).

[5] Jesse Gray was a local activist who organized a rent strike in Harlem. Ramon A. Martinez was a lawyer who was appealing to the Puerto Rican voters in the district. John H. Young was a public relations consultant and former aid to Powell.

largely uncompetitive. In previous chapters we focused on the role primaries can play in the selection of more-qualified candidates in open-seat races. Elections are imperfect, of course, and sometimes candidates unsuited for the office are elected. In addition, politicians may change during their time in office. They may start as talented and diligent officials but fail to maintain the same level of performance as they age or as their life circumstances change.

Do primaries help voters hold incumbents accountable for their performance while in office? In Chapter 7, we presented descriptive evidence that incumbents rarely face significant primary competition, especially in the post-1950 period. However, if the electoral system is effectively selecting high-quality public officials in open-seat races, then perhaps the overall low level of primary competition that we typically observe is an indication that the system is functioning well overall. In parties-balanced constituencies, incumbents can be unseated by a relatively small proportion of the general electorate that is unsatisfied with their performance in office. In districts where the incumbent's party is heavily favored and the incumbent is unlikely to lose in a general election – which we will refer to throughout this chapter as safe districts – primaries provide a way for voters to hold poorly performing incumbents accountable.[6]

The theoretical model and discussion in Chapter 5 provide a rationale for why primaries in these safe districts will be especially competitive when the incumbent's performance in office reveals them to be "low-quality" or at least not "high-quality." As in the case of open-seat primaries with an initial low-quality entrant, challengers – particularly high-quality challengers – will have strong incentives to challenge low-quality incumbents in safe districts. Thus, the strategic entry decisions suggest that low-quality incumbents will face more competition (and be more likely to be removed from office) in advantaged-party primaries compared to parties-balanced primaries.

In this chapter, we examine two situations in which primaries would be expected to hold low-quality incumbents accountable in the primary elections: (1) when an incumbent is involved in a scandal and (2) when an incumbent is viewed as being less effective than his or her peers at performing the duties of their office. We study US House races with incumbents involved in scandals, and North Carolina state legislative

---

[6] In a safe district, the average presidential vote share for the incumbent's party across all elections between redistrictings is greater than 57.5 percent.

races involving incumbents who experts perceive as being relatively ineffective in office.[7] We should expect malfeasant and poor-performing incumbents to face more serious primary challenges and have a higher probability of losing their primary than other incumbents, especially in safe districts.

10.1 LITERATURE ON POLITICAL ACCOUNTABILITY

Most previous statistical studies of performance-based accountability in the US context focus on policy-related outcomes – such as the economy or crime rates or "bringing home the bacon" – but these measures depend heavily on a wide variety of factors beyond the control of politicians. Few such analyses use *direct* evaluations of performance or quality, largely because such measures tend to be unavailable. In the studies focusing on outcomes, it is often unclear what information voters have about outcomes, or even which outcomes they are using.[8] Moreover, a number of studies argue that certain events can affect an incumbent's electoral support even when the incumbent has little influence over the outcome of these events. This claim is currently the subject of a lively scholarly debate.[9]

A few studies have developed indices of legislative effectiveness or quality and shown that they are correlated with general election outcomes. Luttbeg (1992) studies journalists' rankings of legislators in several states, and finds that those with the highest rankings have a significantly higher probability of re-election than those with the lowest rankings. McCurley and Mondak (1995) measure "integrity,"

---

[7] There are other measures of legislative effectiveness for members of Congress, such as roll-call absenteeism and the Volden and Wiseman (2014) Legislative Effectiveness Scores (LES). When we study absenteeism we find patterns roughly similar to those documented below. This is not true when we study the LES scores. One feature of the LES scores is that the distribution is highly skewed to the right. Thus, these scores may be better at identifying the most effective legislators rather than the unusually ineffective legislators. Primaries are probably most useful for holding the particularly bad types accountable.

[8] We know very little about the information voters have regarding their incumbent's performance in "bringing home the bacon." We also know little about the types of indicators voters might be using when evaluating the economy. Do voters use unemployment, inflation, GDP growth, GDP growth in the last six months, or some mixture of these? A large literature has addressed this issue, from the seminal article by Kramer (1971) to more recent work by Fair (2002), Ansolabehere, Meredith, and Snowberg (2014), and Healy and Lenz (2014), but there is still no consensus.

[9] See, for example, Achen and Bartels (2002); Wolfers (2002); Healy, Malhotra, and Mo (2010); Huber, Hill, and Lenz (2012); Fowler and Montagnes (2015); Fowler and Hall (2018). There is also a large literature that studies political accountability outside the US.

"competence," and "quality" by conducting content analysis of the biographical descriptions of US House members in the *Almanac of American Politics* and *Politics in America*. They also focus on the link between incumbent quality and voters' opinions as revealed in the National Election Studies, and find that incumbent integrity directly influences both feeling thermometer scores and voting choices, while competence affects elections indirectly via the behavior of potential challengers. Padró i Miguel and Snyder (2006) use a measure of legislative effectiveness for the North Carolina state legislature, which we describe below, and find that legislators with low effectiveness scores are less likely to be re-elected.

Few studies address accountability in primaries. Among the exceptions are those that examine the effect of political scandals on primary election outcomes involving incumbents.[10] These papers typically find that scandals decrease incumbents' vote shares.[11] However, since incumbent-contested primaries on average tend to attract only minimal competition, the authors typically conclude that primaries matter little or not at all. For example, Brown (2006*a*, 8–9) states: "The scandal variables are statistically significant and large in magnitude in nearly all of the regressions ... Since incumbents, however, typically win primary elections by larger margins than they do general elections, the impact of losing more percentage points in a primary may have little or no effect on the outcome (the constants in these models suggest as much)." Some studies even find small and statistically insignificant effects. Welch and Hibbing (1997, 233) note that for the 1980s, "[p]rimary defeats are even rarer than voluntary departures ... More importantly, [the primary defeat rate] is only slightly higher than the primary defeat rate for incumbents not charged with corruption, despite the fact that an incumbent not charged with corruption almost never loses in the primary."[12]

---

[10] A number of papers also find that scandals significantly hurt US House and Senate incumbents in general elections, including Peters and Welch (1980); Abramowitz (1988, 1991); Alford et al. (1994); Jacobson and Dimock (1994); Stewart (1994); Welch and Hibbing (1997); Brown (2006*a,b*).

[11] See, for example, Jacobson and Dimock (1994) regarding the 1992 House banking scandal, Brown (2006*b*) for a comprehensive study of US House races between 1966 and 2002, and Brown (2006*a*) for a study of the 2006 elections.

[12] Lazarus (2008, 121) describes his findings on US Senate and gubernatorial races as follows: "... the coefficient on scandal is statistically significant and in the predicted direction only for one type of challenger: amateur out-party challengers in gubernatorial

A few studies examine the relationship between expert evaluations of incumbent performance and primary election outcomes. Mondak (1995) employs the McCurley and Mondak (1995) measures of competence and integrity and finds that incumbents with low competence are more likely to face primary opposition and have smaller primary election vote margins. Mondak interprets these findings as evidence of the potential role of primary elections in removing poorly performing politicians: "If we value legislative skills, then it clearly is good news that primary elections serve in part to weed out those congressional incumbents with the lowest levels of competence" (Mondak, 1995, 1060). However, the analysis does not examine whether incompetent incumbents actually lose in primaries. The pessimism regarding the role of primary elections in removing malfeasant incumbents in the above studies is because those authors suspect that primary competition does not ultimately lead low-quality incumbents to be *removed* from office. Most recently, Lim and Snyder (2015) analyze bar association evaluations of incumbents and non-incumbents running for judicial offices and find that candidates with low ratings receive significantly fewer votes and lower probabilities of winning in primary elections.

10.2 US HOUSE INCUMBENTS IN SCANDALS

One situation where it seems clear that an incumbent deserves to be replaced is when he or she has been involved in malfeasance of some sort – activities that are either illegal or violate the norms of proper behavior to an extreme degree. In the period 1978 to 2008, when newspapers endorsed a candidate in the primaries, US House incumbents not involved in a scandal received more than half of the endorsements in 85.4 percent of the races. This is true for only 33.3 percent of the incumbents involved in scandals. Scandals are relatively rare events, but they are useful for estimating a kind of "lower bound" on the value of elections. Specifically, studying scandals allows us to ask whether citizens use elections to remove some of the worst types of politicians from office.[13]

As noted above, when an incumbent is involved in a scandal and runs for re-election, the incumbency advantage that typically reduces

election. Thus, it does not seem as though the presence of a scandal results in the entry of a significant number of serious challengers of either party."

[13] Some of the analyses and background material on US House scandals draw on Hirano and Snyder (2012).

both primary and general election competition should be less of a factor. Thus primary races with a scandal-ridden incumbent should face higher levels of competition, and such incumbents should have a lower probability of winning the nomination, compared to a typical incumbent running for re-election. Similar to the patterns of competition in open-seat primary races, the differences should be larger in safe districts.

The potential role of primaries in holding incumbents accountable for scandals is evident in the 1992 US House banking scandal that affected Mickey Edwards and many other members of Congress who "kited" large numbers of checks at the House bank.[14] In Hirano and Snyder (2012) we found that the 49 incumbents who kited more than 100 checks faced significantly more primary competition in 1992 and were more likely to lose their primary compared to other incumbents. Of these, 15 retired, 20 won re-election, 5 lost in the general election, and 9 lost their primary elections. Five of those who lost their primary represented safe districts. These incumbents were therefore quite likely to win in the general election if they won their primaries, despite the large impact of the scandal on general election vote shares. Two others were from fairly safe districts, where the average presidential vote was more than 55 percent, and therefore had a reasonable chance of winning in the general election if they had not lost in the primary. It is difficult to say what would have happened to the incumbents who retired, in part because of massive redistricting in several cases. Overall, however, it appears that the primary elections played at least as important a role as the general election in giving voters a chance to punish incumbents who seriously abused the House bank.

While illustrative, the House bank scandal was just one case. We now analyze the impact of a broader range of US House scandals on primary and general election competition over four decades, from 1978 to 2016. We use three criteria to identify whether a member of Congress is considered to be involved in a scandal: (i) the House Committee on Standards of Official Conduct investigated the incumbent; (ii) the Department of Justice investigated the incumbent; or (iii) *Congressional*

---

[14] The House bank had been operating under loose rules for years. It did not use a computerized accounting system, it did not provide regular account statements to representatives, and it did not even post representatives' deposits in a timely manner.

Quarterly Weekly Reports discussed the scandal in at least one article.[15] Of course, many scandals appear in two or more sources.[16]

Although relatively few incumbents are implicated in a serious scandal – only 2.2 percent of the congressional races in our sample have an incumbent involved in a scandal running for re-election – we have enough cases to examine whether the effect of being involved in a scandal varies by the general election safety of the incumbent's district. We then plot the various primary election competition variables in safe versus other (not-safe) districts, separating incumbents involved and not involved in scandals.[17]

From 1978 to 2016, 13.5 percent of US House incumbents involved in scandals lost in a primary election compared to only 1.0 percent of incumbents not involved in a scandal. Figure 10.1 shows that the probability that an incumbent involved in a scandal will lose is 0.13 higher when they represent safe districts compared to not-safe districts. For incumbents not involved in scandals, there is little difference between the probability of losing in a primary between the two types of districts.

We can also investigate how scandals are related to other aspects of primary competition. The key variables are: (i) the presence of a primary challenger; (ii) the number of primary election challengers faced by the incumbent; (iii) the presence of a qualified challenger; and (iv) the total vote share for all challengers.[18] These variables are plotted for safe and not-safe districts in Figure 10.2. In all cases, incumbents in scandals face

---

[15] The sources for these are the *Historical Summary of Conduct Cases in the House of Representatives* (2004), the *Summary of Activities* reports published after each Congress by the House Committee on Standards of Official Conduct, the *Report to Congress on the Activities and Operations of the Public Integrity Section* published annually by the US Department of Justice (DOJ), and *Congressional Quarterly Weekly Reports*.

[16] We do not count cases where the House Committee on Standards of Official Conduct simply dismissed a complaint against the incumbent and *Congressional Quarterly* does not discuss it. In a few cases the committee authorized but deferred its investigation at the request of the DOJ. Since these cases involved ongoing DOJ investigations, we include them as scandals. We count all DOJ investigations as scandals even if they did not ultimately lead to a conviction. We considered various ways to try to quantify the relative magnitudes of scandals, but we have not found an objective enough way to do this, especially for different scandals that occur at different times and under different circumstances. The mix of scandals is clearly heterogeneous.

[17] We drop all top-two system cases from our analyses due to the uniqueness of the electoral system.

[18] We drop token challengers who received less than 1 percent of the vote. As in the previous chapters, we classify a challenger as qualified if she has relevant experience, which we define as legislative experience in Congress or a state legislature. The information was gathered from the ICPSR State Legislative data sets, newspaper reports, and various online databases.

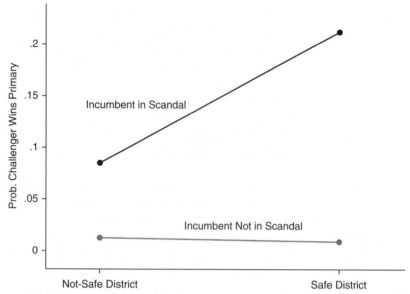

FIGURE 10.1 Scandals, District Safety, and Challenger Success in US Congressional Primaries

stiffer competition in the primary, especially in safe districts. The results of a regression analysis show these same patterns.

To assess the role of primaries in helping to remove malfeasant incumbents, we need to have some idea about how many of those who lost in the primary would have won in the general election. This is challenging due to obvious selection bias issues. To get a rough estimate, we regressed the general election vote shares on the following independent variables: a primary scandal indicator, a cubic polynomial of the presidential vote share, a first-term indicator, and party-year dummies to capture national tides.[19] Based on this model, the expected vote share of incumbents involved in scandals is roughly -0.10 lower than other incumbents. However, scandal-ridden incumbents who lost in the primary tended to represent districts where the presidential vote favored their party, quite heavily in many cases. Thus, the estimates suggest that most of them would probably have won in the general election, and that all but one of those from safe districts would probably have won.[20]

[19] Uncontested incumbents are assigned 100 percent of the vote.

[20] Of those involved in scandals who won their primary and ran in the general election, 94.2 percent won. Since we do not know whether these incumbents would have also lost in conventions or "smoke-filled rooms," we cannot assert that primaries are superior

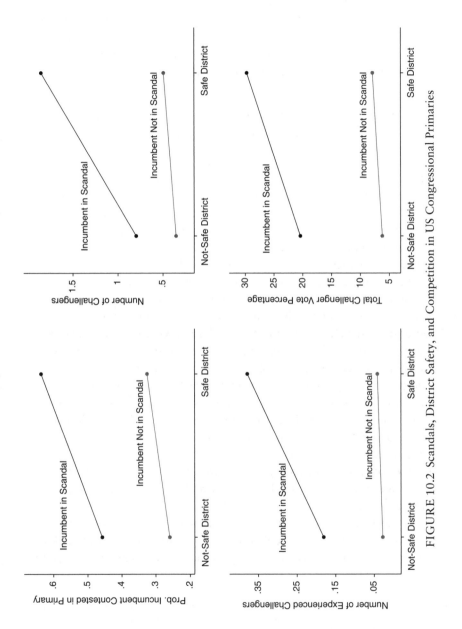

FIGURE 10.2 Scandals, District Safety, and Competition in US Congressional Primaries

The findings above are easily summarized. Incumbents involved in scandals face a higher probability of being challenged in the primary than those who are not, and they are also more likely to lose in the primary, especially in safe districts. Thus, our findings indicate that primaries can improve accountability by removing malfeasant incumbents who face re-election in districts or regions with an advantaged party.

10.3 EFFECTIVENESS OF NORTH CAROLINA LEGISLATORS, 1988 TO 2016

We now analyze a measure of performance in office, legislative "effectiveness." The expectations about primary competition in safe and not-safe districts for ineffective legislators are similar to those for incumbents involved in scandals. The overall level of primary competition, and the likelihood of losing the primary, should be higher for ineffective legislators than for effective legislators, and this difference should be even larger in safe districts compared to not-safe districts.

We examine the North Carolina state legislature. Since North Carolina has a hybrid legislature – that is, an amateur citizens' legislature with some professional characteristics – there is likely to be substantial variation in the effectiveness of the legislators. As discussed in Chapter 8, legislators are ranked according to their effectiveness by the North Carolina Center for Public Policy Research (NCCPPR), an independent non-partisan organization. At the end of each regular legislative session, the NCCPPR asks state legislators, lobbyists and legislative liaisons, and capital news correspondents to rate the "effectiveness" of each member of the General Assembly. Although these evaluations are subjective, they have several desirable characteristics: each ranking is based on a large number of evaluations, the evaluators are all legislative "specialists," and the rankings are constructed in a consistent manner over a long period of time.[21]

To keep the analysis simple and comparable to the other analyses involving incumbents, we collapse the legislator effectiveness rankings into a dichotomous variable identifying the bottom quarter – that is, the

---

to other nomination methods. Moreover, we do not know if the vote shares of those involved in a scandal who lost in the primary would have had a drop of even more than -0.10 in the general election.

[21] See Chapter 8 for a discussion of this measure, and Padró i Miguel and Snyder (2006) for additional checks regarding its validity.

bottom 30 members of the 120 state House members and the bottom 12 senators of the 60 state senators.

We focus on four of the same primary election outcomes as in the analysis of US House incumbents involved in scandals: (1) the probability that a challenger will win the primary; (2) the probability that the primary will be contested; (3) number of challengers; and (4) total challenger vote percentage.[22] Since data on prior political experience (e.g., membership on city councils) is not readily available for state assembly challengers, we are unable to examine the likelihood that the challenger had relevant experience as we did for the analysis of scandals.

Finally, we classify districts as safe or not-safe using a measure of district partisanship that aggregates precinct-level election results for all available statewide offices. We again classify a district as safe for an incumbent if the average vote in the district for the incumbent's party's nominees across these offices is above 57.5 percent.[23]

Figure 10.3 plots the different outcomes for state legislators with low and not-low effectiveness rankings in safe and not-safe districts. The top-left panel shows that incumbents with low effectiveness rankings have a higher probability of losing a primary election compared to those with higher effectiveness rankings, but only in safe districts. Although this difference is relatively modest, 0.06, the pattern is consistent with the predictions from the theoretical discussion. The remaining three panels of the figure display a sizable gap in primary competition between incumbents with low and not-low effectiveness rankings. Although the gap is slightly larger in safe districts compared to not-safe districts, all incumbents face more primary competition in safe districts. The results of a regression analysis reveal the same patterns. While the patterns in this figure are not as dramatic as those in Figures 10.1 and 10.2, they are consistent with our claim that primaries provide an important electoral mechanism for holding incumbents accountable when the general election is not likely to be competitive.

---

[22] The primary election data was obtained from the North Carolina State Board of Elections and the NC State Legislative Library, and we extracted some from the URL: www.sboe.state.nc.us.

[23] The statewide offices we use include the following: US senator, governor, lieutenant governor, secretary of state, treasurer, auditor, attorney general, commissioner of agriculture, commissioner of insurance, commissioner of labor, and superintendent of public instruction. See Hirano and Snyder (2009) for sources. We use all available elections between redistricting periods.

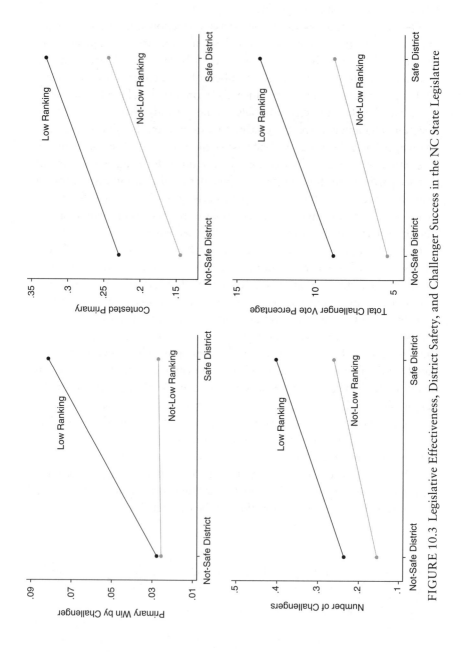

FIGURE 10.3 Legislative Effectiveness, District Safety, and Challenger Success in the NC State Legislature

10.4 PRIMARY VOTING AND INCUMBENT PERFORMANCE

While the evidence suggests that malfeasant and poorly performing incumbents are significantly more likely to lose in a primary than other incumbents, these patterns do not provide direct evidence that primary voters choose to punish malfeasant or ineffective incumbents. As discussed in Chapter 8, the patterns in Figures 10.1, 10.2, and 10.3 may simply reflect differences in the pool of candidates running in primaries for safe and not-safe districts, rather than the decisions of the primary electorate to vote against malfeasant or ineffective incumbents. Here we examine the voting behavior of primary voters who are faced with relatively low-performing incumbents compared to voters whose incumbent is not revealed to be low-performing. Do voters tend to support the latter? We focus on cases where we have indicators of low performance: US House members involved in scandals; North Carolina state legislators who are evaluated as being less effective than their peers; and incumbents who, contrary to the normal pattern, do not receive all of the endorsements in the newspapers covering their race.

We regress primary vote shares on each of the three indicators of incumbent performance.[24] The coefficient estimates on the incumbent performance indicators are presented in Table 10.1. The estimates show that low-performance incumbents receive significantly lower vote shares than others. The primary vote shares of US House members who were involved in a scandal are -19.3 percentage points lower than those who are not. The coefficient is of a similar magnitude when we examine all offices and classify low-performance incumbents as those who do not receive all of the newspaper endorsements, -19.9. The difference in electoral support for North Carolina legislators with low

TABLE 10.1 *Incumbent Vote in Primary versus Incumbent Performance*

	Coeff.	Std. Error	N
US House (Low Performance = Scandal)	−19.3	2.4	630
NC Legislature (Low Performance = Low Effectiveness)	− 4.8	2.0	599
All Offices (Low Performance = Not All Endorsements)	−19.9	1.1	980

Coefficients are OLS regression estimates.

---

[24] Although we control for the number of candidates, we also drop cases in which more than five candidates are competing in the primary.

effectiveness rankings compared to those with relatively higher rankings is less substantial (-4.8 percentage points). However, even this coefficient estimate is statistically significant. These results are consistent with a primary electorate in which enough voters are informed about the performance of elected representatives.

10.5 DISCUSSION

What do these results suggest about the value of primary elections? Overall, the findings indicate that primary elections sometimes improve accountability by removing relatively poorly performing incumbents who represent districts or regions dominated by a single political party.

Our analysis may underestimate the role of primaries in holding incumbents accountable for at least three reasons. First, incumbents in safe districts who run for re-election tend to be more senior and powerful than those from marginal districts. Consider for example the case of US House incumbents involved in scandals. In our sample, the mean number of terms served by incumbents involved in scandals from safe districts was 6.0, while it was just 4.6 for not-safe districts. Party caucuses and conventions might be especially unwilling to remove powerful party members, such as senior members of Congress, and this may give primaries an even more important role. A similar argument likely holds in other contexts.

Second, poorly performing incumbents may often choose to retire, so the estimates presented in this chapter could be biased towards zero due to selection bias. In the analysis of the US House, for example, approximately one-third of the incumbents involved in scandals chose to retire rather than run for re-election, and they are excluded.[25] Anecdotal evidence suggests that many of these incumbents would have faced serious primary opposition had they run.[26]

---

[25] The retirement rates were relatively similar in both safe and competitive districts for incumbents involved in scandals. This is consistent with what we would observe if both primary and general elections provided a significant hurdle for malfeasant incumbents.

[26] For example, in April 2007, the FBI raided the home of John Doolittle (R, CA) because of possible involvement by his wife in the corruption investigation of Jack Abramoff; Doolittle had direct ties with Abramoff as well. In the summer of 2007, three Republicans announced their intention to run against Doolittle in the next primary election. These included a city councilman, and a state assemblyman, Ted Gaines, who stated "I think voters have lost faith in his [Doolittle's] leadership ability ... When you lose the moral ability to lead, you kind of have to re-evaluate." (Peter Hecht, "Doolittle may face big test in GOP race," *Sacramento Bee*, August 31, 2007.) In addition,

Finally, we have not measured the potential deterrent effect. If incumbents in safe states or districts fear losing in the primaries due to poor performance, then they should already be incorporating this into their actions in office.

a prominent county party chairman announced that he would no longer support Doolittle. In January 2008, Doolittle announced that he would not seek re-election.

11

Primaries and Polarization

The evidence presented thus far highlights the positive contributions that primaries make to the US electoral system. What are the drawbacks? One concern, which has received widespread attention recently, is that primaries might be a major cause of partisan polarization – and that this polarization is one of the main factors driving citizens' dissatisfaction with politicians and government. As Phil Keisling, the former Oregon Secretary of State, wrote in a *New York Times* editorial: "Want to get serious about reducing the toxic levels of hyper-partisanship and legislative dysfunction now gripping American politics? Here's a direct, simple fix: abolish party primary elections" (Keisling, 2010).

Numerous scholars have identified theoretical reasons why ideologically extreme candidates might perform better than moderates in primary elections.[1] Extremists might receive more votes simply because those who vote in primaries prefer them, or because they are better at attracting the support of activists who give time, money, endorsements, and other resources. Journalists and academics have stated these arguments in various ways. Jacobson (2004, 16) explains that, "Primary electorates are much more partisan and prone to ideological extremity, and the need to please them is one force behind party polarization in Congress." Sinclair (2006, 29–30) writes that activists "always vote, they vote in primaries, and they give money or work for candidates. To win in the

---

[1] See, for example, Brady, Han, and Pope (2007); Burden (2001, 2004); Fiorina, Abrams, and Pope (2006); Fiorina and Levendusky (2006); Hacker and Pierson (2006); Jacobson (2004); King (2003); Sinclair (2006); Wright and Berkman (1986).

primary, the candidate needs to be especially attentive and responsive to activists who are more polarized than less interested voters. The candidates who emerge from primaries are likely to be acceptable to the activist." Journalists often describe the situation in similar terms: "Voters in primaries are generally political activists who represent the ideological extremes of the two major parties. Thus, Democrats tend to choose candidates who are more liberal than the general electorate and Republicans tend to choose candidates who are more conservative than the general electorate."[2]

Political economy models with candidates competing in primary and general elections formally show that when there is an ideological divide between the primary electorates of the two parties, and primary elections are fully contested, strategic candidates will take policy positions away from the general election median voter and toward the median voter in their primary.[3]

An important point is often missed in the popular and academic discourse, however: in order to argue that primaries "cause" polarization, primaries must be *compared* to alternative nomination systems.

The experience in Utah illustrates why we must carefully consider the alternatives before concluding that eliminating primaries would reduce polarization. Utah's nomination system employs both a convention and a primary. In the spring of 2010, incumbent US Senator Bob Bennett's re-election bid came to an abrupt end when he failed to secure the Republican Party's nomination. He was defeated by Tea Party favorite Mike Lee, who criticized Bennett for supporting the Troubled Asset Relief Program (TARP), co-sponsoring healthcare legislation with a Democratic colleague, and voting to increase the national debt. Although Bennett's overall record was conservative, his opponents all argued that

[2] Vasyl Markus, Jr. in a *Chicago Tribune* article published on May 2, 1992.

[3] See Aranson and Ordeshook (1972); Coleman (1972); Owen and Grofman (2006). Scholars and political observers have, of course, identified and investigated a variety of factors other than primaries that may be important causes of polarization. These include broad political and social forces such as the partisan realignment in the US South, the increasing salience of "social/moral" issues compared to economic issues, changes and fragmentation in the media environment and increasing income inequality, as well as more institutional forces, such as gerrymandering and changes in campaign finance. Barber and McCarty (2015) provide a review of the literature.

he was not conservative *enough*, particularly on fiscal issues.[4] Lee went on to win the general election by close to 30 percentage points.

Bennett's defeat would be consistent with the popular narrative that primary elections contribute to partisan polarization among elites – that is, even candidates who are not particularly moderate are losing their party's nominations to those taking more extreme positions – except for one important detail. Bennett lost the nomination in the Utah pre-primary state party convention, and never made it onto the primary ballot. Nor is this case unique. In recent years, several other Republican incumbents in Utah have faced serious nomination challenges from Tea Party-backed candidates at the state pre-primary conventions. In the 2016 gubernatorial election Gary Herbert lost the state pre-primary convention to the more conservative Jonathan Johnson by 10 percentage points, but Herbert went on to beat Johnson in the primary by over 40 percentage points. In 2012, six-term US Senator Orin Hatch was forced into a primary by convention challenger and Tea Party favorite Dan Liljenquist; Hatch won the primary handily with two-thirds of the vote.

In the cases above, the more ideologically extreme candidates received larger vote shares in the conventions than in the primaries. These cases illustrate that, in order to properly evaluate the extent to which primaries contribute to polarization, we need to compare those nominated under primaries to those nominated under some alternative system(s). That is, we must ask the question, *primaries compared to what?* Caucuses? Conventions? Party committee meetings? A top-two system?[5] National party meetings? Lotteries? The Utah cases raise the possibility that the main alternatives used in the past – that is, caucuses, party committee meetings, or conventions – might systematically produce nominees who are more extreme than those selected in primaries. In addition, there are theoretical reasons to believe that these alternatives would be even more

---

[4] In an article in *The Atlantic*, Good (2010) writes "Incumbent Sen. Bob Bennett (R) will face off against no less than seven challengers tonight, and there's a good chance he will lose out. If that happens, conservatives will have knocked off an incumbent GOP senator – one who isn't liberal by any means, but who just isn't conservative enough for their liking. And it will mean that, in the current electoral climate, GOP incumbents in right-leaning states can't afford to deviate much from a straight fiscal-conservative line." According to votesmart.org, Bennett had an American Conservative Union rating of 86 percent, which, while conservative, was not as conservative as Lee's score of 100 percent.

[5] Recall that in top-two systems, the top two candidates from a first-round ballot compete in a second-round election, even if they are from the same party.

polarizing than primaries. Indeed, caucuses and conventions are likely to be dominated by political activists, who according to prior research are generally more extreme than primary voters. Except in areas with lively inter-party competition, party elites and activists do not have strategic incentives to nominate moderate candidates. Thus, the degree to which primaries lead to more polarization than alternative systems is an open question. In this chapter, we examine a number of cases in which these alternative systems were used to select US House nominees, and find no clear evidence that they produced more moderate representatives than primaries.

In the first half of this chapter, we evaluate the evidence that primaries operate in ways that systematically benefit ideological extremists. We examine key features of the broad historical patterns and conduct detailed analyses of primaries in the current polarized environment. Overall the evidence is mixed or subject to various interpretations. For example, one obvious fact is that primaries were introduced several decades before polarization began rising in Congress. If primaries are involved in magnifying polarization, then something else must have changed in recent decades that interacts with primaries to facilitate polarization. We document four patterns that, at the very least, call into question some of the popular claims about primaries and polarization: (i) ideologically more-extreme US House members are as likely to be elected in high-turnout primaries as in low-turnout primaries; (ii) incumbents rarely face serious competition, and this is equally true for ideologically extreme and moderate incumbents; (iii) incumbents who face a serious primary challenge do not subsequently become more extreme; and (iv) on average, ideologically extreme candidates in open-seat congressional primaries are not more likely to win, except possibly in safe constituencies.

In the second half of the chapter, we turn to our main concern: would an alternative system lead to more moderate representatives? As noted above, when we compare primaries to nominating conventions, caucuses, and party committee meetings, we find that these alternatives are not significantly more likely to nominate more moderate candidates than primaries. In fact, we find that pre-primary conventions endorse extreme candidates more often than the subsequent primaries. These results suggest that the activists and party elites who tend to dominate conventions, caucuses, and party committee meetings are not particularly strategic in their choices – that is, consistent with their ideologically extreme preferences they tend to support relatively ideologically extreme candidates. We also compare closed versus open primaries, as well as partisan primaries versus top-two systems. Overall, there is little evidence that more-open primaries would lead to a substantial increase in the election of moderate representatives. Regarding top-two systems, we find significant evidence of one key force identified by proponents: when the second-round candidates are both from the same party, then voters of the opposite party disproportionately support the more moderate candidate. However, this force is usually not strong enough to overcome the advantage that the more extreme candidate tends to have among co-partisans in the constituency. Our analyses therefore highlight the additional behavioral conditions that are necessary to reduce polarization in alternative systems, as well as some of the challenges in evaluating these systems.

11.1 PRIMARIES AND POLARIZATION OVER THE LONG TERM

It is difficult to argue that primary elections *per se* are the cause of polarization in Congress today, because they were introduced several decades before the current period of polarization even began. As McCarty, Poole, and Rosenthal (2006, 67) point out, the view that primaries drive polarization "has important limitations ... The first is that the widespread adoption of the primary as a nomination device for Congress took place at the end of the nineteenth century and the first half of the twentieth. As we have seen, this corresponds to an era of declining polarization. By the time polarization began escalating, primaries were nearly universal."

Figure 11.1 illustrates the lack of correlation between the introduction of primaries and polarization. It plots the changes in polarization of US House members along with the fraction of House members elected in states using primary elections over the period 1880 to 2014. Partisan polarization is captured by the differences in the roll-call votes of Democratic and Republican US House members. We use W-NOMINATE Common Space (CS) scores as estimates of US House members' roll-call voting positions.[6] The black curve shows the polarization as measured by the distance between the parties – that is, the average 1st-dimension

---

[6] W-NOMINATE, DW-NOMINATE, and other related roll-call based scores are widely used as measures of legislators' ideological positions in studies of Congress and American politics more generally. Roughly speaking these all involve some type of non-linear, parametric latent variable model. See Poole (1998) for a discussion of how these scores

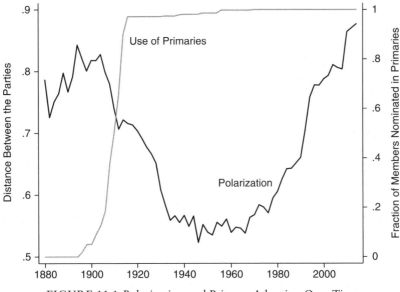

FIGURE 11.1 Polarization and Primary Adoption Over Time

CS score among Republicans minus the average 1st-dimension CS score among Democrats. The gray curve shows the change in primary usage over time weighted by the number of House members elected from states using primaries. The y-axis on the left is for the polarization measure, and the one on the right is for the primary usage measure.

Figure 11.1 shows that polarization: (1) was high until about 1904 and then fell dramatically until the mid-1930s; (2) was low and relatively unchanged (trending gradually upwards) from the mid-1930s through the late 1970s; and (3) increased sharply during the 1980s through the 2010s. The over-time pattern in the proportion of US House members who were nominated through primaries is quite different. There was a rapid growth in the adoption of primary elections between 1900 and 1916, but during this period polarization was declining. Over the subsequent periods of changing polarization there was very little change in use of primary elections. The sharp drop in polarization in the 1920s happened after most US House members were already being nominated in primaries. Similarly, there was essentially no change in the use of primaries during the most recent period of increasing polarization.

can be transformed into a common space score that allows for comparability over time and across chambers.

Although not shown in the figure, the patterns are very similar for the US Senate.

The meaning of "polarization" over the period covered by Figure 11.1 almost certainly changed. For example, the ideological cleavage between the parties on economic issues – Democrats generally espouse more government spending, higher taxes, and more extensive regulation of the economy than Republicans – emerged clearly only during the New Deal realignment in the 1930s. Five states introduced direct primary laws for congressional elections after the New Deal, so for these states we can examine the relationship between ideological extremism of US House members and the use of primaries in the post-New Deal period. The states are: Connecticut (1956), Delaware (1970), New Mexico (1940), Utah (1938), and Rhode Island (1948). If primary elections contributed to polarization, then the House members from these states should have become more extreme after their introduction.[7]

A simple "before-and-after" analysis tells the story. In the five states listed above, the average relative ideological extremism score in the ten years before the adoption of primaries was 0.311 ($N = 16$) and the average score in the ten years after adoption was 0.257 ($N = 15$). The difference, -0.054, is not statistically significant (the standard error of the difference clustered at the House member level is 0.062). Since the CS scores range from -1 to 1, the difference is also not substantively significant. Moreover, as noted in the footnote above, higher scores indicate higher levels of extremism, so, if anything, the average level of extremism in these states relative to that of their co-partisans in Congress fell following the adoption of primaries.

The main conclusion from Figure 11.1 and the "before-and-after" analysis of the late adopting states is that there is essentially no relationship between large changes in the use of primaries and large changes in polarization. The use of mandatory primaries alone does not

---

[7] We measure "relative" ideological extremism by comparing individual House members' CS scores to the average of their party. The relative extremism score for member i is measured as follows: $Relative\,Extremism_{it} = CS_i - \overline{CS}_t^R$ if i is a Republican and $Relative\,Extremism_{it} = -(CS_i - \overline{CS}_t^D)$ if i is a Democrat, where $\overline{CS}_t^R$ and $\overline{CS}_t^D$ are the average CS scores for Republican and Democrat members of Congress t, respectively. Note that the scores are oriented so that higher values of $Relative\,Extremism_{it}$ are associated with greater extremism for both Democrats and Republicans. We compare members to their party in order to account for factors that affect all members of a party. This helps us isolate the effect of primaries by taking advantage of variation in the primary election environment across states within years.

appear to have had a more polarizing effect on roll-call voting behavior compared to the previous nominating procedures used in these states.[8] Thus, if primary elections are implicated in polarization, it must be because they interact with other factors in the political environment that have changed. One factor of particular interest is the distribution of preferences within the primary electorates of the two major parties.

Primaries, Polarization, and Turnout

A popular refrain heard among skeptics of primary elections is that low primary turnout allows a small group of activists with extreme preferences to control the nomination process. For example, Fiorina and Levendusky (2006, 70) write, "turnout in primary elections is usually very low, so a few core committed supporters (at least on the lower rungs of the electoral ladder) can be critically important foundation for a campaign." Political analyst Walter Shapiro writes, "miniscule turnout in primaries feeds political polarization and extremism. The rise of the Tea Party movement was aided by a GOP primary electorate in which militant conservatives were over-represented."[9] Similarly, a *Washington Post* editorial states: "Falling turnout in primary elections, particularly in congressional races in off years, cedes the field to fiery partisans."[10] Thus, the primary system might facilitate polarization by underweighting the preferences of moderates and independents who do not participate, either by choice or because they are ineligible due to the laws governing primaries.[11]

Figure 11.2 shows the long-run relationship between primary election turnout and polarization. Primary turnout in the figure is measured as the maximum total primary turnout for any office divided by the maximum total general election turnout for any office.[12] Turnout is then averaged over four-year presidential election cycles.[13] Focusing

[8] A more comprehensive analysis with essentially the same findings can be found in Hirano et al. (2010).

[9] Shapiro (2014: n.p.).

[10] "A Polarized Nation?" *The Washington Post.* November 14, 2004, p. B6.

[11] The argument is actually more subtle than it appears. For example, if low turnout leads to primaries dominated by activists, and activists strategically nominate moderate candidates in order to win the general election, then low turnout could theoretically lead to the nomination of moderate candidates (see, for example, Hirano, Snyder, and Ting (2009) for an analysis of strategic voting with primaries).

[12] The maximum total primary turnout is the sum of the two parties' primary votes.

[13] In constructing average primary election turnout, we weight each state-year by the number of US House districts the state had in that year. We do this to parallel the weighting that is implicit in the polarization measure.

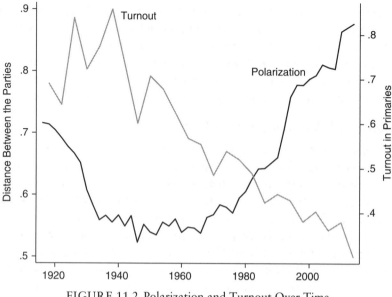

FIGURE 11.2 Polarization and Turnout Over Time

on the period beginning in the late 1970s, there is clearly a negative correlation – that is, as primary turnout steadily declined, polarization was increasing. However, there is no obvious relationship prior to the 1970s. For example, from 1934 through the 1960s, primary turnout was first increasing then generally decreasing, while polarization was essentially flat.

Particular historical episodes also make it difficult to draw general conclusions about turnout and polarization. Consider, for example, the long period of Southern realignment from the 1960s through the 1990s, in which the South transitioned from Democratic to Republican control. During this period, turnout in Republican primaries increased sharply relative to both the voting-age population and overall general election turnout, and even relative to Republican general election support.[14] However, this increase in turnout did not lead to a more moderate Southern Republican House delegation. In fact, Southern Republicans' roll-call voting positions became noticeably more conservative during this period.

---

[14] For example, average turnout in Republican primaries from 1966 to 1990 (relative to overall general election turnout) was 9.5. This increased to 20.1 from 1992 to 2016.

The opposite occurred in the Southern Democratic Party during this period. The size of its primary electorate fell sharply, as did its support in general elections, despite the enfranchisement of large numbers of African-Americans. The Southern Democratic congressional delegation became noticeably more liberal over this period. This is in line with the simple prediction that smaller primary electorates lead to more extremism. However, it is unlikely that this relationship reflected only a decline in the number of "moderates" voting in Democratic primaries. Rather, it was probably due to a variety of changes, including the influx of new, and generally more liberal, African-American voters as well as the movement of conservative whites away from the Democratic Party.

These broad patterns in primary turnout and polarization indicate that there is no simple relationship between the size of a party's primary electorate and the extremism of its nominees. We will return to these claims about the link between primary turnout and extremism in the next section, which focuses on the recent polarized environment. The availability of individual-level survey data and information about candidates' relative positions will allow us to examine the relationship in greater detail.

11.2 PRIMARIES IN THE RECENT POLARIZED ENVIRONMENT

If primaries are linked to the increased polarization in Congress, then it must be because they are interacting with something that is also changing. One possibility is that the parties' primary electorates have changed. Scholars disagree over whether the public as a whole has become more polarized, that is, whether a larger share of citizens hold more extreme policy views than in the past.[15] There is more agreement that – due to sorting, polarization, or some combination of the two – the ideological gap between the supporters of the two parties has been increasing since at least the 1970s.[16] Voters affiliated with the Republican Party have become more conservative, while those affiliated with the Democratic Party have become more liberal.

Fiorina, Abrams, and Pope (2006) and others highlight the connection between this widening ideological gap and the increasing likelihood that

---

[15] See, for example, Fiorina, Abrams, and Pope (2006); Levendusky (2009); Abramowitz (2010); Hill and Tausanovitch (2016).

[16] Layman, Carsey, and Horowitz (2006).

Republican (Democratic) primary electorates will nominate conservative (liberal) candidates. It is difficult to prove that sorting or polarization within the electorate is causing polarization among elites, since the causal arrow might actually be reversed. As Lenz (2012) argues, for example, partisan voters may simply be adopting the positions of the parties and party leaders they favor.[17]

It is reasonable to expect that increasingly ideologically distinct primary electorates would increasingly favor relatively extreme candidates. Thus we should see a growing tendency for open-seat primaries to nominate relatively extreme candidates. We should also expect that, *ceteris paribus*, when an ideological extremist competes head-to-head against an ideological moderate, the extremist will win more often. In addition, since previous studies have shown that incumbents' roll-call voting positions are quite stable over their careers, we might also expect to observe moderate incumbents – especially those who are more senior – to be challenged more often than extremist incumbents, and that the challengers should tend to be more extreme than the incumbents.[18] Even if the incumbents do not lose, they may retire in response to tough challenges by relative extremists.

Previous empirical work has explored some of these hypotheses, and the findings are mixed. For example, Brady, Han, and Pope (2007) find that more extreme candidates have higher vote shares in US House primaries, while Hirano et al. (2010) find no significant evidence that extreme candidates do better than moderates in US Senate primaries.

---

[17] One concern with the simplest sorting claim – that relatively conservative Democrats have been switching to the Republican Party and relatively liberal Republicans have been switching to the Democratic Party – is that they imply a degree of symmetry in the movement of partisan electorates and representatives that does not clearly match the empirical evidence. At the elite level, the roll-call voting measures appear to show that Republicans have moved farther to the extreme than Democrats. Barber and McCarty (2015) note that this pattern is consistent with qualitative accounts of the movements in the parties' positions. This could indicate that the sorting has been occurring at the same time as overall preferences have been trending in a conservative direction. However, on many social issues preferences appear to be moving in a liberal direction.

[18] See, for example, Poole (2007); Stone (1980). McCarty, Poole, and Rosenthal (2015, 55) write, "Ideological positions are also quite stable for politicians throughout their careers … Even a member whose constituency changes quite dramatically, either by elevation to the Senate or through major redistricting, rarely changes positions in a significant way." Other scholars have found evidence of legislators changing their roll-call voting positions, but these changes are usually small and/or limited to particular issues – for example, Stratmann (2000); Kousser, Lewis, and Masket (2007); Feigenbaum and Hall (2015). The exception is when representatives switch parties.

As with many debates regarding polarization, the measurement issues are particularly challenging. In particular, while the positions of elected representatives can be measured well by using roll-call voting records, these data are not observed for those who fail to win office. Here we measure ideological positions using a measure based on roll-call voting records – both in the US Congress and state legislatures – as well as candidate responses to a nationally administered survey. The state legislative roll-call scores (NP scores) are from Shor and McCarty (2011) and cover almost all state legislators who served at some point between 1996 and 2014.[19] The survey-based scores (Project Vote Smart, or PVS, scores) are from Project Vote Smart's Political Courage Test, and cover the period 1996 to 2016.[20] For all candidates who never served in Congress, but have either an NP score, a PVS score or both, we use a standard linear imputation method to impute CS scores.[21] This yields estimates of the ideological positions of thousands of candidates.[22] Overall for the period 1994 to 2016, we have estimates for about 38 percent of our sample of US House and Senate candidates in non-incumbent primaries.[23] Among the more serious candidates – for example, those who gather more than a quarter of the vote – we have scores for 47 percent of House candidates and 58 percent of Senate candidates. For those who win in non-incumbent primary races, we have scores for 54 percent of House candidates and 67 percent of Senate candidates.[24]

[19] The data also cover some states for the 1993-to-1995 period. See Shor and McCarty (2011) and americanlegislatures.com for details.

[20] Project Vote Smart's survey was formerly called the National Political Awareness Test. Previous research often refers to this survey as the NPAT.

[21] We regress incumbents' CS scores on their NP scores and PVS scores when available. We use the coefficient estimates from these regressions to predict the CS scores of non-incumbents for whom we have NP or PVS scores.

[22] More precisely, we have NP scores for more than 1,440 non-incumbents and PVS scores for more than 4,160 non-incumbents.

[23] The winning candidates are disproportionately represented in the sample, but among the losing candidates, the differences in terms of vote share are not particularly striking. The candidates with missing scores are also slightly less likely to be competing for safe seats, but again the differences are relatively small.

[24] Some scholars have used ideological scores based on campaign contributions (Hall, 2015; Rogowski and Langella, 2015). However, campaign contribution-based scores may not be appropriate for investigating polarization, since the campaign donors themselves may be adjusting their behavior in response to changes in the political environment. For example, see Tausanovitch and Warshaw (2017) for a critique of these campaign finance-based scores.

We orient the scores so that higher values indicate more extreme positions. Since the actual and imputed CS scores are oriented so that higher values indicate more conservative positions, we define extremism as follows: $Extremism_i = CS_i$ if i is a Republican member of Congress and $Extremism_i = -CS_i$ if i is a Democrat. Since the range of CS score is -1 to 1, the maximum possible value for *Extremism* is 1. For the period 1994 to 2016, the average value of *Extremism* across all candidates in our sample, including incumbents, is 0.39. Note that this is about half of the gap between the Republican and Democratic average CS scores over this period (see Figure 11.1).[25]

For certain analyses we are mainly concerned with identifying which candidate is more ideologically extreme. For these analyses we can add cases where we are missing one or more imputed CS scores. We classify the candidates' relative positions based on a variety of sources including newspaper archives, candidate and interest group web pages for endorsements and issue positions (for example, Club For Growth, Tea Party Express, Eagle Forum, etc.), and online political commentaries. In some cases, the sources did not highlight a noticeable or consistent difference in the candidates' ideological positions, or they focused on issues unrelated to the candidates' ideological positions. We code these cases as races in which there is no significant ideological difference between the candidates.

11.2.1 Incumbent-Contested Races

The popular perception is that incumbent politicians, particularly in safe constituencies, fear being "primaried." The fact is, however, incumbents are seldom seriously challenged in primaries, and hardly ever lose. As we showed in Chapter 7, for both statewide offices and the US House, the fraction of incumbent-contested primaries that were competitive has been declining for over half-a-century. Overall, incumbents faced a decline in primary competition during the period of increasing polarization. Thus, for example, between 1992 and 2008 only about 3 percent of incumbents had competitive primaries, and only 26 percent of incumbents were even contested. During the same period, only 1.17 percent of US House incumbents and 1.61 percent of US Senate incumbents lost their primary

---

[25] For some analyses, it also makes sense to compare candidates only with their co-partisans or to the chamber average. For example, in Section 11.1 we use the *Relative Extremism* measure defined above.

election. However, since 2010 there has been a noticeable increase in primary contestation and competitiveness. During the period 2010 to 2016, almost 44 percent of incumbents' primaries were contested and more than 8 percent were competitive.[26,27]

As discussed above, as primary voters become more ideologically extreme, we might expect moderate incumbents, especially those who are senior and therefore increasingly "out of step" with their primary electorates, to be challenged more often than extremists. Studying the period 1992 to 2016, we find no evidence that this is true. In fact, senior incumbents – those who have served ten or more years – with relatively moderate positions are less likely to be challenged than senior incumbents with relatively extreme positions. This is perhaps not surprising, since incumbents representing safer constituencies tend to have relatively extreme positions. Even after controlling for constituency safety, we find no statistically significant relationship between incumbent extremism and the probability of being challenged in the primary. We also find no statistically significant relationship between incumbent extremism and the number of primary challengers.[28]

Moreover, incumbents have not been challenged disproportionately by candidates who are more ideologically extreme than they are. The average extremism score of incumbents who were challenged in their primary during the period 1994 to 2016 was 0.42, while the average score among the challengers was only 0.38. Moreover, the top primary challenger – that is, the challenger with the highest vote share – was less likely to be extreme than the incumbent. Again focusing on senior incumbents with ten or more years of service, we find that the top challenger was more extreme than the incumbent only 40 percent

---

[26] This burst of activity did not increase the probability that US House incumbents lose their renomination bids, 1.17 to 1.16 percent. Note that we drop cases where two incumbents face one another in the primary due to redistricting, since in these cases one incumbent must lose. In the US Senate there does appear to be some change, 1.61 to 3.81 percent; however, the number of cases is small. Only four incumbent senators lost in the first period and four in the second period.

[27] Boatright (2013) also examines incumbent-contested primaries and presents results that are qualitatively similar to several of the findings in this section.

[28] These findings are from linear regressions with the following independent variables: incumbent *Extremism*, a third-order polynomial of constituency partisanship, indicator variables for constituency safety, and year-fixed effects. The standard errors are clustered by member. The findings are similar if we extend this analysis back to 1978, approximately the year that the modern increase in congressional polarization began; there is no statistically significant difference in the probabilities that moderates and extremists are challenged in primaries.

of the time.[29] However, there is some evidence that the patterns of primary competition differ for Democrats and Republicans. For US House Democrats, the corresponding figure is 21 percent, and for US House Republicans, 53 percent. For the US Senate, the corresponding figures are 34 percent for Democrats and 60 percent for Republicans.[30] Republican incumbents appear to be more likely to face challengers with relatively extreme positions. It is unclear why primaries would lead only one party's incumbents to be challenged by ideological extremists.

These patterns might not fully capture the extent to which incumbents feel threatened by primary challenges from ideological extremists. The fear of such challenges might drive them to retire. If incumbents are extremely precise in timing their retirements, then we would not observe a correlation between their roll-call voting positions and serious primary challenges by extremists. This type of precision would require accurate and detailed information about the preferences of primary voters and the pool of potential challengers. In our sample of races, we observe 239 cases in which a US House or Senate incumbent faced a serious primary challenge between 1994 and 2014 and won the subsequent general election.[31] Intuitively, if incumbents are more concerned about primary challenges from extremists, and if a serious primary challenge of a particular type (that is, extremist or moderate) reveals an incumbent's vulnerability to future primary challenges of that type, then we should observe incumbents retiring more often after facing significant challenges from the extremes. However, incumbents are only slightly more likely to retire after facing a significant primary challenge from a candidate who is more extreme than they are than when the challenger is not more extreme (17 versus 16.6 percent).[32] More generally, incumbents who retire are, on average, about as extreme as those who continue in office. The largest change in extremism scores following the replacement of an incumbent occurs when an incumbent loses a general election. The average change in extremism scores following a retirement is roughly the same magnitude as the change in extremism scores after a representative

[29] We consider a challenger to be more ideologically extreme when the imputed CS score is more than 0.02 points higher than the incumbent's score or when the imputed score is not available and the challenger is classified as extreme based on other sources.

[30] The number of incumbent-contested cases used to calculate these figures are 150, 165, 38, and 57, respectively.

[31] An incumbent is considered to have faced a serious primary challenge when the top challenger received more than 25 percent of the vote.

[32] Retirement means retirement from Congress. This may include those who retire to seek other offices.

passes away. The smallest change occurs after a representative loses the primary.

The patterns could also understate the threat incumbents face from primary challenges by extreme candidates if incumbents are adjusting their roll-call voting positions in response to these threats. Following conventional wisdom, we have assumed that incumbents typically do not make substantial adjustments to their roll-call voting positions while in office.[33] Since this might not always be the case, we can use the "one Congress at a time" roll-call voting positions of US House members to examine whether incumbents adjusted their positions after facing serious primary challenges – applying the same logic as we used to examine incumbent retirement decisions.[34] Between 1992 and 2012, there were only 55 cases of an incumbent who faced a serious primary challenge from an extreme candidate and went on to be re-elected. The incumbent moved towards the extreme in 49.1 percent of these cases.[35] This is not significantly different from the percentage of incumbents moving toward the extremes who faced no primary challenge, 42 percent. Thus, US House incumbents do not appear to be making substantial movements towards the extreme in response to strong primary challenges.

Another possibility is that incumbents respond strongly to the electoral difficulties of their colleagues in other districts and states, magnifying the effect of any single incumbent losing or even facing a serious challenge. This seems doubtful, however, for at least two reasons. First, such instances are extremely rare: incumbents lost to more-extreme challengers in only 18 out of more than 4,809 congressional races that involved an incumbent.[36] Second, incumbents are almost as likely to lose to a challenger who is more centrist or has a very similar ideological position, 13 cases, as to one who is more extreme. If incumbents are responding to the electoral defeat of colleagues, they must be putting significant weight on the handful of cases in which extremists win and very little weight on the other cases. In the absence of effects such as

---

[33] The CS scores we use to measure roll-call voting positions do not identify changes in representatives' positions over time. Thus the polarization that we are attempting to explain, which is illustrated in Figures 11.1 and 11.2, is due to member replacement.

[34] The one-Congress-at-a-time scores are from Nokken and Poole (2004), and are available until 2012.

[35] Only changes in an incumbent's score of greater than 0.02 are counted as movements.

[36] There are three losing incumbents for whom we do not have CS scores due to their switching parties and losing their primary. In two cases for which we do not have scores because the winning challenger does not have a CS score, we coded the relative positions of the incumbents from various media reports.

these, however, it seems unlikely that the fear of primary challenges is a major factor underlying the polarization we have observed in Congress.

We have not examined all the ways in which incumbents might react to ideological extremists. It is possible, for example, that incumbents respond to threats (and potential threats) in ways that are not apparent in traditional roll-call-based measures. They may adjust their rhetoric to make themselves *appear* more extreme. They may also move on particular issues, even though these changes are not necessarily reflected in overall ideological scores. We have focused on the roll-call-based scores since these are most commonly used to assess trends in polarization.

11.2.2 Non-Incumbent Primaries

Although observers often focus on incumbents' concerns about primary challenges as a source of polarization, the most competitive primaries are those without an incumbent. Furthermore, if elections are mainly about selection rather than accountability, these are the more consequential contests. The lack of primary contestation for incumbents with relatively extreme positions may reflect the electoral success of extremists in open-seat races. Here we investigate the following question: when two candidates with different ideological positions compete in a non-incumbent primary, does the candidate with the relatively extreme position win more often?

Using the imputed CS scores introduced above, we examine whether ideologically extreme candidates have an electoral advantage in non-incumbent primaries. We focus on cases for which the candidates with the highest and the second-highest number of primary votes have distinct ideological positions, and where the two candidates combined won more than 50 percent of the total vote.[37] During the period 1994 to 2016 there were 660 such cases. The more extreme candidate won slightly more than half of the time, 53 percent of the non-incumbent primaries. Overall, the extreme candidate won in 54 percent of the House races and 46 percent of the Senate races. We should note

---

[37] As above, we consider cases in which the extremism scores of the two candidates differed by more than 0.02 points. We drop 55 cases where the absolute difference in candidate scores was less than 0.02. We also include 149 cases where one or more of the imputed scores are not available, but we were able to identify the candidates' relative ideological positions from the various sources described above.

that unlike in incumbent-contested primary races, where we find that Republican incumbents appear more likely to face a relatively extreme challenger than Democrats, we find no significant partisan difference in the likelihood of nominating the relatively extreme candidate in non-incumbent primaries.

When we compare advantaged-party and parties-balanced primaries, the candidate with a relatively extreme score defeats the candidate with a relatively moderate score in more than half of the advantaged-party primaries (73 percent of the cases) but not in parties-balanced primaries (only 44 percent of the cases). The candidates with relatively extreme scores also defeat those with relatively moderate scores in more than half (58 percent) of the disadvantaged-party primaries.[38] These patterns are consistent with strategic voting. In constituencies where the parties are balanced, voters might sometimes choose the moderate candidate even when they prefer the extremist because they understand that the moderate candidate has a greater chance of winning the general election. In safe constituencies, where the outcome of the general election is largely predetermined, there is less need to be strategic in this way. However, the patterns are also consistent with an even simpler hypothesis – that is, compared to constituencies where the parties are balanced, in constituencies with an advantaged party, the distribution of primary election voters in that party is more extreme.[39]

Another way to think about non-incumbent primaries is to ask whether those who win primaries are more extreme than the overall pool of candidates running. We find no significant evidence that this is the case. The average extremism score for candidates who are nominated in non-incumbent US House or Senate primaries is 0.38, and for those who lose it is 0.37 ($n = 3,305$ and $1,608$, respectively).[40] In advantaged-party primaries the winners are slightly more extreme

---

[38] The number of observations is 110 for advantaged-party primaries, 379 for parties-balanced primaries, and 162 for disadvantaged-party primaries. Note that there are relatively few advantaged-party cases, since incumbents in advantaged-party constituencies are rarely defeated and tend to stay in office for long periods.

[39] According to this logic, we might have expected the distribution of primary voters in the disadvantaged party to be more moderate. The electoral success of the extreme candidates in these primaries may reflect something about the pool of candidates.

[40] The average scores of the pools are almost identical for the US House and Senate. Focusing on candidates with state or congressional legislative experience, almost all of whom have ideological extremism scores, we find that those nominated in US House primaries are slightly more moderate than the losers, and the winners of US Senate primaries are noticeably more moderate than the losers.

than the losers – 0.49 to 0.42 – while there is essentially no difference in parties-balanced primaries. Note that in the sample, the number of candidates in parties-balanced primaries (n = 2606) far outnumbers those in advantaged-party primaries (n = 572). Thus, the patterns are broadly consistent with the findings in the analysis above that compares the top two candidates from each contested race.

Finally, we can also investigate the handful of races in which redistricting forced two incumbents of the same party to run against each other in a primary. In these cases we have CS scores for both candidates, and both candidates are likely to be of high quality, from both an electoral point of view and also in terms of qualifications. During the period 1992 to 2016, the candidate with the relatively moderate position won the primary in more than half – 11 out of 19 – of these races.[41]

11.2.3 Polarization and Primary Election Turnout (Again)

As we discussed above, critics of primaries often argue that low turnout skews the distribution of primary voters towards the ideological extremes, resulting in the nomination of more-extreme candidates. However, we show here that the evidence in support of this claim is at best mixed.

The first question is, are voters who turn out for a party's primary more ideologically extreme than those who support that party in the general election? Several previous analyses of individual-level survey data from presidential primary and general elections find little difference in the ideological positions of voters who participate in a party's primary and those who support the party's nominee in the general election.[42] Norrander (1989, 584) writes, "Fears about extremist primary voters selecting extremist candidates unpalatable to the more moderate general election voters are unsupported. Primary voters just are not more ideologically extreme." More recent work examining midterm elections finds some evidence that primary voters are more extreme than the parties' followers.[43] However, Sides et al. (2016) examine surveys using

---

[41] We observe the same pattern if we extend the sample back to 1982. As above, we only consider cases in which the roll-call scores of the two incumbents differed by more than 0.02 points.

[42] See, for example, Geer (1988); Norrander (1989); Boatright (2014); Sides et al. (2016).

[43] See, for example, Hill (2015); Sides et al. (2016). Hill (2015) finds differences even in the presidential election years when congressional district preferences are estimated

validated votes and conclude that the differences in the ideological positions of primary voters and party supporters are not substantively meaningful. Neither Hill (2015) nor Sides et al. (2016) find evidence that primary electorates are particularly extreme in midterm election years compared to presidential election years. Sides et al. (2016, 7) write, "This runs contrary to fears that smaller turnout in midterm elections enhances the power of the ideological extremes."

Analyzing exit polls for presidential primary and general elections between 1992 and 2004, we find one pattern that is consistent with previous work, and one that differs.[44] Similar to the studies summarized above, we find that the average ideological difference between primary and general election voters is approximately zero for Republicans and positive but quite small for Democrats. However, exploiting the variation in primary turnout across states, parties, and years, we find a negative and statistically significant relationship between primary election turnout and the relative ideological extremism of the party's primary electorate.[45]

We measure the ideology of a given party's primary electorate in each state for each available year as the average of the (self-reported) ideological positions of the respondents who voted in that party's presidential primary.[46] We calculate the "ideological gap" in each state for each election by subtracting the average ideological position of a party's supporters in the general electorate from the average for that party's primary electorate. Respondents are considered a supporter of a party if they identify with that party.[47]

On average, there is little difference between the ideological positions of the typical primary and general election voters within states across

---

using multi-level regression with post-stratification (MRP). The differences are much smaller in both the presidential and congressional years using the raw survey responses aggregated by congressional district. Using self-reported voting, Jacobson (2012) compares primary voters to those who vote in the general election but not in the primary, and finds more substantial differences.

[44] The presidential primary exit polls are from ICPSR 9852, 2015, 3913, and 4183. The general election exit polls are from ICPSR 6102, 6989, 3527, and 4181.

[45] This resembles the analysis in Hirano et al. (2010).

[46] Respondents' ideological positions for both the primary and general election were coded on a three-point scale with three being the extreme position. For Republicans, 1 = liberal, 2 = moderate, and 3 = conservative. Democrats were coded in the opposite direction, that is, 1 = conservative.

[47] We code party identification using a three-point scale – Republican, Independent/Other, and Democrat. When we classified party supporters according to the party they voted for in the general election, the qualitative findings discussed below do not change.

elections.[48] The average "ideological gap" is 0.02, which is only 1 percent of the maximum potential difference, and less than 3 percent of the average inter-party difference (that is, the difference between the ideological positions of Democratic and Republican primary electorates).[49] Interestingly, the gap largely reflects differences in the Democratic Party electorates – the gap among Democrats is 0.05 and among Republicans it is -0.01.

Figure 11.3 displays the relationship between the ideological gap and primary turnout. The figure plots the ideological gap in each state and election against the primary turnout in that state and election. Primary turnout is measured as the total primary vote divided by the voting-age population.[50] These turnout percentages are noticeably smaller than general election turnout, in part because primary turnout tends to be smaller than general election turnout, but also because voters can only participate in one party's primary. The relationships are statistically significant for both parties. The figure includes the fitted values from regressing the ideological gap on primary turnout. A one-standard-deviation change in primary turnout for Democrats, which is 4.9 percentage points, is associated with a 0.04 reduction in the ideological gap. For Republicans the figures are similar – a 4.8-percentage-point change in turnout is associated with a 0.04 reduction in the gap. Thus, although the relationships are statistically significant, they are substantively small in magnitude.

Does the modest relationship between the relative ideological extremism of primary voters and primary turnout, which appears to exist at least across states in presidential election years, also affect the positions of elected representatives? We examine this question by exploiting the variation in statewide primary turnout. Figure 11.4 displays the US House members' extremism scores versus turnout in their party's primary in the year they were first elected. Since primary turnout for US House races is largely driven by turnout for high-profile statewide offices, such as governor or US Senate, we measure primary turnout in each state and year as the maximum primary vote a party receives across all top statewide offices, divided by total voting-age population. Contrary to conventional wisdom, Figure 11.4 shows that extremism is

---

[48] We only include states for which a reasonable number of exit poll respondents is available – that is, we dropped states with fewer than 50 respondents.

[49] The average inter-party difference is 0.68.

[50] The primary vote data comes from the *CQ Guide to Elections*, and the voting-age population data comes from the US Bureau of Economic Analysis.

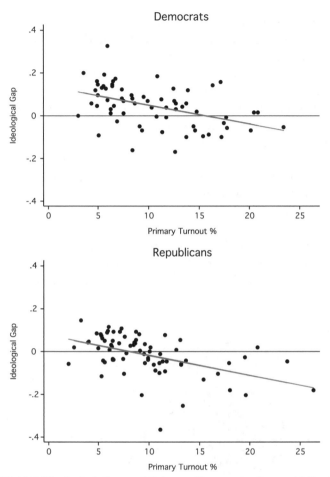

FIGURE 11.3 Ideological Gap and Primary Turnout by State and Presidential Election, 1992 to 2004

essentially unrelated to primary turnout (the correlation is only 0.03). The results from regressions of extremism on primary turnout – both simple bivariate and panel regressions that include state-party and year-fixed effects for representatives first elected from 1992 to 2014 – show no statistically significant relationship between extremism and turnout.[51] The coefficient on primary turnout is positive, which indicates that higher

---

[51] Each US House member is treated as a separate observation, so states with more House members are given more weight in the estimation.

primary turnout in the year a candidate was first elected to office is associated with more-extreme positions. We find the same patterns when we use different measures of primary turnout or extremism – that is, turnout relative to general election total or party votes and extremism relative to the chamber or party average.[52]

As discussed above, primary electorates tend to be slightly more moderate when primary election turnout is high. Why does this not translate into the election of more moderate members of Congress? One possibility is strategic voting – for example, turnout is generally higher in advantaged-party primaries and in these primaries there is less pressure to choose a moderate nominee for the general election. However, we find no significant relationship between extremism and primary election turnout, even after controlling for district safety using the presidential vote. Perhaps the most sensible conclusion is that there is little relationship between the ideological extremism of a US House member and the size of primary electorate that first nominated that member because (i) the

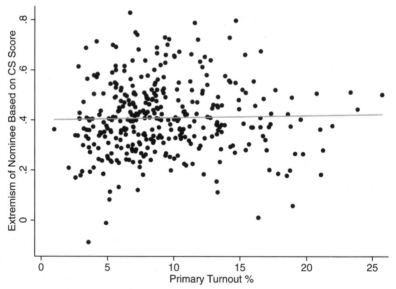

FIGURE 11.4 Extremism of US House Members and Primary Turnout, 1992 to 2014

[52] We also extended the analysis to include all nominees for which we have an imputed CS score, even though the sample only includes a non-random subset of nominees. We find a slightly negative but statistically insignificant relationship between extremism and primary turnout.

relationship between the size of a primary electorate and its ideological leaning is modest; and (ii) primary election voting decisions are typically determined by a variety of non-ideological factors (such as candidates' prior experience).

The broad trends in primary turnout we describe above suggest that the decline in turnout *per se* is unlikely to be a major cause of polarization. Since we rarely observe extremely high levels of turnout in primaries, we still do not know whether more significant and sustained increases in primary turnout levels would lead to the nomination of more moderate candidates.

11.2.4 Bottom Line

The results above suggest that the outcomes of primary elections have not, in fact, directly contributed much to the high levels of polarization in roll-call voting exhibited in Congress since 1992. Ideologically extreme candidates do not appear to be systematically favored in non-incumbent primaries, and incumbents are not defeated in large numbers in primaries by extremists (or by anyone). Low-turnout primaries do not lead to the nomination of extremists significantly more often than high-turnout primaries. One finding potentially connects primaries to polarization: the winners of advantaged-party non-incumbent primaries are more extreme than the losers. However, since the difference in extremism scores, 0.07, is small relative to the overall gap between the parties' average CS scores, 0.81, and since these primaries account for a small percentage of nominations, this factor can only be responsible for a small proportion of the observed growth in congressional polarization.

One potential channel through which primaries could be connected to polarization that we cannot rule out is the pool of candidates seeking office. If moderates who may have sought elected office in the past no longer compete in primaries, then voters may simply be choosing between extreme candidates with relatively minor differences in their positions. This implies that moderates are for some reason more negatively affected than extremists by the various costs and benefits of running in primaries.[53,54]

---

[53] See Hall (2019) for theory and evidence consistent with this argument.

[54] Early skeptics of primaries were concerned that the costs associated with running in primary elections might affect citizens' decisions to seek office.

One reason that moderates may not run is that primary election voters and elites do not have an exceptionally strong incentive to be strategic in their nomination choices. The existing evidence suggests that moderate candidates do better in general elections than extremists, but only by a few percentage points.[55] Of course this may be enough to change the outcome in a significant number of individual races and possibly tip the balance of power in Congress – a consideration that would presumably loom large among national party leaders if the United States had a Westminster-style system. In the decentralized US system, individual races may not internalize these incentives to choose moderates.

However, even if moderates are choosing not to seek office under the current primary system, we must still ask: what would happen under an alternative nomination system? Would moderates seek office and be elected at higher rates if nominations were done via caucuses, conventions, or party committees? In order to determine whether primaries are a major source of polarization, we would need to observe alternative systems that encourage the entry of moderate candidates or that favor the nomination of moderates over extremists when given a choice. We turn to these questions in the next sections.

11.3 PRIMARIES VERSUS CAUCUSES, CONVENTIONS, AND PARTY COMMITTEES

Despite all the attention primaries have received as a cause of polarization, the critics tend to focus on only half of the story. For example, formal models of electoral systems that show how primaries provide incentives to polarize typically compare the outcomes under primaries to a hypothetical nomination system in which party leaders choose their party's platform to maximize their general election support, which is typically assumed to be the median voter's preferred outcome.[56] Political observers who discuss the empirical evidence that primaries cause polarization usually point to reforms, such as more open primaries or a top-two system, with little evidence that these reforms actually yield more moderate candidates. To make a convincing case that we should abandon primaries, reformers must propose an alternative nomination

---

[55] See, for example, Ansolabehere, Snyder, and Stewart (2001); Canes-Wrone, Brady, and Cogan (2002); Hirano et al. (2010); Hall (2015).

[56] See, for example, Aranson and Ordeshook (1972); Coleman (1972); Owen and Grofman (2006); Hirano, Snyder, and Ting (2009). Party leaders might also favor moderate candidates in an effort to boost the collective reputation of their party's ability to govern.

system and at a minimum show that the alternative would result in less polarization. In this section we compare primaries with caucuses, conventions, and party committees.

As a theoretical matter, it is not obvious that caucuses, conventions, and party committees will necessarily produce more ideologically moderate nominees compared to primaries. Voters in primaries, like party elites, have some incentive to act strategically.[57] Party elites – candidates, large campaign donors, and interest group leaders and activists – like voters, have policy preferences.[58] In fact, the available evidence suggests that political elites have more intense and more extreme policy preferences than most voters, even primary election voters. Also, although ideologically moderate candidates on average receive more votes in general elections than extremists, the existing studies suggest that the electoral gains to moderation are modest.[59] Thus, it is not clear that party elites have a strong incentive to nominate moderates, except perhaps in the most competitive constituencies.[60] As a result, it is equally unclear that increasing party elite influence over nominations will lead to more moderate nominees.

The analysis of changes in roll-call voting scores for US House members in states that adopted primaries in the post-New Deal period suggests that those elected under the previous convention system were not significantly more moderate than those initially elected under the primary system. Of course, the discussion above highlights the likely interaction between the political environment and the way the nomination systems operated, so that analysis does not necessarily inform us about how a convention-type system might operate in a highly partisan polarized environment, such as that at the turn of the twenty-first century.

Here we exploit two situations in which nominees are selected by convention delegates in the recent polarized environment. The first is when states hold pre-primary conventions to nominate or endorse a candidate. In these states, candidates' support in the pre-primary conventions affects whether they can compete in the primary or whether

---

[57] See, for example, Hirano, Snyder, and Ting (2009).

[58] Formal models of elections often assume that parties and/or candidates care only about policy, or about policy in addition to winning.

[59] See, for example, Ansolabehere, Snyder, and Stewart (2001); Canes-Wrone, Brady, and Cogan (2002); Hirano et al. (2010); Hall (2015); Hall and Snyder (2013).

[60] Also, party elites might prefer to have some relatively extreme candidates in order to carve out an ideological distinct policy "platform" (Snyder, 1994; Snyder and Ting, 2002; Ansolabehere, Leblanc, and Snyder, 2012; Polborn and Snyder, 2017).

a primary will even be held. The second is when nominees are directly selected through a caucus, convention, or party committee. For example, in Virginia, local parties are allowed to nominate candidates through conventions and in several states, parties use caucuses, conventions, or party committees to nominate special election candidates.

11.3.1 Pre-Primary Conventions

In four states, Colorado, Connecticut, New Mexico, and Utah, parties are required by law to hold pre-primary conventions to formally endorse candidates.[61] In these states, candidates who receive enough support at the pre-primary conventions automatically qualify for the primary election, while those who do not must collect a large number of signatures in order to qualify. In the cases where two or more candidates compete in both the pre-primary convention and the primary election, we can compare the relative appeal of moderate candidates among delegates and voters.

States vary somewhat in terms of the proportion of delegates and the number of signatures candidates needed in order to move on to the primaries. In Colorado, any candidate in the pre-primary convention who received support from more than 30 percent of the convention delegates qualifies for the primary ballot (this threshold was raised from 20 percent in the 1990s).[62] In Connecticut, the threshold was 20 percent of the convention delegates until 1994, when it was lowered to only 15 percent. In New Mexico, the threshold has been 20 percent since 1994.[63] In Utah, the two candidates receiving the most delegate votes automatically proceed to the primary. Prior to 2014, candidates who secured more than 60 percent of the convention delegates would automatically be declared the nominee.[64,65]

---

[61] Other states have used pre-primary conventions in the past, including Idaho, Massachusetts, Minnesota, and Delaware. These states no longer use this system.

[62] The state and congressional pre-primary conventions in Colorado are called assemblies. This is sometimes referred to as the caucus-assembly-primary system.

[63] The pre-primary convention was also used in New Mexico from 1950 to 1954, 1962 to 1966, and 1976 to 1984.

[64] Utah began using the pre-primary convention system in 1947. Those who received more than 70 percent of the convention delegates would automatically be the party nominee. The Democrats lowered the threshold to 60 percent in 1996 and Republicans lowered the threshold to 60 percent in 1999 (Utah Foundation, 2011).

[65] Currently the candidates who lose the pre-primary convention could often petition to be on the ballot. In some cases, candidates would avoid the convention and simply petition to be on the ballot.

In states with pre-primary conventions, we can compare the outcomes in pre-primary conventions with those of primaries for the same pair of candidates.[66] We consider all cases with two candidates who compete against each other in both the convention and the primary. We study the four states mentioned above over the period 1992–2016.[67] We include a handful of races for statewide executive offices, but three-quarters of the observations are from US House or Senate races. For each pair of candidates, we first attempted to identify who was more ideologically extreme based on their imputed CS scores. As above, we use all cases where we have imputed scores for both candidates and the gap between these scores was greater than 0.02. In other cases, we relied on various media reports to classify candidates as extreme or moderate. Then for each pair of candidates, we compare the percentage of votes received by the more extreme candidate in both the primary election and the pre-primary convention. We also record whether the more extreme candidate won the primary election and/or the pre-primary convention.

In the 81 cases for which we know the outcome of the pre-primary convention, we find that the moderate is endorsed by the convention 50 percent of the time. However, when these same candidates face each other in the primary, the moderate wins 62 percent of the time. The difference is similar when we focus on the 61 non-incumbent contested races in our sample: the moderate wins only 45 percent of the time in the convention, but 58 percent of the time in the primary. The pattern is evident in both advantaged-party and parties-balanced constituencies.[68] Based on a simple t-test, the differences in the likelihood that moderates win in conventions versus primaries are statistically significant.[69] Finally, this pattern of the relatively moderate candidate gaining more support

---

[66] In roughly 60 percent of the non-incumbent contested races in these states, the ultimate winner competed in both a pre-primary convention and a primary. On average, US House members who do not also compete in a primary are more moderate than those who are forced to do so. When we control for the presidential vote, this difference is much smaller and no longer statistically significant.

[67] The data on convention votes is from various newspaper reports, state party webpages, and research reports from organizations such as the Utah Foundation. We drop cases in which the winner of the convention does not place among the top two in the primary or if the winner of the primary does not place among the top two in the convention.

[68] The pattern is also evident when we exclude the handful of statewide executive races.

[69] As discussed earlier, there may be stronger strategic incentives to nominate moderates in parties-balanced constituencies than in safe constituencies. We find that in all types of constituencies, the moderate is more likely to win in the primary than in the pre-primary convention.

in the primary than in the pre-primary convention is evident for both Republican and Democratic candidates.[70]

The bottom line is clear: when given a choice between two candidates, one relatively moderate and one relatively extreme, convention delegates are not more likely than primary election voters to choose the moderate candidate. This suggests that substituting conventions for primaries would not automatically lead to the nomination of more moderate candidates.

Of course, it is difficult to generalize from these results to other electoral contexts. First, the primaries come after the conventions, so the convention outcomes may affect the primary election outcomes; convention outcomes might also be affected by the fact that delegates know that subsequent primary elections may be held. So, we do not know what would happen if either the pre-primary conventions or the primaries were eliminated altogether in these states. Second, the set of states that employ the pre-primary convention is not a random sample of states. While they vary in terms of inter-party competition, they are all small or mid-sized states, and all but one are in the West.[71] Nonetheless, the results are at least suggestive.

Convention Delegates Versus Partisan Voters: The Case of Utah

Conventions in Utah illustrate the limits of pre-primary endorsements to facilitate the nomination of moderate candidates. The convention delegates tend to be more ideologically extreme than the primary electorate. In the 2000 gubernatorial election, the incumbent, Mike Leavitt, was not only jeered at the convention but also had his speech interrupted by calls of "liberal" and "Democrat."[72] Although he failed to secure the 60 percent of the convention delegates required to avoid a primary contest, Leavitt went on to win the primary election with 62 percent of the vote.

A survey of convention delegates and active voters conducted by the Utah Foundation reveals the differences in the preferences of pre-primary convention delegates and primary voters. The survey results show that Republican delegates were even more conservative than Republican

---

[70] If anything, the difference is even more pronounced for Republican candidates.

[71] During our period of interest, 1992 to 2014, Colorado was a competitive state, Connecticut was a Democratic leaning to solid Democratic state, New Mexico was a competitive to Democratic-leaning state, and Utah was a solid Republican state.

[72] Bob Bernick, Jr. and Edward L. Carter, "Leavitt, Cook Face Primaries: Both are Booed and Jeered at Republican State Convention." *Deseret News*, May 7, 2000.

TABLE 11.1 *Utah State Convention Delegates and Active Voters, 2010*

| | Percent Choosing 6 or 7 | | | |
| | Republican | | Democratic | |
	Delegates	Voters	Delegates	Voters
Importance Of:				
Expanding Consumer Protections	15	41	39	48
	[522]	[407]	[542]	[42]
Decreasing Pollution	16	41	73	78
	[518]	[416]	[546]	[41]
Expanding the Availability of	19	38	83	83
Healthcare Coverage	[519]	[408]	[545]	[42]
Protecting Gun Rights	73	61	8	21
	[518]	[412]	[538]	[42]
Agreement with Statement:				
Utah Should Increase Funding	23	50	83	76
for Public Education	[523]	[415]	[547]	[42]
The US Should Withdraw from	43	27	1	2
the United Nations	[516]	[403]	[547]	[42]
The 17th Amendment Should be	28	9	2	2
Repealed (Election of Senators)	[518]	[408]	[548]	[42]

Cell entries are percentages; number of respondents in square brackets.

active voters on virtually every item for which there was a clear partisan divide.

We define the "conservative" and "liberal" answers based on the average responses by Democrats versus Republicans overall, as well as current popular discourse. The survey includes two types of items, both on scales from 1 to 7. One type asks whether the respondent thinks a given issue is important. For these, 1 = Not At All Important and 7 = Extremely Important. We define responses of 6 or 7 as indicating that the respondent thinks that the issue is highly important. The other type asks whether the respondent agrees with a given statement. For these, 1 = Strongly Disagree and 7 = Strongly Agree. We define responses of 6 or 7 as indicating that the respondent is in strong agreement with the statement.

Consider for example the item "Expanding Consumer Protections." Republican active voters were almost as likely as Democrat active voters, and even more likely than Democratic delegates, to give the liberal

answer on this issue (that is, to respond that the issue is highly important). They were also more than twice as likely as Republican delegates
to give the liberal answer on this issue. Similarly, on the importance of
"Decreasing Pollution," as well as agreeing with the statement "Utah
Should Increase Funding for Public Education," Republican active voters
were more than twice as likely as Republican delegates to give the
liberal answer.[73] Republican active voters were also about twice as likely
as Republican delegates to give the liberal answer on the importance
of "Expanding the Availability of Healthcare Coverage." They were
also significantly more likely to give the liberal answer on the items
"The United States Should Withdraw from the United Nations," and
"Protecting Gun Rights."

The extreme ideological conservatism of Republican delegates in Utah
can be seen in facts such as the following. The percentage of delegates
responding that the issue is highly important were: 69 percent for
"Allowing Mining and Grazing on Federal Lands in Utah," 73 percent
for "Protecting Gun Rights," and 86 percent for "Protecting States'
Rights," but only 33 percent for "Improving the Quality of Education
at Utah's Colleges and Universities" and 32 percent for "Investing
in Transportation Infrastructure." A larger percentage of Republican
delegates responded that "Allowing Mining and Grazing on Federal
Lands" is highly important compared to the percentages responding
similarly for: "Improving the Quality of Education in Kindergarten
through 12th Grade," "Enhancing Policies that Plan for Utah's Growth,"
"Increasing the Number of Quality Jobs," and "Reducing Crime." It
is even more important than "Reducing Taxes" and "Decreasing State
Government Spending." Republican delegates responded that protecting
states' rights is more important than anything else asked on the survey.
On average Republican delegates are not only more conservative than
the average Utah voter; they are significantly more conservative than the
average Utah Republican voter.[74]

Across the survey, there were 34 policy and ideological items
for which the differences between Democrats and Republicans were
statistically significant and clear. Republican delegates were significantly
more conservative than Republican active voters on 28 of these items.

---

[73] The liberal answer to the first item is that the issue is highly important and the liberal
answer to the second item is strong agreement.

[74] There is only one item on which Republican active voters appear to have more
conservative preferences than delegates – "Abortion of Any Kind Should be Outlawed"
– but the difference is not statistically significant.

Republican active voters were significantly more conservative than Republican delegates on just two of the items.[75] On four other items, the differences between Republican delegates and active voters were statistically insignificant.[76] Overall, the evidence is clear that Republican delegates are more conservative than Republican active voters.

Republican delegates do not appear particularly strategic. Consider the survey item "It is Valuable for the State of Utah to Reelect its Current US Senators and Representatives in Order to Maintain Seniority in the US Legislature."[77] Most careful observers believe that members of Congress become more powerful with seniority. Thus, a "strategic" response would be to agree, rather than disagree, with this statement. However, only 17 percent of Republican convention delegates gave a "strategic" response of 6 or 7 to the statement, while 56 percent gave a "non-strategic" response of 1 or 2. Interestingly, Republican active voters appear slightly more strategic than the delegates: 22 percent of Republican active voters gave a response of 6 or 7, while only 32 percent responded 1 or 2.[78]

Ideological extremism is not limited to Republican delegates. Democratic delegates also appear to be more liberal than Democratic active voters. While the sample of Democratic active voters in the survey is very small (n = 42), across the 34 policy and ideological items for which the differences between Democrats and Republicans were statistically significant and clear, Democratic delegates are significantly more liberal than Democratic active voters in 14 cases, and the reverse is true in only one case.

This difference in preferences between the convention delegates and primary voters is evident to observers of Utah politics. Recent discussions on reforming Utah's nomination system have focused on moving towards primaries to select more moderate nominees. In a *Deseret News* article, Richard Davis writes, "General election voters tend to be more moderate than primary voters, but primary voters are more moderate than convention delegates. Moderate candidates who can cross party lines and build bridges with various and diverse groups

---

[75] The items were about the importance of reducing crime and whether "Abortion of Any Kind" should be made illegal.

[76] There were also four items for which the differences between the parties were statistically insignificant or the patterns were mixed.

[77] This item has the 1-to-7 scale of agreement described above.

[78] It is possible that the convention delegates are not strategic in their nominations in part because Utah is a relatively safe state for Republicans in the general election.

would be advantaged in primary elections."[79] Even more recently, a *US News & World Report* article noted that the 2014 reform that permits candidates to by-pass the Utah pre-primary convention via petitions appears to benefit moderates, with the headline "GOP Primary Shows New Utah System Allows Moderates to Win."[80]

11.3.2 Caucuses, Conventions, and Party Committees

Although political parties in all states employ primaries to nominate candidates for US House elections, even in the recent polarized period a group of Democratic and Republican general election candidates were nominated by caucuses, conventions, or party committees when they were first elected to office. The three situations in which nominees would not be selected in a primary are: (1) special elections; (2) the initial nominee withdraws after the primary; (3) the state allows parties to decide whether or not to hold a primary.[81] There were 136 Democratic and Republican general election candidates not nominated by primaries between 1992 and 2016. We have imputed ideological extremism scores for 81 of these non-primary nominees. In states where the major parties nominated at least one general election candidate in a caucus, convention, or party committee during this period, 339 Democratic and Republican general election candidates were nominated through primaries. We have imputed extremism scores for 213 of these primary nominees.[82]

First we study the change in ideological extremism scores within districts as a function of the nomination method. For this analysis the dependent variable is the within-party difference between the extremism scores of a new nominee and the former incumbent. In most cases, both candidates were nominated via primaries. However, in some cases one of the candidates was nominated via a caucus, convention, or party meeting. In the 235 cases for which we can calculate a difference (26 of which involved a non-primary nominee), there is no systematic relationship between the change in extremism scores and the nomination

[79] Richard Davis, "Still Not Too Late to Reform Nomination Process." *Deseret News*, June 26, 2013.
[80] Price (2017).
[81] Situation 3 only occurs in Virginia.
[82] We also conducted this analysis for both types of nominees where we subtract either the average extremism score for all nominees to the US House in the relevant Congress or the average extremism score among all the co-partisan nominees in the relevant Congress. The substantive findings are the same as when we use the unadjusted extremism scores.

method.[83] Non-primary nominees' and primary nominees' extremism scores are 0.052 and 0.054 higher, respectively, than the incumbents they replaced. The difference between these two changes is not statistically significant.

We can compare the ideological extremism of non-primary and primary nominees in a larger sample of non-incumbent contested US House elections by regressing House candidates' extremism scores on an indicator for whether the candidates were nominated in a primary, the presidential vote of the candidates' parties, and a year trend variable. We find no significant evidence that the House candidates who were nominated by primaries are more extreme compared to those nominated by caucus, conventions, or party meetings.[84]

We might expect the relationship to be more pronounced in competitive districts where the elites and activists in caucuses, conventions, and party meetings may be more responsive than primary voters to general election incentives to nominate moderates. To examine this possibility, we interacted the primary variable with an indicator for district safety. We find no significant evidence that the relative extremism of non-primary compared to primary nominees is greater in parties-balanced constituencies compared to advantaged- or disadvantaged-party constituencies.

Masket and Shor (2013) use a similar approach to examine state legislators in Colorado and Illinois, where vacancies are filled by the incumbent party's central committee for the district. Unlike our analysis of US House elections, in which party elites can only control the nomination, in these two cases the party elites directly fill the vacancies. Masket and Shor (2013) find little evidence that appointed legislators have significantly different roll-call voting scores compared to elected legislators.[85]

---

[83] We could not calculate a difference if an imputed score was missing or if the district boundaries changed due to redistricting.

[84] The coefficient on the primary indicator variable is -0.001 with a standard error of 0.017.

[85] We have not used campaign finance based scores (CF Scores) for our main analyses for the reasons highlighted above. Additional analyses, however, which are not possible with roll-call and survey-based scores, are possible using these CF scores. In particular, since these scores are available for statewide executive offices we can exploit the variation in nomination methods used within states across offices. In three states – Indiana, Michigan, and South Dakota – the nominees for all statewide down-ballot offices, including state attorney general, secretary of state, treasurer, auditor, public utilities commissioner, etc., are nominated via conventions rather than primaries. Like all other states, the nominees for governor and US senator are chosen via primaries. By

The bottom line is that even during the current era of partisan sorting within the electorate, in the cases we are able to study primaries are not more likely than caucuses, conventions, or party meetings to nominate candidates with relatively extreme positions over those with relatively moderate positions. Of course, the set of cases we can study is limited. For example, in the analysis above, other than in Virginia, caucuses, conventions, and party committees were used in rare circumstances. If they were used more regularly, then party elites may have a greater incentive to influence the outcomes, and might also be able to engage in more strategic behavior (for example, log-rolling and ticket-balancing as in the past). This could eventually lead to the nomination of more ideologically moderate candidates. For now however, the available evidence does not indicate that primaries are causing polarization, if the main alternative is a caucus, convention, or party meeting.

11.4 PARTICIPATION IN OPEN VERSUS CLOSED PRIMARIES

A commonly proposed reform to the current primary system, which allows states to restrict participation in a party's primary to those who are registered with the party, is a primary system that allows greater participation in a party's primaries by those not registered with the party. Reformers argue that reducing the barriers to primary participation –

comparing the nominees for the different offices from these states with their neighbors, we can make some tentative inferences about the effects of conventions compared to primaries. We define neighboring states as those that share a border or part of a border with any of the three states that use conventions. The comparison states are Iowa, Illinois, Kentucky, Minnesota, Montana, North Dakota, Nebraska, Ohio, South Dakota, Wisconsin, and Wyoming. More specifically, we calculate the difference in the extremism scores of nominees for top-of-the-ticket and down-ballot offices. We then compare these differences for the states that use conventions to nominate candidates for down-ballot offices to those that use primaries to nominate candidates for down-ballot offices. This difference-in-differences approach provides some indication of whether conventions in general lead to more moderate nominees. The bottom line from the analysis is clear: the down-ballot nominees chosen by conventions are no more likely to be "moderates" than those chosen by primary elections. It appears that in both types of states, the nominees for governor and US senator are more moderate than the nominees for down-ballot offices. This could be due to the measure used: candidates for governor and US senator raise much more money than those for down-ballot offices; thus they may raise more money from "moderate," access-oriented donors, which may give them more moderate scores. While this is suggestive, we might be concerned that extremism is less of an issue for down-ballot offices. Also, as we discussed earlier, primary voters may be less informed about the ideological positions of primary candidates for down-ballot offices than those for top-of-the-ticket offices.

that is, allowing independents to participate or cross-over voting – would move the distribution of the primary electorate in a moderate direction. This would lead to the nomination of ideologically moderate candidates. Richard Pildes writes, "The single institutional change most likely to lead to *some* moderation of candidates and officeholders, across all elections, would be to change the design of primary elections. The change would involve replacing closed primaries, in which only registered party members can vote, with various alternative forms of primary elections" (Pildes, 2011, 298).

States currently differ in the extent to which they restrict participation in primaries. Various scholars have attempted to classify primaries based on these restrictions, often dividing them between those that are open, semi-open, semi-closed, or closed. Open refers to systems that place few, if any, restrictions on which party's primary a registered voter is allowed to participate in. Aside from the blanket or top-two system, primary voters in open systems are still limited to participating in only one party's primary at the polls. Closed systems are at the other end of the spectrum and limit participation in a party's primary to those who are registered with the party prior to the primary election. The semi-open and semi-closed systems that lie in between, which we refer to as mixed systems, differ in whether and how independents, unaffiliated voters, or voters registered with other parties are allowed to participate in a particular party's primary. However, there is some uncertainty about how the specific details of participation requirements associated with each system are predicted to affect participation. This creates challenges for classifying the relative "openness" of these mixed systems. For example, is a system that allows voters to change party registration just before the primary more or less open than one that allows independents, but not registered party members, to vote in either party's primary with no registration restrictions? Is a system that allows parties to choose from election to election whether to let independents participate in their primary more or less open than a system that allows independents to vote in a primary but requires them to become a registered party member on election day?

Existing studies that examine the connection between primary openness and polarization have found mixed or no evidence that openness is correlated with electing ideologically moderate representatives.[86] In a cross-sectional analysis of primaries and congressional roll-call voting scores between 1982 and 1990, Gerber and Morton (1998) find some

---

[86] See, for example, McGhee et al. (2014); Gerber and Morton (1998); Bullock and Clinton (2011); Kanthak and Morton (2001); Rogowski and Langella (2015).

evidence that representatives elected in open primary systems were slightly more moderate than those elected in closed primary systems. However, representatives elected in mixed systems were even more moderate than those elected in open systems. Using state legislative roll-call voting scores or campaign finance-based ideological scores, neither McGhee et al. (2014) nor Rogowski and Langella (2015) find evidence of a systematic association between primary openness and candidate positions. Bullock and Clinton (2011) focus on the 1996 move from a closed to an open primary system in California. They find some evidence that representatives became more moderate in competitive districts but not in safe districts.

Because of the challenges associated with calibrating the relative "openness" of the different mixed primary systems, we focus on differences between open and closed systems. We define an open primary system as having essentially no party registration restrictions for voting in either party's primary. Voters in open primaries may still be limited to choosing from among only one party's candidates for each office in a given election, but they can participate in either party's primary for that election. We do not classify systems that allow same-day party registration as open primaries, since the registration process may have implications that affect participation decisions. We also exclude top-two systems, discussed separately in the next section, since they differ significantly from other primary systems in that they also potentially change the nature of general election contests. We use the standard party registration criteria to identify states with closed primary systems.[87]

We again focus on the period 1992 to 2014. During this period, 22 states nominated candidates at some point in open primaries while 15 states nominated candidates in closed primaries; in the remaining cases states used mixed systems that are commonly labeled semi-open or semi-closed, or a top-two system.[88] Only California elected representatives under both open and closed primary systems during this period.[89] Only two states, Idaho and Washington, switched between open and

---

[87] The classifications are based on data used in McGhee et al. (2014). We thank the authors for sharing their data.

[88] The 22 states that employed an open primary system at some point during this period include: AL, AR, CA, GA, HI, ID, IL, IN, MI, MN, MO, MS, MT, ND, OH, SC, TN, TX, VA, VT, WA, and WI. The 15 states that employed a closed primary system at some point during this period include: AZ, CA, CT, DE, FL, KY, LA, NC, NM, NV, NY, OK, OR, PA, and SD.

[89] This is because we are coding blanket primaries as open. Other studies have coded blanket primaries as non-partisan.

mixed systems, and four (Arizona, North Carolina, Oregon, and South Dakota) switched between closed and mixed systems.[90] The two papers that examine the relationship between primary system openness and representatives' positions within states examine a longer time period, include the variation between the different types of mixed systems, and do not focus on open-seat elections.[91] Because we are focused on open-seat elections in open and closed primary systems during the highly polarized period between 1992 and 2014, the number of within-state observations under the two systems is too limited to provide reasonable estimates of the effects of changing the primary type.

Open primaries are supposed to nominate relatively moderate candidates because of high participation rates by independents and partisan voters who would like to vote in another party's primaries. Thus, we might expect turnout to be higher in open than in closed primaries. Primary turnout is measured as the maximum number of primary votes cast across statewide offices in a given election cycle divided by the voting-age population.[92] Primary turnout does appear to be related to the openness of the primary system. On average, primary turnout in open primaries in non-presidential election years is 17.4 percent. In closed primaries turnout is 13.7 percent.[93] The difference between the two systems is about the same if we include a year trend.[94] However, as discussed above, increasing primary turnout does not necessarily lead to the nomination of more ideologically moderate candidates or even to the participation of more moderate voters. Previous survey analyses of primary electorates find that the distribution of ideological preferences do not vary significantly with the openness of the primary system.[95]

On average, the ideological extremism scores for US House members elected in open-seat elections in states with open primaries is 0.432, and

---

[90] Due to a judicial decision, in 2008 and 2010 Louisiana used closed primaries for US House and Senate elections. In all other years it used its unique top-two system.

[91] See McGhee et al. (2014) and Rogowski and Langella (2015).

[92] We also measured turnout as the number of primary votes cast divided by the maximum number of general election votes cast across statewide offices in a given election cycle.

[93] This difference is statistically significant at the 10-percent level when we cluster by state. In the mixed primary systems turnout resembled the open primaries with a turnout of 16.8 percent.

[94] In a within-state analysis comparing closed systems to either open or mixed systems, we find no significant evidence that changing the primary system is related to changes in turnout. However, as noted above, there are only a few cases of states adjusting their primaries between closed and open or mixed systems.

[95] Geer (1988); Kaufmann, Gimpel, and Hoffmann (2003); Hill (2015); Sides et al. (2016).

0.388 for those elected in states with closed primaries.[96] We estimated a variety of regression models with extremism scores as the dependent variable. These models include an indicator variable for open primaries and different sets of control variables – for example, party indicators, year trends or fixed effects, presidential vote for the winner's party. These analyses provide no evidence that open primaries are associated with the election of ideological moderates. If anything, they point in the opposite direction: the coefficient on the open primary indicator variable is positive in all specifications.[97]

11.5 TOP-TWO SYSTEM

In recent years, many observers concerned with polarization have focused on the top-two system. In a *New York Times* Op-ed quoted at the beginning of the chapter, former Oregon Secretary of State Keisling promoted the top-two system as the alternative electoral system that could reduce polarization: "So what can be done? States should scrap this anachronistic system and replace it with a 'fully open/top two' primary. All candidates would run in a first round, 'qualifying' election, with the top two finalists earning the chance to compete head-to-head in November."[98]

Although these systems vary slightly in their implementation, the basic structure is for candidates from all the different parties to compete against each other in a first-round election, in which voters can vote for any party's candidate for any office. The two candidates with the highest vote shares move on to a second-round election. Thus, the two candidates competing in the second round could come from the same party. While a variant of this system has been used in Louisiana since 1975 for state offices and since 1978 for US House elections, the top-two system for state and federal offices has only been introduced recently in Washington (2008) and California (2012). In the Louisiana top-two

---

[96] For the mixed systems the extremism score is 0.437.

[97] We can include states with semi-open or semi-closed primary systems to examine whether the within-state variation in openness is correlated with the extremism scores of US House members. Since we do not know how to classify all the different variations in the way the primary electorate could be restricted, or what impact these restrictions may have on participation, we compare closed primaries to all other systems. We again find no statistically significant evidence that within-state changes between closed and more open systems are related to the extremism of the US House members elected.

[98] Keisling (2010).

system, the candidates proceed to a second round only if no candidate receives a majority in the first round.[99]

Numerous studies have focused on the most recent reform in California. The various findings do not provide consistent evidence that the top-two system is associated with lower levels of polarization.[100] Part of the issue is that only a few state or federal elections have taken place under this system, which makes it difficult to evaluate.

Examining the ideological extremism scores of US House members in Washington and California elected between 1994 and 2014, we find that both states appear to be electing representatives who were moderate relative to the House members from other states. While US House members overall became more extreme over this period, the representatives from these two states did not. The Washington congressional delegation became gradually more moderate throughout this period. California's 2010 delegation was roughly as extreme as its 1994 delegation. However, there was a noticeable drop in the extremism scores in 2012 and 2014, especially relative to the other states' congressional delegations. This is suggestive evidence that the top-two system may be having a moderating effect, or at least is not contributing to greater polarization.

For Louisiana we examine the period 1950 to 2014. Until recently, the Louisiana delegation nominated under its top-two system appeared, on average, to be less ideologically extreme than the chamber as a whole and even relative to other Southern delegations. One notable exception was the Louisiana delegation elected in 2010, which was the second of two elections during the brief period when the state adopted a closed primary system. While this is suggestive, the pattern is less clear when we compare the roll-call voting behavior of Louisiana members of Congress in the decade-and-a-half before the reform was enacted. Starting with the members elected in 1966, the Louisiana congressional delegation was noticeably less extreme than the US House as a whole (and even relative to other Southern delegations) until the election in 1976, which was just prior to the introduction of the top-two system. Even under the top-two system, the Louisiana delegation followed other Southern delegations in moving in the extreme direction at a faster rate than the non-Southern

---

[99] Municipalities, especially those with non-partisan elections, have been using some variant of a top-two system for several decades.

[100] See Ahler, Citrin, and Lenz (2016); Kousser, Phillips, and Shor (2018); McGhee et al. (2014); Rogowski and Langella (2015).

delegations. Currently the Louisiana representatives elected under its top-two system are more extreme than the average US House member and about as extreme as other Southern delegations. Thus, the Louisiana case does not provide clear evidence that its variant of the top-two system produces more ideologically moderate representatives.

State legislative roll-call data between 1996 and 2014 provide suggestive, but not overwhelming, evidence that the top-two system has some moderating effect. Both the California and Washington state legislative delegations were significantly more extreme, on average, than other state legislative delegations during this period. The average extremism scores of California state legislators relative to those in other states trended up during this period and then remained flat before dropping a bit in 2012. The average extremism scores of Washington state legislators relative to other states trended down during the entire period. Louisiana continues to have one of the smallest gaps in median roll-call voting positions between the two parties. We cannot, however, draw strong conclusions from this evidence.

The theory underlying the claim that top-two systems reduce polarization has not been fully developed.[101] Part of the intuition for why this might occur comes from making the system more open. Since all voters can participate in both rounds, any voter – but moderate voters in particular – will feel free to choose between candidates of either party. Moreover, primary voters in the relatively disadvantaged party may strategically support the more moderate candidate from their party in hopes of attracting centrist voters in the second round. While these claims seem plausible, they have not been well substantiated by the empirical evidence.

In our analyses above in the section on expanding the primary electorate, we found some evidence that the openness of the primary system is associated with higher turnout in primaries, but not with the election of representatives with relatively less extreme positions. We might expect the top-two system to attract even more moderate and independent voters since, similar to the blanket primaries, voters are able to cast a ballot in either party's primary for each office – that is, they do not have

---

[101] We are only aware of one theoretical paper, Amoros, Puy, and Martinez (2016), that directly compares top-two systems with partisan two-round systems. Their model suggests that the top-two system will produce moderate winners more often than the partisan system. However, their model is highly stylized – for example, it restricts attention to the case in which there are exactly two potential candidates from each party.

to vote for nominees from the same party across offices. However, we found no significant evidence in the cross-section or within-state analyses that primary turnout was higher under top-two systems compared to other primary systems. It is possible, but unlikely, that the composition of voters in these systems differs substantially from that of other primary systems.

Prior studies have found little evidence of strategic voting in the California top-two system, at least among survey respondents.[102] For example, Alvarez and Sinclair (2015) argue that survey respondents vote sincerely for the candidate who has the policy position closest to their position. These studies do not examine the strategic voting that may occur in the first round to ensure that at least one candidate from the voter's party is nominated. In a district that leans Democratic (for example, 60-percent Democratic normal vote), two Republicans who gain equal support could both move on to the second round if four or more Democrats enter the primary and split their total vote too evenly. Indeed, in the 2016 Washington state treasurer election, two Republicans competed in the second round in this Democratic-leaning state.[103] Thus, voters from both parties have an incentive to act strategically to avoid splitting the vote. However, it is not clear whether voters actually behave strategically when choosing from among candidates of the same party. Even if voters are strategically coordinating on a particular candidate in the first round, it is not clear that they select the relatively moderate candidate.[104] Coordinating on moderates within a party may require a level of voter knowledge that would be very costly for voters to obtain in the current informational environment.

The top-two system might also facilitate the election of ideologically moderate representatives by attracting more moderate candidates to

---

[102] See Nagler (2015); Alvarez and Sinclair (2015). Previous studies of California blanket primaries find evidence that cross-over voting in the first round varied by election type – for example, top-of-the-ticket versus down-ballot or competitive versus safe. Alvarez and Nagler (2002) find little survey-level evidence that this cross-over voting could have affected the outcomes of most primary elections, and little evidence that it was done for strategic reasons. See Cain and Gerber (2002) for a review of these findings.

[103] The Democrats ran three candidates, John Comerford, Alec Fisken, and Marko Liias, who collectively received 51.6 percent of the first-round vote (18.0, 13.2, and 20.4 percent, respectively). The two Republican candidates, Duane Davidson and Michael Waite, received 25.1 and 23.3 percent of the first-round vote, respectively.

[104] Even if voters are weighing ideology heavily in their decisions, whether to coordinate on a moderate or extreme candidate depends on the distribution of preferences among party supporters. If a majority has relatively extreme preferences, then they should try to coordinate on one of the relatively extreme candidates.

compete in the first round of competition compared to primaries. We explore this possibility using our sample of candidates with extremism scores. This allows us to compare the new primary entrants – that is, those without previous experience running for a statewide or federal office – who competed in a primary between 2006 and 2010 to new entrants who competed in the first round of the top-two system between 2012 and 2016. If the pool of candidates became more moderate under the top-two system, then we would expect the extremism scores of the new entrants to be lower for the 2012-to-2016 elections. However, we find little difference in the extremism scores of the new entrants under the two systems. Of course, there are potential sample selection issues since we are only comparing the candidates for whom we have imputed extremism scores. Nonetheless, the results suggest that the top-two system did not significantly alter the extremism of the pool of primary candidates.

The more consequential difference between this system and other nomination systems appears to be in the second-round election, when voters may end up choosing between two candidates from the same party. If the top-two system were to lead to moderation, then we would expect the effect to be most noticeable in the cases where co-partisans compete against each other in the second-round. In a simple unidimensional spatial voting framework, when a moderate Democrat (Republican) competes against a more extreme co-partisan in the second round, the moderate candidate should attract support from Republican (Democratic) voters and win the election.

Situations where two co-partisans end up competing against each other in the second round election are likely to be relatively rare events. If the electorate is divided with less than two-thirds supporting the Democratic (Republican) Party, and if candidates are strategic in their entry decisions, then we would expect there to be one candidate from each party in the second round. In the typical case, we expect only one serious candidate from the disadvantaged party to run. As long as this candidate attracts most of the support among the disadvantaged party's supporters, she is very likely to proceed to the second round. Even if the advantaged party has the support of more than two-thirds of the voters, they still need to divide the partisan vote relatively evenly among two of their candidates in order to win both nomination positions.

How often has the top-two system led to co-partisans competing against one another in the second-round election? In the first three electoral cycles during which California employed the system, there was only one race for statewide office that involved co-partisans competing in the second round. For the US House, there were eight races in 2012, seven races in 2014, and seven races in 2016. The one race for statewide office was for the 2016 US Senate. Thus, 13.7 percent of the 168 officials elected to statewide or federal office in California during this period faced a co-partisan in the second round. In the five electoral cycles that Washington employed the top-two system between 2008 and 2016, there were only three US House and one statewide second-round elections in which co-partisans competed against each other – that is, only 5.3 percent of 75 federal or statewide elected officials faced a co-partisan in the second round.[105] In Louisiana, where a second round is only held if no candidate receives a majority of the first-round votes, between 1992 and 2016 less than 30 percent of the statewide and federal races went to a second round (40 out of 138). Among the handful of contested races, only nine (that is, less than a quarter) were among co-partisans.

At the state legislative level, where there are perhaps more districts with an extreme partisan imbalance, there were more cases of co-partisan second-round competition. In 2012, less than a quarter of the 80 California state assembly races and only 2 out of 20 state senate races had co-partisans competing in the second round; overall, 20 percent of the state legislative races fell into this category. In 2014, the number of state assembly races with co-partisans competing in the second round dropped to eight; interestingly, there was no overlap with the 2012 districts. The number of state senate races increased to six. In 2016, co-partisans competed against each other in 15 of the 80 state assembly races and 5 of the 20 state senate races. While state legislative races tended to be safe for one party's candidates, the districts with co-partisans competing in the second round tended to be particularly lopsided in partisan support. In Washington, the number of state legislative races with co-partisans competing in the second round was more common than for US House or statewide races, but still less common than for California state legislative races. Between 2008 and 2016 there were 38 out of 490 state assembly races and 11 out of 128 state senate races in which co-partisans competed against each other in the second-round election.

Where voters were given a choice between two co-partisans, there is some skepticism that the supporters of the opposition party would vote

---

[105] The average presidential vote for the favored party in districts with co-partisans competing in 2012 or 2014 was 71 percent. The average presidential vote for the favored party in the remaining districts was 52 percent.

for the more moderate candidate. In the 2014 election in the California 25th Congressional District neither of the two Republican candidates, Steve Knight and Tony Strickland, could secure the endorsement of the Democrat, Lee Rogers, who came in third place. Rogers initially endorsed Knight, but claimed that Knight adopted more conservative policies after the primary. Rogers is quoted as saying, "While I don't support either Republican and I'll be abstaining from voting in the race, the thought of Tony Strickland as my congressman makes me more ill than the honest Steve Knight."[106] Examining survey evidence, Nagler (2015) finds that voters tend to abstain in the second-round election rather than vote for an opposition-party candidate.

For the US House races for which we are able to identify the relatively extreme and centrist candidates in the second round, we find that, overall, moderates do not appear to win the second round at significantly higher rates than extremists: the moderate won in 10 out of a total of 19 races between co-partisans in California (2012–2016) and Washington (2008–2016).[107] Why are moderates not doing better in the second round? Do enough moderates and voters who support the party not on the ballot choose the more moderate candidate? We turn to these questions next and illustrate how even if the top-two system allows moderate candidates to attract a broader base of support in the second round, additional behavioral assumptions are required for the system to yield more moderate representatives.

11.5.1 Voting Behavior under the Top-Two System

The 2016 US Senate race in California illustrates some of the challenges the top-two system faces for electing relatively moderate candidates. This was a high-profile race with two Democrats, Loretta Sanchez and Kamala Harris, defeating 11 challengers in the first round to make it to the second round. Sanchez was a ten-term US House member and was widely perceived to be the more ideologically conservative candidate. Her roll-call voting record placed her to the right (that is, in the direction of the average Republican) of the average Democratic member of Congress. Sanchez tried to appeal to Independent and Republican voters and

---

[106] Rick Orlov, "Strickland, Knight square off for 25th Congressional District seat," *Los Angeles Daily News.* October 19, 2014.

[107] Five of these cases did not involve an incumbent. In four of the cases the moderate won. However, since the sample is so small we do not want to draw any conclusions from these few cases.

received endorsements from several prominent Republicans.[108] Harris was a well-known attorney general and was widely portrayed as having the backing of the Democratic Party. Harris did substantially better than Sanchez in the first round and the poll data prior to the election suggested Harris would win by a considerable margin.

If the intuition behind the moderating effect of the top-two system is correct, then we would expect to observe substantial support for Sanchez among Republicans and some Independents. Using the CCES survey data from the 2016 election we can examine how the Democrats, Republicans, and Independents responded to the two choices in the second round.[109] First we can examine the roll-off rates by voter partisanship.[110] The roll-off was highest among Republicans (32.5 percent); among Independents it was 26.8 percent and only 4.9 percent among Democrats.[111] Thus, even if Sanchez had greater appeal among Republican and Independent voters than Harris, these voters were choosing not to cast a ballot in the race despite casting a ballot for at least one other office.

For those who voted in the race, the patterns are in the direction we would expect: 58.2 percent of the Republicans and 43.4 percent of Independents in the sample report having voted for Sanchez, compared to only 20.4 percent of Democrats.[112]

These patterns highlight the potential obstacles that a relatively moderate candidate can face when competing against a relatively extreme co-partisan when both candidates are from the advantaged party in a safe constituency. Since the disadvantaged party has few supporters in these advantaged-party constituencies, they must turn out in high numbers and vote disproportionately for the moderate, and also combine

---

[108] A *Los Angeles Times* article describes Sanchez's efforts to portray herself as to the right of Harris. Phil Willon, "Hurting for Support in her Own Party, Rep. Loretta Sanchez Tilts her Senate Campaign to the Right." *Los Angeles Times*, September 1, 2016.

[109] This classification is based on self-reported party identification. We classify independent-leaners as partisans. We dropped the few cases in which respondents declared "other" or "unsure" for their party identification.

[110] The roll-off rate for a particular office refers to the percentage of all voters who voted for an office on the ballot but not for this particular office. In this case, the roll-off rate is the percentage of voters who voted for another office but did not vote in the US Senate race.

[111] This is based on 1,266 Republican, 537 Independent, and 2,402 Democratic respondents.

[112] This is based on a sample of 819 Republicans, 379 Independents, and 2,278 Democrats. The percentage of the sample that report voting for Sanchez is close but slightly lower than actual vote shares, 32 versus 38 percent.

TABLE 11.2 *Roll-Off and Voting in Second Round of Top-Two System,*
US House Races in California, 2012 to 2016

Voter Type	Roll-Off		Vote for Moderate	
Both Candidates Same Party				
Same Party as Cands	6.4%	[889]	43.4%	[569]
Opposite Party	24.1%	[435]	68.9%	[228]
Independent	19.6%	[163]	51.6%	[95]
Democrat v. Republican				
Partisan or Leaner	4.0%	[10939]		
Independent	10.4%	[1214]		

Cell entries show the percentages of respondents who exhibit the given behavior (roll-off or vote for moderate) by type of race and respondent. Number of respondents by type in square brackets.

their vote with sufficient support from Independents and those who identify with the advantaged party. The voting behavior even in this high-profile US Senate election does not seem to meet these conditions. There was significant roll-off among Republicans and Independents. Although a majority of Republicans supported Sanchez, she was not able to attract a majority of the Independents and received very little support from Democrats, and therefore lost heavily. It is unclear why these conditions were not met. The roll-off among Republicans and Independents may reflect a lack of information or a lack of concern about the ideological differences between the candidates from the advantaged party.[113] Also, Sanchez's weak support among Independents (and lack of overwhelming support among Republicans) in the second round might indicate that many voters were more concerned with non-ideological differences between the two candidates. Harris was viewed as the clear front-runner just before the election, which may have also reduced the incentives for the Republican or Independent voters to vote in this race.[114] Finally, it is also possible that the pattern reflects features unique to the 2016 election.

---

[113] Ahler, Citrin, and Lenz (2016) find that most voters in the 2012 California primary were not aware of the ideological differences between the candidates.
[114] Harris was elected with 61.6 percent of the second-round vote.

We also analyze the 2012, 2014, and 2016 CCES, focusing on cases in which the two US House candidates in the second round were from the same party.[115] The results in Table 11.2 follow a pattern similar to the 2016 US Senate race. When both candidates are from the same party, roll-off among voters who identify with the opposite party is quite high, as is roll-off among Independents. The roll-off rate among voters who identify with the opposite party is 17.7 percentage points higher than among voters who identify with the party of the candidates, and 20.1 percentage points higher than the roll-off rate among partisans when the candidates are from different parties. These roll-off rates highlight the difficulty that relatively moderate candidates have in mobilizing independents or supporters who do not share their partisan affiliation.

In the races where both candidates were from the same party and we can identify an ideological difference between them, the reported voting patterns are similar to those we found for the 2016 US Senate race. Those who voted and identify with the opposite party disproportionately voted for the relatively moderate candidate, nearly 70 percent of the time (see the last columns of Table 11.2). This is consistent with a key claim by proponents who argue that the top-two system should lead to the election of moderate representatives. Table 11.2 also shows that Independents did not gravitate towards the relatively moderate candidate, as they were about equally likely to support the relatively extreme candidate. Voters who share the party identification of the two candidates were more likely to support the relatively extreme candidate.

These descriptive statistics highlight why ideological moderates in the top-two system are not winning even in second-round races with candidates from the same party. However, we should add some caveats. First, even among those who identify with the opposite party, much of the pro-moderate voting might be anti-incumbent voting (the incumbent was the relatively extreme candidate in more than half of the races). Second, as noted above, roll-off among those who identify with the opposite party is high. Third, as noted above, the districts in which both second-round candidates were of the same party are districts in which that party is advantaged; these districts are therefore likely to be quite liberal or conservative. Voters who share the same party identification as the two candidates dominate the second round, and tend to vote significantly more often for the extreme candidate. Thus, it is not

---

[115] We only examine cases from California and Washington. Louisiana's first round coincided with the November general elections in other states.

surprising that moderate candidates are elected in only about half of the races between co-partisans. Still, this might represent an improvement – in terms of moderation – over what we would observe with partisan primaries.

11.6 CONCLUSION

Would abolishing party primary elections be a "simple fix" to reduce the "toxic levels of hyper-partisanship and legislative dysfunction" in American politics today?[116] We have our doubts. We find little evidence that primaries are operating in the way that critics of the system assert will lead to relatively extreme candidates being nominated over relatively moderate ones. Moreover, the evidence does not suggest that alternative nominating systems produce more moderate candidates. There is some evidence from California and Washington that the top-two system has the potential to elect more moderate candidates. However, since it is such a recent reform in these two states and has only been used in one other state, we cannot yet draw firm conclusions.

Although our discussion has emphasized the importance of comparing primaries to other nomination systems, we have focused on only three alternatives. These are the alternatives often referenced in the debates over polarization and do not exhaust the range of potential alternatives. As pointed out above, even more dramatic reforms are possible – for example, a Westminster-style nomination system or mandatory voting in primaries or non-partisan elections. Whether these arguably more radical reforms would be more successful at reducing polarization is open to debate. Perhaps future work will uncover the moderating effect of these reforms or some other reform that significantly outperforms the current primary system.

---

[116] Keisling (2010).

12

Conclusion

It is now more than 150 years since direct nominations were first used in Crawford County, Pennsylvania, and most US states have been using the direct primary for more than 100 years. They are no longer an experiment but a firmly entrenched part of the American electoral system. And, overall, our evidence suggests that they are contributing to the US electoral system especially in uncompetitive areas, where they are most needed. Throughout much of the US, serious inter-party competition is lacking at the state and local level. Primaries help bring a form of competitive electoral democracy into these areas.

Primaries structure the incentives facing potential candidates and other political elites. For example, qualified candidates have strong incentives to run for open seats, especially in the advantaged party's primary. As a result, in these cases primaries are typically lively affairs, involving two or more serious candidates with strong resumes and campaign skills that make them serious contenders for office. Thus, even though officials elected in these safe constituencies typically only face serious competition in the primaries, we find that on average they tend to be as qualified as those who expect to face both primary and general election competition.

While voting in primaries is difficult because there is little information on the ballot – usually it is just a list of names – and although few voters are well-informed about the candidates' qualifications, a significant number vote "as if" they are informed about these qualifications, enough so that when there is a clear difference between the candidates the more-qualified candidate wins roughly 80 percent of the time.

Primaries involving incumbents tend to be relatively mundane affairs. The incumbent is usually unopposed or faces only token opposition and wins renomination without a serious fight. In most cases, however, this is not an indication of electoral failure, because the primary and general election system works well as a selection mechanism in open-seat races. As a result, the typical incumbent is well-qualified and hard-working and doing a reasonable job in the office he or she holds, so there are seldom compelling reasons to replace him or her with someone new.

12.1 PRIMARIES IN OTHER DEMOCRACIES

Given our sanguine view of primaries, one might also wonder why the direct primary is not in widespread use around the world. Primaries have been used in a number of Latin American countries.[1] They have also occasionally been used elsewhere, but they are far from widespread. Moreover, these primaries typically differ substantially from what we observe in the US – especially in terms of the total number of voters involved, how candidates get on the ballot, and how campaigning is regulated.[2]

Our findings suggest that primary elections might prove useful especially in countries with a strong federal structure and first-past-the-post electoral systems that confer a large plurality bonus. In most European countries this is not the case. They typically use some type of proportional representation system for their national elections. As a result these countries typically have more than two viable parties, so local one-party dominance is less common than in the US. Also, in most European countries government is more highly centralized than in the US, so local one-party dominance is less of a problem when it occurs. Finally, in these countries politicians tend to develop their skills inside political parties with much more structure than US parties.

---

[1] For example, Carey and Polga-Hecimovich (2006) and Aragon (2014) find that presidential candidates in Latin America nominated in primaries receive higher vote shares in the general election. Kemahlioglu, Weitz-Shapiro, and Hirano (2009) critique the data and some of the analyses in Carey and Polga-Hecimovich (2006).

[2] What constitutes a primary is open to debate. Some scholars apply the term in any situation where a leader or party list is selected by a vote of the party membership. In many cases, the number of voters participating is so small that from a US perspective the nomination contest might be considered more of a caucus than a primary. See Hazan and Rahat (2010) and Cross and Katz (2013) for discussions of intra-party democracy outside the US context.

In these contexts, primary elections might severely weaken the ability of "programmatic" parties to formulate and articulate coherent policy platforms and then work in the legislature to pass these into law in a disciplined fashion. We have not analyzed this potential cost because programmatic parties have never been an important part of the US political system. In countries where programmatic parties are arguably more important – for example, Germany, Sweden, Norway, Denmark, the Netherlands, the UK – this cost could be large, and might easily outweigh the benefits.

12.2 A NEW NORMAL? US PRIMARIES FROM 2010 TO 2016

In recent years, some political observers have become skeptical of primaries even in US politics. As we discussed in the previous chapter, a number of academics, journalists, and politicians argue that primaries are contributing to the increasingly polarized political environment. We find little evidence that primaries are responsible for polarization. However, the past few election cycles, with the birth of the Tea Party in 2010 and the election of Trump in 2016, have fueled the popular perception that intra-party divisions have been increasing, and that primaries have either facilitated this trend, or at least have become increasingly important venues for resolving intra-party conflicts. In this final section we investigate whether the primary competition we have been observing in recent years differs significantly from the type of competition we documented over the preceding century. If so, do primaries have less of a role than in the past in helping elect qualified candidates?

One thing is clear: primaries have become more competitive since 2010, particularly inside the Republican party. In Chapter 7, we noted an uptick in primary competition that appeared to deviate from the general trends in competition that existed since the mid-twentieth century.[3] The change is evident when we compare competition in Republican primaries in the 2002-to-2008 and the 2010-to-2016 periods. In the earlier period 23.2 percent of Republican incumbents were challenged. This jumps to 46.3 percent over the period 2010 to 2016. Open-seat races also experienced an increase in primary competition during this period; the

---

[3] See Figures 7.5 and 7.6.

percentage of contested Republican primaries grew from 42.6 percent to 59.9 percent between the two periods.[4,5]

The increasing competition in incumbent-contested primaries is consistent with the popular narrative that there is rising anti-incumbent or anti-establishment sentiment among voters within both parties, but perhaps even more so in the Republican party. If this shifting voter sentiment against incumbents is behind the rise in primary competition, then we should expect challengers to draw support from similar groups of anti-incumbent primary voters. Lacking individual-level data, we used data at the county level to examine whether incumbents in three solidly Republican states (Kansas, Texas, and Utah) all tended to lose primary vote share in the same localities.[6] The correlation in the county-level primary vote among the Republican incumbents running for statewide office between 2010 and 2016 is relatively weak, only 0.24, and very close to the correlation for the earlier period, 0.22. To the extent that support for Donald Trump in 2016 tapped into an anti-incumbent and anti-establishment sentiment in the Republican electorate, we might expect the county-level primary election support for Trump and incumbents running for statewide office in 2016 to be negatively correlated. We find no significant evidence for this type of structure in the 2016 primary votes.[7] Thus, overall there is little evidence that the Republican primary electorates in these states are organized into anti-incumbent voting blocs.

Even if the increase in primary competition is partly fueled by some anti-incumbent or anti-establishment sentiment, the change has not brought about a wave of incumbent defeats, at least not yet. Although the percentage of incumbents losing in primaries almost doubled between the 1998-to-2008 and the 2010-to-2016 periods, only 1.6 percent of incumbents running for re-election lost their primary race. In 2016 only five US House incumbents running for re-election lost their primary

---

[4] The open-seat Republican primaries were particularly competitive in 2010, with 72.3 percent of the races being contested.

[5] For Democrats the patterns are more mixed. The percentage of contested Democratic primaries for incumbents increased from 22.9 to 34.0 percent. However the contestation in open-seat Democratic primaries declined slightly from 42.8 to 41.6 percent.

[6] This is similar to the analysis of factions in Chapters 6 and 9. The analysis assumes that the anti-incumbent sentiment is geographically concentrated within states.

[7] The average correlation between Trump's county-level primary vote shares and the primary vote shares of incumbents running for statewide offices is only -0.04. The 2016 county-level presidential primary data is from www.politico.com/mapdata-2016/2016-election/primary/results/map/president/.

elections, and at most only one of these outcomes was plausibly the result of anti-establishment forces. Here is a brief account of the incumbents who lost their primaries: Corrine Brown (D-FL) and Chaka Fattah (D-PA) were both implicated in serious scandals, so their losses would appear to be cases of primaries operating as we would expect, i.e., a mechanism to hold malfeasant incumbents accountable.[8] Redistricting forced Renee Ellmers (R-NC) into a race with fellow House incumbent George Holding (R-NC), so in this race one incumbent had to lose. Tim Huelskamp (R-KS) was chairman of the House Tea Party Caucus and a leader in the attempted revolt against Speaker John Boehner. In 2012 the House Republican Steering Committee removed Huelskamp from both the Budget Committee and the Agriculture Committee. He also voted against a key farm bill in 2013. Many groups in Kansas began to see Huelskamp as a liability, especially farm groups such as the Kansas Farm Bureau, the Kansas Livestock Association, and the National Association of Wheat Growers.[9] Roger Marshall ran against Huelskamp in the primary with the support of these groups as well as the US Chamber of Commerce, and won the primary with nearly 57 percent of the vote. Finally, Randy Forbes (R-VA) was another casualty of redistricting and, possibly, anti-incumbent sentiment. His former district (the 4th) was redrawn to cover most of the majority-black areas in and around Richmond, and he switched to run in the 2nd district even though he continued to live in the 4th district. He was defeated by Scott Taylor, a Navy SEAL and member of the Virginia House of Delegates. Forbes outspent Taylor by almost ten to one, and some analysts attribute Taylor's victory to "a feisty grassroots campaign." Ideologically, Taylor was a bit more conservative, but only slightly.[10]

The surge in Republican primary competition may also reflect intra-party conflict along a dimension other than the establishment and

---

[8] Brown was indicted in May of 2016 and later convicted in 2017 on corruption charges. Fattah was convicted in 2016 on a number of charges, including racketeering conspiracy, bribery, bank fraud, mail fraud, money laundering, making false statements to a financial institution, and falsification of records.

[9] Huelskamp was already in trouble in 2014. He won the 2014 Republican primary with only 55 percent of the vote, and was not endorsed by either the Kansas Farm Bureau or the Kansas Livestock Association.

[10] Using the ideology scores from Chapter 11, Taylor's imputed ideology score is 0.46 while Forbes' score is 0.41. This is less than 7 percent of the difference in the average ideological score between Democratic and Republican incumbents elected in 2014 (see Figure 11.1).

anti-establishment divide. If these intra-party divisions are reflected in primary voter sentiments that are not distributed evenly across counties, then we expect to observe a large positive correlation in the primary electoral support among candidates competing in different primary races but who share a similar position in the intra-party divide.[11] Again, focusing on the county-level primary vote in the same three solidly Republican states, we find little evidence that Republican primary voters are divided into clear voting blocs or factions. The average magnitude of the correlation in the county-level primary vote among Republican candidates competing in different primary races between 2010 and 2016 is only 0.25, which is similar to the correlation for the period 1998 to 2008, 0.28.[12]

Even in specific cases where, based on their issue positions and other attributes, we would expect candidates to have similar bases of support, the county-level primary votes do not reveal behavior suggesting strong factional or issue division. For example, in the 2014 Kansas Republican primary, the county-level vote shares of Milton Wolf, the Tea Party challenger to US Senator Pat Roberts, were negatively correlated with the support for Governor Sam Brownback, the conservative governor and Tea Party favorite who led the "Kansas experiment" to implement large cuts in taxes and government spending.[13] In that same year, the correlation in county-level support among Tea Party favorites in the Texas statewide Republican primaries, Dan Patrick for lieutenant governor, Ken Paxton for attorney general, and Steve Stockman for US senator, were positive but none above the 0.60 threshold used to identify factions in Chapter 6.[14] For the Utah statewide races we identified the extreme and the moderate candidates and even here the correlation among the conservative candidates is only 0.10.

The recent uptick in Republican primary competition does not appear to reflect an organized divide within the Republican electorate. This

---

[11] Of course this analysis would miss cleavages that entail little or no geographic variation.

[12] This is well below the threshold of 0.6 that we used to identify states with factional divisions in Chapter 6. For all three states – Kansas, Texas, and Utah – over the period 2010 to 2016 the average correlations are less than 0.29. It is possible that the establishment and anti-establishment divide was more salient in certain states outside the three we are considering, but these were three states in which the divide featured prominently during this period.

[13] The correlation was -0.30.

[14] The correlation between Patrick and Paxton was 0.32, Patrick and Stockman was 0.50, and Paxton and Stockman was 0.34. The 2012 US Senate primary vote for Tea Party favorite, Ted Cruz, was not highly correlated with the 2014 support for Stockman or Paxton (Patrick is not considered because he faced the same opponent as Cruz).

is not to say that coherent preference divisions do not exist within the primary electorates, but rather these divisions, if they exist, have not yet produced blocs of voters that systematically support candidates across races on the same side of the intra-party divide. Our discussion of intra-party factions in Chapters 6 and 9 highlights the difficulty in detecting patterns of intra-party factions that provide structure to primary electoral outcomes across multiple primary races within states. In the handful of cases where this occurred, the factions, such as the Non-Partisan League, tended to be highly organized, often providing voters with clear slates of candidates. The recent intra-party factions, such as the Tea Party, have avoided creating formal organizations with clear slates. Another possible reason for the low correlations is that almost all Republican candidates today consider themselves conservative. Tea Party candidates are often indistinguishable from their opponents in terms of actual issue positions and differ instead in their rhetoric and style.[15]

In terms of the role primaries play in facilitating the election of qualified officials, the recent intra-party conflicts may interfere with voters' decisions to support the relatively qualified candidates. The theoretical and empirical discussions in Chapters 6 and 9 highlight the way that intra-party cleavages orthogonal to qualifications can reduce the salience of qualifications in voting decisions. (Of course, sustained intra-competition between factions gives factional leaders an incentive to feature well-qualified candidates on their slate in order to increase their chances of winning in the primary election. But for this to happen the factions must be organized, and such organization would seem to be lacking today.) Moreover, if the primary competition reflects some anti-incumbent and anti-establishment sentiment then this could further reduce the support for candidates with relevant experience. Has the connection between qualifications and primary outcomes weakened in recent elections?

The 2016 Missouri Attorney General Republican primary is an example of how divisions over non-qualification-related issues dominated a race with a clear difference in the candidates' relevant experiences. In this race, Josh Hawley, law professor at the University

---

15 For example, in the Roberts-versus-Wolf race mentioned above, the *Kansas City Star* wrote, "Roberts's ultra-conservative voting record and Wolf's positions on issues are almost identical ... Because there really was not much difference in ideology, both campaigns did resort to personal attacks." (September 13, 2014.)

of Missouri, was competing against Kurt Schaefer, who had a long record of public service including general counsel and deputy director of the Missouri Department of Natural Resources, special counsel to the Governor, special counsel to the Missouri Department of Agriculture, Missouri assistant attorney general, and special assistant United States attorney general. Schaefer was the candidate with more-relevant experience. However, millions of dollars were spent on television and radio advertisements, both by candidates and by outside groups, and the advertisements focused on topics unrelated to qualifications such as connections to terrorist groups, votes on legislation to allow Chinese nationals to buy farms in Missouri, and positions on abortion. One of the Democratic candidates, Jake Zimmerman, said of the Republican primary campaign: "They are fighting with each other not just accusing each other of being terrorist sympathizers who have sold us out to the Chinese, but they are also fighting with each other over who will shut down Planned Parenthood clinics the fastest and who hates gay marriage the most and who hates President Obama the most. To me, all of that misses the point. You are running to be the top law enforcement officer of the state of Missouri, not to be the top Republican of the state of Missouri."[16] Hawley won the Republican nomination with over 60 percent of the primary vote. His opponent in the general election, Democrat Teresa Hensley, was a former elected county prosecutor – that is, had more-relevant experience than Hawley. She stated, "I've practiced law for 25 years, including 10 as a county prosecutor. My opponent is a young man who has never represented a client in a Missouri courtroom. He's never practiced law in Missouri or stood in front a judge in Missouri. He's not qualified for this job."[17] Hawley went on to defeat Hensley with close to 60 percent of the general election vote.

Is the Missouri Attorney General race emblematic of a weakening relationship between qualifications and voting in recent elections? In the US House, US Senate, and gubernatorial races across all states between 2010 and 2016, we do observe a slight decline in the electoral advantage given to primary candidates with relevant experience. This change, which is noted in Chapter 6, is evident when we compare US House primary races in 2010-to-2016 versus those in 1998-to-2008. While the primary election advantage that incumbents and non-incumbents with relevant

---

[16] Kurt Erickson, "Radio stations pull ads in heated attorney general race." *St. Louis Post-Dispatch*, July 13, 2016.

[17] Jason Hancock, "Teresa Hensley-Josh Hawley race for Missouri attorney general has stark differences." *Kansas City Star*, October 11, 2016.

experiences have over candidates without relevant experience is smaller in the recent period, the advantage in the recent period is actually similar in magnitude to the advantage in the pre-1970 period when there was less candidate-centered voting. Moreover, in statewide races, we observe very little decline in this electoral advantage. Thus, overall, qualifications have remained strongly connected to primary election support despite the increased competition and any anti-establishment sentiment. The most significant decline in an electoral advantage occurred for incumbents in general elections, which is consistent with the expectations about voting behavior in a polarized electoral environment.[18]

Finally, we have argued that primaries are particularly consequential in the open-seat primaries of the advantaged party in constituencies where the nominees are expected to win the general elections with little difficulty. The patterns in competition and nomination decisions across disadvantaged, parties-balanced, and advantaged party primaries in the most recent elections continue to be consistent with the theoretical expectations discussed in Chapter 5. In the period 2010 to 2016, the average number of candidates competing in the disadvantaged-party primary for US House, US Senate, governor, state treasurer, or state auditor was 1.5, and 4.9 percent of these candidates had relevant experience. In the parties-balanced primaries the average number of candidates and the percentage with relevant experience increased to 2.3 and 22.0 percent, respectively. In the advantaged-party primary these figures climb to 4.1 and 38.7 percent. The probability that the nominee has relevant experience increases from 0.07 to 0.30 to 0.55 in the disadvantaged party, parties-balanced, and advantaged-party primaries.[19]

---

[18] While voters continue to give more support to candidates with relevant experience over those without relevant experience when given the choice, it is possible that the pool of qualified candidates competing in primaries may have been changing in this recent period. We do not observe any obvious change in the proportion of primary candidates with relevant experience in non-incumbent primary races between 2010 and 2016 compared to the preceding four electoral cycles. For example, averaging across all open-seat primary races, the percentage of candidates with relevant experience is 16.2 percent for the 2010-to-2016 period compared to 15.6 percent for the 2002-to-2008 period. Even within the Republican primaries the change is not very substantial, 15.6 percent for the recent period compared to 16.1 percent for the earlier period.

[19] During the 1998-to-2008 period the probability that the nominee has relevant experience increased from 0.06 to 0.25 to 0.61 in the disadvantaged party, parties-balanced, and advantaged-party primaries.

12.3 WHAT NEXT?

While the recent uptick in primary competition may deviate from long-running trends, the evidence does not reveal any significant change in the way primaries function in the US electoral system. Primaries continue to provide the important escape from one-partyism that was a major motivation for the original nomination reforms.

Moreover, no one is seriously considering a return to party caucuses, conventions, or committees to nominate candidates for federal or state offices. Nor does there appear to be strong support for using non-partisan elections for any federal offices or for major statewide offices or for state legislatures (Nebraska aside). There is some interest in the top-two system as practiced in California, Louisiana, and Washington, but so far there has been no major national movement in this direction. California's top-two system was even subject to some criticism in 2018 for tactics used by some of the major candidates.

Thus, the direct primary will continue to be the major nomination method for the foreseeable future, and we predict that it will continue to contribute to the US electoral system much as it has for the past century.

References

Aaron, Paul and David Musto. 1981. "Temperance and Prohibition in America: A Historical Overview." In *Public Policy: Beyond the Shadow of Prohibition*, ed. Mark H. Moore and Dean R. Gerstein. Washington, DC: National Academy Press, pp. 127–181.

Abramowitz, Alan I. 1988. "Explaining Senate Election Outcomes." *The American Political Science Review* 82(2):385–403.

1991. "Incumbency, Campaign Spending, and the Decline of Competition in US House Elections." *The Journal of Politics* 53(1):34–56.

2010. *The Disappearing Center: Engaged Citizens, Polarization, and American Democracy*. New Haven, CT: Yale University Press.

Achen, Christopher H. and Larry M. Bartels. 2002. "Blind Retrospection: Electoral Response to Drought, Flu and Shark Attacks." Unpublished manuscript.

2016. *Democracy for Realists: Why Elections Do Not Produce Responsive Government*. Princeton, NJ: Princeton University Press.

Adam Clayton Powell, Jr. 1992. In *Contemporary Black Biography*. Detroit: Gale. http://link.galegroup.com/apps/doc/K1606000004/BIC?u=columbiau&sid=BIC&xid=df6be534.

Ahler, Douglas J., Jack Citrin, and Gabriel S. Lenz. 2016. "Do Open Primaries Improve representation? An Experimental Test of California's 2012 Top-Two Primary." *Legislative Studies Quarterly* 41(2):237–268.

Aldrich, Charles and N. M. Hubbard. 1884. "Bribery by Railway Passes." *The North American Review* 138(326):89–99.

Aldrich, John H. 1995. *Why Parties? The Origin and Transformation of Political Parties in America*. Chicago: University of Chicago Press.

Aldrich, John H. and Richard G. Niemi. 1990. "The Sixth American Party System: The 1960s Realignment and the Candidate-Centered Parties." Unpublished manuscript, Duke University Program in Political Economy.

Alford, John R. and David W. Brady. 1989. "Personal and Partisan Advantage in US Congressional Elections." In *Congress Reconsidered*, 4th edition, ed. by Lawrence C. Dodd and Bruce I. Oppenhemier. New York: Praeger Publishers, pp. 153–169.

Alford, John R., Holly Teeters, Daniel S. Ward, and Rick K. Wilson. 1994. "Overdraft: The Political Cost of Congressional Malfeasance." *The Journal of Politics* 56(3):788–801.

Alvarez, Michael R. 1997. *Information and Elections*. Ann Arbor, MI: University of Michigan Press.

Alvarez, Michael R. and Jonathan Nagler. 2002. "Should I Stay or Should I Go?" In *Voting at the Political Fault Line*, ed. Bruce E. Cain and Elizabeth R. Gerber. Berkeley, CA: University of California Press, pp. 107–123.

Alvarez, Michael R. and J. Andrew Sinclair. 2015. *Nonpartisan Primary Election Reform: Mitigating Mischief*. New York: Cambridge University Press.

Amoros, Pablo, M. Socorro Puy, and Ricardo Martinez. 2016. "Closed Primaries versus Top-Two Primaries." *Public Choice* 167(1–2):21–35.

Ansolabehere, Stephen, J. Mark Hansen, Shigeo Hirano, and James M. Snyder, Jr. 2006. "The Decline of Competition in US Primary Elections, 1908–2004." In *The Marketplace of Democracy*, ed. Michael McDonald and John Samples. Washington, DC: Brookings Institution Press, pp. 74–101.

2007. "The Incumbency Advantages in US Primary Elections." *Electoral Studies* 26(3):660–668.

Ansolabehere, Stephen, Shigeo Hirano, and James M. Snyder, Jr. 2007. "What Did the Direct Primary Do to Party Loyalty in Congress?" In *Process, Party and Policy Making: Further New Perspectives on the History of Congress, Volume 2*, ed. David Brady and Mathew D. McCubbins. Palo Alto, CA: Stanford University Press, chapter 2, pp. 21–36.

2010. "More Democracy: The Direct Primary and Competition in US Elections." *Studies in American Political Development* 24(2):190–205.

Ansolabehere, Stephen, William Leblanc, and James M. Snyder, Jr. 2012. "When Parties are not Teams: Party Positions in Single Member District and Proportional Representation Systems." *Economic Theory* 49(3):521–547.

Ansolabehere, Stephen, Marc Meredith, and Eric Snowberg. 2014. "Mecro-Economic Voting: Local Information and Micro-Perceptions of the Macro-Economy." *Economics & Politics* 21(1):159–177.

Ansolabehere, Stephen and James M. Snyder, Jr. 2002. "The Incumbency Advantage in US Elections: An Analysis of State and Federal Offices, 1942–2000." *Election Law Journal* 1(3):315–338.

Ansolabehere, Stephen, James M. Snyder, Jr., and Charles Stewart, III. 2001. "Candidate Positioning in US House Elections." *The American Journal of Political Science* 45(1):136–159.

Aragon, Fernando M. 2014. "Why do Parties Use Primaries? Political Selection versus Candidate Incentives." *Public Choice* 160(1–2):205–225.

Aranson, Peter and Peter Ordeshook. 1972. "Spatial Strategies for Sequential Elections." In *Probability Models of Collective Decision Making*, ed. Richard Niemi and Herbert Weisberg. Columbus, OH: Charles E. Merrill, pp. 298–331.

Ashworth, Scott and Ethan Bueno de Mesquita. 2008. "Electoral Selection, Strategic Challenger Entry, and the Incumbency Advantage." *The Journal of Politics* 70(4):1006–1025.

Aylesworth, Leon E. 1908. "Primary Elections." *The American Political Science Review* 2(4):417–421.

1912. "Primary Elections – Legislature of 1909–1910." *The American Political Science Review* 6(1):60–74.

Baker, John D. 1973. "The Character of the Congressional Revolution of 1910." *The Journal of American History* 60(3):679–691.

Banks, Jeffrey S. and D. Roderick Kiewiet. 1989. "Explaining Patterns of Candidate Competition in Congressional Elections." *The American Journal of Political Science* 33(4):997–1015.

Barber, Michael J. and Nolan McCarty. 2015. "The Causes and Consequences of Political Polarization." In *Solutions to Polarization in America*, ed. Nathaniel Persily. New York: Cambridge University Press, pp. 15–58.

Beard, Charles A. 1924. *American Government and Politics*, 4th edn. New York: MacMillan Company.

Becker, Gary S. 1964. *Human Capital: A Theoretical Analysis with Special Reference to Education*. New York: Columbia University Press.

Beman, Lamar T. 1926. *The Direct Primary*. New York: The H.W. Wilson Company.

Berelson, Bernard, Paul Felix Lazarsfeld, and William N. McPhee. 1954. *Voting*. Chicago: University of Chicago Press.

Bernstein, Robert A. 1977. "Divisive Primaries Do Hurt: US Senate Races, 1956–1972." *The American Political Science Review* 71(2):540–545.

Berry, William D. and Bradley C. Canon. 1993. "Explaining the Competitiveness of Gubernatorial Primaries." *The Journal of Politics* 55(2):454–471.

Besley, Timothy J. 2006. *Principled Agents? The Political Economy of Good Government*. Oxford: Oxford University Press.

Besley, Timothy J. and Stephen Coate. 1997. "An Economic Model of Representative Democracy." *The Quarterly Journal of Economics* 112(1):85–114.

Boatright, Robert G. 2013. *Getting Primaried: the Changing Politics of Congressional Primary Challenges*. Ann Arbor, MI: University of Michigan Press.

2014. *Congressional Primary Elections*. New York: Routledge.

Bond, Jon R., Cary Covington, and Richard Fleisher. 1985. "Explaining Challenger Quality in Congressional Elections." *The Journal of Politics* 47(2):510–529.

Bond, Jon R., Richard Fleisher, and Jeffrey C. Talbert. 1997. "Partisan Differences in Candidate Quality in Open Seat House Race, 1976–1994." *Political Research Quarterly* 50(2):281–300.

Boots, Ralph Simpson. 1917. *The Direct Primary in New Jersey*. New York: Columbia University Press.

Born, Richard. 1981. "The Influence of House Primary Election Divisiveness on General Election Margins, 1962–76." *The Journal of Politics* 43(3):640–661.

Brady, David W. 1972. "Congressional Leadership and Party Voting in the McKinley Era: A Comparison to the Modern House." *The Midwest Journal of Political Science* 16(3):439–459.

Brady, David W. and Phillip Althoff. 1974. "Party Voting in the US House of Representatives, 1890–1910: Elements of a Responsible Party System." *The Journal of Politics* 36(3):753–775.

Brady, David W., Richard Brody, and David Epstein. 1989. "Heterogeneous Parties and Political Organization: The US Senate, 1880–1920." *Legislative Studies Quarterly* 14(2):205–223.

Brady, David W., Joseph Cooper, and Patricia A. Hurley. 1979. "The Decline of Party in the US House of Representatives, 1887–1968." *Legislative Studies Quarterly* 4(3):381–407.

Brady, David W., Hahrie Han, and Jeremy C. Pope. 2007. "Primary Elections and Candidate Ideology: Out of Step with the Primary Electorate?" *Legislative Studies Quarterly* 32(1):79–105.

Brown, George Rothewell. 1922. *Leadership in Congress.* Indianapolis, IN: Bobbs-Merrill Company.

Brown, Lara M. 2006a. "It's Good to Be an Incumbent: Scandals, Corruption, and the 2006 Midterm Election." Unpublished manuscript, California State University, Channel Islands.

  2006b. "Revisiting the Character of Congress: Scandals in the US House of Representatives, 1966–2002." *The Journal of Political Marketing* 5(5):149–172.

Bullock, Will and Joshua D. Clinton. 2011. "More a Molehill than a Mountain: The Effects of the Blanket Primary on Elected Officials' Behavior from California." *The Journal of Politics* 73(3):915–930.

Burden, Barry C. 2001. "The Polarizing Effects of Congressional Primaries." In *Congressional Primaries and the Politics of Representation*, ed. Peter F. Galderisi, Marni Ezra, and Michael Lyons. Lanham, MD: Rowman and Littlefield, pp. 95–115.

  2004. "Candidate Positioning in US Congressional Elections." *The British Journal of Political Science* 34(2):211–227.

Burnham, Walter Dean. 1965. "The Changing Shape of the American Political Universe." *The American Political Science Review* 59(1):7–28.

Cain, Bruce E. and Elizabeth R. Gerber. 2002. *Voting at the Political Fault Line: California's Experiment with the Blanket Primary.* Berkeley, CA: University of California Press.

Campbell, Andrea L. 2007. "Parties, Electoral Participation, and Shifting Voting Blocs." In *The Transformation of American Politics: Activist Government and the Rise of Conservatism*, ed. Paul Pierson and Theda Skocpol. Princeton, NJ: Princeton University Press, pp. 68–102.

Campbell, Angus, Philip E. Converse, Warren E. Miller, and Donald E. Stokes. 1960. *The American Voter.* New York: Wiley.

Canes-Wrone, Brandice, David W. Brady, and John F. Cogan. 2002. "Out of Step, Out of Office: Electoral Accountability and House Members' Voting." *The American Political Science Review* 96(1):127–140.

Canon, Bradley C. 1978. "Factionalism in the South: A Test of Theory and a Revisitation of V.O. Key." *The American Journal of Political Science* 22(4):833–848.

Carey, John and John Polga-Hecimovich. 2006. "Primary Elections and Candidate Strength in Latin America." *The Journal of Politics* 68(3):530–543.

Carson, Jamie L., Erik J. Engstrom, and Jason M. Roberts. 2007. "Candidate Quality, the Personal Vote, and the Incumbency Advantage in Congress." *The American Political Science Review* 101(2):289–301.

Carson, Jamie L. and Jason M. Roberts. 2005. "Strategic Politicians and US House Elections, 1874–1914." *The Journal of Politics* 67(2):474–496.

2013. *Ambition, Competition, and Electoral Reform: The Politics of Congressional Elections Across Time.* Ann Arbor, MI: University of Michigan Press.

Castanheira, Micael, Benoit Crutzen, and Nicolas Sahuguet. 2010a. "The Impact of Party Organization on Electoral Outcomes." *Revue Economique* 61(4):677–696.

2010b. "Party Organization and Electoral Competition." *The Journal of Law, Economics and Organization* 26(1):212–242.

Claggett, William, William Flanigan, and Nancy Zingale. 1984. "Nationalization of the American Electorate." *The American Political Science Review* 78(1):77–91.

Clubb, Jerome M. and Howard W. Allen. 1967. "Party Loyalty in the Progressive Years: The Senate, 1909–1915." *The Journal of Politics* 29(3):567–584.

Clubb, Jerome M. and Santa A. Traugott. 1977. "Partisan Cleavage and Cohesion in the House of Representatives, 1861–1974." *The Journal of Interdisciplinary History* 7(3):375–401.

Coleman, James S. 1972. "The Positions of Political Parties in Elections." In *Probability Models of Collective Decision Making*, ed. Richard Niemi and Herbert Weisberg. Columbus, OH: Charles E. Merrill, pp. 332–357.

Connelley, William E. 1918. *Kansas and Kansans.* Chicago: Lewis Publishing Company.

Cooper, Joseph, David W. Brady, and Patricia A. Hurley. 1977. "The Electoral Basis of Party Voting: Patterns and Trends in the US House of Representatives, 1887–1969." In *The Impact of the Electoral Process*, ed. Louis Maisel and Joseph Cooper. Beverly Hills, CA: Sage Publications, pp. 133–165.

Cotter, Cornelius P., James L. Gibson, John F. Bibby, and Robert J. Huckshorn. 1984. *Party Organization in American Politics.* New York: Praeger.

Cox, Gary W. and Jonathan N. Katz. 1996. "Why Did the Incumbency Advantage in the US House Elections Grow?" *The American Journal of Political Science* 40(2):478–497.

Cox, Gary W. and Mathew D. McCubbins. 1991. "On the Decline of Party Voting in Congress." *Legislative Studies Quarterly* 16(4):547–570.

1993. *Legislative Leviathan: Party Government in the House.* Berkeley, CA: University of California Press.

Cross, William P. and Richard S. Katz. 2013. *The Challenges of Intra-Party Democracy.* Oxford: Oxford University Press.

Dallinger, Frederick William. 1897. *Nominations for Elective Office in the United States.* Vol. 4. New York: Longmans, Green, and Company.

Davis, Oscar K. 1924. "Can You Trust the Primaries?" *Collier's, The National Weekly* 73(13):8–9.

Deckard, Barbara Sinclair 1976. "Electoral Marginality and Party Loyalty in House Roll Call Voting." *The American Journal of Political Science* 20(3):469–481.

1977. "Determinants of Aggregate Party Cohesion in the US House of Representatives, 1901–1956." *Legislative Studies Quarterly* 2(2):155–175.

Delli Carpini, Michael X. and Scott Keeter. 1997. *What Americans Know about Politics and Why it Matters.* New Haven, CT: Yale University Press.

Dewan, Torun and Kenneth A. Shepsle. 2011. "Political Economy Models of Elections." *The Annual Review of Political Science* 14:311–330.

Dimock, Michael A. and Gary C. Jacobson. 1995. "Checks and Choices: The House Bank Scandal's Impact on Voters in 1992." *The Journal of Politics* 57(4):1143–1159.

Downs, Anthony. 1957. *An Economic Theory of Democracy.* New York: Harper and Row.

Epstein, Leon D. 1986. *Political Parties in the American Mold.* Madison, WI: The University of Wisconsin Press.

Evrenk, Haldun, Timothy Lambie-Hanson, and Yourong Xu. 2013. "Party-Bosses vs. Party-Primaries: Quality of Legislature under Different Selectorates." *The European Journal of Political Economy* 29:168–182.

Ewing, Cortez A. M. 1953. *Primary Elections in the South: A Study in Uniparty Politics.* Norman, OK: University of Oklahoma Press.

Fair, Ray C. 2002. *Predicting Presidential Elections and Other Things.* Stanford, CA: Stanford University Press.

Feigenbaum, James J. and Andrew B. Hall. 2015. "How Legislators Respond to Localized Economic Shocks: Evidence from Chinese Import Competition." *The Journal of Politics* 77(4):1012–1030.

Fiorina, Morris. 1981. *Retrospective Voting in American Elections.* New Haven, CT: Yale University Press.

Fiorina, Morris P., Samuel J. Abrams, and Jeremy C. Pope. 2006. *Culture War? The Myth of a Polarized America.* New York: Pearson Longman.

Fiorina, Morris P. and Matthew S. Levendusky. 2006. "Disconnected: The Political Class versus the People." In *Red and Blue Nation? Characteristics and Causes of America's Polarized Politics,* ed. Pietro S. Nivola and David W. Brady. Washington, DC: Brookings Institution Press, pp. 49–71.

Fowler, Anthony and Andrew B. Hall. 2018. "Do Shark Attacks Influence Presidential Elections? Reassessing a Prominent Finding on Voter Competence." *The Journal of Politics* 80(4):1423–1437.

Fowler, Anthony and Pablo B. Montagnes. 2015. "College Football, Elections, and False-Positive Results in Observational Research." *Proceedings of the National Academy of Science* 112(45):13800–13804.

Galderisi, Peter F., Marni Ezra, and Michael Lyons. 2001. *Politics, Parties, and Elections in America.* Lanham, MD: Rowman and Littlefield.

Geer, John. 1988. "Assessing the Representativeness of Electorates in Presidential Primaries." *The American Journal of Political Science* 32(4):929–945.

Gentzkow, Matthew, Jesse M. Shapiro, and Matt Taddy. 2019. "Measuring Polarization in High-Dimensional Data: Method and Application to Congressional Speech" (NBER Working Paper No. 22423). Retrieved from National Bureau of Economic Research website (www.nber.org/papers/w22423).

Gerber, Elizabeth R. and Rebecca B. Morton. 1998. "Primary Election Systems and Representation." *The Journal of Law, Economics, and Organization* 14(2):304–324.

Gibbons, Robert and Michael Waldman. 2004. "Task-Specific Human Capital." *American Economic Review: Papers and Proceedings* 94(2):203–207.

Good, Chris. 2010. "Conservatives Look to Bounce Bennett in Utah Caucuses." *The Atlantic*. www.theatlantic.com/politics/archive/2010/03/conservatives-look-to-bounce-bennett-in-utah-caucuses/37908/.

Goodliffe, Jay. 2001. "The Effect of War Chests on Challenger Entry in US House Elections." *The American Journal of Political Science* 45(4):830–844.

    2007. "Campaign War Chests and Challenger Quality in Senate Elections." *Legislative Studies Quarterly* 32(1):135–156.

Gordon, Sanford G. and Dimitri Landa. 2009. "Do the Advantages of Incumbency Advantage Incumbents?" *The Journal of Politics* 71(4):1481–1498.

Gosnell, Harold F. 1937. *Machine Politics: Chicago Model*. Chicago: University of Chicago Press.

Grau, Craig H. 1981. "Competition in State Legislative Primaries." *Legislative Studies Quarterly* 6(1):35–54.

Green, Donald P., Bradley Palmquist, and Erik Schickler. 2002. *Partisan Hearts and Minds*. New Haven, CT: Yale University Press.

Groseclose, Timothy and Keith Krehbiel. 1994. "Golden Parachutes, Rubber Checks, and Strategic Retirements from the 102d House." *American Journal of Political Science* 38(1):75–99.

Grossman, Gene M. and Elhanan Helpman. 1996. "Electoral Competition and Special Interest Politics." *The Review of Economic Studies* 63(2):265–286.

Hacker, Andrew. 1965. "Does a 'Divisive' Primary Harm a Candidate's Election Chances?" *The American Political Science Review* 59(1):105–110.

Hacker, Jacob S. and Paul Pierson. 2006. *Off Center: The Republican Revolution and the Erosion of American Democracy*. New Haven, CT: Yale University Press.

Hall, Andrew B. 2015. "What Happens When Extremists Win Primaries?" *American Political Science Review* 109(1):18–42.

    2019. *Who Wants to Run? How the Devaluing of Political Office Drives Polarization*. Chicago: University of Chicago Press.

Hall, Andrew B. and James M. Snyder, Jr. 2015. "Information and Wasted Votes: A Study of US Primary Elections." *Quarterly Journal of Political Science* 10(4):433–459.

    2013. "Candidate Ideology and Electoral Success." Unpublished manuscript, Harvard University.

Hall, Melinda G. and Chris W. Bonneau. 2006. "Does Quality Matter? Challengers in State Supreme Court Elections." *The American Journal of Political Science* 50(1):20–33.

Hand, Samuel B. 2002. *The Star that Set: The Vermont Republican Party, 1854–1974*. Lanham, MD: Lexington Books.

Hansen, J. Mark, Shigeo Hirano, and James Snyder, Jr. 2016. "Parties within Parties: Parties, Factions, and Coordination Politics, 1900–1980." In *Governing in a Polarized Age: Elections, Parties, and Political Representation in America*, ed. Peter F. Galderisi, Marni Ezra, and Michael Lyons. New York: Cambridge University Press, pp. 143–190.

Hardy, Leroy Clyde, Alan Heslop, and George S. Blair, eds. 1993. *Redistricting in the 1980s: A 50-State Survey*. Claremont, CA: Rose Institute of State and Local Government, Claremont McKenna College.

Harvey, Anna and Bumba Mukherjee. 2006. "The Evolution of Partisan Conventions, 1880–1940." *American Politics Research* 34(3):368–398.

Hazan, Reuven Y. and Gideon Rahat. 2010. *Democracy within Parties: Candidate Selection Methods and Their Political Consequences*. New York: Oxford University Press.

Healy, Andrew and Gabriel S. Lenz. 2014. "Substituting the End for the Whole: Why Voters Respond Primarily to the Election-Year Economy." *The American Journal of Political Science* 58(1):31–47.

Healy, Andrew, Neil Malhotra, and Cecilia Mo. 2010. "Irrelevant Events Affect Voters' Evaluations of Government Performance." *Proceedings of the National Academy of Sciences* 107(28):12506–12511.

Herrnson, Paul S. 1988. *Party Campaigning in the 1980s*. Cambridge, MA: Harvard University.

Herrnson, Paul S. and James G. Gimpel. 1995. "District Conditions and Primary Divisiveness in Elections." *Political Research Quarterly* 48(1): 101–116.

Hershey, Marjorie Randon. 2006. *Party Politics in America*. New York: Longman.

Hill, Seth J. 2015. "Institutions of Nomination and the Policy Ideology of Primary Electorates." *Quarterly Journal of Political Science* 10(4):461–487.

Hill, Seth J. and Chris Tausanovitch. 2016. "Southern Realignment, Party Sorting, and the Polarization of American Primary Electorates, 1958–2012." Public Choice (special issue in honor of Keith Poole) 176(1–2):107–132.

Hirano, Shigeo. 2008. "Third Parties, Elections, and Roll-Call Votes: The Populist Party and the Late Nineteenth-Century US Congress." *Legislative Studies Quarterly* 33(1):131–160.

Hirano, Shigeo, Jaclyn Kaslovsky, Michael P. Olson, and James M. Snyder, Jr. 2018. "Primary Elections and Campaign Advertising." Unpublished manuscript, Harvard University.

Hirano, Shigeo, Gabriel S. Lenz, Maksim Pinkovskiy, and James M. Snyder, Jr. 2015. "Voter Learning in State Primary Elections." *American Journal of Political Science* 59(1):91–108.

Hirano, Shigeo and James M. Snyder, Jr. 2007. "The Decline of Third-Party Voting in the United States." *The Journal of Politics* 69(1):1–16.

2009. "Using Multimember District Elections to Estimate the Sources of the Incumbency Advantage." *The American Journal of Political Science* 53(2):292–306.

2012. "What Happens to Incumbents in Scandals?" *Quarterly Journal of Political Science* 7(4):447–456.

2014. "Primary Elections and the Quality of Elected Officials." *Quarterly Journal of Political Science* 9(4):473–500.

2018. "The Direct Primary and Voting in US General Elections." In *Routledge Handbook of Primary Elections*, ed. Robert G. Boatright. New York: Routledge, pp. 161–174.

Hirano, Shigeo, James M. Snyder, Jr., and Michael M. Ting. 2009. "Distributive Politics with Primary Elections." *The Journal of Politics* 71(4):1467–1480.

Hirano, Shigeo, James M. Snyder, Jr., Stephen Ansolabehere, and J. Mark Hansen. 2010. "Primary Elections and Partisan Polarization in the US Congress." *Quarterly Journal of Political Science* 5(2):169–191.

Hogan, Robert E. 2003. "Sources of Competition in State Legislative Primary Elections." *Legislative Studies Quarterly* 28(1):103–126.

Holt, James. 1967. *Congressional Insurgents and the Party System, 1909–1916.* Cambridge, MA: Harvard University Press.

Hopkins, Daniel J. 2018. *The Increasingly United States: How and Why American Political Behavior Nationalized.* Chicago: Chicago University Press.

Hortala-Vallve, Rafael and Hannes Mueller. 2015. "Primaries: The Unifying Force." *Public Choice* 163(3–4):289–305.

Huber, Gregory A., Seth J. Hill, and Gabriel S. Lenz. 2012. "Sources of Bias in Retrospective Decision-Making: Experimental Evidence on Voters' Limitations in Controlling Incumbents." *The American Political Science Review* 106(4):720–741.

Hurley, Patricia A. and Rick K. Wilson. 1988. "Partisan Voting Patterns in the US Senate, 1877–1986." *Legislative Studies Quarterly* 14(2):225–250.

Jacobson, Gary C. 1989. "Strategic Politicians and the Dynamics of US House elections, 1946–86." *The American Political Science Review* 83(3):773–793.

1992. *The Politics of Congressional Elections.* New York: Harper Collins.

2004. *The Politics of Congressional Elections*, 6th edn. New York: Pearson.

2009. *The Politics of Congressional Elections*, 7th edn. New York: Longman.

2012. "The Electoral Origins of Polarized Politics Evidence From the 2010 Cooperative Congressional Election Study." *American Behavioral Scientist* 56(12):1612–1630.

2015. "It's Nothing Personal: The Decline of the Incumbency Advantage in US House Elections." *The Journal of Politics* 77(3):861–873.

Jacobson, Gary C. and Michael A. Dimock. 1994. "Checking Out: The Effects of Bank Overdrafts in the 1992 House Election." *The American Journal of Political Science* 38(3):601–624.

Jacobson, Gary C. and Samuel Kernell. 1983. *Strategy and Choice in Congressional Elections.* New Haven, CT: Yale University Press.

Jewell, Malcolm E. 1955. "Party Voting in American State Legislatures." *The American Political Science Review* 49(3):773–791.

1967. *Legislative Representation in the Contemporary South.* Durham, NC: Duke University Press.

1977. "Voting Turnout in State Gubernatorial Primaries." *The Western Political Quarterly* 30(2):236–254.

1984a. "Northern State Gubernatorial Primary Elections Explaining Voting Turnout." *American Politics Research* 12(1):101–116.

1984b. *Parties and Primaries: Nominating State Governors*. New York: Praeger.

Jewell, Malcolm E. and David Breaux. 1991. "Southern Primary and Electoral Competition and Incumbent Success." *Legislative Studies Quarterly* 14(1):129–143.

Jewell, Malcolm E. and David M. Olson. 1978. *American State Political Parties and Elections*. Homewood, IL: Dorsey.

1982. *American State Political Parties and Elections*. Homewood, IL: Dorsey.

Johnson, Donald and James Gibson. 1974. "The Divisive Primary Revisited." *The American Political Science Review* 68:67–77.

Joint Committee of the Senate and Assembly of the State of New York. 1910. *Primary and Election Laws of This and Other States, Volume 1*. Albany, NY: J.B. Lyon Company.

Kanthak, Kristin and Rebecca B. Morton. 2001. "The Effects of Electoral Rules on Congressional Primaries." In *Congressional Primaries and the Politics of Representation*, ed. Peter F. Galderisi, Marni Ezra, and Michael Lyons. Lanham, MD: Rowman and Littlefield Publishers, pp. 116–131.

Kaufmann, K. M., J. G. Gimpel, and A. H. Hoffmann. 2003. "A Promise Fulfilled? Open Primaries and Representation." *The Journal of Politics* 65(2): 457–476.

Keisling, Phil. 2010. "To Reduce Partisanship, Get Rid of Partisans." *New York Times*, p. A27.

Kemahlioglu, Ozke, Rebecca Weitz-Shapiro, and Shigeo Hirano. 2009. "Why Primaries in Latin American Presidential Elections?" *The Journal of Politics* 71(1):339–352.

Kenney, Patrick J. 1986. "Explaining Primary Turnout: The Senatorial Case." *Legislative Studies Quarterly* 11(1):65–73.

Kenney, Patrick J. and Tom W. Rice. 1984. "The Effect of Primary Divisiveness in Gubernatorial and Senatorial Elections." *The Journal of Politics* 46(3):904–915.

1986. "The Effect of Contextual Forces on Turnout in Congressional Primaries." *Social Science Quarterly* 67(2):329–336.

Kernell, Samuel and Michael P. McDonald. 1999. "Congress and America's Political Development: The Transformation of the Post Office from Patronage to Service." *The American Journal of Political Science* 43(3):792–811.

Key, V.O., Jr. 1949. *Southern Politics in State and Nation*. New York: Vintage Books.

1956. *American State Politics: An Introduction*. New York: Alfred A. Knopf.

1964. *Politics, Parties and Pressure Groups*. 5th edn. New York: Thomas Y. Crowell.

King, David. 2003. "Congress, Polarization, and Fidelity to the Median Voter." *Typescript*.

Klein, Philip S. and Ari Hoogenboom. 1973. *A History of Pennsylvania, Second and Enlarged Edition.* University Park and London: The Pennsylvania State University Press.

Kleppner, Paul. 1979. *The Third Electoral System, 1853–1892: Parties, Voters, and Political Cultures.* Chapel Hill, NC: Chapel Hill University of North Carolina Press.

Kousser, J. Morgan. 1974. *The Shaping of Southern Politics.* New Haven, CT: Yale University Press.

Kousser, Thad, Jeffrey B. Lewis, and Seth E. Masket. 2007. "Ideological Adaptation? The Survival Instinct of Threatened Legislators." *The Journal of Politics* 69(3):828–843.

Kousser, Thad, Justin H. Phillips, and Boris Shor. 2018. "Reform and Representation: Assessing California's Top-Two Primary and Redistricting Commission." *Political Science Research Methods* 6(4):809–827.

Kramer, Gerald H. 1971. "Short-Term Fluctuations in US Voting Behavior, 1896–1964." *The American Political Science Review* 65(1):131–143.

La Follette, Robert M. 1913. *Autobiography: A Personal Narrative of Political Experiences.* Madison, WI: La Follette Co.

Layman, Geoffrey, Thomas M. Carsey, and Juliana Menasce Horowitz. 2006. "Party Polarization in American Politics: Characteristics, Causes, and Consequences." *The Annual Review of Political Science* 9:83–110.

Lazarus, Jeffrey. 2008. "Incumbent Vulnerability and Challenger Entry in Statewide Elections." *American Politics Research* 36(1):108–129.

Lee, Frances E. 2016. *Insecure Majorities: Congress and the Perpetual Campaign.* Chicago: University of Chicago Press.

Lengle, James I. 1980. "Divisive Presidential Primaries and Party Electoral Prospects 1932–1976." *American Politics Quarterly* 8(3):261–277.

Lenz, Gabriel S. 2012. *Follow the Leader? How Voters Respond to Politicians Performance and Policies.* Chicago: University of Chicago Press.

Levendusky, Matthew. 2009. *The Partisan Sort: How Liberals Became Democrats and Conservatives Became Republicans.* Chicago: University of Chicago Press.

Lim, Claire and James M. Snyder, Jr. 2012. "Elections and the Quality of Public Officials: Evidence from US State Courts" (NBER Working Paper No. 18355). Retrieved from National Bureau of Economic Research website (www.nber.org/papers/w18355).

2015. "Is More Information Always Better? Party Cues and Candidate Quality in US Judicial Elections." *The Journal of Public Economics* 128: 107–123.

Loeb, Isidor. 1910. "Direct Primaries in Missouri." *Proceedings of the American Political Science Association* 7:163–174.

Lublin, David. 1994. "Quality, Not Quantity: Strategic Politicians in US Senate Elections, 1952–1990." *The Journal of Politics* 56(1):228–241.

Lupia, Arthur. 1994. "Shortcuts versus Encyclopedias: Information and Voting Behavior in California Insurance Reform Elections." *The American Political Science Review* 88(1):63–76.

Luttbeg, Norman R. 1992. "The Validity and Electoral Impact of Media Estimations of 'Best' or 'Worst' State Legislators." *Legislative Studies Quarterly* 17(3):395–408.

Martis, Kenneth C. 1982. *The Historical Atlas of United States Congressional Districts, 1789–1983*. New York: Free Press.

Masket, Seth E. and Boris Shor. 2013. "Primary Electorates versus Party Elites: Who Are the Polarizers?" Unpublished manuscript.

Mayhew, David. 2002. *Electoral Realignments: A Critique of an American Genre*. New Haven, CT: Yale University Press.

McCarty, Nolan M., Keith T. Poole, and Howard Rosenthal. 2006. *Polarized America: The Dance of Ideology and Unequal Riches*. Cambridge, MA: MIT Press.

2015. *Political Bubbles: Financial Crises and the Failure of American Democracy*. Princeton, NJ: Princeton University Press.

McCurley, Carl and Jeffrey J. Mondak. 1995. "Inspected by #1184063113: The Influence of Incumbents' Competence and Integrity in US House Elections." *The American Journal of Political Science* 39(4):864–885.

McDermott, Monika L. 1997. "Voting Cues in Low-Information Elections: Candidate Gender as a Social Information Variable in Contemporary United States Elections." *The American Journal of Political Science* 41(1):270–283.

1998. "Race and Gender Cues in Low-Information Elections." *Political Research Quarterly* 51(4):895–918.

2005. "Candidate Occupations and Voter Information Shortcuts." *The Journal of Politics* 67(1):201–219.

McGhee, Eric, Seth Masket, Boris Short, Steven Rogers, and Nolan McCarty. 2014. "A Primary Cause of Partisanship? Nomination Systems and Legislator Ideology." *The American Journal of Political Science* 58(2):337–351.

McKenzie, Charles W. 1938. *Party Government in the United States*. New York: The Ronald Press Company.

Melendy, H. Brett. 1964. "California's Cross-Filing Nightmare: The 1918 Gubernatorial Election." *Pacific Historical Review* 33(3):317–330.

Merriam, Charles E. 1908. *Primary Elections*. Chicago: The University of Chicago Press.

Merriam, Charles E. and Louise Overacker. 1928. *Primary Elections*. Chicago: University of Chicago Press.

Meyer, Ernst C. 1902. *Nominating Systems: Direct Primaries versus Conventions in the United States*. Madison, WI: the author.

Millspaugh, Arther C. 1917. *Party Organization and Machinery in Michigan Since 1890*. Baltimore, MD: Johns Hopkins University Press.

Mondak, Jeffrey J. 1995. "Competence, Integrity and the Electoral Success of Congressional Incumbents." *The Journal of Politics* 57(4):1043–1069.

Morehouse, Sara M. 1996. "Legislative Party Voting for the Governor's Program." *Legislative Studies Quarterly* 21(3):359–381.

1981. *State Politics, Parties, and Policy*. New York: Holt, Rinehart & Wilson.

Morlan, Robert L. 1955. *Political Prairie Fire: the Nonpartisan League, 1915–1922*. Minneapolis, MI: University of Minnesota Press.

Munro, William Bennett. 1919. *The Government of the United States: National, State, and Local.* New York: Macmillan Company.

Nagler, Jonathan. 2015. "Voter Behavior in California's Top 2 Primary." *The California Journal of Public Policy* 7(1):1–14.

Neal, Derek. 1995. "Industry-Specific Human Capital: Evidence from Displaced Workers." *The Journal of Labor Economics* 13(4):653–677.

Nie, Norman H., John R. Petrocik, and Sidney Verba. 1979. *The Changing American Voter.* Cambridge, MA: Harvard University Press.

Nokken, Timothy P. and Keith T. Poole. 2004. "Congressional Party Defection in American History." *Legislative Studies Quarterly* 29(4):545–568.

Norrander, Barbara. 1989. "Ideological Representativeness of Presidential Primary Voters." *The American Journal of Political Science* 33(3):570–587.

Norris, George W. 1923. "Why I Believe in the Direct Primary." *Annals of the American Academy of Political and Social Science* 106(1):22–30.

Nye, Russel Blaine. 1951. *Midwestern Progressive Politics: A Historical Study of Its Origins and Development, 1870–1950.* East Lansing, MI: Michigan State College Press.

Osborne, M. J. and A. Slivinski. 1996. "A Model of Political Competition and Citizen-Candidates." *Quarterly Journal of Economics* 111(1):65–96.

Owen, Guillermo and Bernard Grofman. 2006. "Two-Stage Electoral Competition in Two-Party Contests: Persistent Divergence of Party Positions." *Social Choice and Welfare* 26(3):547–569.

Padró i Miguel, Gerard and James M. Snyder, Jr. 2006. "Legislative Effectiveness and Legislative Life." *Legislative Studies Quarterly* 31(3):347–391.

Page, Benajmin I. and Robert Y. Shapiro. 1992. *The Rational Public: Fifty Years of Trends in Americans' Policy Preferences.* Chicago: University of Chicago Press.

Patterson, Samuel C. and Gregory A. Caldeira. 1988. "Party Voting in the United States Congress." *The British Journal of Political Science* 18(1):111–131.

Pennock, Pamela E. and K. Austin Kerr. 2005. "In the Shadow of Prohibition: Domestic American Alcohol Policy since 1933." *Business History* 47(3):383–400.

Persson, Torsten and Guido Tabellini. 2000. *Political Economics: Explaining Economic Policy.* Cambridge, MA: MIT Press.

Peters, John G. and Susan Welch. 1980. "The Effects of Charges of Corruption on Voting Behavior in Congressional Elections." *The American Political Science Review* 74(3):697–708.

Piereson, James E. and Terry B. Smith. 1975. "Primary Divisiveness and General Election Success: A Reexamination." *The Journal of Politics* 37(2):555–562.

Pildes, Richard H. 2011. "Why the Center Does Not Hold: The Causes of Hyperpolarized Democracy in America." *The California Law Review* 99(2):273–333.

Polborn, Mattias K. and James M. Snyder, Jr. 2017. "Party Polarization in Legislatures with Office-Motivated Candidates." *Quarterly Journal of Economics* 132(3):1509–1550.

Pollack, James K. 1943. *The Direct Primary in Michigan, 1909–1935.* Ann Arbor, MI: University of Michigan Press.

Pomper, Gerald. 1966. "Ethnic and Group Voting in Nonpartisan Municipal Elections." *Public Opinion Quarterly* 30(1):79–97.

Poole, Keith T. 1998. "Recovering a Basic Space From a Set of Issue Scales." *The American Journal of Political Science* 42(3):954–993.

  2007. "Changing Minds? Not in Congress!" *Public Choice* 131(3–4): 435–451.

Popkin, Samuel L. 1994. *The Reasoning Voter: Communication and Persuasion in Presidential Campaigns.* Chicago: University of Chicago Press.

Price, Michelle L. 2017. "GOP Primary Shows New Utah System Allows Moderates to Win." *US News & World Report.* www.apnews.com/2db8c050e65d40dd8274c7da174acee8.

Quinones, Miguel A., J. Kevin Ford, and Mark S. Teachout. 1995. "The Relationship between Work Experience and Job Performance: A Conceptual and Meta-analytic Review." *Personnel Psychology* 48(4):887–910.

Rahn, Wendy M. 1993. "The Role of Partisan Stereotypes in Information Processing about Political Candidates." *The American Journal of Political Science* 37(2):472–496.

Ranney, Austin. 1975. *Curing the Mischiefs of Faction: Party Reform in America.* Berkeley, CA: University of California Press.

Ranney, Austin and Willmoore Kendall. 1956. *Democracy and the American Party System.* New York: Harcourt, Brace, and World.

Ray, Perley Orman. 1924. *An Introduction to Political Parties and Practical Politics,* 3rd edn. New York: Charles Scribner's Sons.

Remele, Larry. 1981. "Power to the People: the Nonpartisan League." In *The North Dakota Political Tradition,* ed. Thomas W. Howard. Ames, IA: Iowa State University Press, pp. 66–92.

Reynolds, John F. 2006. *The Demise of the American Convention System, 1880–1911.* New York: Cambridge University Press.

Rice, Tom. 1985. "Gubernatorial and Senatorial Primary Elections: Determinants of Competition." *American Politics Quarterly* 13(4):427–446.

Roberts, Peter. 1904. *Anthracite Coal Communities: A Study of the Demography, the Social, Educational and Moral Life of the Anthracite Regions.* London: The Macmillan Company.

Robinson, Elwyn B. 1995. *History of North Dakota.* Lincoln, NE: University of Nebraska Press.

Rogowski, Jon C. and Stephanie Langella. 2015. "Primary Systems and Candidate Ideology: Evidence from Federal and State Legislative Elections." *American Politics Research* 43(5):846–871.

Rohde, David. 1991. *Parties and Leaders in the Post-Reform House.* Chicago: The University of Chicago.

Rosenthal, Alan. 1981. *Legislative Life.* New York: Harper and Row.

Rothman, David. 1966. *Politics and Power: The US Senate 1869–1901.* Cambridge, MA: Harvard University Press.

Sait, Edward M. 1927. *American Parties and Elections.* New York & London: The Century Co.

Sanders, Elizabeth. 1999. *The Roots of Reform: Farmers, Workers and the American State, 1877–1917.* Chicago: The University of Chicago.

Schantz, Harvey L. 1980. "Contested and Uncontested Primaries for the US House." *Legislative Studies Quarterly* 5(4):545–562.

Schattschneider, E. E. 1942. *Party Government*. Westport, CT: Greenwood Press.

1960. *The Semi-Sovereign People: A Realist's View of Democracy in America*. New York: Holt, Rinehart, and Winston.

Scher, Richard K. 2015. *The Politics of Disenfranchisement: Why Is It So Hard to Vote in America?* Abingdon, Oxon and New York: Routledge.

Schier, Steven E. 2000. *By Invitation Only: The Rise of Exclusive Politics in the United States*. Pittsburgh, PA: University of Pittsburgh Press.

Serra, Gilles. 2011. "Why Primaries? The Party's Tradeoff Between Policy and Valence." *The Journal of Theoretical Politics* 23(1):21–51.

Shade, William G., Stanley D. Hopper, David Jacobson, and Stephen E. Moiles. 1973. "Partisanship in the United States Senate: 1869–1901." *The Journal of Interdisciplinary History* 4(2):185–205.

Shapiro, Walter. 2014. "Embrace Primaries to Restore the Sensible Center." URL: www.brennancenter.org/blog/embrace-primaries-restore-sens ible-center.

Shively, W. Phillips. 1992. "From Differential Abstention to Conversion: A Change in Electoral Change, 1864–1988." *The American Journal of Political Science* 36(2):309–330.

Shor, Boris and Nolan McCarty. 2011. "The Ideological Mapping of American Legislatures." *The American Political Science Review* 105(3):530–551.

Sides, John, Chris Tausanovitch, Lynn Vavreck, and Christopher Warshaw. 2016. "On the Representation of Primary Electorates." Unpublished manuscript.

Sinclair, Barbara. 2006. *Party Wars: Polarization and the Politics of National Policy Making*. Norman, OK: University of Oklahoma.

Sniderman, Paul M., Richard A. Brody, and Philip E. Tetlock. 1991. *Reasoning and Choice. Explorations in Social Psychology*. Cambridge: Cambridge University Press.

Snyder, James M., Jr. 1994. "Safe Seats, Marginal Seats, and Party Platforms: The Logic of Platform Differentiation." *Economics and Politics* 6(3): 201–213.

Snyder, James M., Jr. and Tim Groseclose. 2000. "Estimating Party Influence in Congressional Roll-Call Voting." *The American Journal of Political Science* 44(2):193–211.

Snyder, James M., Jr. and Michael M. Ting. 2002. "An Informational Rationale for Political Parties." *The American Journal of Political Science* 46(1):90–110.

2011. "Electoral Selection with Parties and Primaries." *The American Journal of Political Science* 55(4):782–796.

"Solomon Francis Prouty." 1928. *The Annals of Iowa* 16(4):310–311.

Sorauf, Frank J. 1963. *Party and Representation: Legislative Politics in Pennsylvania*. New York: Atherton Press.

1972. *Party Politics in America*, 2nd edn. Boston: Little, Brown and Company.

Squire, Peverill. 1992. "Legislative Professionalization and Membership Diversity in State Legislatures." *Legislative Studies Quarterly* 17(1):69–79.

Standing, William H. and James A. Robinson. 1958. "Inter-Party Competition and Primary Contesting: The Case of Indiana." *The American Political Science Review* 52(4):1066–1077.

Stewart, Charles, III. 1994. "Let's Go Fly a Kite: Correlates of of Involvement in the House Bank Scandal." *Legislative Studies Quarterly* 19(4):521–535.

Stone, Walter J. 1980. "The Dynamics of Constituency: Electoral Control in the House." *American Politics Quarterly* 8(4):399–424.

Stratmann, Thomas. 2000. "Congressional Voting Over Legislative Careers: Shifting Positions and Changing Constraints." *Legislative Studies Quarterly* 94(3):665–676.

Sundquist, James L. 1983. *Dynamics of the Party System.* Washington, DC: Brookings Institution.

Talbot, Ross B. 1957. "North Dakota – A Two-Party State?" *North Dakota Quarterly* 25:93–104.

Tausanovitch, Chris and Christopher Warshaw. 2017. "Estimating Candidates' Political Orientation in a Polarized Congress." *Political Analysis* 25(2):167–187.

Turner, Julius. 1953. "Primary Elections as the Alternative to Party Competition in 'Safe' Districts." *The Journal of Politics* 15(2):197–210.

Tweton, D. Jerome. 1981. "The Anti-League Movement: The IVA." In *The North Dakota Political Tradition*, ed. Thomas W. Howard. Ames, IA: Iowa State University Press, pp. 93–122.

Utah Foundation. 2011. "Nominating Candidates: The Politics and Process of Utah's Unique Convention and Primary System." *Research Report* (704):1–8.

United States Bureau of the Census. Various years. *Congressional District Atlas of the United States.*

Van Dunk, Emily. 1997. "Challenger Quality in State Legislative Elections." *Political Research Quarterly* 50(4):793–807.

Volden, Craig and Alan E. Wiseman. 2014. *Legislative Effectiveness in the United States Congress: The Lawmakers.* New York: Cambridge University Press.

Ware, Alan. 1979. "Divisive Primaries: The Important Questions." *The British Journal of Political Science* 9(3):381–384.

2002. *The American Direct Primary.* Cambridge: Cambridge University Press.

Wattenberg, Martin P. 1990. *The Decline of American Political Parties, 1952–1988.* Cambridge, MA: Harvard University Press.

1991. *The Rise of Candidate-Centered Politics: Presidential Elections of the 1980s.* Cambridge, MA: Harvard University Press.

Welch, Susan and John R. Hibbing. 1997. "The Effects of Charges of Corruption on Voting Behavior in Congressional Elections, 1982–1990." *The Journal of Politics* 59(1):226–239.

Wilson, William H. 1916. "Primary Elections as an Instrument of Popular Government." *Case and Comment: The Lawyer's Magazine* 23:396–399.

Wolfers, Justin. 2002. "Are Voters Rational? Evidence from Gubernatorial Elections." *Stanford GSB Working Paper #1730*.

Wright, Gerald C., Jr. and Michael B. Berkman. 1986. "Candidates and Policy in United States Senate Elections." *The American Political Science Review* 80(2):567–588.

Wright, Stephen G. and William H. Riker. 1989. "Plurality and Runoff Systems and Numbers of Candidates." *Public Choice* 60(2):155–175.

Wyman, Roger E. 1964. *Insurgency and the Elections of 1910 in the Middle West*. Unpublished master's thesis, University of Wisconsin–Madison.

Index

Note: Page numbers in *italic* refer to tables.

Daniel W. Gingerich,
Political Institutions and Party-Directed Corruption in South America
Avner Greif,
Institutions and the Path to the Modern Economy: Lessons from Medieval Trade
Jeffrey D. Grynaviski,
Partisan Bonds: Political Reputations and Legislative Accountability
Stephen Haber, Armando Razo, and Noel Maurer,
The Politics of Property Rights: Political Instability, Credible Commitments, and Economic Growth in Mexico, 1876–1929
Ron Harris,
Industrializing English Law: Entrepreneurship and Business Organization, 1720–1844
Anna L. Harvey,
Votes Without Leverage: Women in American Electoral Politics, 1920–1970
Murray Horn,
The Political Economy of Public Administration: Institutional Choice in the Public Sector
John D. Huber,
Rationalizing Parliament: Legislative Institutions and Party Politics in France
Sean Ingham,
Rule of Multiple Majorities: A New Theory of Popular Control
John E. Jackson, Jacek Klich, Krystyna Poznanska,
The Political Economy of Poland's Transition: New Firms and Reform Governments
Jack Knight,
Institutions and Social Conflict
Michael Laver and Kenneth Shepsle, eds.,
Cabinet Ministers and Parliamentary Government
Michael Laver and Kenneth Shepsle, eds.,
Making and Breaking Governments: Cabinets and Legislatures in Parliamentary Democracies
Michael Laver and Kenneth Shepsle, eds.,
Cabinet Ministers and Parliamentary Government
Margaret Levi, Consent, Dissent, and Patriotism Brian Levy and Pablo T. Spiller, eds.,
Regulations, Institutions, and Commitment: Comparative Studies of Telecommunications
Leif Lewin,
Ideology and Strategy: A Century of Swedish Politics (English Edition)

Gary Libecap,
Contracting for Property Rights
John Londregan,
Legislative Institutions and Ideology in Chile
Arthur Lupia and Mathew D. McCubbins,
The Democratic Dilemma: Can Citizens Learn What They Need to Know?
C. Mantzavinos,
Individuals, Institutions, and Markets
Mathew D. McCubbins and Terry Sullivan, eds.,
Congress: Structure and Policy
Gary J. Miller,
Above Politics: Bureaucratic Discretion and Credible Commitment
Gary J. Miller,
Managerial Dilemmas: The Political Economy of Hierarchy
Ilia Murtazashvili,
The Political Economy of the American Frontier
Douglass C. North,
Institutions, Institutional Change, and Economic Performance
Elinor Ostrom,
Governing the Commons: The Evolution of Institutions for Collective Action
Sonal S. Pandya,
Trading Spaces: Foreign Direct Investment Regulation, 1970–2000
John W. Patty and Elizabeth Maggie Penn,
Social Choice and Legitimacy
Daniel N. Posner,
Institutions and Ethnic Politics in Africa
J. Mark Ramseyer,
Odd Markets in Japanese History: Law and Economic Growth
J. Mark Ramseyer and Frances Rosenbluth,
The Politics of Oligarchy: Institutional Choice in Imperial Japan
Stephanie J. Rickard,
Spending to Win: Political Institutions, Economic Geography, and Government Subsidies
Jean-Laurent Rosenthal,
The Fruits of Revolution: Property Rights, Litigation, and French Agriculture, 1700–1860
Michael L. Ross,
Timber Booms and Institutional Breakdown in Southeast Asia
Meredith Rolfe,
Voter Turnout: A Social Theory of Political Participation